# ALBUERA
# EYEWITNESS

# ALBUERA EYEWITNESS

Contemporary Accounts of
the Battle of Albuera,
16 May 1811

GUY DEMPSEY

FRONTLINE
BOOKS

First published in Great Britain in 2023 by
Frontline Books
An imprint of
Pen & Sword Books Ltd
Yorkshire – Philadelphia

Copyright © Guy Dempsey 2023

ISBN 978-1-39906-640-2

Typeset by Lapiz Digital
Printed and bound by CPI UK

Pen & Sword Books Limited incorporates the imprints of Atlas,
Archaeology, Aviation, Discovery, Family History, Fiction, History,
Maritime, Military, Military Classics, Politics, Select, Transport,
True Crime, Air World, Frontline Books, Leo Cooper, Remember
When, Seaforth Publishing, The Praetorian Press, Wharncliffe Local History,
Wharncliffe Transport, Wharncliffe True Crime, White Owl
and After the Battle.

For a complete list of Pen & Sword titles please contact

PEN & SWORD BOOKS LIMITED
47 Church Street, Barnsley, South Yorkshire, S70 2AS, England
E-mail: enquiries@pen-and-sword.co.uk
Website: www.pen-and-sword.co.uk

or

PEN AND SWORD BOOKS
1950 Lawrence Rd, Havertown, PA 19083, USA
E-mail: Uspen-and-sword@casematepublishers.com
Website: www.penandswordbooks.com

# CONTENTS

# LIST OF MAPS

These maps from my 2008 study of the battle are intended to help readers visualise the phases of the battle described in the sources set out in this volume. For comparison and contrast, see the Illustrations section of this book for a selection of historical maps showing different versions of the battlefield topography.

1. Spain and Portugal 1811

2. Southern Portugal/South-Western Spain February 1811

3. Extremadura and Adjoining Regions May 1811

4. The Initial French Advance 8:00 a.m.

5. The French Flank Attack 10:00 a.m.

6. Girard's Attack against Zayas 11:00 a.m.

7. Colborne's Attack against Girard 11:30 a.m./Colborne's Defeat 12:00 noon

8. The Musketry Duel between Hoghton and Maransin 12.30 p.m.

9. The Advance of the 4th Division 2:00 p.m.

10. The Fight for the Village 2:00 p.m.

**Cartographic note**

These maps are based on the terrain depicted in Spanish Mapa Topográfico Nacional No. 802-III, scale 1:25,000 (2003). All unit placements and movement timings represent reasoned conclusions based on analysis of primary source information.

# KEY TO MAPS

## KEY TO MAP SYMBOLS

| | British | $\equiv$ | Artillery | ——— | Road |
| | Portuguese | ※ | Skirmishers | ——— | River |
| | Spanish | → | Allied advance | · · · · · | Seasonal river |
| | French | → | French advance | ⸬ | Buildings |
| | Cavalry | | Woods | | |

## ARMY ABBREVIATIONS

| | | | |
|---|---|---|---|
| CH | Chasseurs | D | Dragoons |
| VL | Vistula Legion Lancers | LM | Latour-Maubourg |
| KGL | King's German Legion | CG | Combined Grenadiers |
| LD | Light Dragoons | PV | Penne-Villemur |
| DG | Dragoon Guards | HUS | Hussars |

# MAPS

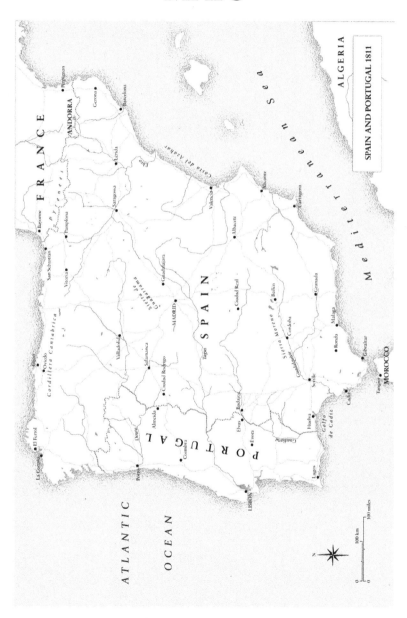

SPAIN AND PORTUGAL 1811

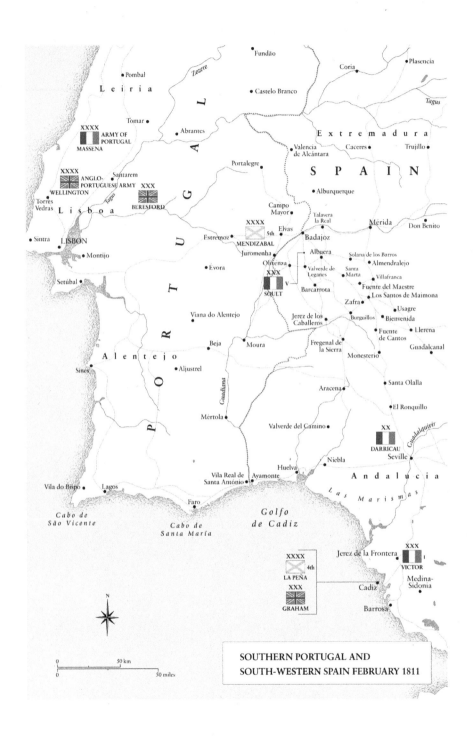

Fundão

Coria

Plasencia

Pombal

*Zezere*

L e i r i a

Castelo Branco

Tomar

*Tagus*

Abrantes

E x t r e m a d u r a

XXXX
ARMY OF
PORTUGAL
MASSENA

Portalegre

Valencia
de Alcántara

Cáceres

Trujillo

S P A I N

XXXX
ANGLO-
PORTUGUESE ARMY
WELLINGTON

Santarem

XXX

BERESFORD

Torres
Vedras

*Tagus*

L i s b o a

Alburquerque

Campo
Mayor

Talavera
la Real

Mérida

Don Benito

Sintra

LISBON

Montijo

Estremoz

XXXX
5th
MENDIZABAL

Elvas

Badajoz

Juromenha

Albuera

Solana de los Barros

Évora

Olivenza

Almendralejo

XXX
V
SOULT

Valverde de
Leganes

Santa
Marta

Villafranca

Setúbal

Barcarrota

Fuente del Maestre

Zafra

Los Santos de Maimona

Viana do Alentejo

Jerez de los
Caballeros

Burguillos

Usagre

Bienvenida

P     O     R     T     U     G     A     L

Beja

Moura

Fregenal de
la Sierra

Fuente
de Cantos

Llerena

Guadalcanal

A l e n t e j o

*Guadiana*

Monesterio

Sines

Aljustrel

Aracena

Santa Olalla

Mértola

Valverde del Camino

El Ronquillo

XX
DARRICAU
Seville

*Guadalquivir*

Vila Real de
Santa António

Ayamonte

Huelva

Niebla

A n d a l u c í a

Vila do Bispo

Lagos

Faro

Cabo de
São Vicente

Cabo de
Santa María

*L a s     M a r i s m a s*

Golfo
de Cadiz

N

XXXX
4th
LA PEÑA

Jerez de la Frontera

XXX
I
VICTOR

XXX

GRAHAM

Cadiz

Medina-
Sidonia

Barrosa

0        50 km
0                    50 miles

SOUTHERN PORTUGAL AND
SOUTH-WESTERN SPAIN FEBRUARY 1811

P O R T U G A L

to Portalegre

Caia

Gevora

to Lisbon

Alburquerque

Aljucen

Villanueva
de la Serena

Campo Mayor

Mérida

to Madrid

Talavera
la Real

Elvas

Badajoz

Guadiana

Guarena

Corte de
Peleas

Juromenha

Albuera

Solana de los Barros

Olivenza

Valverde de
Leganes

Royal Road

Almendralejo

Almendral

Santa Marta

Villafranca

Hornachos

Cheles

Barcarrota

Fuente del Maestre

Los Santos de Maimona

Zafra

Villanueva
del Fresno

Jerez de los
Caballeros

Usagre

Granja

Oliva de
la Frontera

Valencia
del Ventoso

Viar

Fregenal de la Sierra

Fuente de Cantos

Llerena

Barrancos

Canaveral
de Leon

Monesterio

Guadalcanal

Rosal de
la Frontera

Aroche

to Constantino

Aracena

Zufre

Paymogo

S P A I N

El Ronquillo

N

Alosno

Valverde del Camino

Las Pajanosas

Cantillana

Royal Road

Guadalquivir

0                    25 km

0                              25 miles

Gibraleon

Niebla

Seville

Bollullos
del Condado

Huelva

Almonte

Venta de Cruce

Dos Hermanas

Isla Cristina

EXTREMADURA AND ADJOINING
REGIONS MAY 1811

El Rocio

L a s    M a r i s m a s

to Cadiz

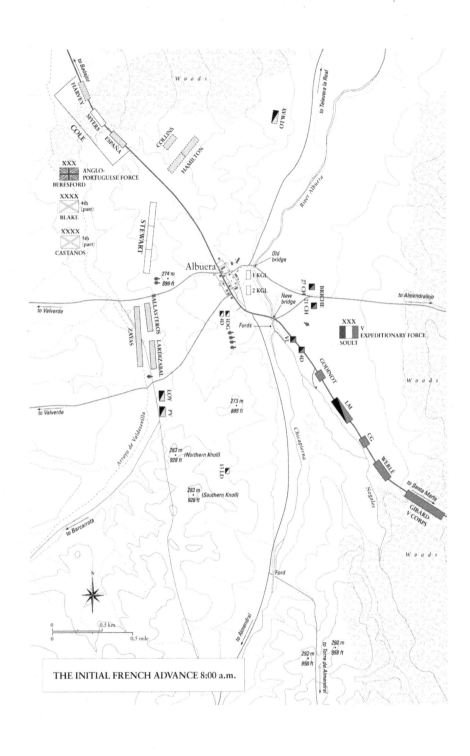

to Badajoz

HARVEY
MYERS
COLE
ESPAÑA

Woods

COLLINS

HAMILTON

OTWAY

River Albuera

to Talavera la Real

XXX
ANGLO-
PORTUGUESE FORCE
BERESFORD

XXXX
4th
(part)
BLAKE

XXXX
5th
(part)
CASTAÑOS

STEWART

Albuera

274 m
899 ft

Old
bridge

1 KGL

2 KGL

27 CH 21 CH

BRICHE

to Almendralejo

to Valverde

BALLASTEROS

ZAYAS

LARDIZABAL

HCG
4D

New
bridge

Fords

VI
4D

XXX
V
EXPEDITIONARY FORCE
SOULT

GODINOT

Woods

LOY

PV

273 m
895 ft

LM

to Valverde

CC

WERLÉ

Arroyo de Valdesevilla

283 m
928 ft

(Northern Knoll)

11 LD

283 m
928 ft

(Southern Knoll)

Chicapierna

Nogales

to Santa Marta

GIRARD
V CORPS

to Barcarrota

Woods

N

Ford

0       0.5 km

0            0.5 mile

to Almendral

292 m
958 ft

292 m
958 ft

to Torre de Almendral

THE INITIAL FRENCH ADVANCE 8:00 a.m.

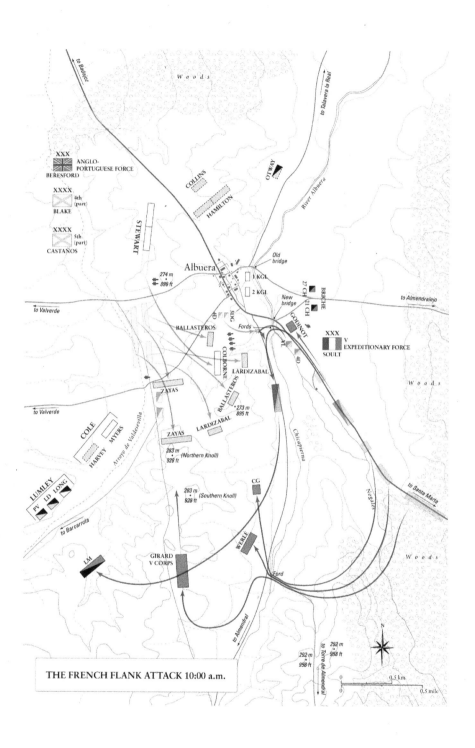

Woods

to Badajoz

to Talavera la Real

River Albuera

COLLINS

OTWAY

HAMILTON

STEWART

Old
bridge

Albuera

274 m
899 ft

to Valverde

1 KGL

2 KGL

New
bridge

27 CH 21 CH

BRICHE

to Almendralejo

4D

3DG

BALLASTEROS

Fords

GODINOT

to Valverde

COLBORNE

4D

XXX
V
EXPEDITIONARY FORCE
SOULT

LARDIZABAL

Woods

ZAYAS

BALLASTEROS

• 273 m
895 ft

COLE

LARDIZABAL

MYERS

ZAYAS

Arroyo de Valdeсevilla

HARVEY

283 m (Northern Knoll)
928 ft

Chicapierna

to Valverde

LUMLEY

283 m (Southern Knoll)
928 ft

CG

Nogales

PV    LD    LONG

to Santa Marta

to Barcarrota

WERLE

Woods

LM

GIRARD
V CORPS

Ford

to Almendral

N

to Torre de Almendral

292 m
958 ft

292 m
958 ft

0        0.5 km
0            0.5 mile

THE FRENCH FLANK ATTACK 10:00 a.m.

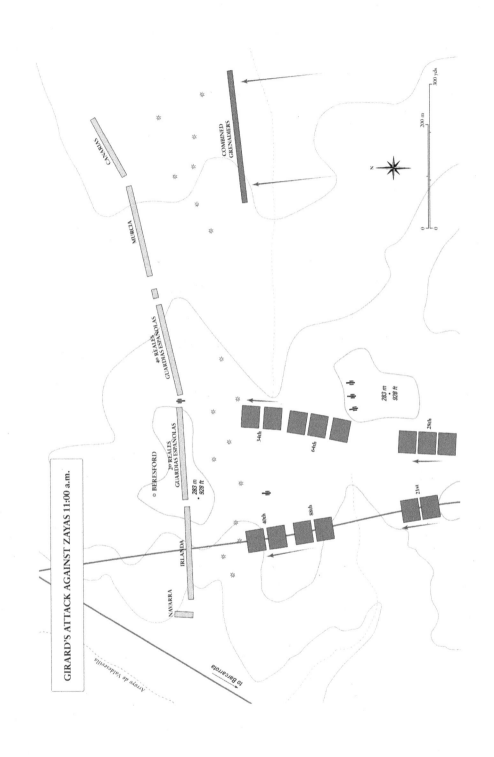

GIRARD'S ATTACK AGAINST ZAYAS 11:00 a.m.

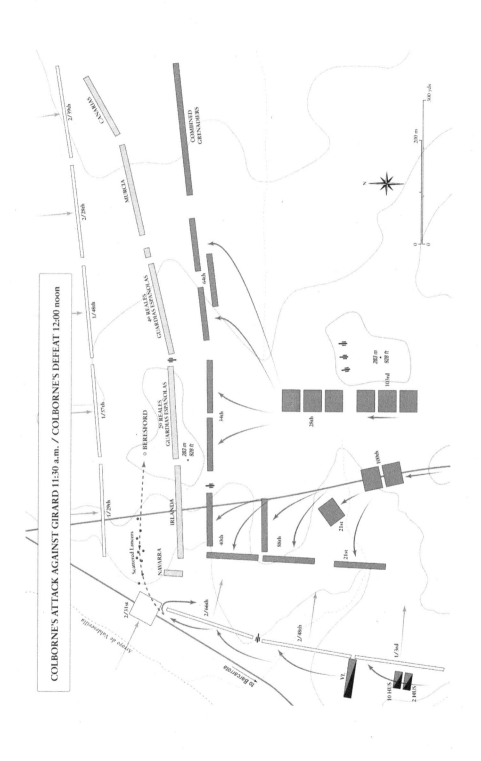

COLBORNE'S ATTACK AGAINST GIRARD 11:30 a.m. / COLBORNE'S DEFEAT 12:00 noon

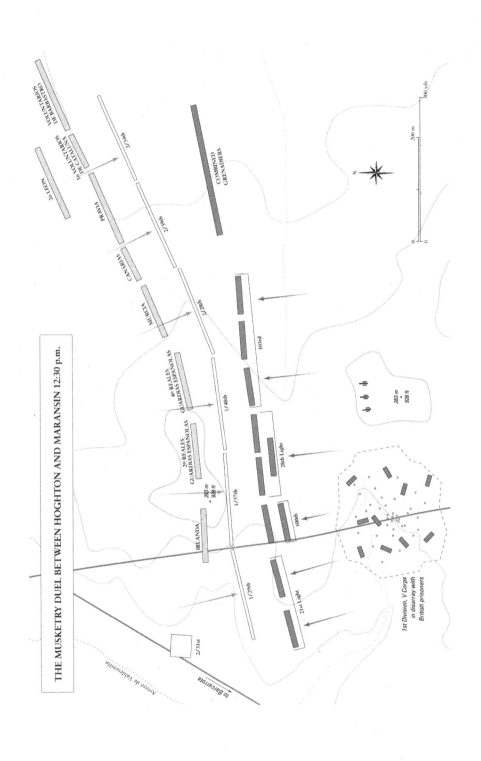

THE MUSKETRY DUEL BETWEEN HOGHTON AND MARANSIN 12:30 p.m.

2o LEON

VOLUNTARIOS DE BARBASTRO

1o VOLUNTARIOS DE CATALUÑA

PRAVIA

2/34th

CANARIAS

2/39th

MURCIA

2/28th

4o REALES GUARDIAS ESPAÑOLAS

1/48th

2o REALES GUARDIAS ESPAÑOLAS

1/57th

IRLANDA

1/29th

2/31st

COMBINED GRENADIERS

103rd

283 m
528 ft

28th Light

100th

21st Light

283 m
528 ft

1st Division, V Corps in disarray with British prisoners

Arroyo de Valdecetilla

to Barcarrota

N

0        200 m        300 yds

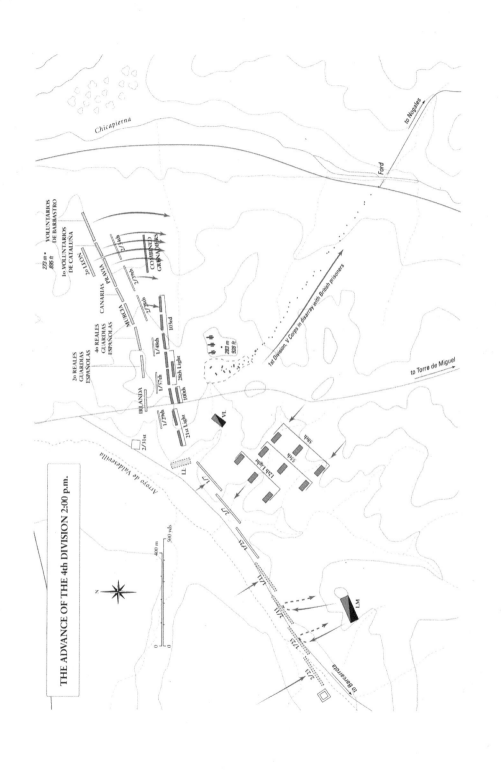

THE ADVANCE OF THE 4th DIVISION 2:00 p.m.

400 m
500 yds

N

Chicapierna

273 m
895 ft

VOLUNTARIOS
DE BARBASTRO

1o VOLUNTARIOS
DE CATALUÑA

2o LEÓN

CANARIAS    PRAVIA

MURCIA

4o REALES
GUARDIAS
ESPAÑOLAS

2o REALES
GUARDIAS
ESPAÑOLAS

IRLANDA

COMBINED
GRENADIERS

2/34th

2/39th

2/28th

1/48th

1/57th

28th Light

100th

1/29th

21st Light

103rd

2/31st

283 m
928 ft

1st Division, V Corps in disarray with British prisoners

to Torre de Miguel

Ford

to Nogales

Arroyo de Valdesevilla

VL

TL

1/7

2/7

3/27

1/27

1/31

2/31

2/23

1/23

LM

to Berrocua

12th Light

5/60th

5/60th

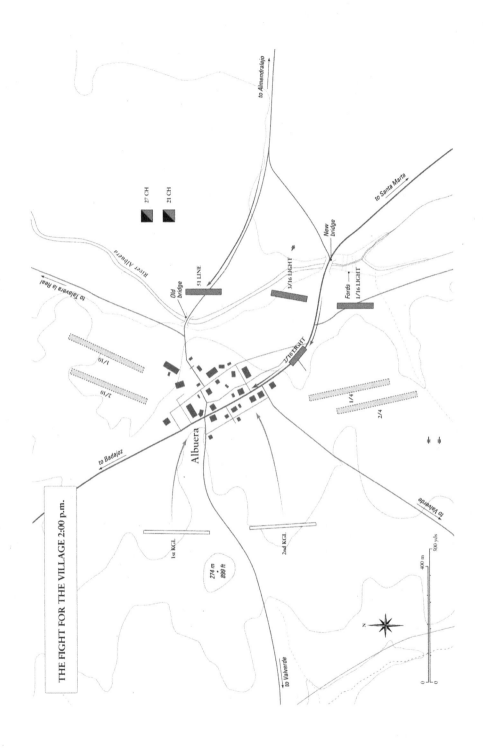

THE FIGHT FOR THE VILLAGE 2:00 p.m.

to Almendralejo

to Santa Marta

27 CH

21 CH

River Albuera

to Talavera la Real

51 LINE

Old bridge

3/16 LIGHT

New bridge

Fords

1/16 LIGHT

1/10

2/10

2/16 LIGHT

1/4

2/4

to Badajoz

Albuera

to Valverde

1st KGL

274 m
899 ft

2nd KGL

to Valverde

N

0

400 m

500 yds

# LIST OF ILLUSTRATIONS

# NOTE FOR READERS AND ACKNOWLEDGEMENTS

This book consists primarily of accounts and narratives about the Battle of Albuera (fought on 16 May 1811) that were written by participants in that action. These accounts and narratives have not been edited for substance, but some punctuation has been changed and some blocks of text have been broken into multiple sentences and paragraphs to enhance readability. In cases where the original account is in the form of a handwritten manuscript, the transcription is faithful to the content but does not always exactly replicate all the abbreviations and stylistic quirks of the original. When a word is indecipherable in a manuscript original, that is so indicated; if a word is identified without certainty, it is followed by a question mark in brackets. I have also given individual and place names consistent spelling across all sources for the convenience of the readers.

Most of these accounts and narratives are referenced in my 2008 book about the battle, but the advantage of this format is that they can be quoted at much greater length, and thus can provide greater detail. Where an account or narrative covers other events in addition to the battle, only passages describing the days leading up to the battle and those in its immediate aftermath have been included.

All texts originally in French have been translated by me, with significant assistance from Yves Martin and Donald Graves, and I have given the original French military terminology in brackets in certain instances where I thought that might be useful. The translators of text originally in other languages are identified in each case in the relevant footnote, but Mark Thompson and Oliver Schmidt deserve particular mention for providing most of the Spanish and German translations for this work.

The maps in the text of this book come from my 2008 book about the battle. In addition, I have included as illustrations a selection of historical maps of the battle for comparison and contrast.

There were many individuals and institutions who provided assistance with the sources for my 2008 book on the battle that serve as the foundation for this work. With respect to this project in particular, I would like to acknowledge the help I have received from Natalia Griffon de Pleineville, Gareth Glover, Markus Stein, Rob Griffith, Tom Holmberg, Jonathan North, Joao Centeno, Antonio Millan, Bob Burnham, Moisés Gaudêncio, Geoffrey Whaley, Simon Roberts of Bonhams (London), Jonas Baker of the Yale University Library (New Haven, CT), Alison Metcalfe of the National Library of Scotland, Paul Evans of the Royal Artillery Library (Woolwich), Bethany Slater of the National Army Museum (London), John Martino of the Newberry Library (Chicago), and Ifan Roberts of the Anglesey Archives.

I give thanks to John Grehan of Frontline Books for supporting this project and Linne Matthews, my editor, for saving me from errors. Any that remain are mine, not hers.

My family (Nancy, Katie, Elizabeth, Laura and Matt) continues to support my fascination with Albuera and they rally for a commemoration each 16 May.

# INTRODUCTION

The most enduring question for the study of history is, how can one truly know what happened at a particular moment in the past? The enduring answer (albeit an incomplete answer) is that one must collect and analyse all available evidence about the relevant events in the hope that the key facts can be established beyond a reasonable doubt, or at least by a preponderance of the evidence. History is a set of mysteries that are unravelled using primary source information to determine facts and then using those facts to reach interpretive conclusions about the way events actually transpired.

The purpose of this volume is to present all the currently known significant eyewitness and first-hand accounts of the Battle of Albuera so that each reader will have an opportunity to investigate the story of Albuera for herself or himself and have the experience of sifting through these sources to determine the relevant facts and produce their own version of the Albuera story. It is certainly the case that '[t]he soldier on the field of battle . . . knows little of what is going forward save as far as his own individual self or those more immediately surrounding him may be concerned', but each account written by a combatant contains unique details.[1] The challenge is to form a coherent narrative from these shards of information, each of which may be insignificant when viewed in isolation but which together make up a complete story. I wrote my own version of the Albuera story in my book *Albuera 1811 – The Bloodiest Battle of the Peninsular War* (Barnsley, 2008). I now invite others to take the Albuera challenge and determine their own version of events with the help of these primary sources, which include several that I have discovered since my previous book was written.

---

1     Gazzola, Jean, *Scenes in the Life of a Soldier of Fortune* (London, 1846), p. 110.

The challenge is not an easy one. The Duke of Wellington pointed out the first level of difficulty in a letter responding to a request for him to write an account of the battle of Waterloo:[2]

Paris, 8th August, 1815

My Dear Sir,

I have received your letter of the 2nd, regarding the battle of Waterloo. The object which you propose to yourself is very difficult of attainment, and, if really attained, is not a little invidious. The history of a battle is not unlike the history of a ball. Some individuals may recollect all the little events of which the great result is the battle won or lost; but no individual can recollect the order in which, or the exact moment at which, they occurred, which makes all the difference as to their value or importance.

Then the faults or the misbehaviour of some gave occasion for the distinction of others, and perhaps were the cause of material losses; and you cannot write a true history of a battle without including the faults and misbehaviour of part at least of those engaged.

Believe me that every man you see in a military uniform is not a hero; and that, although in the account given of a general action, such as that of Waterloo, many instances of individual heroism must be passed over unrelated, it is better for the general interests to leave those parts of the story untold, than to tell the whole truth.

The words of those who were present at the battle are the foundation stones for this exercise, but different words, like stones, have different weights and attributes. Those written close to the event can be vivid and fresh but can also be inaccurate because of the limits of what any one individual can see or hear, the frailty of human memory or self-censorship to suppress disturbing or scandalous details. Those written long after may be clearer and better composed because the author has had time to collect his thoughts and understand what happened, but time can adversely affect the accuracy of recollections and even cause them to become confused with relevant narratives from other sources. Words written for public consumption as opposed to a private audience can be manipulated for political and military purposes. Consequently, all primary sources in this book must be carefully analysed to make judgments about their accuracy and the reliability of the facts they contain.

---

2    Wellington, Duke of, *The Dispatches of Field Marshal The Duke of Wellington During His Various Campaigns in India, Denmark, Portugal, Spain, The Low Countries and France* (J. Gurwood, ed.) (13 vols., London, 1838), v. 12, p. 590.

The writing skills of each recorder of events are highly relevant to the evaluation of sources, since some writers have a knack for clear presentation of information and others do not, with the latter in particular struggling to express themselves using the flowery and oblique stylistic conventions of the era. Moreover, even the best writers struggle with the inadequacy of words to convey the full range of human experience in the battlefield.

A particularly difficult aspect of the Albuera challenge comes from the fact that no two sources use the same language to describe relevant terrain features and military formations and the vocabulary that is used is often maddeningly imprecise and often susceptible to multiple translations and meanings. In terms of terrain such as the famous 'heights' of the Albuera battlefield, the resulting confusion is only partially rectified by reference to modern topographical maps. In terms of descriptions of military formations such as lines and columns and right flanks versus left flanks, it is sometimes impossible to be exactly certain as to what a particular writer may have been trying to describe, although some possible interpretations may be logically excluded.

Another difficulty arises when facts discovered in primary sources conflict with the information contained in later accounts of the battle written by professional historians, who presumably engaged in their own version of the exercise contemplated by this book. However, William Napier, Charles Oman and John Fortescue, just to name the most prominent chroniclers of Albuera, all faced limits on the research they were able to conduct and the materials to which they had access, and all were engaged in writing projects of which the story of Albuera was only a small part. Even more importantly, they were not subject to the discipline of having to cite sources for their most significant conclusions. Their accounts nevertheless have an almost mythic importance for any study of the battle, but persistent and persuasive myths such as those created by Napier's stirring description of the charge of the Fusilier brigade and Oman's description of the French advancing in a mixed order (*ordre mixte*) can be as much an enemy of the truth as actual mistakes of fact.

Even after facts have been established, there can be multiple versions of any historical narrative reflecting multiple points of view. In the case of the Battle of Albuera, there is at least a British version, a French version, a Portuguese version and a Spanish version, as well as numerous individual versions. Each of these versions is theoretically based on the same facts as the other versions, but in different proportions given that an important fact for one version (such as an instance of individual heroism) may not be particularly relevant for another version. No one version can represent the 'truth' about the events of that day – that elusive objective can only be approximated by taking all the versions into account.

This collection does not purport to include <u>all</u> the primary written sources for the study of Albuera, just the most important ones that qualify as eyewitness or first-hand accounts. As the term implies, an eyewitness account is a written record of things seen directly by the writer. A first-hand account, however, includes information obtained from other participants that was not observed or created directly by the writer. Most of the accounts in this volume are actually both of these at the same time. For example, a narrative may be an eyewitness account to the extent that the writer is recounting what he saw happen to his own regiment, but would only be a first-hand account with respect to overall casualty figures he mentions, since he could only have obtained those from other participants. The common element is that all the information included in these sources comes from individuals who were present on the battlefield on 16 May.

The preponderance of English sources is not a result of selection bias, just a practical reflection of the fact that the victors of Albuera seem to have been more interested in memorialising the battle than the vanquished since English sources outnumber others by a wide margin. Some readers may be disappointed by the relative lack of Spanish and Portuguese accounts. I share that disappointment, but after countless years of researching the battle with the help of experts from those countries, I have reluctantly concluded that additional sources from those perspectives (especially in the form of individual eyewitness narratives) simply do not exist. It would be great if some future researcher could demonstrate that conclusion is wrong.

There are additional eyewitness and first-hand accounts of the battle sprinkled here and there in the extraordinary set of pamphlets attacking and defending the military reputation of Marshal Beresford that were exchanged between William Napier and Beresford and his defenders in the 1830s, but I have not included them systematically in this volume because most were written long after the event and usually for the express purpose of making or refuting a specific factual point as opposed to reflecting an intent to write an accurate account of the battle.

A couple of recurring points about the sources are worthy of note. First and foremost, almost every source includes information about the relative losses of the combatant forces. This may be in part a reflection of the common view that a defeated army should have greater losses than a victorious army. It may also be a reflection of the fact that the participants in the battle were shocked by the exceptionally high casualty figures for individual units and could not find words better than figures to convey that shock to others. Similarly, almost every account contains some statement of the view that the battle had been fierce and bloody to an unprecedented degree. Finally, the roster of authors of these accounts suggests that junior officers are the most diligent chroniclers of historical events, perhaps because they were better educated than the rank and file and not constrained by military politics from being candid.

One old soldier turned author has stated that combat experience is the sole measure of merit for a work of military history:

> To undertake the history of a campaign or to describe a battle, you must have been a participant – you must have smelled the intoxicating aroma of gunpowder, you must have experienced all the emotions of hand-to-hand combat, as well as those resulting from having to passively endure the fire of enemy batteries; finally, you must have slept and eaten on a battlefield littered with corpses!!! Otherwise, however skilful the writer may be, his work will always lack that cachet of authenticity, which cannot be counterfeited.[3]

Reading this book will not change the personal military status of any reader, but it will give them the raw facts of Albuera through the unfiltered words of actual combatants. And that should be sufficient to enable a reader to address the big questions about the battle:

1. Did Soult know he was seriously outnumbered when he launched his attack?
2. Was Beresford fooled by the French flank attack?
3. Did Blake jeopardise the Allies by failing to respond to the French flank attack?
4. Did the French capture the 'key' to the Allied position?
5. What circumstances led to the destruction of Colborne's brigade by the French cavalry?
6. How many colours were lost by Colborne's brigade?
7. What tactical formation did the French use for their flank attack?
8. Did Colonel Inglis of the 57th actually urge his men to 'die hard'?
9. Who ordered the attack by Cole's division?
10. Did Beresford order a retreat of his army?
11. Did Godinot fail to press his attack?
12. How did the French escape total disaster after the defeat of their reserves?
13. Who 'won' the battle?

---

3    Mauduit, Hippolyte de, *Les derniers jours de la Grande Armée, ou, Souvenirs, documens et correspondance inédite de Napoléon en 1814 et 1815* (2 vols., Paris, 1847–8), v. 2, p. 114.

# PART I

## 1. Strategic Context

1811 was the fourth year of Napoleon's effort to depose the Bourbon monarchs of Spain and replace them with a new line of royalty starting with his older brother, Joseph. The year began with the French army of Portugal besieging the British and Portuguese armies in the Lines of Torres Vedras around Lisbon and the French Army of the South (Armée du Midi) besieging a Spanish army plus the provisional Spanish government in Cadiz while many other French forces were doing battle elsewhere throughout the land with assorted Spanish regular army and guerilla forces. French Marshal Jean-de-Dieu Soult, the Duke of Dalmatia, commander of the Army of the South, launched an offensive in February 1811 with the Vth Corps of his army to assist the French forces in Portugal. The offensive did not have its intended strategic effect, but it was militarily successful in the short run in that Soult besieged and captured the important border fortress of Badajoz on 10 March after having defeated the Spanish 5th Army under its walls. He then returned to the headquarters of the Army of the South in Seville in Andalusia, leaving a strong garrison in the captured town.

When the French army of Portugal retreated from Lisbon, the Duke of Wellington detached two British divisions and some Portuguese troops from his army to recover Badajoz. Command of this detachment was given to William Carr Beresford, a British general who had been appointed as the commander of the Portuguese army in 1809 with the Portuguese rank of field marshal. After retaking the subsidiary fortresses of Campo Mayor and Olivenza, Beresford moved on to Badajoz. After reaching agreement on coordination with Captain General Don Francisco Xavier Castaños, commanding the remains of the Spanish 5th Army, and Lieutenant General Don Joaquín Blake, commanding units of the Spanish 4th Army detached from the garrison of Cadiz to reinforce Castaños, Beresford began a siege of the fortress on 8 May.

1

Soult, however, was unwilling to lose Badajoz without a fight. He accordingly organised a relief force consisting of the Vth Corps and some other available units of the Army of the South and he left Seville on 9 May, moving swiftly towards the threatened town. Wellington had given Beresford detailed instructions for conducting his campaign, but left him discretion to fight or retreat if the French advanced to relieve the Badajoz garrison. After multiple meetings with Castaños and Blake on 14 May, Beresford decided that the Allies had a sufficient numerical superiority to meet the French in battle. He accordingly ordered the dismantling of the siege works and a concentration of all the Allied forces at Albuera on 15 May to confront Soult's advance.

## 2. Chronology of Events, Early 1811

| | |
|---|---|
| 11 March 1811 | Badajoz surrenders to Marshal Soult |
| 25 March | Beresford captures Campo Mayor |
| 15 April | Olivenza surrenders to General Cole |
| 22 April | Beresford and Wellington reconnoitre Badajoz |
| 23 April | Wellington (1) authorises Beresford to fight at Albuera, and (2) proposes plan for cooperation between Spanish and Anglo-Portuguese forces |
| 8 May | Castaños agrees to cooperate and allows Beresford to command the joint force |
| 8 May | Beresford commences siege of Badajoz |
| 9 May | Soult leaves Seville with relief force |
| 12 May | Beresford learns of Soult's advance and orders dismantling of siege works |
| 13 May | Soult's relief force makes contact with French Vth Corps |
| 14 May | Beresford meets with Castaños and Blake at Valverde and they agree to offer battle at Albuera |
| 15 May | Bulk of Anglo-Portuguese forces arrive at Albuera and are joined at night by Spanish forces |

## 3. Chronology of Events, Thursday, 16 May
(All times are approximate)

| | |
|---|---|
| 2:00 a.m. | Cole's division leaves Badajoz for Albuera |
| 3:20 a.m. | Opposing forces stand to arms on opposite sides of the Albuera River |
| 4:20 a.m. | Dawn |
| 6:00 a.m. | Opposing forces stand down; Spanish forces complete alignment |
| 8:00 a.m. | French infantry arrives from Santa Marta; Cole's division arrives from Badajoz |
| 9:00 a.m. | French begin advance towards Albuera |
| 10:00 a.m. | French advance against the Allied right flank |
| 11:00 a.m. | French Vth Corps attacks Spanish position |
| 11:30 a.m. | Colborne's brigade attacks flank of French Vth Corps |
| 12:00 noon | French cavalry routs Colborne's brigade |
| 12:30 p.m. | Musketry duel between French Vth Corps and Hoghton's brigade |
| 1:00 p.m. | Beresford orders a withdrawal; Cole attacks French flank |
| 1:30 p.m. | Werlé's brigade attacks Cole |
| 2:00 p.m. | Alten reoccupies Albuera |
| 3:00 p.m. | French artillery and cavalry cover French retreat |
| 4:00 p.m. | End of combat |

# PART II
# ANGLO-PORTUGUESE
# ACCOUNTS

## A. Command and Staff Accounts

### 1. Beresford's Dispatch

*The official Anglo-Portuguese account of the battle was published in* The
Times *of London on 4 June 1811. We know that the original version of
Beresford's dispatch was significantly more negative in tone and was rejected
by the Duke of Wellington, but no copy of that first version has survived.*[1]

Albuera, 18th May, 1811
My Lord,
I have infinite satisfaction in communicating to your Lordship that
the Allied army, united here under my orders, obtained, on the 16th
instant, after a most sanguinary contest, a complete victory over that of
the enemy, commanded by Marshal Soult; and I shall proceed to relate
to your Lordship the circumstances.

In a former report I have informed your Lordship of the advance of
Marshal Soult from Seville, and I had in consequence judged it wise
entirely to raise the siege of Badajoz, and prepare to meet him with our
united forces, rather than, by looking to two objects at once, to risk the
loss of both.

Marshal Soult, it appears, had been long straining every nerve to
collect a force which he thought fully sufficient to his object for the
relief of Badajoz; and for this purpose he had drawn considerable
numbers from the corps of Marshal Victor and General Sebastiani,

---

1    The story of how the initial version was revised is told in Woolgar, C.M., 'Writing
     the Dispatch: Wellington and Official Communication', *Wellington Studies II*
     (Southampton, 1999), pp. 1–25.

and also, I believe, from the French army of the centre. Having thus completed his preparations, he marched from Seville on the 10th instant, with a corps then estimated at 15,000 or 16,000 men, and was joined on descending into Extremadura by the corps under General Latour-Maubourg, stated to be 5,000 men.

His Excellency General Blake, as soon as he learned of the advance of Marshal Soult, in strict conformity to the plan proposed by your Lordship, proceeded to form his junction with the corps under my orders, and arrived at Valverde in person on the 14th instant, where, having consulted with his Excellency and General Castaños, it was determined to meet the enemy and to give him battle.

On finding the determination of the enemy to relieve Badajoz, I had broken up from before that place, and marched the infantry to the position in front of Valverde, except the division of Major General the Hon. G.L. Cole, which, with 2,000 Spanish troops, I left to cover the removal of our stores.

The cavalry, which had, according to orders, fallen back as the enemy advanced, was joined at Santa Marta by the cavalry of General Blake; that of General Castaños, under the Conde de Penne-Villemur, had been always with it.

As remaining at Valverde, though a stronger position, left Badajoz entirely open, I determined to take up a position (such as could be got, in this widely open country) at this place, thus standing directly between the enemy and Badajoz.

The army was therefore assembled here on the 15th instant. The corps of General Blake, though making a forced march to effect it, only joined in the night, and could not be placed in its position till the morning of the 16th instant; when General Cole's division, with the Spanish brigade under Don Carlos de España, also joined, and a little before the commencement of the action. Our cavalry had been forced on the morning of the 15th instant to retire from Santa Marta, and joined here.

In the afternoon of that day the enemy appeared in front of us. The next morning our disposition for receiving the enemy was made, being formed in two lines, nearly parallel to the river Albuera, on the ridge of the gradual ascent rising from that river, and covering the roads to Badajoz and Valverde, though your Lordship is aware that the whole face of this country is everywhere passable for all arms. General Blake's corps was on the right in two lines; its left, on the Valverde road, joined the right of Major General the Hon. William Stewart's division, the left of which reached the Badajoz road, where commenced the right of Major General Hamilton's division, which closed the left of the line.

General Cole's division, with one brigade of General Hamilton's, formed the second line of the British and Portuguese army.

The enemy, on the morning of the 16th, did not long delay his attack. At 8 o'clock he was observed to be in movement, and his cavalry was seen passing the rivulet of Albuera, considerably above our right; and shortly after he marched out of the wood opposite to us a strong force of cavalry, and two heavy columns of infantry, pointing them to our front, as if to attack the village and bridge of Albuera. During this time, under cover of his vastly superior cavalry, he was filing the principal body of his infantry over the river beyond our right; and it was not long before his intention appeared to be to turn us by that flank, and to cut us off from Valverde.

Major General Cole's division was therefore ordered to form an oblique line to the rear of our right, with his own right thrown back; and the intention of the enemy to attack our right becoming evident, I requested General Blake to form part of his first line, and all his second, to that front, which was done.

The enemy commenced his attack at 9 o'clock, not ceasing at the same time to menace our left; and after a strong and gallant resistance of the Spanish troops, he gained the heights upon which they had been formed. Meanwhile the division of Major General the Hon. William Stewart had been brought up to support them, and that of Major General Hamilton brought to the left of the Spanish line, and formed in contiguous close columns of battalions, to be moveable in any direction. The Portuguese brigade of cavalry, under Brig. General Otway, remained at some distance on the left of this, to check any attempt of the enemy below the village.

As the heights the enemy had gained, raked and entirely commanded our whole position, it became necessary to make every effort to retake and maintain them; and a noble one was made by the division of General Stewart, headed by that gallant Officer.

Nearly at the beginning of the enemy's attack a heavy storm of rain came on, which, with the smoke from the firing, rendered it impossible to discern anything distinctly. This, with the nature of the ground, had been extremely favourable to the enemy in forming his columns, and in his subsequent attack.

The right brigade of General Stewart's division, under Lieut. Colonel Colborne, first came into action, and behaved in the most gallant manner; and finding that the enemy's column could not be shaken by fire, proceeded to attack it with the bayonet; and, while in the act of charging, a body of Polish lancers (cavalry), which the thickness of the atmosphere and the nature of the ground had concealed (and which was, besides, mistaken by those of the brigade, when discovered, for Spanish cavalry, and therefore not fired upon), turned it; and, being thus attacked unexpectedly in the rear, was unfortunately broken, and suffered immensely. The 31st regiment, being the left one of the brigade, alone escaped this charge, and, under the command of Major L'Estrange, kept its ground until the arrival of the 3rd brigade, under Major General Hoghton. The conduct of this brigade was most conspicuously gallant; and that of the 2nd brigade, under the command of Lieut. Colonel the Hon. A. Abercromby, was not less so. Major General Hoghton, cheering on his brigade to the charge, fell pierced by wounds.

Though the enemy's principal attack was on this point of the right, he also made a continual attempt upon that part of our original front at the village and bridge, which were defended in the most gallant manner by Major General Baron Alten, and the light infantry brigade of the German Legion, whose conduct was, in every point of view, conspicuously good. This point now formed our left, and Major General Hamilton's division had been brought up there; and he was left to direct the defence of that point, whilst the enemy's attack continued on our right, a considerable proportion of the Spanish troops supporting the defence of this place.

The enemy's cavalry, on his infantry attempting to force our right, had endeavoured to turn it; but, by the able manoeuvres of Major General the Hon. William Lumley, commanding the Allied cavalry, though vastly inferior to that of the enemy in number, his endeavours were foiled. Major General Cole, seeing the attack of the enemy, very judiciously bringing up his left a little, marched in line to attack the enemy's left, and arrived most opportunely to contribute, with the charges of the brigades of General Stewart's division, to force the enemy to abandon his situation, and retire precipitately, and to take refuge under his reserve. Here the Fusilier brigade particularly distinguished itself.

He was pursued by the Allies to a considerable distance, and as far as I thought it prudent, with his immense superiority of cavalry; and I contented myself with seeing him driven across the Albuera.

I have every reason to speak favourably of the manner in which our artillery was served, and fought; and Major Hartman, commanding the British, and Major Dickson, commanding the Portuguese, and the Officers and men, are entitled to my thanks. The four guns of the horse artillery, commanded by Captain Lefebvre, did great execution on the enemy's cavalry; and one brigade of Spanish artillery (the only one in the field) I saw equally gallantly and well served. We lost in the misfortune which occurred to the brigade commanded by Lieut. Colonel Colborne (whom General Stewart reports to have acted, and was then acting, in a most noble manner, leading on the brigade in admirable order) one howitzer, which the enemy, before the arrival of the gallant General Hoghton's brigade,[2] had time to carry off with 200 or 300 prisoners of that brigade. After he had been beaten from this his principal attack he still continued that near the village, on which he never could make any impression, or cross the rivulet, though I had been obliged to bring a very great proportion of the troops from it, to support the principal point of attack; but the enemy seeing his main attack defeated, relaxed in his attempt there also. The Portuguese division of Major General Hamilton in every instance evinced the utmost steadiness and courage, and manoeuvred equally well with the British.

Brig. General Harvey's Portuguese brigade, belonging to General Cole's division, had an opportunity of distinguishing itself when marching in line across the plain, by repulsing, with the utmost steadiness, a charge of the enemy's cavalry.

It is impossible to enumerate every instance of discipline and valour shown on this severely contested day; but there never were troops that more valiantly or more gloriously maintained the honour of their respective countries. I have not been able to particularise the Spanish divisions, brigades, or regiments, that were particularly engaged, because I am not acquainted with their denominations or names; but I have great pleasure in saying that their behaviour was most gallant and honourable: and though, from the superior number and weight of the enemy's force, that part of them that were in the position attacked were obliged to cede the ground, it was after a gallant resistance, and they continued in good order to support their allies; and I doubt not his Excellency General Blake will do ample justice on this head, by making honourable mention of the deserving.

The battle commenced at 9 o'clock, and continued without interruption till 2 in the afternoon, when, the enemy having been driven over the Albuera, for the remainder of the day there was but cannonading and skirmishing. It is impossible by any description to do justice to the distinguished gallantry of the troops; but every individual most nobly did his duty, which will be well proved by the great loss we have suffered, though repulsing the enemy; and it was observed that our dead, particularly the 57th regiment, were lying

---

2    The name of this officer is often written as 'Houghton', but 'Hoghton' is how his name appears in the 1811 Army List and a modern biography.

as they had fought in ranks, and every wound was in front. Major General the Hon. William Stewart most particularly distinguished himself, and conduced much to the honour of the day; he received two contusions, but would not quit the field. Major General the Hon. G.L. Cole is also entitled to every praise; and I have to regret being deprived for some time of his services by the wound he has received. Lieut. Colonel the Hon. A. Abercromby, commanding the 2nd Brigade, 2nd Division, and Major L'Estrange, 31st regiment, deserve to be particularly mentioned; and nothing could exceed the conduct and gallantry of Colonel Inglis at the head of his regiment. To Major General the Hon. William Lumley, for the very able manner in which he opposed the numerous cavalry of the enemy, and foiled him in his object, I am particularly indebted. To Major General Hamilton, who commanded on the left during the severe attack upon our right, I am also much indebted; and the Portuguese brigades of Brig. Generals Fonseca and Archibald Campbell deserve to be mentioned. To Major General Alten, and to the excellent brigade under his orders, I have much praise to give; and it is with great pleasure I assure your Lordship that the good and gallant conduct of every corps, and of every person, was in proportion to the opportunity that offered for distinguishing themselves. I know not an individual who did not do his duty. I have, I fear, to regret the loss to the service of Colonel Collins, commanding a Portuguese brigade, his leg having been carried off by a cannon shot. He is an Officer of great merit; and I deeply lament the death of Major General Hoghton, and of those two promising Officers, Lieut. Colonel Sir William Myers and Lieut. Colonel Duckworth. It is most pleasing to me to inform your Lordship, not only of the steady and gallant conduct of our allies, the Spanish troops under his Excellency General Blake, but also to assure you that the most perfect harmony has subsisted between us; and that General Blake not only conformed in all things to the general line proposed by your Lordship, but in the details; and in whatever I suggested to his Excellency I received the most immediate and cordial assent and co-operation; nothing was omitted on his part to ensure the success of our united efforts; and during the battle he most essentially, by his experience, knowledge, and zeal, contributed to its fortunate result.

His Excellency the Captain General Castaños, who had united the few troops he had in a state to be brought into the field to those of General Blake, and placed them under his orders, assisted in person in the field; and not only on this, but on all occasions, I am much indebted to General Castaños, who is ever beforehand in giving whatever can be beneficial to the success of the common cause.

10

Though I unfortunately cannot point out the corps, or many of the individuals of the Spanish troops, that distinguished themselves, yet I will not omit to mention the names of General Ballesteros, whose gallantry was most conspicuous, as of the corps he had under his command; and the same of General Zayas and of Don Carlos de España. The Spanish cavalry have behaved extremely well; and the Conde de Penne-Villemur is particularly deserving to be mentioned.

I annex the return of our loss in this hard contested day: it is very severe; and in addition to it is the loss of the troops under his Excellency General Blake, who are killed, missing, and wounded, but of which I have not the return. The loss of the enemy, though I cannot know what it is, must be still more severe. He has left on the field of battle about 2,000 dead, and we have taken from 900 to 1,000 prisoners. He has had five Generals killed and wounded: of the former, Generals of Division, Werlé and Pépin; and Gazan and two others amongst the latter. His force was much more considerable than we had been informed of, as I do not think he displayed less than from 20,000 to 22,000 infantry, and he certainly had 4,000 cavalry, with a numerous and heavy artillery. His overbearing cavalry cramped and confined all our operations, and, with his artillery, saved his infantry after its rout.

He retired after the battle to the ground he had been previously on, but occupying it in position; and on this morning, or rather during the night, commenced his retreat on the road he came, towards Seville, and has abandoned Badajoz to its fate. He left a number of his wounded on the ground he had retired to, and to whom we are administering what assistance we can. I have sent our cavalry to follow the enemy; but in that arm he is too powerful for us to attempt anything against him in the plains he is traversing.

Thus we have reaped the advantage we proposed from our opposition to the attempts of the enemy; and, whilst he has been forced to abandon the object for which he has almost stripped Andalusia of troops, instead of having accomplished the haughty boasts with which Marshal Soult harangued his troops on leaving Seville, he returns there with a curtailed army, and, what perhaps may be still more hurtful to him, with a diminished reputation.

In enumerating the services received from the Officers of my own staff, I must particularly call your Lordship's attention to those of Brig. General d'Urban, Quarter Master General to the Portuguese army; and which I cannot sufficiently praise, though I can appreciate. On all occasions I have felt the benefits of his talents and services, and more particularly on this, where they very essentially contributed to the success of the day: and I cannot here omit the name of Lieut. Colonel

11

Hardinge, Deputy Quarter Master General to the Portuguese troops, whose talents and exertions deserve my thanks. To Brig. General Mozinho, Adjutant General of the Portuguese army, and to Lieut. Colonel Rooke, Assistant Adjutant General to the united British and Portuguese force, and to Brig. General Lemos, and to the Officers of my own personal staff, I am indebted for their assistance.

To the services of Lieut. Colonel Arbuthnot (Major in His Majesty's service) I am also much indebted; and he is the bearer of this to your Lordship, and is fully enabled to give you any further information you may desire, and is most deserving of any favour your Lordship may be pleased to recommend him for to his Royal Highness the Prince Regent.

I have the honour to be, &c.

W.C. Beresford,

P.S. Major General Hamilton's division, and Brig. General Madden's brigade of Portuguese cavalry, march tomorrow morning to reinvest Badajoz on the south side of the Guadiana.

## 2. Beresford Comment on Blake

*During his long pamphlet war with Peninsular War historian William Napier, Beresford made numerous statements about events of the day, but the reliability of many of them is suspect because Beresford's primary purpose in writing the pamphlets was to refute statements made by Napier, not to provide his own coherent account of the battle. One exception is the following factual passage, which describes the interaction between Beresford and Blake when the Marshal ordered the Spaniards to form a new battle line to receive the French flank attack.[3] Napier alleged that Blake insubordinately disputed the order, but that does not appear to have been the case. Equally intriguing is the statement that Blake and Beresford had no further contact during the battle.*

No one can know better than Colonel Napier, that the Spanish armies were not precisely in the same state of discipline as the English, nor, like them, supplied at all times with every requisite, and ready to march at the tap of the drum. So far was I from perceiving any arrogance in General Blake, that I did not even observe any want of cordiality in that officer; and the delay which occurred may very easily be accounted for on any one of the grounds intimated above. With regard to my order for the change of front, as far as I am acquainted with it, all the circumstances are fairly stated in the 'Strictures'. I delivered my first instructions to Blake himself, and he not only did not object to them,

---

3    Beresford, William, *Refutation of Colonel Napier's Justification of his Third Volume* (London, 1834), pp. 150–1.

but he left me with the intention, as it appeared, of carrying them into effect. His doubts of the enemy's designs were afterwards brought me by his aide-de-camp, who simply reported that, as there was as yet no enemy to be seen on our right, and he 'thought their principal attack was still intended against the village and bridge, he would suspend the execution of the orders I had given him, until he received my further directions'. I instantly dispatched one of my own staff to him, desiring him to execute my original instructions; and, as I immediately proceeded to the threatened point, and there formed the Spanish line, with the assistance of Ballesteros and Zayas, whom I found upon the spot, I neither saw, nor heard, anything more of General Blake till after the conclusion of the battle.

## 3. D'Urban's Journal

*Benjamin D'Urban was Beresford's chief of staff. His campaign journal provides objective details of the army's movements but, oddly, he makes no mention of the successful French cavalry attack.*[4]

May 15. Headquarters Albuera. Marched the divisions of Hamilton and Stewart and the brigade of Alten to Albuera. Took up with Hamilton and Stewart a line following the contour of the ground parallel to the Albuera, about ¾ of an English mile from the river, the right upon the high road from Valverde. Orders sent to Long to fall back upon Albuera from Santa Marta; to Madden to march from Solana upon Talavera, and to General Blake to march his Spanish Division from Almendral to Albuera. The prolongation of the English line was destined for the Spanish troops and Blake, his left upon the Valverde road, his front along the contour of the ground parallel to the Albuera. This was not a good position, but it is the only one. Blake's division did not arrive till past midnight and then in spite of all instructions took up [the] wrong ground in the dark. Alten held the village of Albuera and Campbell's Portuguese brigade was attached to him. Cole ordered to March at 2 o'clock tomorrow from the bivouac, and Kemmis's brigade by Jerumenha after the stores should all be sent off to Elvas.

Long was driven rather faster than one could have wished from Santa Marta and retiring precipitately [*sic*], cross the Albuera, and gave up the whole right bank to the enemy. This haste is a bad thing, because the woods masque all the enemies' movement. Madden ordered to Albuera.

---

4     D'Urban, B., *The Peninsular Journal of Major-General Sir Benjamin d'Urban* (I.J. Rousseau, ed.) (London, 1930), pp. 213–16.

May 16. At daybreak the Spaniards commenced to get into their general alignment, which they are total want of all system of movement, and consequent and wielding us, took up such a length of time that they were not in till 7 a.m. The cavalry which had covered the ground destined for the Spaniards, we are now moved to a bivouac in the rear of the right of the British, for rest and forage. Cole arrived at 8 o'clock. The officer sent to Madden returned from Talavera without finding him – it appears he has retired from thence without orders, where no one knows.

At 8 o'clock the enemy were seen beginning to pass the river. He menaced our centre and left pretty strongly and directed his real attack upon our right. (The Spaniards' second line thrown *en potence* upon the heights of the right.) For this he had good reason, it was the key of the position and was also the direct road to cut off our communications. The firing began at half past 8. The enemy advanced upon the right and drove the Spaniards from the heights. It was necessary to retake them promptly. The enemy had rapidly established himself upon them and got up a powerful artillery. The Spaniards to save time as being the nearest troops were to attack and General Stewart's division to support. General Hamilton remaining in reserve to move to either point and sustain if required, either the centre or right. Meanwhile the division of Cole was placed obliquely, behind the right of the British line, to cover its flank or support its rear. General Lumley with the cavalry, British in Spanish, was in front of Cole upon the plain, and Colonel Otway with the Portuguese cavalry covered and watched the left of the whole, beyond the town of Albuera. The French occupied the heights they had gained with 18,000 infantry and some cavalry. Of the latter they had an overwhelming superior superiority, and with 26 squadrons to Lumley's 12, manoeuvred on our right.

*The contest was bloody and obstinate, it lasted from 10 a.m. till 2 p.m.* [Emphasis in original.] An uninterrupted fire of artillery and musketry, the latter frequently at 20 paces asunder, varied at short intervals by partial charges of the bayonet, continued for the four hours. From 12 till 2 it was the hottest action of the Peninsular War and unequalled in the memory of the oldest soldier. The enemy brought up reserve upon reserve, but at 2 he could make no further efforts, he was turned by both flanks. The heights were carried and the battle gained by the invincible valour of the British and Portuguese troops. The Spaniards behaved gallantly but were so devoid of discipline that they stood in the way and did more harm than good. The enemy retired to his camp, a fusillade and cannonade lasted until nightfall, and each army occupied itself in repairing its disasters as far as practicable, in sending off its wounded, and making arrangements for a renewal of the action tomorrow. Soult will probably attack again. An officer dispatched to hasten Kemmis's brigade. Even that small reinforcement is necessary to us, for the loss has fallen heavily upon her most precious people, our British. Out of about 6,000 of them engaged, I'm afraid we should find nearly 3,000 *hors de combat*. They have nobly upheld the honour of their name, and whatever may be the fruits of the victory of Albuera, it has been desperately fought for and brilliantly achieved.

May 17. The enemy quiet. His loss has been severe. Three generals of division killed, three dangerously wounded, with a host of officers *supérieurs*, 2,000 dead upon the field and more than 4,000 wounded. This he has paid for his attempt. I doubt his renewing it. Kemmis arrived. This makes us better and if he saw the brigade arrive he'll give up the task.

May 18. At daybreak the enemy had abandoned the bridge, and there was a reason to suppose he was moving to his right or rear. Early in the morning this became manifest and by 11 o'clock he was in full march covering his rear with all his cavalry; he took the road of Solano and Almendralejo. The cavalry followed. The infantry remained. Hamilton ordered to Badajoz at daybreak.

## 4. D'Urban's Report

*In 1817, D'Urban wrote a complete history of the 1811 campaign, the tone of which suggests he was anxious to justify the command decisions Beresford made in the field.[5] The description of Albuera in that volume is much more detailed than the one in this journal and contains cross-references to a plan of the battle that was included with the work. That plan can be found in the Illustrations section of this volume but the various changes of position are still hard to follow.*

Upon the morning of the 15th, the troops in the camp at Valverde advanced to the Albuera, and were placed in position about noon, as in **A.A** [these and other bold letters and numbers in this text are references to positions marked in the accompanying map of the battle] of the annexed plan.

The brigade of Baron Alten, occupying the village and bridge of Albuera; the 2nd Division (to which the 4th Division was destined

---

5     D'Urban, Benjamin, *Report of the Operations of the Right Wing of the Allied Army under Field Marshal Sir William Beresford in the Alentejo and Spanish Estremadura during the campaign of 1811* (London, 1817), pp. 21–31.

on its arrival to form the second line) extending from the Valverde to the Badajoz Road; and the line being thence prolonged by General Hamilton's Portuguese division and the Portuguese brigade of Colonel Collins (these troops forming their own second line), and following the contour of the ground as it falls towards the stream, and in the direction of the Cortijo of Ignacio Payano.

About 3 o'clock, the cavalry, which had been pushed back from Santa Marta rather more briskly than had been looked for, by that of the enemy, arrived, and upon the return of Sir William Beresford to the right, from placing the left of the line, and examining the country immediately beyond it, he found that it had already crossed the rivulet, and that the whole of the opposite bank was in possession of that of the enemy. Under the actual circumstances, this mistake once made, it was too late to repair it.

As the Spaniards under General Blake had not yet arrived, the horse artillery, the British cavalry, and that of Count Penne-Villemur, were stretched provisionally along the ground on the right of the Valverde road, which the former were destined to occupy, having pickets and posts of observation, well to the right in the direction of Torre de Almendral and Almendral, and the Portuguese brigade of Colonel Otway was placed on the left of the line in **f.f**, and charged with the outposts of the left, and the communications with General Madden at Talavera.

An officer was sent to General Blake at Almendral, to press his march, and to conduct him to the ground.

Meanwhile, it having been judged by Colonel Fletcher and Major Dickson, that the ordinance stores would be all got over the Guadiana on the night of the 15th, the Honourable Major General Cole had received directions on that day to send a battalion of Don Carlos España's troops to occupy Olivenza, and to hold himself in readiness to concentrate and march at the shortest notice to withdraw Colonel Kemmis's brigade from St Cristobal's by the ford above Badajoz, if it should be found practicable, but, if not, to send it round by Jerumenha and Olivenza, as soon as the remaining ordinance and stores before Saint Christophers should have all been sent off to Elvas, and to send back the 17th regiment and the cavalry to that place.

The Honourable Major General Lumley had been previously ordered to repair to the front, to take command of the cavalry of the army, which it was necessary should be under the orders of a major general, in consequence of the jarring ranks of several brigadier generals of the different nations actually with it, and which required the whole to be placed under a general of whose superiority of rank no doubt could exist.

The Major General, although at the moment commanding infantry brigade, was an officer of cavalry, and was well calculated for the duty he was called upon to perform, as the ability with which he afterwards discharged it proved. He arrived and took command of the cavalry, accordingly, in the morning the 16th, about an hour before the beginning of the battle.

At this period, the *tête de pont* [bridgehead] which had been constructed in front of Jerumenha, was in an excellent state of preparation, and, in case of any unforeseen misfortune, would have served to receive the army, and to afford the necessary protection for repassing the Guadiana.

In the afternoon the 15th, the enemy's infantry began to arrive (continuing to do so during the greater part of the night), and encamped in the wood upon the Santa Martha Road, in **B.B**.

It was now certain that his whole force assembled at Los Santos had moved upon Solana and Santa Martha, and his army was collecting in front of Albuera.

Sir William Beresford, therefore, sent orders to the Honourable Major General Cole before Badajoz, to march at 2 o'clock in the morning of the 16th, with Major Hawker's 9-pounder brigade (which had arrived a few days before from Elvas), the two squadrons of Portuguese cavalry, the 4th Division and the remainder of Don Carlos España's corps, upon Albuera, by the high road from Badajoz; and to Brigadier General Madden, to march immediately from Talavera (where his presence was no longer any used), and join the left to the army near the Cortijo of Ignacio Payano.

Four Spanish 4-pounders had now joined General Castaños, in addition to the two which had originally accompanied the army, and were all under the command of Colonel Don José de Miranda.

Meanwhile, the Spanish corps, under General Blake, which had little more than a league to march from Almendral, by a good road, guided by an officer sent for the purpose, and which the General had engaged should be upon its ground at noon, did not commence arriving till 11 at night, and was not all up until three in the morning of the 16th.

These troops were disposed of as soon as it was practicable, in the ground which had been marked out for them on the right of the 2nd Division, and the two lines, as shown in the plan.

This was at length effected, after much delay upon the part of General Blake; and the cavalry and horse artillery, which had provisionally

17

covered that part of the position, was withdrawn to rest and refresh, in rear of the centre.

The corps from before Badajoz, under the Honourable Major General Cole, having marched at the ordered hour, arrived at six in the morning by the high road, and halted, and rested in column, in rear of the 2nd Division, to which they thus formed the second line, or reserve.

Brigadier General Kemmis's brigade had not accompanied the 4th Division, because the fords of the Guadiana had become impracticable, and it had therefore been sent round by Jerumenha.

The two squadrons of Portuguese cavalry, which had come with General Cole, joined Colonel Otway's brigade on the left; that of General Madden to which they belonged, not arriving from Talavera-Real.

Don Carlos España, was sent to the right, to join the Spanish forces.

The Allied army was thus united up on the Albuera, having regulated all its successive movements by the progressive advance of the enemy, equally avoiding a late or premature assembly, and having combined the removal of all the ordinance and siege stores with a timely arrival at the proposed position.

It now stood across the roads leading from Albuera to Talavera-Real, Badajoz and Valverde as in **A a d f g k**; and thus posted, equally ready to give battle where he was, or to move by his right upon Valverde, or by his left upon Talavera, as circumstances might require. Sir William Beresford observed the movements of the enemy, and awaited the further developments of his projects.

The ground which the army occupied was by no means strong; it was a range of heights gradually falling into the Albuera in front and into the Arroyo de Valdesevilla in the rear. It was of gentle undulation, and easy for cavalry throughout; it was nevertheless good fighting ground, and very well calculated for a position of assembly in which to meet and observe the enemy, and be guided by his subsequent measures.

Marshal Soult, having reconnoitred the position of the Allies on the evening of the 15th, determined to attack their right, which ground afforded scope for using his superior cavalry to advantage, and which he expected to find but weakly occupied, because the Spanish infantry not having arrived when he made his reconnaissance, there had been an appearance of very few troops.

Here, therefore, he thought to roll up the army by its right flank, establishing himself upon the height **Z.Z**, and penetrating to the Valverde road, to take the position in reverse, place himself upon its communications, and pursue his success to the utmost that such an advantage would have put in his power.

This was undoubtedly the most decisive mode of bringing matters to a conclusion; and, as he received information that one British division still remained before Badajoz, he was naturally desirous to attack before it should have joined, and resolved to do so the instant his infantry should have all arrived, notwithstanding its fatigue, part of it having marched eight leagues (or 32 English miles), and not reaching the camp till the middle of the night.[6]

The ground which he encamped upon in **B.B** was covered with wood, which afforded great facility for making his real assembly for attack, particularly on his extreme left, where it was thick, and extended down to the banks of the Feria, and where an abrupt shoulder of the tongue between the fork of that rivulet and the Albuera formed a hollow V, capable of holding a large body of troops, and concealing them from any part of the opposite heights. In this hollow, then, he had, early in the morning of the 16th, formed the elite of his infantry in three columns of attack, and a large proportion of his cavalry and artillery, **4.4** and **5.5**; and, having completed his preparation, the remainder of his infantry in three columns, **1.1**, and of his cavalry and artillery, **2.2** and **3.3**, moved out of the wood, and directed themselves between eight and nine in the morning up on the bridge and village of Albuera. When this force had proceeded so far as to give him reason for supposing that the principal attention of his antagonist would be drawn to the left and centre, two of the three columns of infantry, **1.1**, rapidly countermarched, and hastened back to his left to form the reserve of his real attack, while part of the cavalry, **3.3**, turned to its left, crossed Albuera, and, proceeding up its left bank at a gallop, came round the right flank of the Allies.

The third column of infantry, **2.2**, with the artillery, continued its march, and commenced a sharp cannonade and tiraillade upon the bridge and village of Albuera, and the opposite bank of the stream, in front of and to the flank of it; while the cavalry, proceeding further on, took post near the Cortijo de Campanello, in observation and menace of the Portuguese cavalry in **F.F**.

Meanwhile the artillery, cavalry, and three columns of infantry, which had been prepared upon the enemy's left, moved from the ground where they had been formed in the V, as soon as the troops at the bridges and village were warmly engaged, and advanced with great rapidity to **Y**, where the artillery opened its fire upon the right of

---

6    In a letter dated 29 August 1811 in the D'Urban archive in the National Army Museum, London, D'Urban states: 'The first question he [Soult] asked of the officers who were made prisoner early in the action was "What is the strength of the division you have left before Badajoz?"'

the Allies; while the infantry formed in **7.7** for the attack of **Z.Z**, the two columns which had countermarched from **1.1** forming the reserve in **6.6**, and part of the cavalry remaining with these columns to cooperate in their attack, the rest joined that which had already crossed from **3.3**, and stretched round to their left in **S.S**, to penetrate into the rear of the right of the position.

While these arrangements were going on, Sir William Beresford, observing the troops which were in march upon Albuera, judged that they were not in sufficient strength to be the sole or principal attack, penetrated the enemy's design, and saw that this was either a feint altogether, or that the movement upon the village would be combined with one upon his right.

Under this conviction he ordered General Blake to form all his first line, and the right of his second, to his right, and so occupy **Z.Z**, and he put the 2nd Division from the centre in movement to the right to support him, and, bringing the Portuguese division and the brigade of Colonel Collins from the left, formed them upon the ground quitted by the right of the 2nd Division near the Valverde road, in contiguous close columns of battalions in **t.t**, instructing General Hamilton (while he remained in readiness to move in whatever direction he might ultimately be ordered) to advance a brigade near the village for the support of Baron Alten, and to take care that that post was maintained.

This division was thus at once a support to the centre and the right, could be rendered to the left, if any an unforeseen exigency should demand it, and secured against all accidents the important hill upon the Valverde road in the centre, which commanded, and was the key of the whole position.

At the same time he moved the 4th Division, which was in column at **1d**, to **3d**, and placed it obliquely in rear of the right. Here it stood secure upon strong ground, forming a powerful reserve for the right and centre, covering the right flank and Valverde road, and holding out an *appui* [support] to his inferior cavalry, from the protection of which that of the enemy, though more than double in number, could never drive it. In the event, this division answered every purpose that Sir William Beresford expected from it when he posted it so ably.

Finally, he placed the British and Spanish cavalry (under the Honourable Major General Lumley) in advance of the 4th Division on the right, upon the plain in (**e.k**), within the little channel formed by the Arroyo de Valdesevilla. Here it was disposable to move towards the position by its left, or to stretch along the Valverde road by its right; and Sir William Beresford, aware of its numerical inferiority to that of the enemy, as well as of the infinite importance of preserving it entire for emergencies, instructed General Lumley to have these considerations in view, and to adventure nothing against the enemy which might lead to a wide movement, to separating his force, or to removing him from the *appui* of the 4th Division; but at the same time to watch the enemy's movements, and act according to his own discretion for the main object of impeding his attempts to penetrate to the Valverde road, and double round the rear of the position.

The Portuguese cavalry remained on the left in **f.f**, in observation of the flank at the French cavalry in the Cortijo de Campanello; and the 13th light dragoons in the hollow **h.h**, watched the cavalry which the enemy had opposite the village.

The artillery was disposed of in just proportions to support the different points, and the horse artillery of captain Lefebvre accompanied the cavalry.

These dispositions were promptly and precisely carried into effect, with the exception of that General Blake, whose delay in executing it had very nearly led to the most fatal consequences; for so much time was lost, that, instead of being prepared upon the ground he was to hold, his troops had scarcely placed themselves there when the enemy fell upon them.

About 9 o'clock, the enemy in **7.7** moved rapidly from **Y** under a very heavy fire of artillery, and attacked the Spanish corps upon **Z.Z**.

The Spaniards made a gallant and an obstinate resistance, but were at length obliged to yield their ground, upon which the enemy took post.

This height was of great importance, inasmuch as it commanded the right of the position; and the 2nd Division, under the Honourable Major General Stewart, which was now rapidly advancing to support the Spaniards, and which arrived just as they had been forced to abandon it, was immediately ordered by Sir William Beresford, to attack and recover it, the Spaniards in their turn supporting. This attack was made an echelon of brigades from the right, and led by General Stewart with equal intrepidity and precision.

There fell at this time a heavy rain, which combining with the smoke of the firing, caused such a darkness, that it was impossible to distinguish any object, even at a few paces distant. Favoured by this, as the 1st brigade, under Colonel Colborne, fell upon the enemy with the bayonet and were driving him before them, some squadrons of Polish Lancers and hussars, which had lodged themselves unperceived behind the knoll **x**, charged the brigade in the rear, and many of these gallant soldiers perished.

The 31st regiment, which was on the left of the brigade, commanded by Major L'Estrange, extricated itself from the confusion, and continued

21

the attack alone, and with the best effect, unshaken by the disaster of the other regiments.

The wind at this moment blowing aside the smoke and rain, General Lumley in the plain, perceived the enterprise of the enemy, and instantly detached two squadrons of the 4th Dragoons led by Lieutenant Colonel Leighton, directed by the Honourable Colonel de Grey, and two squadrons of Spanish cavalry, under Count de Penne-Villemur, to the spot. These troops fell upon the lancers and hussars with so much fury, that the greater part of them were cut to pieces, and then returned without delay to the cavalry in the plain.

The 3rd Brigade of the 2nd Division, under Major General Hoghton, following the first, with equal intrepidity, and better fortune, deployed very judiciously and with admirable precision, under cover of the lower falls of the heights, moved on in line to the attack, and supported and followed by the 2nd Brigade under the Honourable Colonel Abercromby, and the Spaniards under Generals Ballesteros and Zayas, carried all before it, gained the contested ground, and took post upon it.

In this glorious exploit, General Hoghton fell, pierced with bullets, having still continued to lead the troops after receiving several wounds, and cheering them to the charge with his last breath. Lieutenant Colonel Duckworth was also killed at this period of the battle, at the head of the 1st battalion of the 48th.

Scarcely had Sir William Beresford (who had conducted this attack of the 3rd Brigade in person) placed the troops and artillery to the best advantage upon the ground they had gained, when the enemy, who had taken breath for a moment under the fire of his artillery from **Y**, and reinforced himself from his columns of reserve in **6.6**, again moved upon the height **Z.Z**, in three columns, from 4,000 to 5,000 men in each, and here commenced the most desperate and sanguinary conflict of infantry that perhaps had ever been witnessed. It was an incessant fire of musketry, very often at the distance of 20 paces, only interrupted at intervals, upon the part of the British, by partial charges of the bayonet. The French, treble in number, fought in their best manner, and made incredible efforts, but in vain; nothing could shake or overcome the troops who opposed them; and this period of the battle was fruitful beyond all former example, in traits of devoted heroism and contempt of death.

Here the 29th and 48th regiments were conspicuous for their invincible steadiness, and the immense number of the enemy's dead in their front showed how well their prowess was directed; and here the 57th regiment, commanded by Colonel Inglis, had their Colonel and 22, out of 24, officers killed or wounded, and here, after the battle was won, their dead were found (as described in Sir William Beresford's dispatch) lying in the ranks as they fought, and with all their wounds before.

The Honourable General Stewart received two wounds, but would not quit the field; and from the general to the soldier, all were animated with the same feeling, and all resolved to conqueror or to fall.

The heavy loss sustained by the right brigade, and the destructive struggle now continuing, had so diminished the force of the 2nd Division, that the enemy was able to lodge one of his columns which he had constantly fed from his reserves rather forwarder than he had hitherto done upon the right of the contested ground, and Sir William Beresford dispatched orders to the Honourable General Cole to send his left brigade to this point. The order had been anticipated, for Colonel Hardinge had perceived the necessity, and, with his characteristic promptness and decision, had hastened to the point to point it out to General Cole, who instantly directed the Fusilier brigade under Sir William Meyers, and the battalion of the Loyal Lusitanian Legion commanded by Colonel Hawkshaw, upon this duty.

These troops moved to their point with rapidity and in the most perfect order; and, in a few minutes, the greater part of the French column which had required their presence, perished under their fire.

In this glorious and successful achievement, they suffered, however, severely; the Honourable General Cole (who had, himself, led the Fusiliers to the attack), and the Colonels Ellis, Blakeney, and Hawkshaw, were wounded, and Sir William Myers killed.

The enemy now, foiled in his attempts to gain the long disputed height Z.Z, and pushed back upon Y from whence he had originally attacked, maintained himself there, and the battle continued upon this point with unabated fury.

The 2nd brigade of the 2nd Division had behaved throughout the day with the most distinguished prowess; the 28th, 34th, and 39th regiments, vied with each other in discipline and valour, and executed various movements under the hottest fire with admirable precision. The conduct and able dispositions of the Hon. Colonel Abercromby were worthy [of] the renown of his father.

Colonel Collins's Portuguese brigade having arrived from the centre to support the 2nd Brigade, suffered considerably, and its commander, an officer of the highest promise, lost his leg by a cannon shot.

The Spanish 4-pounders under Colonel Don José de Miranda, were well served.

The Allied artillery under Major Dickson, was directed with consummate ability by that excellent officer and all under his orders.

23

Meanwhile, the enemy had not ceased to continue a vigorous attack upon the left of the Allies at the bridge and village of Albuera (which had been ably resisted throughout the day by the German light brigade, under Baron Alten, and the 5th Caçadores, under Lieutenant Colonel M'Creagh, supported by the Portuguese brigade of Brigadier General Campbell), while at the same time, his superior cavalry on the right had made various efforts to envelop, and penetrate by, that flank. In all of these he failed, through the prompt and judicious measures of the Honourable Major General Lumley, who, manoeuvring with 15 squadrons against 26, constantly found means, by availing himself with the trifling obstacle of the Arroyo de Valdesevilla, and leaning upon the 4th Division, to baffle his endeavours, moving down upon him, whenever he showed a disposition to pass the Arroyo, with so determined a countenance, that, although he often made the attempt, he as often abandoned it, and he was deterred from stretching very widely round by his left towards the Valverde road and the baggage, by the apprehension that, if he withdrew from the front of the cavalry and the 4th Division, these corps would throw themselves, perhaps with fatal effect, upon the left flank of his infantry engaged on the heights.

When General Cole moved the Fusilier brigade to the assistance of the 2nd Division, he advanced the 4th Division to **4d**, and then closed the Portuguese brigade nearer to the heights to preserve the connection; at this moment, some squadrons from the right of the French cavalry made an attempt upon the Portuguese brigade, and were received by Colonel Harvey with the most perfect coolness, and such a well-directed fire giving it about 40 paces, that they dispersed, and fled in all directions.

General Lumley advancing as the 4th Division advanced, the French cavalry fell back as their infantry gave ground to take post in **Y**.

Sir William Beresford now saw that the moment for deciding the fortune of the day was arrived. The whole of the enemy was before him on the right; to conquer him there, then, was victory, and he determined to fall upon him with the flower of his force united.

To this end, he ordered the left of the Spanish front line (which still remained in its original ground, and had not been engaged), to occupy the village of Albuera from whence he called Baron Alten to support the left, in turning the enemy's right in **p.p.** He directed General Hamilton to close up the whole of the Portuguese division to the rear of the centre of this attack, and the 2nd Division thus reinforced, were to move straight upon the enemy in **Y**; while General Lumley, with the cavalry, combining with a Fusilier brigade and the Portuguese brigade of the 4th Division united, turned his flank in **w**.

The orders for this simultaneous movement were immediately given, and promptly obeyed. The troops all moved accordingly, and the enemy turned by both flanks, and perceiving the close column of General Hamilton advancing in support of the attack upon centre, made all possible haste to send back his reserve and artillery to **D.D**, and then, unable to make any further effort, his troops at **Y** fled in the greatest confusion over the Albuera, and took refuge under that protection.

They were bayonetted to the edge of the stream by the British infantry, and there Sir William Beresford recalled the troops from further pursuit, which their fatigue, their loss, and the superior cavalry of the enemy, combined to forbid.

Baron Alten hastened to reoccupy Albuera, and the troops of the Portuguese division which were for the most part fresh and untouched immediately placed in position **C.C**. Those who had been engaged were formed in columns of reserve in the rear; the cavalry were stretched well round to the right, the necessary posts and pickets established, and everything secured.

The wounded were removed from the immediate field of battle, the soldiers cooked, got an additional ration of spirits, and their ammunition was completed.

The battle, which had begun at nine, ceased at a little after two, and all these arrangements were completed by four.

D'Urban Note – A report appears to have been for some time in circulation, that, at one period of the battle of Albuera, orders had been given by Sir William Beresford for a retreat. The above, which is a faithful statement of what passed, and of the order actually issued, as well as of the motives and circumstances by which they were successfully dictated, will suffice to show that this report was unfounded.

## 5. Stewart's Account

*Major General William Stewart was the commander of the 2nd Division of the Anglo-Portuguese army. The 2nd Division was composed of three brigades of British infantry – the 1st, commanded by Lieutenant Colonel John Colborne, the 2nd, commanded by Lieutenant Colonel Alexander Abercromby, and the 3rd, commanded by Major General Daniel Hoghton – and was considered by Marshal Beresford to be his most reliable available strike force for responding to Soult's attacks. The way that force was used is recounted in a letter written by Stewart soon after the battle that appears in edited form in a published collection of his papers.[7]*

---

7    Stewart, Sir William, *Cumloden Papers* (Edinburgh, 1871), pp. 88–91.

Bivouac of Albuera, May 18, 1811

The arduous combat in which we were engaged having been fought under your own immediate eye, it may be almost unnecessary that I should on this occasion enter upon that which is certainly the most pleasing of all our duties – the giving praise to the survivors and recording the gallantry of those who may fall in a well-contested action. The memory and martial virtue, however, of those who entered the field that day are too strongly impressed upon my mind for me willingly to lose the opportunity which you have given me of asserting, that more brave men never defended the honour of His Majesty's arms or more firmly supported the glory of their country than those who fell in, as well as those who survived, the contest of the 16th instant. The conduct of the 1st Brigade, which was first brought into action by Lieutenant Colonel Colborne, was very gallant. Although the loss in prisoners and colours has fallen on this portion of the division, you are probably aware, Sir, that the brigade was suddenly attacked in flank and rear by a body of the enemy's cavalry while engaged in the almost desperate effort of charging nearly the whole of the enemy's attacking force. The form of the hill up which the brigade was led to the charge, and the obscurity occasioned by the smoke of musketry, and by a heavy fall of rain, prevented the enemy's cavalry from being seen, or their charge sufficiently early resisted. The colours of the 2nd battalions of the 48th and 66th regiments were unfortunately lost on this occasion, but not until the officers who bore them were killed, and the commanding officers, Major Brooke and Captain Benning, ceased to command. The former was severely wounded and made prisoner, and the latter was killed.

The 31st Regiment, the left of the brigade, not having been attacked by the cavalry, retained, by its steadiness and spirit, the summit of the hill which had been gained by the rest of the brigade. The conduct of this small corps (it had only 320 firelocks in action), under the command of Major L'Estrange, was so particularly remarked by me during the whole of the action that I feel it to be my duty to state the same in the warmest terms. Wherever the fire or the bayonets of that battalion could be directed, although against the heaviest columns of the enemy, they never failed of being so directed until the defeat of the enemy closed the operations of the day.

[The General then speaks of the 3rd Brigade, which had opportunely been brought up by General Hoghton to supply the place of the 1st Brigade, and says its great gallantry was the admiration of the Allied army. Aided by an equally bold attack on the part of the

Fusilier brigade of General Cole's Division, the height was effectually maintained against the repeated attacks of the enemy.]

The death and severe wounds of every commander in the 3rd Brigade, and the fall of two-thirds of both officers and men on the spot which was so warmly contended for, sufficiently bespeak the unconquerable spirit of the corps which composed that brigade. A noble example was shown by the Major General (Hoghton) who commanded it. He fell with many wounds while in the act of encouraging the 29th Regiment to the charge.

[General Stewart next gives praise to the 2nd Brigade, which he says was ably commanded by the Hon. Lieutenant Colonel Abercromby, and greatly contributed by its gallantry and spirit to the enemy's defeat. Words of high and ardent praise are bestowed on all for their conduct that victorious day. In conclusion, he says:]

On none of the many occasions on which British armies have been accustomed to evince high conduct in battle has there been more high or, I believe, more general good conduct than was shown on the 16th instant. The contest was arduous, and our situation was critical. The enemy was more obstinate than usual; and your own expression of determination to myself on the field called forth a more than ordinary degree of exertion and of self-devotion from all. It is my hope that the 2nd Division did its duty on that day.

## B. Colborne's (1st) Brigade, 2nd Division Accounts

### 1. Colborne's Account
*Lieutenant Colonel Colborne provides more details than General Stewart concerning the successful French charge against his brigade.[8] Not surprisingly, he was particularly concerned that he might be blamed for the disaster.*

May 18, 1811
To the Reverend Duke Yonge
My dear Duke,
Since April of the brigade I commanded has been in continual movement. During the siege of Badajoz I was sent into the Sierra Morena as a movable column to attract the enemy's attention, and we performed a march of about 260 miles in a very short time. Marshal Soult was collecting his force at Seville, and on the 15th his advance card arrived at Santa Marta, three leagues from our position.

---

8    Smith, G.C. Moore, *The Life of John Colborne, Field Marshal Lord Seton* (London, 1903), p. 160.

Marshal Beresford was obliged to retire from his lines before Badajoz and concentrate his force. The Spaniards, under Blake and Ballesteros, joined the army on the night of the 15th, and we occupied a position near Albuera.

Soult began his attack at 8 a.m., and having menaced the village of Albuera, I was ordered into it, but as soon as I had marched there, the enemy commenced his attack on the right, and was in the act of turning it. Our brigade was then ordered to occupy the ground where the Spaniards should have been, and we were brought up under very disadvantageous circumstances, and obliged to deploy under the enemy's fire.

The regiments were ordered to charge before the deployment was complete, and without support; in the act of charging to very heavy columns, a regiment of Polish cavalry passed by our right, which was unprotected, and having gained our rear, the three right-hand regiments were almost destroyed. The Spaniards on our left behaved very well, but, as we had not any support, the few who are not killed or wounded were taken prisoners.

The 4th Division came up and drove the enemy, supported by the 2nd and 3rd brigades of the division. Soult retreated about 2 p.m. Our loss has been immense, nearly 6,000, the greater part British. The enemy retreated to Almendralejo last night, and I believe we are to pursue him immediately.

This has been a most unfortunate affair for me, although I had nothing to do with the arrangement, but merely obeyed the orders of General Stewart. Yet, it being my first trial, and having so considerable command, it is truly unfortunate for your brother. I did not receive any injury personally, although in the hands of the Poles some minutes.

Poor Colonel Duckworth was killed leading on the 48th; he received three shots at the same time. His horse was wounded. Pray communicate this sad intelligence to Mrs. Duckworth. I was very intimate with him. The poor fellow had been long sighing to revisit his home.

You can easily conceive what a stroke this has been on me, and yet if Bonaparte had been in my place nothing could have saved the three battalions. The enemy had 4,000 cavalry and 20,000 infantry.

Yours sincerely,

J. Colborne

## 2. Gordon's Letter

*An officer of the 3rd Foot or Buffs (identified as Captain Arthur Gordon in C.R.B. Knight's regimental history)[9] catalogued the horrendous casualties suffered by his regiment in a letter written shortly after the battle. The letter was published in the* Star *newspaper on 8 June 1811 and reprinted in a French translation in* Le Moniteur Universel *in Paris on 20 June 1811.*

Extract of a letter from a Captain of the Buffs, who is wounded in the action at Albuera, to his Brother Officer in England.

Elvas, in Portugal, 20th May, 1811

Before this reaches you, many statements of the battle fought at Albuera on the 16th instant, will be received in England.

I shall endeavour, however, to give you some facts respecting the first Battalion of the Buffs:

Captain Burke is killed, Captain Cameron shot in the neck, wounded in the breast with a pike, and a prisoner.

Captain Marley was wounded twice in the body with a pike, badly.

Captain Stephens was shot in the arm, was a prisoner, and made his escape.

Lieutenant Woods had his leg shot off by a cannonball.

Lieutenant Latham's hand is shot off, also part of his nose and cheek.

Lieutenant Juxon is wounded in the thigh with a pike.

Lieutenant Hooper shot through the shoulder.

Lieutenant Hoghton has received a severe sabre cut on the hand, and through the skull.

Lieutenant Herbert is dead; Ensigns Chadwick and Thomas also dead.

Lieutenants O'Donnell and Tetlow, with Ensign Walsh, were wounded and made prisoners, [but] they have since escaped and joined.

Twenty-four officers, and 750 rank and file, were actually engaged. Out of that number there only remained to draw rations on the following day five officers and 34 men.

This immense slaughter occurred in consequence of our charging the enemy, halting at the muzzles of their heavy guns, when a tremendous fire was opened on both sides.

So soon as our ranks were thinned by cannon shot, the enemy's cavalry (Polanders) armed with long spikes, charged over our dead and wounded men. It was this circumstance that caused the destruction of

---

9      Knight, C.R.B., *Historical Records of the Buffs East Kent Regiment (3rd Foot) 1704–1914, Part 1: 1704–1814,* (London, 1953), p. 343, n. 1.

many of the Buffs. I was stabbed at the time with a pike in the breast, in the back, and elsewhere, and the enemy's cavalry galloped over me, when the British cavalry appeared in sight, and they very soon came up to our assistance, the enemy's cavalry galloped off in all directions. Our colours were taken and retaken three times, and they are now in our possession, fixed on two halberts. Lieutenant Colonel Stewart, Major King, and another field officer of the Buffs are all safe.

The French have retreated in great confusion, and have suffered severely. Marshal Beresford is in pursuit of the enemy.

### 3. Stephens-Matthews Letter

*Fifteen-year-old Ensign Edward Thomas of the Buffs lost his life at Albuera defending the regimental colour of his unit. His courageous behaviour was so impressive that it was discussed in Parliament in connection with the vote of thanks to Marshal Beresford and his army for the victory. Unfortunately, the Members of Parliament had some of their facts wrong, so the utterance 'I will surrender it [the colour] only with my life' was incorrectly attributed to him even though those words were actually spoken by Lieutenant Matthew Latham, the officer who defended the King's colour of the regiment. The last moments of Ensign Thomas's short life are described in a letter written by Captain William Stephens (called 'Stevens' in this letter), his company commander, to Thomas's aunt, Mrs E. Matthews. Mrs Matthews subsequently communicated the details to Lord Londonderry in a letter dated 14 September 1828.[10]*

The subject to which I allude is the notice your Lordship has been pleased to particularly take of the gallant conduct of my nephew, Ensign Thomas of the Buffs, who fell in that battle bravely defending a colour of his regiment. The little hero was born in Jamaica, and being an orphan, was committed to my care at the age of four years, and was educated and provided for by my husband Doctor Matthews, who was then the surgeon of the same regiment. . . .

He had, previously to his regiment's being broken by the French cavalry, taken the command of Captain Stevens's company, there being no other subaltern officer but himself attached to the company, and the captain being wounded at the commencement of the battle. The circumstances are detailed by Captain Stevens in a letter he wrote to Dr. Matthews from Olivenza four days after the action, which letter

---

10    Vane, Charles William [Marquis of Londonderry], *Narrative of the Peninsular War from 1808–1813* (2 vols., London, 1829) v. 2, pp. 317–19.

I now have before me, and I beg leave to transcribe an extract for your Lordship's information. . . .

The extract runs thus: 'I cannot refrain from tears, while I relate the determined bravery of your gallant little subaltern, who fell on the 16th instant, covered with glory; and it must in some measure alleviate the grief I know you will feel at his loss, to know he fell like a hero. He rallied my company after I was wounded and taken prisoner, crying out, "Rally on me, men, I will be your pivot." Such glorious conduct must surely meet its reward in that world where all troubles cease, and all grief is at an end. He was buried with all care possible by a sergeant and a private, the only two survivors out of my company, which consisted of sixty-three men when taken into action.

'The colours he died in protecting, it appears he took possession of at the moment the officer who held them was killed, his company being dispersed. This gallant little fellow was not sixteen years of age when he so bravely sacrificed his life for the honour of King and country. His loss was, and still is most painfully felt by me, for he was as truly amiable in his private life as he was gallant and brave in performing his duty to King and country as a soldier.'

## 4. Morrison's Letter

*John Morrison was an assistant surgeon of the 3rd Foot (the Buffs). In 1834, he decided to write a letter to the* United Service Gazette *to clarify once and for all the role played by Lieutenant Matthew Latham in the fight for the unit's colours.*[11]

At the battle of Albuera, on the 16 May, 1811, the 3rd Regiment of Foot, or Buffs (owing to an error to which I shall allude more particularly) was surrounded by a large force of French and Polish cavalry. The ensign (Thomas) who carried the regimental colour was shot dead in the commencement of the struggle, and the colour captured. The King's Colour was carried by Lieutenant Matthew Latham. He was attacked by several French hussars, one of whom seizing the flag-staff, and rising in his stirrup, aimed a stroke at the head of the gallant Latham, which failed in cutting him down, but which sadly mutilated him, severing one side of the face and nose; he still however, struggled with the dragoon, and exclaimed, 'I will surrender it only with my life.' A second sabre struck severing his left arm and hand, in which he held the staff, from his body. The brave fellow, however, then seized

---

[11]   'Preservation of the Colours of the Buffs at Albuera', *United Service Gazette*, 25 April 1840 (No. 382), p. 3.

the staff with his right hand, throwing away his sword, and continued to struggle with his opponents, now increased in number; when ultimately thrown down, trampled upon and pierced by the spears of the Polish lancers, his last effort was to tear the flag from the staff as he thus lay prostrate, and to thrust it partly into the breast of his jacket. The number of Latham's adversaries impeded their efforts to destroy him, and the dragoons were ultimately driven off by the 7th Fusiliers, and 48th Regiment, which came up to support the Buffs. The greater part of the latter corps, was, however, made prisoners, and sent to the rear. The brave Latham was turned over by a soldier of the 7th Fusiliers, and the colour which he had thus preserved found under him. Latham was left on the field, supposed to have been killed, and the flag was sent on the evening following the battle to the headquarters of the Buffs, with a statement of the manner of its recovery.

Latham, however, although so desperately wounded, was not killed; in two hours afterwards he crawled on his remaining hand and knees towards the river of Albuera, and was found by some of the orderlies of the army attempting to slake his thirst in the stream; he was carried into the convent, where his wounds were dressed, the stump of his arm amputated, and he ultimately recovered. . . .

Captain Latham retired from the service some years subsequently; in fact, 'the weak piping times of peace' ill-suited the heroic ardour of his character, and he lives *at this moment* in a secluded part of France, where for years he has remained, *unnoticed and unknown*. This, however, is his *choice* and his wish, and even friendship claims no right to interfere with his selection; but *history* still remains to be vindicated. Latham's name belongs to that of his country, and he *must* not complain that this tardy debt to truth should at length be paid.

Colonel Napier, in his splendid History of the Peninsular War, in narrating the battle of Albuera, and the disaster of the Buffs, and speaking of the capture and rescue of the Standard, gives the honour to Ensign Thomas (who, as I have stated, was killed on the spot), and never even mentions the name of Latham, to whom all the honour belongs. He also puts the sentiment I have quoted into the mouth of Thomas. The high and honourable fame of Napier is a sufficient guarantee, that when he shall have satisfied himself of the correctness of this detail, he will correct that page of his history in which the error occurs, which it is almost inconceivable should have remained uncorrected during so many years, whilst so many officers survive to whom the facts are known; but 'what is everyone's business is no one's', and this, added to Latham's determination to abandon the world, has left the matter unquestioned to this day.

In the history and achievements of the Buffs, which has been lately published, by authority, uniformly with that of other regiments, the story of the affair of Albuera has been taken from Colonel Napier's history, and of course does not contain the name of Latham.

Should I have been the means of doing justice to the fame of an old brother officer, and of assisting historical truth, I shall feel proud and gratified.

## 5. Smith Comment

*Although Lieutenant Harry Smith of the 95th Rifles was not present at Albuera, he was close with General Stewart and included a comment in his autobiography that sheds some technical light on the formation used by the 3rd Foot just before the French cavalry attack.*[12]

It is true the Buffs were awfully mauled at Albuera, but what did my kind patron, Sir William Stewart, order them to do? They were in open column of companies right in front, and it was necessary at once to deploy into line, which Sir William with his light 95th had been accustomed to do on any company. He orders them, therefore, to deploy on the Grenadiers; by this the right would become the left, what in common parlance is deemed 'clubbed'; and while he was doing this, he kept advancing the Grenadiers. It is impossible to imagine a battalion in a more helpless position.

## 6. Close Diary

*Another dramatic account of the rout of Colborne's brigade was penned by Lieutenant Edward Close of the 2nd Battalion of the 48th Foot.*[13] *He provides some specific, if confusing, details of the English formation and confirms that the Allied cavalry did come to the aid of the brigade. In his opinion, some effort was made to obscure the number of colours captured by the French.*

May 16th – Albuera. We formed a line along a ridge of hills with a small stream passable in various places along the front, the town of Albuera and its bridge being almost opposite the centre, the Portuguese infantry on the left of our line, and the Spaniards on our right. After a few cannon shot from the enemy, he began to move forward his troops as if to attack the centre by the bridge, which was occupied by a rifle German regiment, just joined. The morning was heavy and misty,

---

12    Smith, Harry, *The Autobiography of Lieutenant General Sir Harry Smith* (G.C. Moore Smith, ed.) (London, 1903), p. 278.

13    Close, Edward Charles, *Diary of E.C. Close* (London, nd [1900?]).

and prevented us from observing the enemy's movements distinctly, in consequence of which the real point of attack was not perceived. Our brigade, however, were sent down to the protection of the bridge, which had been in our immediate front all along. The rain now fell in torrents. We remained here some time. The enemy having approached pretty near the bridge halted, whilst they pursued their attack to our right, where lay the key of our position.

We at last got orders to move off to the right, which we did in open column of companies, right in front, and arrived at the right just as the French were driving in the Spanish sharpshooters. A very heavy cannonading was scattering destruction amongst us at this time. Our brigade began to form line, the Buffs on the right, 2nd Battalion 48th next, and the 66th Grenadiers being all that could be said to be formed – in line they were not, our left and rear companies being in the act of forming – and the 66th moving in echelon to form. Before the 31st Regiment, which was the last of our brigade, could open out, we were bayonet to bayonet with the enemy, and the hostile armies were met to decide the fate of many, if not of the day. We found the enemy, all grenadiers, kneeling [in] several ranks, and pouring in a dreadful fire up the hill, for they had formed on one side before we could affect a similar purpose on the other. Two or three shots were fired by our regiment, when irregularly formed as we were, we charged. The left column of the French became opposed to the left wing of the Buffs, and our right. Their centre column faced our two left companies and the 66th Grenadiers. The right column, which had escaped our notice, found its way to our rear.

In less time than I can write it, although we were literally cut to pieces, we stood on the hill like extended light infantry, many of the intervals filled up by the Spanish sharpshooters. The French left column was broken, and was the only part of their troops which stood the charge. They remained as if powerless until they were bayonetted by our men. The rear companies fled. The centre column to which we were opposed, however, gave way as soon as we charged. We kept advancing until we received an order to retire, when upon facing about we beheld the mass in our rear firing away handsomely. Those of the French left and centre columns that had fled and laid down their arms, resumed the fight and commenced a murderous fire.

Thus we were situated – our colours in the intervals between two columns of the enemy – when their cavalry filed through the intervals of their infantry and rode through us in every direction, cutting down the few that remain on their legs. There was nothing left for it but to run. In my flight I was knocked down by some fugitive like myself, who, I suppose, was struck by a shot. This was in a road among furze bushes. Whilst on the ground I was ridden over by a number of Lancers, one of whom in passing close to me was about to save me the trouble of recording this event, when a Spanish dragoon rode up to him and struck him with his sabre, which brought him over his horse's head. I then got up and ran again, when I found myself between the French right column and the 4th English Dragoons, who were in the act of charging that body. On arriving at the foot of the hill I found the Fusilier brigade formed in line pouring a dreadful fire into the enemy.

The rest of the division arrived, and were soon hotly engaged. We kept, however, masters of the field, after eight or nine hours as hard fighting as the greatest glory hunter could desire. The Buffs, 2nd Battalion 48th, and the 2nd Battalion 66th lost their colours and were destroyed. The 31st from remaining in column escaped such a disaster. There was much effort made to prove that the Buffs had not lost their colours; but they were seen, along with the others, in the hands of the enemy after the battle. A piece of the one of the Buff's colours was preserved in an officer's pocket, it was said; and again, that Colonel Stewart ordered a sergeant to put by a scrap in his pack. One of the Buffs' standards was afterwards retaken by the Fusiliers, and returned to the regiment. Our muster on coming out of the field was, including noncommissioned officers and drummers, just 25 and six officers, and I was one of that number. . . .

At Albuera my sword, or rather sabre – for it was a Spanish weapon – was broken in two, in what way I never could tell – whether it was done by a shot or from the tread of the Cavalry I never could decide, but think a shot must have done it. My cap was left on the field, and brought to me by a fellow soldier.

## 7. Brooke Narrative

*Another vivid description of the successful French cavalry attack is provided by Major William Brooke, also of the 2nd Battalion, 48th Foot. His narrative is a rare first-person account of the experience of being wounded and captured on the battlefield.[14] According to the writer of the next account in this volume, Major Brooke was a grey-haired old man, 66 years of age.*

---

14 'A Prisoner of Albuera' in Oman, Charles, *Studies in the Napoleonic Wars* (London, 1929), pp. 175–206. According to Oman, 'The manuscript journal here printed was found among the papers of Sir James Stevenson Barnes. . . . [T]he Journal is without signature or title. Internal evidence makes it certain that the author was Major William Brooke.'

On the morning of May 16, 1811 our whole army, English and Spanish, was drawn up in two lines along the heights of Albuera. We of the 2nd Division were in the right centre. The enemy commenced their attack by a lively advance against the bridge and village in front of us. The 2/48th and its neighbours in Colborne's brigade suffered very considerably from the cannonade, losing several men killed and wounded by random cannon shot that came over the hill in our front. But this was an evil that did not long continue. The fire becoming extremely warm at the village and bridge, Sir William Beresford ordered forward our brigade to support the fatigued battalions of the German Legion, who were gallantly defending those posts. But before we reached the village the attack there slackened, and the most tremendous fire commenced on the extreme right of our line, at the hill on which Blake Spaniards were posted. It obliged them to retire, and to take shelter in good order under cover of the slope. In consequence of the retreat of the Spaniards our brigade (first brigade of the 2nd Division, consisting of the 3rd or Buffs, 31st, 66th, and 2/48th) received orders to mount the hill and dislodge the enemy. On gaining the summit of the hill we discovered several very heavy columns of French troops ready to receive us. The British line deployed, halted, and fired two rounds; the heads of the French columns returned the fire three deep, the front rank kneeling.

Finding these columns were not to be shaken by fire, the three leading battalions of the brigade prepared to charge with the bayonet, by order of Major General the Hon. William Stewart, who led them on in person to the attack in the most gallant manner. The charge being delivered, the French 28th Léger gave way, as did also the front ranks of their Grenadiers.[15] In the latter we could see the officers trying to beat back the men with the flats of their swords.

During this contest a body of French cavalry, that had been judiciously posted on the left rear of their heavy column, took advantage of our brigade's being unsupported, galloped around the hill, some 2,500 strong, and coming into the rear of our most unfortunate battalions, cut them off. Two squadrons of our 4th Dragoons were dispatched by General Lumley for the purpose of giving us assistance, but they only shared the same fate as our infantry, and their commanding officers, Captains Phillips and Spedding, were both of them made prisoners. The 31st Regiment, the left battalion of our brigade, alone escaped; it

---

15    Note by Oman: Apparently Brooke means the three battalions of *Grenadiers réunis* of the 1st and 4th corps, which were acting along with Gazan's division, to which the 28th Léger belonged. I have no other evidence that the Grenadiers were in the front line.

was still at the foot of the hill in solid column, not having had time to deploy along with the 3rd, 66th, and 48th.

Part of the victorious cavalry were Polish lancers; and from the conduct of this regiment on the field of action I believe many of them to have been intoxicated, as they rode over the wounded, barbarously darting their lances into them. Several unfortunate prisoners were killed in this manner, while being led from the field to the rear of the enemy's lines. I was an instance of their inhumanity; after having been most severely wounded in the head, and plundered of everything that I had about me, I was being led as a prisoner between two French infantry soldiers, when one of these Lancers rode up, and deliberately cut me down. Then, taking the skirts of my regimental coat, he endeavoured to pull it over my head. Not satisfied with his brutality, the wretch tried by every means in his power to make his horse trample on me, by dragging me along the ground and wheeling his horse over my body. But the beast, more merciful than the rider, absolutely refused to comply with his master's wishes, and carefully avoided putting his foot on me!

From this miserable situation I was rescued by two French infantry soldiers, who with a dragoon guarded me to the rear. This last man had the kindness to carry me on his horse across the river Albuera, which from my exhausted state I could not have forded on foot. The cause of my being so carefully looked after was that my captors would not believe that I was of no higher rank than a major. I was led to some rising ground on the left rear of the French army, from which the remaining part of the action was clearly to be seen. I was a prisoner, dreadfully wounded, and loss of blood made me faint and weak, yet, notwithstanding all my misfortune, my whole heart was with my countrymen, and from the brisk fire they kept up I augured a successful end of the battle. About 2 o'clock I had the happiness of seeing the French run, and English mounting the hill and giving three cheers. At this moment I was sent to the rear.

When I arrived at the French hospital, one of their surgeons, seeing me so badly wounded, left his own people and examined my head. He cut off much of my hair, and, having put some lint on my two wounds, tied up my head so tightly, to keep the skull together, I could not open my mouth for three days, except to take a little to drink. He told me that at the expiration of that time I might venture to loosen the bandage a little. The surgeon spoke English tolerably well; having been a prisoner in our country, and well treated, he had a respect for us. Of my final recovery he gave me little hope, as my skull had received fractures of whose consequences he was fearful. The French soldiers abused him for attending to me before them; he left, promising to see me again, but I never met him after.

Weak as I was, I reconnoitred the French guard over the prisoners in the evening; it had been reinforced, and their sentries being posted three deep, I found it impossible to get past them, although on the other side of the river I could see my friends resting on their arms after the victory. The night was extremely cold and damp; we had but few clothes left, and no blankets. We made a fire by gathering boughs from the trees near us, but could get no sleep from the pain of our wounds, the loss of blood, and our distressing circumstances.

May 17. On the morning, and during the day following the battle, part of the dispirited French army was left under the command of General Gazan, who was wounded himself, to make preparation for the evacuation of their hospitals to the rear. The French are generally well supplied with conveyances for this purpose; on this occasion they had not less than 80 or 100 large covered wagons for the use of the worst cases, exclusive of many horses, mules, and asses. These wagons had been brought up laden with provisions to the field of battle, and after being emptied were applied to any other purpose necessary. But on this occasion, from the enormous number of wounded that they had to remove, they found it necessary to force the British soldiers, who had fallen into their hands as prisoners, to carry some of the generals and other officers of note on litters. Being disgusted with his burden, through fatigue and the heat of the sun, one of the prisoners exclaimed his comrades: 'D–n this rascal, let us throw him down and break his neck.' To the surprise of the soldiers, the wounded general lifted his head and replied 'No, I hope not.' Those of the prisoners who did not escape were handsomely paid for their trouble.

## 8. Wood letter

*Lieutenant William Wood of the 2nd Battalion, 48th Foot, wrote a letter to his family explaining that he had an extremely busy day of battle since, in quick succession, he received a battlefield promotion, was wounded and was captured.*[16]

Almendralejo, May 29th 1811
My dear Eliza and Mary,
... At daybreak on the 16th, the pickets were skirmishing and at 8 o'clock there was a heavy cannonade. At this time the rain began to descend in torrents, and in a great measure obscured the distant prospect.

---

16    Koch, Timothy, 'A Second Prisoner at Albuera', *The Waterloo Journal*, Vol. 26, No. 3 (Winter 2004), pp. 3–9, at 6–7.

The enemy forded the river two miles below the town. Already they had occupied some commanding heights, and were attempting to secure another on which almost the fate of the day depended. The first brigade, consisting of the Buffs, 2nd Battalion 48th, 66th, and 31st regiments, were ordered to check them. We advanced rapidly, under a most unparalleled fire of grape, musketry and 12-pound shot.

At the foot of the hill, my worthy captain (Captain Wood) was shot through the thigh and the command of the company devolved upon me. As well as I could amidst an incessant roar of artillery, I entreated the men to be firm and steady. They, however, needed no caution. We were soon halted and began a brisk fire, but trifling compared to that of the enemy. In a few minutes, the drum beat for it to cease, and General Stewart ordered us to charge.

The men Huzzaed [sic] and advanced with the greatest spirit. A column of grenadiers of gigantic stature, rendered hideous by their huge fur caps and enormous beards and mustachios which they wore, were opposed to us. When within a few feet of them, the bayonets so terrified these formidable heroes that numbers dropped their arms and attempted to fly. Our men made dreadful havoc among them. This column was completely routed and two others were giving away. Had another brigade been near to support us at this juncture the fate of the day would in a few minutes have been decided. But alas! No support was immediately near.

The French general saw it and got a regiment of hussars and a new species of troops armed with lances and mounted, amongst us. At this time more than half the brigade was either killed or wounded, and I found myself left with only four men of the company, surrounded on all sides. In a minute after, I was struck smartly on the right leg by a ball which had rebounded from the ground, and the next minute a number of hussars came upon us and rode me and the four men all down together. Before I could get up, a French officer came. I called out in French, 'I am an English officer.' The scoundrel made no reply, but spurred his horse violently to get him over me. He was followed by several dragoons, and I was trampled upon and bruised in several places, but not half so severely as I expected. I got up as soon as I could, and was cut at by two dragoons in all directions. I evaded many cuts and expected to have got away, as some of our dragoons were coming up the hill, when someone gave me a blow on the back of my neck which brought me down again.

At this instance a French officer came up and saved my life. The two villains with horrid imprecations robbed me of everything, pockets and all. I was then taken to the rear where to my regrets and horror,

I found Major Brooke, two captains and five subalterns with a number of our men prisoners, besides about 17 officers of other regiments all but about three wounded.

They used us most cruelly, many of my brother officers could not get their wounds dressed, they were completely drenched in blood, which was still fast flowing from the deep cuts of the sabres. Neither age nor rank seemed to soften their feelings. Major Brooke is a grey-haired old man 66 years of age and although he was cut in the head severely, they would not allow him to ride, but even made him wade up to the middle through rivers, which were running rapidly from the late heavy rains.

## 9. Girdlestone Letter

*Captain James Girdlestone, 31st Foot, wrote to his mother the day after the battle.[17] A fellow officer described Girdlestone in 1813: 'My captain, however – poor Girdlestone, who had only just rejoined us from the rear, recovered from his second wound in the Pyrenees – was again severely wounded. His left arm was so shattered that he wore it in a leather case for the rest of his life; it would have been better if it had been amputated on the spot. . . . A braver solder never stepped, or a more perfect gentleman.'[18]*

Albuera, May 17th, 1811
Dear Mother,
. . . Marshal Beresford was consequently obliged to raise the siege of Badajoz and withdraw the whole of the British and Portuguese troops from there except one brigade of the 4th Division. On the morning of the 16th, our army was formed on this ground with the Spanish army under Blake, Castaños and Ballesteros, about 10,000.

I have now to give you an account of one of the most desperate and hardest fought battles the British were ever engaged in. Our line was formed with the left on the village of Albuera. From the nature of the ground we had not a very advantageous defensive position. About seven in the morning of the 16th, the French began to advance upon us with their skirmishers, at eight our brigade was ordered in rear of the town. At this time a most tremendous rain fell that concealed the enemy from our view when they moved to the right where the Spaniards had been directed to post themselves on some small hills. However, from the slowness of their movements it became necessary

17    Girdlestone, James, Albuera Letter dated 17 May 1811, sold at Bonham's, London, 12 June 2012.
18    L'Estrange, George B., *Recollections of Sir George B. L'Estrange* (London, 1903), p. 136.

40

to bring the Second Division under Genl. Stewart to their assistance. At this time the enemy were pressing the Spaniards with such vivacity that our brigade (the first of the division) was ordered to charge with the bayonet. The instant they had deployed, eight hundred Polish lancers (dragoons with long pikes) penetrated by the right where the Spaniards should have been and attacked the brigade in the rear then engaged with the French infantry. The consequence was such as might be expected – three regiments of the brigade (the 3rd, the 2nd Batt. 48th & 66th regiments) were nearly annihilated. We fortunately escaped by being the rear regiment of the brigade and advancing in an oblique direction we fell close upon a French regiment who instantly opened a tremendous fire upon us. We gave three cheers and drove them considerable to the rear with that never failing weapon, the bayonet. This charge separated us from the brigade, whom we never saw again. The 2nd Brigade then formed on the left of our regiment and we continued hotly engaged to the end of the action, at the close of which we were dri[hole in letter, possibly 'driving'] a column of French Grenadiers before us in confusion. When we got within about fifteen yards of them [a] strong body of the enemy's cavalry suddenly made their appearance from behind a hill close upon us which not only saved their column from destruction by the bayonet but also saved two pieces of artillery close to us from which we afterwards suffered much.

The British troops have sustained a most dreadful loss. Our division, the 2nd, went into action four thousand and about 300 men and they had in killed & wounded & prisoners two thousand and nine hundred including officers. Our brigade in going into battle had 1,700 men and we can scarcely now muster four hundred firelocks. The strength of our regiment was about three hundred & thirty going into the field and we had two sergeants & 26 men killed and two captains & five subalterns and 115 men wounded and although that is nearly half of our men we have suffered considerably less than most of the regiments which I can attribute only to our good fortune for we were engaged the whole of the action. Almost every officer of our regiment that was not wounded received balls through their hats or some part of their dress. My sword was knocked out of my hand by a cannon shot. Our commanding officer had a horse shot under him. In fact, all the officers say it was the hottest action they were ever in. Talavera was upon a larger scale but not near so severe.

The French fought more desperate than was ever known before. That division were never before engaged with British troops and consequently advanced with much greater confidence being accustomed to drive the Spaniards whenever they met them. Their loss is not yet

41

ascertained but supposed to be about seven or eight thousand in killed and wounded, two generals killed & four wounded. The British have lost between 3,500 and 4,000 in killed, wounded & prisoners. The Spaniards lost from 1,500 to 2,000. The Portuguese very few out of not being much engaged, they formed the rear line.

The Spaniards in general behaved well & on this occasion showed more bravery than in any during the war. The cause of the British suffering so much was from the French making their attack upon the Spaniards with such resolution & spirit that it became necessary to bring the British to their assistance at once, who then had the whole of their force to contend with, which was driven back only by repeated charges, while we stood and fired they remained within twenty yards but the moment we charged, they fled. Genl Stewart (Mr. Wing's friend) was slightly wounded in two places. He behaved most gallantly. He was a considerable time with our regt and we understand has made a most particular report of the conduct of our regiment to the Marshal. You will see the dispatches before us – they go today to Ld Wellington who is expected here in two or three days, also two divisions of his army. We want them much. We had here only one brigade of British (the Fusiliers) besides our division; the other brigade of General Cole's division, left at Badajoz, joined us this morning.

We are now laying on the field of battle amongst the dead and dying, the weather cold and most dreadfully wet and, what is worse than all to a John Bull, but little to eat. The French occupy the same ground as on the 15th and show no inclination to renew the attack and we have no wish that they should, our British being so small, but if they come on we must serve them in the same friendly manner as yesterday. Altho we have suffered so severely, the bravery and obstinacy of British troops never shown more conspicuous. John Bull on reading the account will rub his eyes, but he is a character difficult to please.

## 10. Bayley Letter

*Lieutenant Charles Andrew Bayley, 31st Foot, described the battle in a detailed letter to his fiancée, Miss Sally Smith.[19] Since he was also Deputy Assistant Adjutant General of the 2nd Division, he was with General Stewart rather than his regiment when the French cavalry charged Colborne's brigade.*

---

19   This letter was sold, along with a set of decorations belonging to Bayley, at an Auction of Medals and Honours at Sotheby's (London) on 18 December 1990. It is currently in a private collection.

Camp near Albuera
May 18, 1811
10 O'clock, Morning
Thank God, my ever dearest beloved Sally, once more your Charles
has been spared. The day before yesterday we have had one of the
greatest battles ever fought and not till this moment have we had a
moment to spare. We now see the enemy in full retreat towards
Seville. I am sorry to say that our division has lost severely – we had
4,200 in action, and we have lost killed, wounded and taken prisoner
2,903. Poor Shewbridge [Lieutenant Lewis S., 66th Foot] is killed; he
died most gloriously leading his company. Colonel Ellis is wounded
through the hand. I believe [he] is doing extremely well. I have not
time now my Love to give you a long account, as we are about to move
to the ground the French have left where we shall find a great number
of their wounded. Their loss is between 6,000 & 7,000 men, so we hear
from deserters who have come over to us.

My horse was shot in the head & a ball lodged in the hind part of the
saddle & one passed through my coat. My poor General Stewart was
wounded twice, in the foot & breast. General Cole, who commanded
the 4th Division, his two aides-de-camp & his Adjutant General were
all wounded. The 31st have behaved most gloriously – they have
seven officers wounded, and if you should see Harmsworth, tell him
this: Captain Fleming shot thro' the eye, Captain Knox I believe in
the shoulder, Lt. Butler in the leg, Lt. Cashel through the breast, Lt.
Gethen, Lt. Nangle and Lt. Nicolson, all badly wounded. The French
had about 22,000 and we 10,000 British, 5,000 Portuguese and about
9,000 Spaniards, who I assure you behaved tolerably well. They have
lost nearly 2,000, but you will see the full account in the Gazettes. . . .

Poor Shewbridge's regiment, the 66th, and the 2nd Battalion, 48th
have lost their colours. Whilst charging the enemy down a hill they
were charged in their rear by a large body of cavalry. General Stewart,
myself and Hon. Captain Waller, our quartermaster general (who was
cut down) actually cut our way through. Then we saw them coming
on, but expected our cavalry would have assisted us and continued
our charge at the head of the 66th until we were all surrounded. The
slaughter that ensued was most horrid to behold. In the midst of all
this confusion and with cavalry cutting down everything in their rear,
the 31st charged a column of about 6,000 and drove them down the
hill like so many sheep. After this check, they never again returned,
but kept at long shot. General Hoghton was killed, who commanded a
brigade in our division. You may fancy the slaughter when a brigade
is now commanded by a young captain, all the officers above him in

43

the 1st Batt. 48th, 29th, & 57th are either killed or wounded. Captain Cimetière of the 48th commands the above three regiments.

The moment we get a little settled I shall write you a long account. I have a great deal to do now owing to our division being so cut up. The 4th Division is attached to us and I am the only adjt. general with the British troops here.

Take every care of yourself. In the midst of all this, you, Sally dear, were never from my thoughts one moment.

God bless you and spare you for your loving and faithful,
Charles

## 11. Clarke Narrative
*Lieutenant John Clarke, 66th Foot, wrote a graphic letter or memoir about the battle that is reproduced in a regimental history.*[20]

On the evening of 15 May, we arrived at the heights of Albuera. After we had been a couple of hours in line, I had to parade for picket. My picket was placed in front of the bridge [of] Albuera – a narrow stone bridge, wide enough for two horses to walk abreast. About 8 a.m. on the 16th, the enemy sent a brigade of guns and a force of cavalry towards the bridge. The guns commenced a smart fire and the cavalry dashed forward, as if they were going to charge the bridge. Marshal Beresford, who had come down to my picket, asked me what remarks I had been able to make during the night. I told him.

He then asked some questions of another officer. I said to a friend, 'This is a feint, they are going to turn out right.' The Marshal heard me and quickly said, 'They are going to retreat, gentlemen, I expect to attack their rear guard by 9 o'clock.'

A few moments after, an aide-de-camp galloped up from the right, where the Spaniards under Blake and Castaños were stationed, and Colborne's brigade was ordered to move to the right in open column of companies at the double. The fact was, our right was turned. The rain was falling fast and the ground was very heavy. When near the point on which we were to form, it was perceived that we were marching rear rank in front; we counter marched, on the march, under a tremendous cannonade, I can safely say that the movement was never better performed by the 66th on its own parade ground.

Fifty yards from us was an isolated hill, its summit enveloped in a heavy fog. We wheeled into line and opened a destructive fire upon

---

20    Reproduced in Groves, J. Percy, *The 66th Berkshire Regiment* (London, 1887), pp. 51–4.

the enemy, who were in close column. The order was given to 'charge'; when quite close to the enemy the 'halt' was sounded, followed by the 'retire'; then we were again ordered to advance. At this moment the French enemy cavalry got round to our right flank under the cover of the fog.

The Buffs had been ordered to reform column, their right wing to cover the rear of the brigade; to effect this they faced about, a very dangerous manoeuvre when near an enemy. The enemy's cavalry suddenly appearing in their rear, great confusion ensued. We advanced again, but at that moment a crowd of Polish Lancers and Chasseurs à Cheval swept along the rear of the brigade; our men now ran into groups of six or eight, to do as best they could; the officers snatched up muskets and joined them, determined to sell their lives dearly. Quarter was not asked, and rarely given. Poor Colonel Waller, of the Quarter-Master-General's staff, was cut down close to me; he put up his hands asking for quarter, but the ruffian cut his fingers off. My ensign, Hay, was run through the lungs by a lance which came out of his back; he fell and got up again. The lancer delivered another thrust, the lance striking Hay's breast bone; down he went, and the Pole rolled over in the mud beside him. In the evening I went to seek my friend, and found him sitting up to his hips in mud and water. He was quite cool and collected, and said there were many worse than him.

The lancers have been promised a doubloon each, if they could break the British line. In the melee, when mixed up with the Lancers, Chasseurs à Cheval and French infantry, I came into collision with a lancer and, being knocked over, was taken prisoner; an officer ordered me to be conducted to the rear. Presently a charge was made by our Dragoon Guards in which I liberated myself, and ran to join the Fusilier brigade at the foot of the hill. When I got close to the 7th regiment, they knelt to receive cavalry, and I threw myself down to avoid the fire; I got up, and passing through the regiment met Lieutenant Anderson carrying a colour. He said, 'I thought, my dear fellow, you must have been riddled, it was only presence of mind saved you.' I went a few paces to the rear, and fell exhausted.

## 12. Dobbin letter

*Lieutenant Robert Dobbin was assigned to Captain Benning's light company of the 66th Foot. In his letter, he says explicitly that his men crossed bayonets with the French.*[21]

---

21    Extracts from a letter of Lieutenant Dobbin, 23 May 1811, included in a Sale of
      Captain Conway Benning's Albuera medal and gold watch, Sotheby's (London),
      19 July 1988, Lot 4.

Almendralejo 23rd May 1811

About 8 o'clock in the morning of the 16th, our brigade marched to attack the French who were moving on the right of our position. We commenced the attack at 9 o'clock, but not before the French had got possession of the hill and were sending their shells very thick among us. We had got to the top of the hill, and were come bayonet to bayonet when the French sent a regiment of Polanders round our left flank, and another of hussars round our right, which came on our rear and cut the three right regiments to pieces before our cavalry could come to their assistance.

These Polanders were all mounted, and armed with lances which they handled with great dexterity, and killed a vast number of our regiment, but not without great loss on their side. I am sorry to say that the French got our colours, but not until we had two officers killed, two wounded, and nine sergeants killed and wounded, defending them. Our loss in officers has been very great, having four killed and 11 wounded; among the former, Captain Benning who fell gallantly leading the battalion he commanded to the charge. His horse was first shot under him, and he afterwards received a ball in his right side, which killed him on the spot. I was for two hours after the battle, searching for him among the dead, and when I found him, Surgeon S[hackleton] and I paid the last sad offices to the best and bravest of men, seeing him covered in the spot on which he fell.

I have now been in four general engagements, but never saw the French fight so well as they did on this occasion. We were often firing at not more than 10 yards distance, before we came to the charge, and that for the two or three minutes together; and, when we did charge, the French never moved until we came bayonet to bayonet, and as soon as we dispersed one column another appeared which we served as the former. Sergeant Hogan and my own servant fell by my side while I was clapping him on the shoulders for his gallant behaviour.

I suppose you will be glad to hear that I have been thanked for my conduct on that day. We have got great credit in Orders.

Out of our battalion we have only 91 men left, most of whom have received some slight wounds. The French have left 400 wounded in this town, and our cavalry are taking them every hour.

You may say I am a lucky fellow in having escaped without a scratch. A Frenchman made a snap at me when I was in front, and not 5 yards distant, but his piece misfired, and he was taken down in a moment by a man of the company name Boland.

## 13. Crompton Letter

*Lieutenant George Crompton, 66th Foot, was another officer who wrote to his mother after the battle, despite the obvious shame he felt concerning what happened to his regiment.*[22]

Albuera 18 May, 1811

A few lines, my dearest mother, I, in haste, sit down to write, to say, that under the protection of Almighty God, I have escaped unhurt in one of the severest actions that ever was contested between France and England; to describe the horrors that were witnessed on the ever memorable 16th of May would be impossible, but as the part the unfortunate first brigade of the second division took on that day might be a little interesting to you, I will relate it as far as I am able.

I think it was about 10:00 a.m. when the French menaced an attack on our left; we immediately moved to support it. It proved, however, to be a feint, and the right of the line was destined to be the spot (Oh, never to be effaced from my mind) were Britons were to be repulsed; three solid columns attacked our regiment alone. We fought them till we were hardly a regiment.

The commanding officer was shot dead, and the two officers carrying the colours close by my side received their mortal wounds. In this shattered state our brigade moved forward to charge. Madness alone would dictate such a thing, and at that critical period cavalry appeared in our rear. It was then that our men began to waver, and for the first time (and God knows I hope the last) I saw the backs of English soldiers turned upon the French. Our regiment once rallied, but to what avail! We were independent of infantry; outnumbered with cavalry. I was taken prisoner, but retaken by the Spanish cavalry.

Oh, what a day was that. The worst of the story I have not related. Our colours were taken. I told you before that two ensigns were shot down under them; two sergeants shared the same fate. A lieutenancy seized a musket to defend them, and he was shot to the heart; what could be done against cavalry? General Stewart, who marched us wildly to this desperate attack without any support, praised rather than censored our conduct, but I should think that the malicious world will take hold of it with scandal in their mouths. Our brigade, which entered the field 2,000 strong, collected after the action 350 men. Our regiment that was 400, came out 80 men. We had one captain, two lieutenants, and two ensigns killed, and one captain, five lieutenants and two ensigns wounded.

---

22    *Journal of the Society for Army Historical Research*, Vol. 1 (1921–2), p. 130.

*Adieu*, my dear mother for the present. Give my most affectionate and kindest love to father, Annie, William and all at home, and believe me to be your most affectionate son,

G. Crompton,

A miserable lieutenant of the unfortunate 66th regiment.

P.S. The Fusilier brigade afterwards came on, also the other brigades in the division with some Spanish and Portuguese beat back to French getting to complete victory. The French lost, they say, killed and wounded, 10,000 men.

## 14. St George Anecdote

*This anecdote about Stepney St George, a lieutenant in the 66th Foot, comes from the pen of his brother-in-law, George L'Estrange, who was a nephew of Major Guy L'Estrange, who commanded the 31st Foot at Albuera.[23] The nephew also served in the 31st, but not at Albuera.*

In the few observations which I made referring to my late brother-in-law, Stepney St. George, I forgot to mention what had happened to him at the battle of Albuera, before my time but related to me by himself and his brother officers. In that very bloody and almost doubtful victory he received a very severe wound, and lay upon the field of battle. A Polish lancer, probably attracted by his bright Scarlet coat and gold epaulets (for he, having plenty of private means, was always well dressed), gave him a poke with his Lance, and finding there was life in him, thought he should perhaps secure an officer of high rank [as a prisoner]. He took him by the collar, and was dragging him into the French lines in a state of insensibility, when Saint George was aroused from his swoon by something warm trickling down upon his head. It proved to be the lifeblood of the Pole, who had received a mortal wound from a musket shot, which relieved him of his burden, and poor St. George managed to crawl back into the British lines and was saved.

## 15. Letter from a Private of the Buffs

*More details of the annihilation of Colborne's brigade comes from a letter written by an unidentified private in the 3rd Regiment of Foot who was taken prisoner but eventually made his escape from the enemy.[24]*

---

23    L'Estrange, George B., *Recollections of Sir George B. L'Estrange* (London, 1903), pp. 193–4.

24    Quoted in *The Soldier's Companion, or Martial Recorder* (London, 1824), v. 1, pp. 240–1.

I was knocked down by a horseman with his lance, which luckily did me no serious injury. In getting up, I received a lance in my hip, and shortly after another in my knee, which slightly grazed me. I then rose, when a soldier hurried me to the rear a few yards, striking me on the side of the head with his lance. He left me, and soon another came up, who would have killed me, had not a French officer came up, and giving the fellow a blow, told him to spare the English, and to go on and do his duty with those of my unfortunate comrades. This officer conducted me to the rear of the French lines, and here the sight that struck the eye was dreadful! Men dead, where the column had stood, heaped on each other; the wounded praying for assistance, and human blood flowing down the hill! I came to where the baggage was, where I found a vast number of my own regiment, with a good proportion of officers, prisoners like myself, numbers of them desperately wounded, even after they were prisoners! Here then I offered up my most fervent thanks to heaven for having escaped so safe. I remained prisoner seven days, and the whole I received from our enemy (marching six leagues every day on the road to Madrid) was three ounces of rice, nine ounces of bread, and a pound of meat. . . .

## 16. Letter from an Officer of the 2nd Battalion, 48th Foot

*An unidentified officer of the 48th Regiment wrote a letter about the battle to a friend in Edinburgh that was eventually published in a Scottish newspaper.*[25]

Almendralejo, 25 May 1811
Our brigade, after a very fatiguing march into the interior of Spain, of about 70 leagues through the Sierra Morena for 14 days, join the rest of the army previous to the battle of the Albuera, after escaping by 30 hours march being taken prisoner by Marshal Soult.

Before recovering from the fatigues of our march, in consequence of the enemy making a disposition to cross the river on the right of the village of Albuera, our brigade was ordered down to the rear of that place to dispute the passage; which, when the enemy saw, they filed off to our right, where it appeared they had from the beginning intended to attack us, the river being fordable all along our front. We were then ordered, with the four pieces of artillery attached to us, to the right of the British line, to support the Spaniards, who were then engaged with the enemy. After much hurry, we ascended the height under a tremendous cannonade of shot and shells, with

---

25     *Caledonian Mercury*, 4 July 1811.

continued discharges of musketry. They had at that time got about 32 pieces of artillery to play on us. At this period a very heavy shower of rain fell, which prevented many of the firelocks going off. However, after firing about seven rounds, two regiments only being hurriedly formed, viz. the 3rd (or Buffs) and ours, before the other two regiments on our left had formed, and before our pieces of artillery could come up to flank the three solid columns in our front, besides a grenadier battalion, and two regiments of cavalry, we were ordered to charge, which our noble fellows did with three cheers, broke through the grenadier battalion, which could not stand the bayonet, but turned their backs.

At this time the carnage was most dreadful. Every man of that battalion was put to death. However, our brigade being outflanked on the left; and receiving continual volleys of musketry, and the cavalry getting into our rear, was annihilated in a few minutes after.

Of 28 officers belonging to our regiment, who went into action in the morning, six only escaped, four were killed, nine made prisoners, and carried off by the enemy, the others severely wounded, and since gone to Elvas. I thank God I had such a providential escape. I was struck with a blunt edge of a pole or pike, with which the Polish cavalry are armed, which bruised and cut me, and brought me to the ground, where I lay for some time senseless. But our cavalry coming up, the enemy made off, and I made my escape, suffering severely, having been rode over, and much hurt. Thank God I am now nearly well. So desperate and sanguinary a contest I believe never was fought. Soult had persuaded his men that there was no English to oppose them – that those who are clothed in scarlet were Portuguese troops in British pay. It is well ascertained the enemy lost, in killed and wounded, 9,000 men; we had 4,030 killed, and about 2,000 wounded and prisoners; the latter have nearly all escaped. One of our officers made his escape; he says the French use their prisoners very ill.

They left on the field of battle, on the morning of the 18th inst. when they commenced their retreat, 800 of their worst wounded; 330 wounded we found in the hospitals here.

Our cavalry, in conjunction with the Spaniards, have hung on their rear, and two days ago killed 300 men, and took 135 prisoners – one colonel, two majors, and a subaltern have come in. The French brought into the field on the 16th inst. 23,000 men; we about 8,300 British and 12,000 Spaniards. The Portuguese were not very much engaged.

## C. Abercromby's (2nd) Brigade, 2nd Division Accounts

### 1. Sherer's Account
*The most comprehensive unofficial description of the battle comes from the memoirs of Moyle Sherer, then a lieutenant in the 34th Foot.[26] His narrative mixes detailed information with philosophical musings.*

Albuera, the scene of a most murderous and sanguinary conflict, it may not be amiss to describe. It is a small inconsiderable village, uninhabited and in ruins; it is situated on a stream from which it takes its name, and over which there are two bridges; one about two hundred yards to the right of the village, large, handsome, and built of hewn stone; the other, close to the left of it, small, narrow, and incommodious. This brook is not above knee-deep: its banks, to the left of the small bridge, are abrupt and uneven; and, on that side, both artillery and cavalry would find it difficult to pass, if not impossible; but, to the right of the main bridge, it is accessible to any description of force. The enemy occupied a very large extensive wood, about three quarters of a mile distant, on the other side of the stream, and posted their picquets close to us. The space between the wood and the brook was a level plain; but on our side the ground rose considerably; though there was nothing which could be called a height, as from Albuera to Valverde every inch of ground is favourable to the operations of cavalry – not a tree, not a ravine, to interrupt their movements.

I shall here interrupt my private Recollections, to give a rapid and general sketch of the battle, which took place on the morrow. On the morning of the 16th our people were disposed as follows: The Spanish army, under the orders of General Blake, was on the right, in two lines; its left rested on the Valverde road, on which, just at the ridge of an ascent, rising from the main bridge, the right of our division (the second) was posted, the left of it extending to the Badajoz road, on ground elevated above the village, which was occupied by two battalions of German rifle-men, General Hamilton's Portuguese division being on the left of the whole. General Cole, with two brigades of the fourth division (the Fusilier brigade and one of Portuguese), arrived a very short time before the action, and formed, with them, our second line. These dispositions the enemy soon compelled us to alter. At eight o'clock he began to move; and menacing, with two columns, the

---

26    Sherer, Moyle, *Recollections of the Peninsula* (London, 1824), pp. 150–66. The title page announces that the book was written 'by the Author of Sketches of India', but all bibliographic sources identify Sherer as that person.

village and bridges, under cover of his cavalry, he filed the main body of his infantry over the rivulet, beyond our right, and attacked that flank with very superior numbers, and with great impetuosity. The greater part of the Spaniards hastily formed front to the right to meet the attack; and, after a short and gallant resistance, were overpowered and driven from their ground. The enemy now commanded and raked our whole position: the fire of his artillery was heavy, but fortunately for us, not very well directed.

It became now imperiously necessary to retake, at any price, the important post, unfortunately, not blamably, lost by the Spaniards. The three brigades of the division Stewart marched on it in double quick time, led by that General. The first, or right brigade, commanded by Colonel Colborne, was precipitated into action under circumstances the most unfavourable: it deployed by corps as it arrived near the enemy, fired, and was in the act of gallantly charging with the bayonet on a heavy column of their infantry, when a body of Polish lancers, having galloped round upon its rear in this most unfortunate moment, (for a charge is often a movement of exulting confusion), overthrew it with a great and cruel slaughter. The 31st regiment, not having deployed, escaped this misfortune; and the third brigade, under General Hoghton, and second, under Colonel Abercromby, successfully arriving, re-established the battle, and, with the assistance of the Fusilier brigade under Sir William Myers, the fortunes of this bloody day were retrieved, and the French driven in every direction from the field. I should not omit to mention, that, during the whole of the day, there was very heavy skirmishing near the village, which was occupied and held, throughout the contest, by the German light infantry, under the orders of Major-General Alten. General Lumley, who commanded the Allied cavalry, displayed great ability, and foiled every attempt of the enemy's horse to turn our right, [Sherer Note – This may sound inconsistent; but it will be understood that the order of battle was changed from its commencement; and again, the Polish horse were but a small body, detached for a particular object.] who were in that arm very superior, and who directed their efforts repeatedly to that object. The Portuguese troops, with the exception of one brigade, were very little engaged in this affair, and numbers of the Spanish troops never came into action.

The brunt of the battle fell on the British, who lost 4,103 killed and wounded, including in this number 120 of the German legion. The Portuguese lost about 400; the Spaniards 1,800: making a total of about 6,300. The French lost, at the lowest calculation, 9,000. Soult had about 24,000; and we were, perhaps, in point of numbers, a little superior to him altogether, but had only 7,000 English. The two British brigades, who more particularly distinguished themselves on this glorious day, were the Fusilier brigade, commanded and led by Sir William Myers, and the third brigade of the second division, headed by General Hoghton. The first of these, composed of two battalions of the 7th regiment, and one of the 23d, lost upwards of 1,000 men; and the other, composed of the 29th, first 48th, and 57th regiments, lost 1,050 men killed and wounded, having entered the field about 1,400 strong. This last brigade went into action led by a major general, and with its due proportion of field-officers and captains. I saw it at three in the afternoon: a captain commanded the brigade; the 57th and 48th regiments were commanded by lieutenants; and the junior captain of the 29th regiment was the senior effective officer of his corps. Not one of these six regiments lost a man by the sabre or the lance; they were never driven, never thrown into confusion; they fought in line, sustaining and replying to a heavy fire, and often charging; and when the enemy at length fled, the standards of these heroic battalions flew in proud, though mournful triumph, in the centre of their weakened but victorious lines. I have read the annals of modern warfare with some attention, and I know of little, which can compare with, nothing, which has surpassed, the enthusiastic and unyielding bravery, displayed by these corps on the field of Albuera. Yet this dear-bought, and, let me add, not useless victory, won by unaided courage, graced with no trophies, and followed by no proportionate result, has almost sunk into oblivion, or is remembered only, and spoken of, as a day of doubtful success, if not of positive disaster. It was certainly not useless, because the object of Marshal Soult, which was the relief of Badajoz, and the expulsion of our troops from Spanish Extremadura, was wholly defeated; but it had yet a higher, a nobler, a more undying use, it added one to the many bright examples of British heroism; it gave a terrible and long-remembered lesson to the haughty legions of France; and, when Soult rode by the side of his Imperial master on the field of Waterloo, as the cheering of the English soldiery struck upon his ear, Albuera was not forgotten, and he could have whispered to him, that they were men, who could only be defeated, by being utterly destroyed.

So much for the battle, generally considered: I would now relate what fell under my own observation, and describe, if it be possible, my feelings on that day. We stood to our arms an hour before break of day: it was a brilliant sight, at sun-rise, to see the whole of the French cavalry moving on the plain; but in a short time they retired into the wood, leaving their picquets as before, The battalion being dismissed, I breakfasted, and immediately afterwards set out to walk towards the Spanish troops, little dreaming, that day, of a general action. But the sound of a few shots caused me to return; and I found our line getting hastily under arms, and saw the enemy in motion. The prelude of skirmishing lasted about an hour and a half, and our division lost a few men by random gunshot; all this time we were standing at ease, and part of it exposed to a heavy, chilling, and comfortless rain. Sounds, however, which breathed all the fierceness of battle, soon reached us; the continued rolling of musquetry, accompanied by loud and repeated discharges of cannon on our extreme right, told us, convincingly, that the real attack was in that quarter. The brigades of our division were successively called to support it. We formed in open column of companies at half distance, and moved in rapid double quick to the scene of action. I remember well, as we moved down in column, shot and shell flew over and through it in quick succession; we sustained little injury from either, but a captain of the twenty-ninth had been dreadfully lacerated by a ball, and lay directly in our path. We passed close to him, and he knew us all; and the heart-rending tone in which he called to us for water, or to kill him, I shall never forget. He lay alone, and we were in motion, and could give him no succour; for on this trying day, such of the wounded as could not walk lay unattended where they fell: all was hurry and struggle; every arm was wanted in the field.

When we arrived near the discomfited and retiring Spaniards, and formed our line to advance through them towards the enemy, a very noble-looking young Spanish officer rode up to me, and begged me, with a sort of proud and brave anxiety, to explain to the English, that his countrymen were ordered to retire, but were not flying. Just as our line had entirely cleared the Spaniards, the smoky shroud of battle was, by the slackening of the fire, for one minute blown aside, and gave to our view the French grenadier caps, their arms, and the whole aspect of their frowning masses. It was a momentary, but a grand sight; a heavy atmosphere of smoke again enveloped us, and few objects could be discerned at all, none distinctly. The coolest and bravest soldier, if he be in the heat of it, can make no calculation of time during an engagement. Interested and animated, he marks not the flight of the hours, but he feels that, 'Come what may, time and the hour run through the roughest day.'

This murderous contest of musketry lasted long. We were the whole time progressively advancing upon and shaking the enemy. At the distance of about twenty yards from them, we received orders to charge; we had ceased firing, cheered, and had our bayonets in the charging position, when a body of the enemy's horse was discovered under the shoulder of a rising ground, ready to take advantage of our impetuosity. Already, however, had the French infantry, alarmed by our preparatory cheers, which always indicate the charge, broken and fled, abandoning some guns and howitzers about sixty yards from us. The presence of their cavalry not permitting us to pursue, we halted and recommenced firing on them. The slaughter was now, for a few minutes, dreadful; every shot told; their officers in vain attempted to rally them; they would make no effort. Some of their artillery, indeed, took up a distant position which much annoyed our line; but we did not move, until we had expended every round of our ammunition, and then retired, in the most perfect order, to a spot sheltered from their guns, and lay down in line, ready to repulse any fresh attack with the bayonet.

To describe my feelings throughout this wild scene with fidelity would be impossible: at intervals, a shriek or a groan told that the men were falling around me; but it was not always that the tumult of the contest suffered me to catch these sounds. A constant feeling to the centre of the line, and the gradual diminution of our front, most truly bespoke the havoc of death. As we moved, though slowly, yet ever a little in advance, our own killed and wounded lay behind us; but we arrived among those of the enemy, and those of the Spaniards who had fallen in the first onset: we trod among the dead and dying, all reckless of them. But how shall I picture the British soldier going into action? He is neither heated by brandy, stimulated by the hope of plunder, or inflamed by the deadly feeling of revenge; he does not even indulge in expressions of animosity against his foes; he moves forward, confident of victory, never dreams of the possibility of defeat, and braves death with all the accompanying horrors of laceration and torture, with the most cheerful intrepidity. . . .

Incredible as it may appear, Marshal Beresford evidently thought a renewal of their attack, on the 17th, very possible; for he had us under arms two hours before break of day, and made arrangements, which certainly indicated anything rather than intention to advance. It is to be presumed, that could the Marshal have guessed the dreadful slaughter he had made in the ranks of the enemy, and their consequent disorganisation and discontent, he would have entered the wood, to which they retired on the evening of the sixteenth, and thus have achieved a more complete triumph than any up to that period gained in the Peninsula. . . .

The whole of the seventeenth we never ventured across the stream, but stood looking at the enemy's picquets, and videttes, posted impudently on the little plain between us and their bivouac. On the eighteenth they retired, destroying the contents of many of their tumbrils and ammunition cars, to facilitate the conveyance of their wounded; and they were followed, at a respectful distance, by our cavalry and light infantry.

## 2. Dickens Letter

*This letter is unsigned but internal evidence suggests that the writer was Lieutenant S. Dickens, 34th Foot, who was promoted to be captain in place of Captain Gibbons, killed in action.*[27]

May 15.
At noon marched for Albuera and halted on a position – at six in the afternoon we observed the French cavalry in a wood, on the other side of the river, 1 mile and a half distant. The village of Albuera is a wretched place, forsaken by the inhabitants, and the greater part of the houses are unroofed. It is situated on a small river of the same name, has a bridge over it, but this time of the year is fordable in every part. This separated the two armies. The French infantry did not show themselves, but remained close in a thick wood; nor had we a view of them until the following morning, when they advanced to the attack. The town, which was on our side of the river, was occupied by a battalion of German rifleman, under the command of Colonel Halkett. These lined the walls, outhouses, and fences about the town, and had complete command of the bridge. This was the left of the position.

From the town, indeed, was, to the right, a line of elevated ground, which left the river obliquely to its front. This line of defence was occupied by the French infantry. The British was considerably to the left; and the Allied cavalry on the banks of the river observed the enemy's, whose squadrons were strongly posted on the opposite side.

May 16 at 7 a.m., the enemy's cavalry supported by infantry drove in our out pickets, crossed the river and directed the heads of their columns to that part of the line where the Spaniards were posted. A range of hills in front of the Spaniards (and which, in my opinion, ought to have been occupied as they completely commanded the position) was the place where the French posted their artillery, which was admirably served during the whole of the action. The Spanish line was formed three deep, and received the approach of the French with the greatest fortitude. Their number, I believe, amounted nearly to 15,000, under the command of the Generals Blake, Castaños, Carrera;

---

27    Historical Manuscripts Commission, *Report on the Manuscripts of the Late Reginald Rawdon Hastings, Esq.* (Francis Bickley, ed.)(3 vols., London, 1934), v. 3, pp. 289–93.

and I can assure you that during the whole of the engagement, they were as composed as if going through their evolutions on a field day, but with a great deal more glee. On the advance of the French upon the Spaniards, the British troops were ordered immediately to their support, and were moved to the right in open column of companies, and formed line in rear of the Spaniards, who at this time were briskly engaged with the enemy, in succession of battalions.

During our advancing open column, the French artillery played upon us, and did great execution, and this gives me the idea that it must have been very advantageously posted.

As we were under cover of our position, it is impossible for me to give you a particular account of the occurrences that took place in the army in general, for I do assure you we were ourselves unacquainted with them, until we had them detailed in the general dispatches. With respect to the regiment, I can give you an account of all our operations.

When the British line was formed, the Spaniards retired through it, and we advanced under a heavy fire of musketry and artillery, which soon thinned our ranks. Very soon we had a glimpse of a massive column of the enemy advancing. It was a regiment of Imperial Grenadiers, which we distinguished by their immense caps. We kept up a lively fire as we advanced against them, [and] they as briskly returned it until we came within 20 or 30 yards. We then gave three cheers, and prepared for the charge.

This had an instantaneous effect. They went to the right about in the utmost confusion and disorder, and we after them. For a short time our firing ceased, as they were ingenious enough to pass themselves for Spaniards. We soon discovered our error and pursued them from hill to hill until they reached their reserve, which consisted of cavalry and a train of artillery, which was extremely well served. If we had had cavalry and artillery to have supported us and to have kept up with us, their loss would have been infinitely greater, and their artillery would have been taken, as their infantry had abandoned it. We should have advanced and taken it, had we not observed a column of the cavalry ready to attack us, and our line, as you may conceive, was rather in confusion, from the pursuit and number of casualties.

Their column, I am sure, consisted of 5,000 or 6,000 men, and were pursued by our brigade of 1,100. We had advanced so far, that the Colonel ordered us to halt and await further orders; and during that time the enemy's artillery was not idle, for there is not anything to occupy their attention but firing deliberately at us, who were unsupported by artillery, and we received their fire without returning a shot. We afterwards retired under the cover of the hill in our rear, where they threw shells at us, but happily they did but little execution. The enemy in the afternoon retired to the wood to contemplate on the result of the day.

My company had one ensign, one sergeant and five men killed, and 15 wounded. We took 46 into the field.

Amongst the wounded I have to regret my servant, who had his left leg carried off by a cannon shot, in the latter part of the action. Have you sufficient interest to get him into Chelsea?

I should like to do something for the poor lad – he came up with me from Lisbon, but a few days before, and he bore the shock with the greatest fortitude. That there are not braver troops in the world than the British, I will now affirm, for I have had the opportunity of observing them. . . .

Our total loss is one captain, one lieutenant and one ensign killed. Two captains, two lieutenants and about 100 men wounded – 30 men killed. Two companies were not in the action, as they were left on the baggage guard. We took 378 rank and file into the field. During the action we had some very heavy rain, which continued during the night without our having any earthly shelter, and 3,000 or 4,000 wounded laying in the same state.

On the morning of the 17th we stood to our arms very early, but they did not evince any inclination to attack us. . . .

I am now in command of a company, vacant by the death of Captain Gibbons.

### 3. Saunderson Letter

*Both Captain Hardress Saunderson and Lieutenant George Beard of the 39th Foot became casualties during the battle, but only Saunderson survived. He wrote a letter to Beard's father detailing his last recollections of his friend.[28] His postscript serves as a reminder of the limitations of eyewitness accounts.*

Camp near Albuera, May 19, 1811
To Beard, Esq.
Father of the late Lieutenant Beard, of the 39th Regiment of Foot,
Supposed of Finsbury Square.

Sir,
To me is left the painful duty of communicating to you the untimely, though glorious, death of your son, who expired in the arms of victory on the 16th instant.

---

28    Saunderson, Hardress W.R., Letter dated 19 May 1811, British Library.

If it could be any consolation, or could possibly alleviate the tender feelings of a parent, to know that the whole regiment participates in the grief for the loss of his son, I feel particularly happy in informing you of it. For my own part, sir, I have lost a most estimable friend and companion; our intimacy has existed ever since we came to the Peninsula, and from the circumstances of my ever-to-be regretted friend belonging to my company, and being always together, our friendship seemed established forever, until his untimely death deprived me of him.

He was wounded early in the action through the wrist, when I recommended him to go to the rear, to have his wound bound up. 'No!' exclaimed he, 'as long as I am able to fight with you, I'll never retire.' Sometime afterwards, when we beat the enemy from the field, and the heat of the action had in some measure subsided, I turned around to my friend to know how he was, when a shell instantly deprived me of all sensation. I woke out of my trance unhurt, and the first object which presented itself to my eyes, was my dear companion stretched on the ground close to me. His soul had already winged its flight to a better world; peace be to it!

A more sincere friend or brave soldier never existed. He fell in one of the most sanguinary conflicts that ever interested the pages of military history. For four hours did Victory hover over in doubt about the hostile armies, till at length she perched upon our banners, and yielded herself to British courage. Out of 7,000 Britons who were engaged, 4,000 were numbered in the list of killed and wounded. I must plead the hurry of the moment, as an excuse for me not writing a more detailed account; but as long as I draw breath, and reflect on the laurels gained at Albuera, I should be ever mindful of how much it cost me, and the loss of my much-esteemed friend.

That heaven may console you, sir, in this hour of distress, is my most anxious wish; and believe, I remain,

Your distressed friend,

Hardress W.R. Saunderson,

Captain 39th Regiment.

P.S. As this letter is written in the greatest hurry on the field of battle, and consequently must contain many inaccuracies, it is therefore only written to gratify an anxious family.

## 4. 39th Foot Court Martials

*Two junior officers of the 39th Foot who fought at Albuera were court-martialled in 1813.[29] The facts of their cases suggest that there was some controversial behaviour in their regiment during the battle, but the full story will never be known unless other relevant sources are discovered.*

On March 1, 1813, Lieutenants Alexander Morrow and Matthew Moore, both of the 39th Regiment, were found guilty of the offence of 'making use on, or about, 16 May, 1811, near Albuera, in Spain, of the most gross and improper language to each other in the presence of many officers assembled in the rear of the regiment'. The nature of the language was unspecified. The Prince Regent was pleased to grant clemency to both officers and they were restored to the functions of their commissions in the army with a severe reprimand and admonition to be more circumspect in their future conduct.

This outcome, however, did not prevent Lieutenant Morrow from being court-martialled again the very next day 'for scandalous and infamous conduct'. The conduct in question was that Lieutenant Morrow had cast aspersions on the character of Lieutenant Colonel Lindsay, his superior officer, 'by asserting that, during an engagement in the Peninsula [most likely Albuera], Lieutenant Colonel [Patrick] Lindsay, then commanding the 2nd Battalion of the 39th Regiment, was called on by General Stewart, commanding the division, to do his duty, and 'not to skulk behind a rock', or words to that effect.

Lieutenant Morrow was found guilty of that charge and this time the sentence was approved and confirmed by the Prince Regent, so Morrow was dismissed from the army and the sentence of the court was read at the head of every corps of the army, and entered into the general order book.

## D. Hoghton's (3rd) Brigade, 2nd Division Accounts

### 1. Wilson Narrative

*The account of Albuera by Captain James Wilson of the 1st Battalion, 48th Foot, can be found in his manuscript daily journal, to which he occasionally added later comments.[30] His comments on some of his fellow officers make him one of the most candid chroniclers of the battle.*

---

29    James, Charles, *A Collection of the Charges, Opinions, and Sentences of General Courts Martial, as Published by Authority; From the Year 1795 to the Present Time* (London, 1920), pp. 482–5.

30    Journal of Captain James Wilson, 1st Battalion, 48th Foot, Newberry Library, Chicago, IL.

May 15th. About 2 o'clock [we] marched to La Albuera, where the troops have taken up a position waiting for the enemy. Our cavalry fell back this morning from Santa Marta followed by the French advanced guard. Some skirmishing. Towards evening, the advance of the cavalry threw out their pickets in front of our line, the main body forming in the wood on the other side of the river Albuera, which is fordable at nearly all points.

[Later text addition.] The position selected for the army is behind a little river Albuera, where the roads leading from Seville to Olivenza and Badajoz separate after crossing the river by a bridge close to the village of Albuera. The Albuera runs into the Guadiana and the village is on its left bank. The ground on the west [left] side rises from the river in gentle swells and easy slopes. At the summit of this rise, nearly parallel to the river, the army is formed, its left having the village of Albuera in front of it. The swellings of the ground on the right succeed each other so rapidly that every extension to one knoll renders it desirable to prolong the line to the next. Therefore after drawing it out to the uttermost and placing the right on a commanding feature there still remained ground on that flank very favourable to the enemy. Above the point forming the right of the line, the Albuera is only a rivulet.

On the eastern [right] side of the river, in front of the left of the position, the ground is perfectly flat and open for an extent of 600 or 700 yards. At that distance are gentle rises covered with thick woods, and which opposite to the right wind round in a semicircular form till they meet the Albuera stream above that part of the ridge occupied by the Allies. Marshal Soult in the wood in front of the position with 20,000 infantry, 3,000 cavalry and 40 pieces of Cannon. [End of later addition.]

May 16th. By daylight, General Blake with the Spanish army, composed of the corps of Ballesteros, Castaños, [and] Don Carlos España, consisting of 12,000, joined our army and took up their position on the right. General Cole's division arrived from Badajoz. The army had been under arms a considerable time before daylight and had been dismissed. At about 7 o'clock, we observed their columns to be in motion and shortly after it was evident their intention was to attack us. Our line was ordered under arms and, immediately after, the artillery on both sides began to play, whilst the French columns having formed in the wood, debouched some of their cavalry with a strong column of infantry and some artillery, [and] moved towards the village of Albuera. The 1st Brigade, Second Division was ordered there. Some shot was thrown from their guns and our artillery did execution among their cavalry. Three heavy columns were evidently

61

moving on our right. Nearly the whole of their cavalry and artillery took that direction and crossed the Albuera. It became extremely dark and heavy and rained very hard, scarcely anything could be seen. During this time they commenced the attack, about 8 o'clock, on the high ground on the right, the position of the Spaniards, who after considerable resistance were overpowered.

The British were moved from their position in double quick time to the right. The Portuguese under General Hamilton, formed columns of reserve in the rear. By the time we reached the right of the line, the Spaniards had been obliged to abandon the high ground on the right and were closely followed by the French columns.

The 1st Brigade of the 2nd Division moved up in column and had scarcely time to deploy when they were in the act of charging the French columns in their front (one column consisting of 9,000, another of 5,000, and a third of 3,000) when three regiments of French cavalry, one of which was a regiment of Houlans [*sic*] or Poles with pikes (called Lancers), got round their flank and completely routed the brigade. Nearly the whole of the Buffs, with our Second Battalion and the 66th Regiment where in about five minutes *hors de combat*. The 31st being on the left was not broken.

[Later text addition] The confusion and rout of the 1st Brigade appears to have originated in some little misunderstanding between Lieutenant Colonel Colborne of the 66th Regiment who commanded it and General Stewart. The latter being in charge of the division could not have been supposed to interfere in the immediate formation of his brigade. He, however, directed it himself, and, contrary to the wishes and suggestion of Colonel Colborne, who is a most excellent officer, advanced under cover of rising ground in the front, and on its arrival at the commencement of the ascent gave orders to deploy. But the enemy's columns had gained the summit of the height and the 1st Brigade had not time to deploy more than the right regiment (the Buffs) and two or three companies of the centre regiments, when the order was given to charge.

They charged in great confusion and by companies or grand divisions and perfectly repulsed the French, but before the line was properly reformed, the enemy, seeing their confusion, moved three regiments of cavalry undiscovered, which the nature of the ground enabled them to do, round the right flank of the brigade. The Buffs being then in line was requested by Captain Waller of the Quartermaster General's Department to refuse their right and received the charge of cavalry. This was communicated to Major [Henry] King, who not being in command of the regiment, very injudiciously and imprudently hesitated in instantly making this movement with the right wing, replying to [Lieutenant] Colonel Stewart commanded the regiment. Consequently, at so critical a period, not a moment ought to have been lost, as by this delay, the rapid advance of the French cavalry enabled them to move round the flanks of the Buffs, when the soldiers became panic struck at seeing the enemy's cavalry in their rear and instantly proclaimed 'the cavalry are in our rear'. This like wildfire spread through the brigade. The soldiers lost all presence of mind, broke, and fled in every direction, the French cutting them down and showing no quarter at the moment. The whole brigade was, in consequence of this unfortunate occurrence, immediately in the hands of the enemy, either killed, wounded or prisoners. In the confusion, some few men and officers contrived to escape in the consequence of the arrival of our brigade, the 2nd, and the movement of our cavalry, which obliged the enemy to fall back, taking with them nearly all the survivors of the 1st Brigade prisoners.

The colours of the three regiments of the Buffs, 2nd Battalion 48th and 66th were taken. Some feats of valour were performed by individuals in self-defence – particularly by an ensign of the Buffs who had his arm sabred off, and covered with wounds, in endeavouring to preserve the colour which he carried, wrapping it around his body when torn from the staff. But to the conduct of this regiment may be imputed this sad disaster, or perhaps to the indecisive, hesitating and imbecile Major. Colonel Stewart in the confusion and took himself to the rear and left his regiment to its fate, and when all prisoners, returned to the field enquiring for them. Poor Waller was terribly mauled by a lancer, but got off with the loss of some of his fingers.

The 2nd Brigade [*sic*, should be 3rd Brigade] behaved nobly, standing the ground to the very last, particularly my excellent regiment (1st Battalion). The 29th and 57th from loss of men retired to the rear, but our battalion maintained themselves and afterwards making a charge drove the enemy at the commencement of the retreat and came out of the action with about 90 men. [End of later addition.]

At this time our brigade, the 3rd, arrived, and parallel to us on the right the Fusiliers and on the left the 2nd [Brigade] under Colonel Abercromby. We passed through the Spaniards who, though behaving very well, were in some confusion. The intervals through which the regiment had to pass were scarcely sufficient for a company. The Spaniards suffered a good deal, both from the enemy and from our brigade, which charging the French when they retired fired on them. General Hoghton who commanded us early, fell pierced with four balls. Our brigade stood their ground most gallantly and behaved in the most glorious manner, keeping up a most destructive fire on the enemy's columns which were endeavouring to gain the ground which we had driven them from and maintained. Every field and mounted officer of the brigade was either killed or wounded. Lieutenant Colonel Duckworth, who commanded the 1st [Battalion] of the 48th, was killed early in the action and the command devolved on myself.

[Later text addition] Shortly after our brigade was warmly engaged with the enemy, I had repeatedly urged Duckworth to charge. At one time he appeared disposed to do it, and ordering the drums to beat cease firing, moved in front of the line to ascertain the precise position of the columns we were opposed to, [and] in so doing his horse was wounded in the flank. He returned and ordered his men to commence firing, and stopping close to my side, asked if his mare bled much. He had no sooner put the question when he observed, 'I am wounded myself,' raising his left hand to his right shoulder. Scarcely had he uttered the words when a musket ball passed my own head within a hair's breadth and entered the neck of Duckworth. He immediately fell on the withers of his horse, his left arm falling on my thigh, and instantly expired. His remark in the morning immediately came to my recollection and I had no other feeling but regret at his loss. His body was immediately conveyed from the field by Sergeant McDonald and lamentable it is to observe that when the wounded soldiers at Elvas heard of his death, they shouted and exclaimed 'G— D— him, he is now in hell!' Such was the feelings of soldiers who themselves were (at least many of them) on the point of death from their wounds, respecting their commanding officer, who was certainly a zealous officer, and desirous at all times of doing his duty and making those under him equally attentive to duty, but who unfortunately from erroneous ideas, considered that tyranny, opprobrium and violent manner could alone enforce discipline and obedience; and no man appeared more determined to gain the ill will and hatred of every one under his command, and in this he generally most fully succeeded. He had, however, some good qualities – [he was] an affectionate and tender husband, a good father, and an excellent son and a brave and zealous soldier, but ignorant of human nature, and the art of governing soldiers. [indecipherable word] to his [indecipherable word]. I bear his memory no ill will, and lament the loss his wife and family must sustain in his fall. [End of later addition.]

The glorious conduct of the soldiers was most conspicuous. They never attempted to assist the wounded but, conscious that every man ought to remain, stood their ground to the last. Out of the 400 odd men we took into action, not 100 remained. The 29th and 57th suffered in the same proportion. A captain ultimately commanded the brigade and a subaltern the regiment. The loss of this brigade was very great as likewise that of the Fusiliers who behaved with great gallantry. The 3rd Brigade of that division was not much engaged.

Towards the close of the action I received a musket ball through my leg and another near my ankle. My horse had likewise one through his hind quarters. The cavalry had not an opportunity of distinguishing itself, the enemy being four times its number. Two squadrons of the 4th Dragoons made a successful charge and handsomely cut up the enemy. The French regiment of Houlans behaved in the most dastardly manner to our officers in soldiers when wounded and prisoners, thrusting their pikes at them and wounding them in several places.

After a most sanguinary and obstinate contest of more than six hours, the enemy drew off his columns and re-passed the river, leaving above 1,000 wounded on the field. Their loss is estimated at 10,000, 6,000 of which are wounded. Five general officers, two killed and three wounded. Gazan the chief of staff badly. Our force in the field 12,000 Spaniard, 8,000 Portuguese, 6,200 British infantry, 800 British cavalry, 1,000 Portuguese in Spanish cavalry. Total 28,000, 32 pieces of artillery. French 23,000 infantry, 4,000 cavalry, 40 pieces of artillery. Our loss better than 4,000 British, 1,500 Spaniards and 300 Portuguese.

The Portuguese were not much engaged.

Being obliged to quit the field from my wounds I had not an opportunity to seeing it after the action, but from every account it was most dreadful. Carnage on both sides was horrible, and considering nearly the whole of it fell on the British, against whom was the whole of the enemy's force, it is astonishing how many escaped. Never was British valour more conspicuous, and in the annals of our military history there never was an action in which it was more put to the test.

Thus the object for which Soult advanced had been frustrated. Badajoz for the present abandoned, the French retiring with great and serious loss and the British covered with glory.

Out of our two battalions we have 41 officers killed, wounded or prisoners and not 100 remaining for each battalion. Marshal Beresford was himself for a short time prisoner but by superior strength overcame his antagonist and got away.

The wounded were removed as expeditiously as possible to Valverde. Got my wound dressed and in evening reached Olivenza where General Kemmis's brigade had halted from Badajoz, but moved on in the evening.

## 2. Hobhouse Letter

*One of the most detailed accounts concerning the musketry duel that took place between the French Vth Corps and the 3rd Brigade of the 2nd Division comes from a letter written by Ensign Benjamin Hobhouse of the 57th Foot.[31] It is remarkable to imagine someone able to compose such a complete narrative a mere day after the battle.*

Field of Battle before Alburah [*sic*], May 17, 1811

My dear Father,

I have to thank God for my preservation during one of the most severe actions that the older officers on the field ever experienced. I have not much time to give you an account of the action, nor, indeed, have I it in my power to mention any further than what happened to our own regiment. Our line, consisting of about 6,000 British and as many Portuguese upon our left, which formed in the rear of the small village of Albuera with a rivulet in our front. About 6 in the morning, 10,000 Spaniards under Blake and Ballesteros formed upon our right. About 8, the French made their appearance from an extensive cork wood some distance from the village, advancing in massy [*sic*] columns upon the right of the line. Some large columns of their artillery with cavalry pushed forward to menace an attack on the bridge, which was directly in front of our centre; but the whole weight of the infantry fell upon the Spaniards on our right. To withstand this the Spaniards were not sufficient; the British were called upon for their support, which was not long at arriving. General Cole's and Stewart's divisions marched to their relief in open column (the whole of them, I believe, like ourselves) during one of the most tremendous and destructive fires that has ever been witnessed.

What I mention at present is particularly of our own brigade. During our advance in column, the incessant and well-directed fire the French artillery mowed down many of our poor fellows. Of course our object was, and should have been sooner, to deploy into line, which we did about 20 yards in the rear of the right of a small body of Spaniards, who are supporting and returning the enemy's fire with the greatest bravery. We immediately passed in front of them, and received the most raking and continued cross-fire of musketry from a large body of the enemy's infantry whose heads scarcely exposed above the brow of a hill. At this time our poor fellows dropped around us in every

---

31    The letter resides in the Royal Archives, Windsor Castle. The letter is quoted in part in *The Times*, 24 June 1811, and printed in full in *The Times* on 25 February 1915.

direction. In the activity of the officers to keep them firm, and to supply them with ammunition of the fallen men, you could scarcely avoid treading on the dying and the dead. But all was still firm. In passing the Spaniards, the different regiments of our brigade were separated, and fought alone, during the remainder of the action. Tho' alone, our fire never slackened nor were the men the least disheartened. Tho' by closing to the right we appear to be no more than a company, we still advanced and fired; and the Spaniards moved upon the left with the greatest bravery.

Just before this, our colonel, major, every captain and 11 subalterns fell; the King's colour was cut in two; the regimental had 17 balls through them, many companies were without officers, and as the light company was next to me, I could not do otherwise than take command of it which I did, until it was my turn to take up the shattered colours. After an engagement of at least four hours (which was the time our regiment was actually engaged) a general shout passed down the lines, and immediately after a cry of 'they run, they run'. Just as we mounted the heights from which they had fought we saw them running over the plain in the greatest disorder. Marshal Beresford passed us at the time, and ordered us to halt; upon which we drew up, and a shell that was thrown from a great distance blew up the horse of our last field officer, and wounded him slightly. The French artillery, which was covering their retreat, annoyed us most dreadfully on the height; and we went under the brow to count our numbers.

This was indeed a lamentable sight; we entered the field with 3 field officers, 7 captains, 19 subalterns and 572 men. We appeared on the field, 1 field officer who is wounded, 6 subalterns, 2 of which were slightly wounded, the adjutant without his horse, and 118 men. Among all the officers in the regiment, another and myself were the only ones who had not some scratch or shot through their clothes. We were in vain looking for some holes to show our brother officers; our anxiety to find one, and our want of success created a laugh against us. Were we not fortunate, my dear father, or rather can we be sufficiently thankful to divine providence which preserved us during one of the most dreadful fire of shot, shells and musketry the heroes of Egypt, Maida, and Talavera, who were with us, ever witnessed? In the commencement our General of brigade, Hoghton, was killed; our General of division, Stewart, was wounded; our brigade, which went into the action so strong, returned commanded by a junior captain; and our regiment was commanded by a young lieutenant.

In this situation, as you may suppose, we could not do more; the Portuguese troops which had not yet been engaged, were brought up in our place, and appeared firm and ready for fresh attack; while the light troops skirmished with retreating parties of the enemy. As for us, we were occupied in looking out for the shattered remains of our brigade. After a short time we found the 48th regiment equally reduced as ourselves. General Stewart, though wounded, was still on horseback, actively employed in collecting the different regiments. The second brigade, which was on our left, was found some distance to our left, where they retired after having been relieved by the Portuguese, and behaving, as General Stewart said, most gallantly. Their loss, however, was by no means so great as ours.

The firing ended late in the afternoon after the French were seen to have reformed their scattered forces and marched back into the wood they left in the morning. The Portuguese and Spaniards remained on the field of battle, and we, like skeletons, marched back to the left of the lines.

The place, which had been the scene of action, afforded a sight which I cannot attempt to describe as I cannot think of it but with horror. The mangled bodies of the dead, the groans of the dying, and the complaints of the wounded are too horrible to reflect upon. The hill was actually covered with the French who were opposed to us, and proved that our fire had been successful and that our brave fellows did not die unavenged. During the principal part of the action it rained most violently and the wind blew in our teeth, which prevented us from seeing the enemy during the thickest part of the fire. Their loss was immense, and from some of the wounded officers we learned that they came into action 25,000 strong. A sergeant to whom I spoke told me there was a corps of 6,000 men on the ground where he lay, and it was with this body that we were engaged. Soult commanded. A French general's uniform was found on the field of battle. Ballesteros seized it and cried out, though I believe he knew to the contrary, 'Soult is dead, my lads, look at his coat' as he rode in front of the lines, and he held up the embroidered coat. He said this in my hearing, and it produced an admirable effect; for both Spaniards and British advanced to the attack with redoubled vigour.

Though wet to the skin we slept soundly during the night, expecting another attack this morning. The enemy however, has not as yet thought proper to attempt it. They are still in the wood just in our front. We have been occupied the whole day in collecting our wounded and burying our dead, who were this morning lying on the field of battle in two distinct lines where we stood the fire. We found the bodies of our major and a captain, who was my particular friend and mess mate. I mentioned to you the number of officers who suffered; some men have since joined, which makes it so much stronger than I told you.

You will, of course, soon see correctly lists of our killed and wounded; and I trust some mention will be made of the conduct of our (the 57th) regiment. Not a single man of ours was taken prisoner, for we never lost our ground.

Previous to the action we had been seven days employed in the siege of Badajoz; and the night before we raised the siege, on account of Soult's approach, we dug a trench in the face of 12 pieces of cannon within 500 yards of the walls. Of course, all our work there was night work, and from continual watching at Badajoz, our business since, and the almost incessant rains the few officers that are left are nearly overcome by fatigue. Thank God I am myself as well as I ever was in my life, and, as you may suppose, in great spirits, although deprived of every comfort. I have suffered much from the losses of baggage and baggage animals, but I am thankful it is no worse.

Your affectionate son,

Benj. Hobhouse

## 3. Inglis Narrative

*Lieutenant Colonel William Inglis of the 57th Foot made only two written public comments about the battle. This one is in the form of a letter he wrote to the editor of the United Service Journal explaining the 'friendly fire' incident of Hoghton's brigade firing on their Spanish allies.[32] Inglis refers to himself in the third person in the letter.*

The 2nd Division of the British army engaged at Albuera was under the command of Major General the Right Hon. William Stewart. The 3rd Brigade in that division was the one that was commanded by Major General Hoghton, and was composed of the 29th, 1st Battalion 57th, and 1st Battalion 48th. The whole division moved from its ground in open column of companies, right in front, about a mile, where the line was to be formed on the leading company.

At this period the Spaniards were warmly engaged with the enemy and behaving most gallantly. General Stewart's division was brought up to support them and to form the second line.

After the 29th, and the right wing of the 57th had formed, a body of French lancers got between the two lines. The right platoon of the 29th was ordered to disperse them. The fire from this body flew rapidly to the left, and in consequence was taken up by the 57th.

---

32   Letter to Editor from W. Inglis, *United Service Journal* (1832), Pt. II, pp. 241–2. The other public statement was a terse refutation of a claim that the 57th had lost their colours in the battle: 'The colours are in my possession', *United Service Journal* (1829), Pt. I, p. 349.

Colonel Inglis, who commanded the latter regiment, was, it so happened, at that moment wholly employed in the act of correcting an error which had occurred in the formation of the centre of his regiment, in which, owing to the rain that fell, and the thickness of the atmosphere which it occasioned, joined to their having met with a piece of hollow ground, the 5th company had lost its perpendicularity, and doubled behind the 4th, whereby the centre of the regiment became crowded; Colonel Inglis having also at the same time his horse shot under him.

It was at this moment, and whilst Colonel Inglis's attention was thus unavoidably taken off, that the firing which has been mentioned happened; but almost instantly Colonel Inglis was again, though dismounted, in front of his right wing, and gave the command to order arms, which was immediately obeyed.

Whilst speaking to his men on what had occurred, General Hoghton and a Spanish officer came up to him, and complained that the Spaniards had been fired upon. Colonel Inglis expressed his concern, of course, at such an occurrence; but it was a great satisfaction to him to perceive that the Spaniards themselves had happily not suffered – a circumstance which was attributable to their position with respect to the hill at the time of firing, which occasioned the balls to pass over their heads.

Colonel Inglis then called the General's attention to the steadiness evinced by his regiment, who were standing with ordered arms under so heavy a fire from the enemy. General Hoghton directed Colonel Inglis not to engage till he should receive his orders so to do, and said, that he himself was going to the right of his brigade, and would take off his hat to the Colonel, as a signal to him when he wished him to commence. When the signal was given (the Spaniards having retired) it was returned by the Colonel, who then ordered arms to be shouldered, and his regiment then threw in a very heavy well-directed fire, by files from the right of companies.

From this period nothing more was heard of General Hoghton by Colonel Inglis, until his Aide-de-camp, Captain Ramsden, acquainted Colonel Inglis that he was killed.

## 4. Lindenthal Manuscript

*The text below comes from a manuscript found in the George Murray Papers in the National Library of Scotland that is catalogued as 'Series of general abstracts of military events in Portugal from 27 September 1810 to 31 July 1811'. The manuscript includes information about Albuera that was compiled from official and unofficial sources. The compiler is likely to have been Major General Lewis Lindenthal serving on assignment to the Horse Guards.*

*The text is included in this volume because it provides the earliest source for the 'Die Hard' quotation attributed to Colonel Inglis.*[33]

The conduct of every corps was so distinguished that it is difficult to particularise that of any without doing injustice to others. Yet there were some circumstances attaching to that of the 57th Reg't which seem to call for peculiar notice. Sir Wm. Beresford states 'It was obvious that our dead, particularly those of the 57th Reg't, were lying as they had fought, in ranks, and every wound was in the front.' Other letters state that they stood alone against a heavy French column, forced it to halt and eventually to retire. An officer of the Reg't, 'tho badly wounded, remained sitting on the ground at the head of his company, giving orders to his men to level [?] low.'[34] Colonel Inglis, their commanding officer, a man rather advanced in years showed upon this occasion all the energy & activity of youth. His horse being killed under him, he went up & down the ranks encouraging the men, and when wounded in the neck by grape, he called out to the men to die game [emphasis in original].

## 5. Leslie Narrative
*Lieutenant Charles Leslie of the 29th Foot wrote a compelling memoir of his long military service that includes many unique details concerning Albuera.*[35]

On the afternoon of the 15th May, 1811, after a long march, the English army took up their ground on the heights in rear of Albuera; but, as the Spanish army had not arrived, General Hoghton's brigade, consisting of the 29th, 57th, and 1st battalions of the 48th Regiment, was moved to the right and formed *en potence*. The Spaniards having come up during the night, our brigade, after standing some hours under arms, was ordered, about six or seven o'clock on the morning of the 16th, to resume its place in the line. We had scarcely time to get a little tea and a morsel of biscuit, when the alarm was given – 'Stand to your arms! The French are advancing.'

We accordingly instantly got under arms, leaving tents and baggage to be disposed of as the quartermaster and batmen best could. We moved forward in line to crown the heights in front, which were

---

33  Inglis himself never publicly claimed the quote. For more detailed information about the 'Die Hard' quotation, see Appendix D of my 2008 book about the battle.

34  This officer was most likely Captain Ralph Fawcett. See Warre, H.J., *Historical Records of the Fifty-Seventh, or, West Middlesex Regiment of Foot* (London, 1878), p. 53.

35  Leslie, Charles, *Military Journal of Colonel Leslie, K.H. of Balquhain* (Aberdeen, 1887), pp. 216–25.

intended for our position, and which may be shortly described as follows. The rivulet of Albuera ran nearly parallel to the front of the heights, at about six hundred yards' distance, which sloped down to it, these being perfectly open for all arms; but beyond our right they swelled into steeper and more detached ones. The village of Albuera was nearly opposite the centre of our line, and on the same side of the water; at which point was the only bridge. The banks of the rivulet were at some places steep and abrupt. On the opposite, or French side, they were rather low, and the ground flat and open for some little distance; then gradually rose to a gentle height, covered with wood, particularly at some distance from the bridge up the river, where the French army lay concealed from our view, they having only some detached parties of cavalry in the open ground.

In occupying the position the army was formed as follows: The Portuguese, in blue, on the left; the English, in red in the centre-viz., General Hoghton's brigade, the 29th, 57th, and 1st battalions of the 48th Regiment; General Lumley's, 28th, 39th, and 34th regiments; Colonel Colborne's, the 3rd, the 2nd battalion of the 48th, the 66th, and 31st regiments; and the Spaniards, in yellow or other bright colours, formed the right. The whole were drawn up as for a grand parade, in full view of the enemy, so that Soult could see almost every man, and he was also enabled to choose his point of attack; which would not have been the case if we had been kept under cover a few yards farther back, behind the crest of the heights, or had been made to lie down, as we used to do under the Duke of Wellington. That part of the 4th Division under Sir Lowry Cole, which had just arrived from Badajoz, were posted in second line in our rear.

Before we had time to halt in our position, we observed two large columns of the enemy, supported by cavalry and artillery, moving towards the bridge and village of Albuera, which was occupied by the light corps of the German Legion under Colonel Halkett. The first attack here commenced, under cover of a heavy cannonade, upon the village and our line in its rear. The Germans made a gallant defence, and maintained their post; but as the enemy apparently seemed to make a push at this point, Colborne's brigade was ordered to move down in support of the troops in the village.

Soult must have been much delighted on observing this movement: it, no doubt, was precisely what he most wished; because the columns which appeared to threaten the village and our line was only a ruse to distract our attention and neutralise the English force which he most dreaded. Our skilful adversary was, in the meantime, throwing his masses directly across our right flank, or Spanish army, which extended to a great distance from us; and it was with no small surprise that we most unexpectedly heard a sharp fire commence in that quarter.

The error our chief had been led into now became evident. We were suddenly thrown into open column, and moved rapidly along the heights to our right flank for nearly a mile under a tremendous cannonade, for the French had already established themselves on some commanding heights, which raked us as we advanced, Captain Humphrey and several men being killed. They were, at the same time, attacking the Spaniards with great vigour, having put them into some confusion when in the act of throwing back their right to meet this flank attack. Colborne's brigade also, which had moved to cover the village, as stated above, had been recalled and brought up in a hasty manner in column, obliquing to their right towards the heights now occupied by the enemy, and formed line at a right angle perpendicular to the first position.

It has been understood that Colonel Colborne wished to move to the attack with the two flank regiments in quarter distance columns, and the two centre ones in one line; but Sir William Stewart, anxious to show a large front, was deploying the whole. The 3rd, 48th, and 66th regiments were in line, and the 31st Regiment still in column; when a body of French Lancers, taking advantage of the thick weather and heavy showers of rain, got round the right of this brigade, made a dash from the rear through those regiments which were in line, broke them, and swept off the greater part as prisoners into the French lines. The 31st Regiment stood firm, and fortunately escaped the disaster; and the Spaniards continued with some difficulty to hold their ground. Just as this misfortune had occurred our brigade came up, the 29th leading. We closed up into quarter distance columns under cover of the heights and deployed; but before the 57th and 48th regiments had completed the formation, a body of Spaniards in advance of our left flank gave way, and in making off ran in our front, and then came rushing back upon us. We called out to them, urging them to rally and maintain their ground, and that we would shortly relieve them.

On these assurances, with the exertions of some of the officers and of our Adjutant, who rode amongst them, they did rally, and moved up the hill again, but very shortly afterwards down they came again in the utmost confusion – mixed pell-mell with a body of the enemy's Lancers, who were thrusting and cutting without mercy. Many of the Spaniards threw themselves on the ground, others attempted to get through our line, but this could not be permitted, because we being in line on the slope of a bare green hill, and such a rush of friends and foes coming down upon us, any opening made to let the former pass would have admitted the enemy also. We had no alternative left but to stand firm, and in self-defence to fire on both. This shortly decided the business; the Lancers brought up and made the best of their way back to their own lines, and the Spaniards were permitted to pass to the rear.

The formation of our brigade being now completed, and Lumley's brigade having taken post on the left, and all being now ready for the attack, Sir William Stewart rode up to our brigade, and after a few energetic words, said, 'Now is the time – let us give three cheers!' This was instantly done with heart and soul, every cap waving in the air. We immediately advanced up the hill under a sharp fire from the enemy's light troops, which we did not condescend to return, and they retreated as we moved on. On arriving at the crest of the height we discovered the enemy a little in rear of it, apparently formed in masses, or columns of grand divisions, with light troops and artillery in the intervals between them. From the waving and rising of the ground on which some of these stood, the three or four front ranks in some cases could fire over the heads of one another, and some guns were posted on a bank and fired over one of these columns. Notwithstanding this formidable array, our line went close up to the enemy, without even a piece of artillery to support us; at least near us there were none. We understood that the nine-pounder brigade had been withdrawn in consequence of the disaster above related. On the other hand, Soult has since stated that he had forty pieces of cannon vomiting death at this point. The 29th Regiment being on the right of this line, its flank was *en l'air* and completely exposed without any strong point to rest upon, while the Fusilier and Portuguese brigades of the 4th Division, which had also been brought up to the new front, were a considerable way to our right on the plain below.

This was the moment at which the murderous and desperate battle really began. A most overwhelming fire of artillery and small arms was opened upon us, which was vigorously returned. There we unflinchingly stood, and there we fell: our ranks were at some places swept away by sections. This dreadful contest had continued for some time, when an officer of artillery – I believe a German – came up and said he had brought two or three guns, but that he could find no one to give him orders, our superior officers being all wounded or killed. It was suggested that he could not do wrong in opening directly on the enemy, which was accordingly done. Our line at length became so reduced that it resembled a chain of skirmishers in extended order; while, from the necessity of closing in towards the colours, and our numbers fast diminishing, our right flank became still further exposed.

The enemy, however, did not avail himself of the advantage which this circumstance might have afforded him.

We continued to maintain this unprecedented conflict with unabated energy. The enemy, notwithstanding his superiority of numbers, had not obtained one inch of ground, but, on the contrary, we were gaining on him, when the gallant Fusilier brigade was moved up from the plain, bringing their right shoulders forward. They thus took the enemy obliquely in flank, who, although already much shattered, still continued to make a brave resistance; but nothing could withstand the invincible and undaunted bravery of the British soldiers. The enemy's masses, after a desperate struggle for victory, gave way at all points, and were driven in disorder beyond the rivulet, leaving us triumphant masters of the field.

To the credit of the troops engaged it ought to be recollected that, in all other battles fought either before or afterwards in the Peninsula, our gallant army, under a skilful commander, had only either to march up to the enemy or to await his attack, and that after a conflict of more or less duration the victory was won; but in this terrible contest, error, confusion, and misfortune attended our first disposition. Victory had to be retrieved from a brave and experienced foe, under many untoward and disheartening circumstances, and it seems universally agreed that the annals of war scarcely afford an instance of so bloody a battle having ever been fought in proportion to the numbers engaged.

Mustering the living and recording the dead became afterwards our melancholy duty. On reckoning our numbers, the 29th Regiment had only ninety-six men, two captains, and a few subalterns remaining out of the whole regiment; the 57th Regiment had but a few more, and were commanded out of action by the Adjutant; the first battalion of the 48th Regiment suffered in like manner: not a man of the brigade was prisoner; not a colour was lost, although an eloquent historian most unwarrantably stated that the 57th had lost theirs. The 57th lose their colours! – never! Major General Hoghton, commanding the brigade, and Lieutenant Colonel Duckworth of the 48th Regiment were killed; Lieutenant Colonel White of the 29th Regiment mortally wounded; Colonel Inglis of the 57th and Major Way of the 29th regiments were very severely wounded. In fact, every field-officer of the whole brigade was either killed or wounded, so that at the close of the action the brigade remained in command of a captain of the 48th Regiment, and, singular enough, that captain was a Frenchman, named Cimetière (cemetery).

The field afterwards presented a sad spectacle, our men lying generally in rows and the French in large heaps, from their having fought principally in masses, they not having dared to deploy, as they afterwards told us, from a dread of our cavalry, as they supposed that we would not have ventured to act in such an open country without a great superiority in that description of force.

The French were driven in such confusion from the field that their brigades and regiments lost all order and were completely mixed, so that numbers of our men and several of the officers who had been taken prisoners made their escape out of the enemy's bivouac during the night, and many deserters came over; but notwithstanding their great disorder, which must have been known to our chief, we remained all the next day looking at one another, while the enemy was actively employed in reorganising his shattered forces. It struck many people that if only a demonstration of advancing had been made even on the following morning, their total rout would have been complete, because General Hamilton's division of Portuguese were still almost entire, nor had Halkett's fine corps, or even Lumley's brigade, or our cavalry been rendered unserviceable, and the remaining part of the 4th Division, which had been detained at Badajoz, were momentarily expected to arrive, exclusive of the Spanish army. On the third day, even after the enemy had recovered his order, as soon as he observed that we were about to advance, he immediately commenced his retreat without offering the smallest resistance.

Some affecting incidents which occurred on this memorable occasion may not prove uninteresting. When in our first position Major General Hoghton was on horseback in front of the line, in a green frock-coat, which he had put on in the hurry of turning out. Some time afterwards his servant rode up to him with his red uniform coat, and without dismounting he immediately stripped off the green and put on the red one. It may be said that this public display of our national colour and of British coolness actually was done under a salute of French artillery, as they were cannonading us at the time.

There had been a general court martial held some time previous to the action. The prisoner, Lieutenant Ansaldo, was found guilty and sentenced to be suspended for six months. He, however, instead of quitting his corps during that period, remained with the army, and gallantly went into action by the side of his prosecutor. They both fell; and what is still more extraordinary, the president, General Hoghton, the Judge Advocate, Captain Benning, 66th Regiment, and many of the members and witnesses were also killed and were almost all of them entombed near the same spot.

A few days after the battle five regiments who suffered most were embodied into one, forming a provisional battalion – viz., the 3rd Regiment, one company; the 66th, one company; the 29th, two companies; the 57th, three; and the 31st three companies, placed under the command of Lieutenant Colonel L'Estrange of the 31st Regiment.

## 6. Hamilton Narrative

*Thomas Hamilton was a mere ensign in the 29th Foot when he fought and was wounded at Albuera. In 1827, he wrote a very popular novel recounting the adventures of a fictional British soldier named Cyril Thornton in the Napoleonic Wars. Although he went on to publish a formal history of the Peninsular War in 1829, the chapter in his novel describing the experiences of Cyril Thornton at Albuera is probably autobiographical and accurately reflects Hamilton's personal experiences, including the speech he attributes to General Stewart.[36]*

Heavily rose the sun on the eventful morning of the sixteenth of May 1811. Dark volumes of clouds obscured his disk, and his rays lost more than half their brightness in penetrating the dense masses of vapour which on all sides overspread the horizon. We were under arms two hours before day-dawn; and thousands of eyes which that morning watched his rising, were destined never to see him set. The morning, though still and dark, was not misty. Objects, even at a considerable distance, were distinctly visible. There was not wind to stir a leaf upon the smallest spray, and the scene before us, though gloomy, was peaceful.

It was seven o'clock before we returned to our tents, and at that time no enemy was visible. Two of my brother-officers that morning shared my breakfast; and of the whole party, including the three servants who ministered to our wants, I was in the course of two hours the only individual alive.

While we were at breakfast, a few shots were fired by our artillery, which did not at all influence our meal; but that concluded, my curiosity led me to advance a considerable distance in front of the line, to observe the motions of the enemy, who were reported to be fast approaching. The report was correct. Their advancing masses covered the road for several miles, and their cavalry, formed in column of squadrons on the plain, had already menaced an attack on the bridge of Albuera. Fast as their infantry came up, they halted in column on either side of the road,

---

36    Hamilton, Thomas, *The Youth and Manhood of Cyril Thornton* (3 vols., London and Edinburgh, 1827), v. 3, pp. 160–70.

without indicating, by any demonstration, what part of our position was about to become the chief object of their attack. I spent about half an hour – it might be more – in thus gratifying my curiosity; and when I returned, the tents were struck, the baggage sent to the rear, and the whole army drawn up in line of battle.

The pain I felt at this sight was excruciating. To have been absent from my post at such a moment, when the sound of the artillery, which had already opened on the advancing enemy, showed that the battle had even now begun, was to incur the possibility of an imputation which I could brook no lips to utter. I ran madly to the rear, and found with some difficulty the place where my tent had stood. I was in dishabille; and it was necessary, on such an occasion, to appear in uniform. My coat, hat, and sash, had been left on the ground; but in the hurry my sword had been removed with the baggage. I changed my dress as speedily as possible, casting from me that which I wore, for plunder either to our own soldiers or those of the enemy, and having supplied the place of my own sword by that of a sergeant, I joined my regiment. . . .

In order to render the subsequent account of this, to me, most eventful and memorable battle, more clear and intelligible, I shall here take leave to say something of the relative situation of the hostile armies.

Our position was a chain of eminences, along the front of which flowed the river Albuera, a shallow stream, and in many places fordable. Through the centre of it ran the road to Badajoz and Valverde, crossing the river by a bridge, which Beresford evidently expected would have been the main object of the enemy's attack. To the left of the road lay the village of Albuera, apparently deserted and in ruins. Near this was stationed our artillery. The enemy, however, merely menacing this point, crossed the river about a mile higher up, where its course was nearly at right angles with that which it subsequently took in front of our position. By this movement our right flank, consisting of Blake's army, was laid completely open to attack, and instantly driving the Spaniards from the heights they occupied, Marshal Soult drew up his army in a commanding position, which completely raked the line of the Allies. Thus an immediate change of front, on our part, became necessary; and the object to which our efforts were directed, of course, was to dislodge the enemy from the very important heights of which he had already gained possession. In truth, on the success of these efforts depended the whole issue of the battle; for if the French succeeded in maintaining their position, ours became untenable, and no resource was left but a retreat, which, situated as we then were, could not fail to be both disgraceful and calamitous.

78

Such were the circumstances in which both armies stood, when the order, which I have already mentioned, arrived for our brigade to march instantly to attack the enemy on the heights he occupied.

The morning, which had been overcast . . . had now changed to one of storm and rain, so heavy, that less than forty days of it would have sufficed for a second deluge; and it was with every part of our apparel perfectly saturated with water that we commenced our movement. The enemy soon opened on us a tremendous fire of artillery, which did considerable execution in the column, and dashed the earth in our faces as we advanced. One cannon-ball struck close to my foot, and bounding onwards with terrific velocity, passed through the body of the officer commanding the company immediately in rear of my own, and killed two soldiers in its further progress.

As we approached the spot where the courage of both armies was about to be tested, a sight of the most dispiriting description presented itself at some distance on our right. The first brigade, in the act of forming line, was charged by a large body of Polish lancers, and thus taken at a disadvantage, were thrown into disorder, which it was found impossible to retrieve. By this attack, nearly the whole of the Buffs and second battalion of the 48th were made prisoners.

We had reached the bottom of the heights, which we were about to ascend, and for that purpose were deploying from column into line, when Sir William Stewart, the second in command, rode up to us at full speed.

His appearance arrested my attention. The day, as I have already said, was cold and wet, but the perspiration stood in large drops on his forehead, and ran down his cheeks. He was always a man of martial appearance, but at that moment particularly so. There was strong agitation visible in his countenance and manner, but there was a striking expression of high courage in his eye, and as he spoke his utterance was quicker, and his voice more animated than I had ever heard it. He addressed us as follows:

Men of the third brigade, you are about to fight for the honour of your country, and I am not afraid to tell you that the fate of this army is in your hands. I have committed a great and unfortunate error with the first brigade, but I am sure you will repair all. You will crown the height, and then charge the enemy with the bayonet. Go on, my brave fellows, and may God bless you!

To this inspiriting address the men answered by a loud and hearty cheer, and General Hoghton, waving his hat, led the way up the side

79

of the hill. On reaching its summit, we were instantly, assailed by a dreadful fire, both of musketry and artillery, and the men fell thickly in the ranks. For a moment the line first wavered, and then recoiled for a pace or two, but General Hoghton, again waving his hat, spurred on to the front, and we advanced once more, in double quick, to the charge.

The other regiments of the brigade, being in rear, had not yet taken up their position in the line, and we enjoyed the honour of leading them into action. As we advanced, I remember passing Marshal Beresford on the height. He was on foot, with no staff near him, and in a situation of extreme exposure. His look and air were those of a man perplexed and bewildered.

Our intention of charging the enemy was unfortunately defeated by the intervention of a small ravine, on the opposite bank of which the French were stationed, and were enabled, by the acclivity on which they stood, to fire on us eight deep. It was on the edge of this ravine that we halted, and opened our fire. The carnage in our ranks was dreadful. General Hoghton had been killed in the advance, and bullets flew like hailstones. I saw my friends and brother officers fall around me; and it seemed as if I bore a charmed life, and that I alone moved secure and scatheless amid the surrounding havoc.

Such had been our situation for some time, when the sergeant major came to inform me that the command of the regiment had devolved on me, all the officers senior in rank having been killed or wounded. In the rear I found the horse of the adjutant, who had been killed, and mounting him, I rode along the ranks, and saw that I had indeed succeeded to a melancholy command. We had taken upwards of seven hundred men into action, of whom not a third remained; and it was evident, if we continued much longer in our present situation, few even of those could expect to escape the fate of their companions.

The firing, which had somewhat slackened on the part of the enemy, had, from the exhaustion of ammunition, almost entirely ceased on ours, yet we had received no orders to retire. In this situation, a brigade of artillery was advanced to the front, and instantly opened their fire. It was charged by the French cavalry, and we had the mortification to observe the artillerymen driven from their posts, and the guns remain in possession of the enemy. The regiment were already retiring when this unfortunate event took place; but even destitute as we were of an ammunition, I determined to make an effort to recover the guns, thus disgracefully sacrificed, at the point of the bayonet. Once more we faced the enemy; and calling on the small remains of the regiment to follow me, I led the charge, trampling as we advanced on the bodies of our dead and dying companions. The charge was successful. The enemy were driven back, and the guns were once more in our possession.

The Fusilier brigade was seen at that moment advancing to our support, and everything seemed to indicate a happy termination of the contest. Before the arrival, however, of this seasonable reinforcement, we were charged by the Polish lancers, who had already done so much execution in the commencement of the action, supported by a heavy column of infantry. At this moment I received a shot in the body, but did not fall from my horse. I was immediately surrounded by the lancers, and remember receiving a dreadful sabre-cut on the face, and a pistol-shot in the left arm.

I fell to the ground, and of what passed afterwards my memory gives me no intelligence.

## E. 4th Division Accounts

### 1. Broke Narrative
*Major Charles Broke was a staff officer of the 4th Division who kept its journal of operations, which he published in 1841.[37] (He took the surname Vere after the war, and is sometimes referred to by that name.) His journal makes the case that General Cole alone was responsible for ordering the advance of the 4th Division in violation of the orders he had received earlier from Beresford to hold his position.*

When General Cole joined Sir William Beresford with the two brigades of the 4th Division on the morning of 16 May, the enemy's movement on the right of the position of Albuera had just been announced, and the advance posts on the right were engaged. General Cole was ordered to place his division in contiguous columns in the rear of the 2nd Division; in the plain on the reverse of the position, in reserve to the troops that occupied the high ground, which was crossed by the Albuera road, and looked to the approaches by the bridge of Albuera. It was on that side [that] the attack had been expected; but Marshal Soult profiting by the shelter of the woods which cover the country to the right, on the side of Santa Marta, unexpectedly collected there the principal part of his force, and showed his columns of attack directed upon the heights on the extreme right of the position – the most commanding ground, and part of which was not then occupied by the Allies.

---

37    *Marches, Movements, and Operations of the 4th Division of the Allied Army in Spain and Portugal in the Years 1810, 1811 & 1812* by the Assistant Quarter-master-General of the Division (Ipswich, England, 1841), pp. 9–16.

The Spanish corps, which had joined Sir William Beresford on the 15th May, acted immediately under General Blake, and was on the right of the troops in the position. It had to change its front and to take ground to the right, to meet the flank attack, and as the movement of the Spaniards was slow; the ground was imperfectly occupied, when they had to bear the brunt of the attack.

The cavalry of the Allies, at that time, was collected on the right of the Spaniards, on their new front.

The enemy's cavalry, much superior in force to that of the Allies, spread around the right and rear of the Allies towards the Valverde road, but gradually closed to its right, keeping the Allied cavalry in check.

The battle was now decidedly on the right; the enemy's columns had gained the highest summits of the heights, and pressed hard upon the Spaniards.

Sir William Beresford moved the British brigades of the 2nd Division to the right, to the support of the Spaniards.

As those brigades went into action at a quick pace, the column of the brigade on the right was attacked in the flank by a corps of Polish lancers, which was kept close up with the French infantry, and the column was broken. The brigade rallied, and advanced, but was again broken by the same cavalry. At this instant the Hon. Colonel De Grey with two squadrons of British dragoons, charged upon the French infantry, which was halted, and fell in with the Polish cavalry, which were mixed with English infantry, and several of the enemy's cavalry suffered in the charge.

When the French cavalry were extended to their left, and round the right of the Spaniards, an order was brought to General Cole by Colonel D'Urban to change the position of the division to the right, and form it at right angles to its original front. General Cole immediately executed the order; and deployed his columns into line, with the exception of one, and the light companies of the Fusilier brigade, which he kept in column on the right and rear of the Portuguese brigade, which was on the right of his line.

The division was still under the heights of the position: the left on its new front, resting at the foot of those heights, and its right was extended in the plain; but the division was advanced in no way more towards the right of the position where the troops were engaged.

General Cole continued anxiously to watch the progress of the contest, and he sent his aide-de-camp [Captain Roverea] to Sir William Beresford to request authority to carry his division in support of the troops engaged.

Colonel Rooke, the Deputy Adjutant General, and also Major Hardinge, Deputy Quartermaster General, had suggested, and the latter strongly urged on the general, the necessity of his advancing to reinforce the 2nd Division; but they brought <u>no order</u> from Sir William Beresford, neither did his aide-de-camp return with any answer. General Cole was impatient with being compelled to withhold support under an evident demand for succour – and such at length appeared to be the critical state of the conflict, that he took upon himself the responsibility of moving his division to reinforce the battle, without receiving any order from his superior to do so.

And the manner in which he directed his line should be moved forward, was such as showed his desire to effect with promptness the immediate object of the movement; and at that same time, his care to secure the army, his protection on its right, of the extended formation of his division to that flank, which was one of the advantages afforded in its position in reserve.

Having directed that the flank companies of the division in column of quarter distance, and the brigade of guns, should keep on the right of the Portuguese brigade; that being the extreme right, he moved forward with the Fusilier brigade, supported by the 7th Caçadores [originally the Loyal Lusitanian Legion], to reinforce the troops engaged, so as to bring the brigade up to their right, by a forward and flank movement across the slopes of the heights, and at the same time, he directed the remainder of the division (the Portuguese brigade, artillery, and light companies) should follow the movement of the Fusilier brigade, with as much celerity, as keeping their order in line, and place in echelon with the Fusiliers, would admit of.

As the whole had to take ground to the left during a quick and forward movement in the face of the enemy, the operation was one of some difficulty, required precision, and constant attention to execution.

The Fusiliers advanced rapidly, and approached the right of the 2nd Division just after another charge of Polish Lancers. The Fusiliers fired on the enemy's cavalry – closed to their left – and were soon in line, and in action with the 2nd Division against the French columns.

The remainder of the division followed the movement of the Fusiliers, but could not make the same forward progress, and also to keep its order, so as to preserve the echelon to the Fusiliers; but every effort was made, and effectually, to keep the Portuguese line well to the left, to cover the right of the Fusiliers, which at every step became more exposed.

The cavalry of the Allies had been brought by General Lumley to the right of the infantry as it advanced on the plain, having there the support of the guns of the 4th Division and the troops in column on that flank.

The French cavalry, under General Latour-Maubourg, was in front of the advancing line in the plain, and charged twice on the line of the Portuguese infantry during its movement. The French cavalry was received with, and repulsed by, a well-directed fire from the line, and the artillery on its flank, in both charges. The line showed great steadiness; and conduct, that would have done honour to the best and most experienced troops.

The Fusilier brigade was now hotly engaged, and the Portuguese line was closing up to it and covering well its right, and in echelon to it; when the right of the Fusilier brigade was charged and partially broken, by the same Polish cavalry which attacked the right of the 2nd Division.

The Portuguese received the lancers with a steady fire. The Poles were repulsed, and the Fusiliers resumed their formation.

The ranks of the infantry were thinning fast, whilst standing under the fire of the dense and crowded columns of the enemy; which made no progress.

The left brigade of the 2nd Division, and the guns on the left, were doing execution; and the fire of the Fusiliers was marking its effect.

Every effort of the enemy to deploy his columns had failed – they became closely crowded – his fire slackened; and suddenly the unmanageable and confused mass turned about and fled in disorder down the heights under the fire of the Allies. The light companies of the 4th Division followed them on the right to the stream, through which they had moved to the attack in the morning.

General Latour-Maubourg had wholly drawn off his cavalry, after the fruitless advance he had made against the Portuguese.

In this battle General Cole and all his personal staff, and all the officers of the staff of the division, except one, were severely wounded.

The temporary command of the division devolved for the remainder of the day on Brigadier General Harvey of the Portuguese brigade. Major General Kemmis joined with the right brigade on the following day, and took command of the division.

## 2. Hardinge Narrative

*Lieutenant Colonel Henry Hardinge wrote a later account of his discussions with General Cole that adds additional details, but does not contradict the essential point that the responsibility for the advance of the 4th Division was*

*Cole's alone since Hardinge was urging the advance on his own initiative, not delivering an order from Marshal Beresford.*[38]

I reported to Sir L. Cole, that the loss was so heavy it would be impossible for Hoghton's brigade to hold their ground; having described the state of things on the hill, I told him I came down for the purpose of proposing to him to move his division immediately to the attack of the enemy's column.

Sir L. Cole objected to the move, on account of the injunction he had received, when placed in his position by Sir Benjamin D'Urban in the morning, not to move without orders. I earnestly represented that this order had been given four hours before, under a very different state of things, and that the gain or loss of the battle depended on the immediate advance of his division. I was personally well known to Sir L. Cole. I spoke as an eyewitness, and I was the Deputy Quartermaster General of the Portuguese army, and next to Sir Benjamin D'Urban, senior officer of that department in the field; and as such my responsibility and authority were pledged for the accuracy of my report, and for the necessity of the movement I proposed.

During this discussion, Lieutenant Colonel Rooke, the senior officer of the Adjutant General's department, rode up. He confirmed my report of the critical state of things on the hill; he made no proposal for the division to attack the enemy; but Sir L. Cole observed to him, 'Hardinge is pressing me to attack the enemy's column.' Upon which, Colonel Rooke coincided with me; and as Colonel Wade states, we both urgently recommended the movement to be made; Sir L. Cole agreed with us, that under the circumstances, it was the best thing that could be done; and I need not say with what energy, ability and success, the movement was made. . . .

I then rode to Abercromby's brigade, and put it in motion.

## 3. De Roverea Account
*Alexander de Roverea was a native of Switzerland whose father had raised a regiment of Swiss infantry in British pay during the French Revolutionary Wars. In 1811, he was a captain in the Sicilian regiment in British service acting as an aide-de-camp to General Lowry Cole. His entertaining account of the battle was published in his father's memoirs, which were written*

---

38    Henry Hardinge, Letter to the Editor of the *United Service Magazine*, 9 September 1840, reproduced in Cole, G.L., *The Correspondence of Colonel Wade, Colonel Napier, Major General Sir H. Hardinge and General the Honourable Sir Lowry G. Cole* (London, 1841), pp. 10–11.

*in French.*[39] *His experiences highlight the difficulties of command and control on a battlefield where the only communication possible involved sending staff officers to and fro on horseback. Surgeon Guthrie, mentioned in this account, wrote a description of de Roverea in 1812: 'my poor friend, although a most excellent, honourable and upright man, was certainly not handsome; he was short, with a large face, having high cheekbones, and as small a portion of nose as was ever allocated to man.'*[40]

On the evening of May 15 . . . we received the order to raise the blockade and to join the army at Albuera. I was on horseback all night – at 2 o'clock in the morning the advance posts were withdrawn, the columns formed and set in motion. General Cole had with him two brigades of his division and 3,000 badly armed Spaniards without uniforms under the orders of D'España. During the same night Marshal Beresford been joined at the camp of Albuera by the corps commanded by under General Ballesteros and by the troops brought by General Blake from Cadiz by way of Ayamonte. Ballesteros had 4,000 men who had long experience skirmishing in the western region of the Sierra Morena; Blake had 8,000 very fine troops. . . .

We arrived at Albuera at 8 o'clock in the morning. Our force consisted of 30,000 men, of which 15,000 Spanish, 7,000 English and 8,000 Portuguese. We only had 1,500 horsemen since a brigade that was supposed to join us from Talavera went to Elvas by mistake. Generals Blake and Castaños asked Marshal Beresford to take overall command and agreed to follow his orders, thus making the largest and most noble sacrifice that Spanish vanity could accept.

A small stream, the Albuera, flows near the village of the same name. It has muddy banks and is crossed by a stone bridge. On the right of the stream there is an immense plain covered with forest. On the left bank the ground is more varied – there is a chain of small hills, uncultivated and treeless, covered with heather.

Marshal Beresford did not believe that Soult would attack him, but that if he did, he would attack his centre by seizing the bridge. As a result, he placed the Spaniards on the right (where he thought they

---

39  Alexander de Roverea, Letter to Father, [?] October 1811, in Roverea, Ferdinand de, *Memoires* (4 vols., Paris, 1848), v. 4, pp. 27–45 at pp. 30–43. The father describes the account as follows: 'I only learned on July 29 that my son had been so seriously injured on May 16 at the battle of Albuera, that he was counted among the dead, then threatened with insanity. . . . This murderous day, whose significance was almost nil, offers particularities so characteristic and so bizarre though generally little known, that I insert here the report sent to me by my son, when he had fully recovered the use of his faculties . . .'

40  Quoted in Crumplin, Mark, *Guthrie's War* (Barnsley, 2010), at p. 94.

would be less threatened), the English in the centre, and the Portuguese on the left, forming a line more or less parallel with the stream. The Fourth Division was placed in reserve at a certain distance on the right of the Spaniards.

Some 500 paces from the right of the Spanish line was a hill that dominated our position. This hill was an essential point which ought to have been fortified in advance and, in any case, should have been strongly occupied. The Marshal thought it sufficient to occupy it with 500 Spanish light troops. The enemy made a feint towards the bridge, and while we debated whether or not Soult's attack was serious, the French army crossed the stream further above the village. We did not see this movement because it was screened by General Latour-Maubourg moving his numerous cavalry towards Almendral. At 11 o'clock, the fatal hill was occupied by the enemy. Five minutes later we could see all the French infantry formed in close columns with 40 pieces of cannon enfilading our line. One had to admire the skilful dispositions of Marshal Soult, but he had committed a significant fault – he should have attacked at dawn before the arrival of the 8,000 [sic] men led by General Cole.

Our Marshal left the centre and rode over to the Spaniards. The brigade of 4 battalions led by Colonel Colborne also moved in that direction and began to attack the French army on its own, without having received any clear orders to do so. General Stewart accompanied that brigade, which mounted the hill and arrived near the summit. They found the whole enemy army before them and just then a regiment of Polish lancers burst into their rear. The fruit of this beautiful manoeuvre was the capture of 5 colours, 3 pieces of artillery and 800 prisoners. The 31st Regiment was the only unit to survive, it having formed square and saved its colours.

It was necessary to change the direction of the Spanish army, an operation that would be difficult with new troops subject to a fierce cannonade. This was nevertheless accomplished and the Spaniards were deployed in several lines on the reverse slope of the knoll closest to the hill occupied by the enemy. The first battalions to arrive were attacked many times at bayonet point but held firm. The French lost the favourable moment – instead of halting they should have pressed forward to prevent our new formation. Because they remained stationary and in columns as they did, their loss was increased. The combat dissolved into an affair of artillery. We had like the enemy 40 well-served pieces of artillery that horribly ravaged them. We made successful use of an English invention consisting of an explosive shell filled with balls [shrapnel] that were spewed over a distance of 50 *toises*.

Our general [Cole] exposed himself bravely, but hardly gave any orders so the officers on his staff acted as they thought best. The rest of the 2nd Division was brought up from the centre and deployed in line behind the Spaniards. Our men, never having seen these troops, mistook them for the French and, while the Polish Lancers charged the Spaniards in front, the English opened fire on them. I think that in the confusion and noise of the battle our allies did not realise this before we ceased firing.

The English then relieved the Spanish line and advanced a few paces to the crest of our hill, from where they commenced the type of well-directed musketry that, combined with their great bravery and perfect discipline, makes the British infantry superior to all others on the day of battle.

At the first sound of cannon fire, I was sent by my general to the Marshal to accompany him and receive his orders. He gave me none, but as I was with him behind the Spaniards when the English fired on them, I galloped to them to help end that situation. During this time, several Polish lancers pierced the Spanish line and one of them seized Beresford's collar, but the Marshal pulled the lancer from his horse and threw him to the ground, where he was killed.

Bright sunshine alternated with spring showers. Generals Blake and Castaños, followed by their large staffs, mounted on imposing Andalusian horses covered with long embroidered saddle cloths, promenaded gravely back and forth. Their men, even though not relieved, kept up steady and strong volleys and occasionally shouted the national battle cry of *'Viva, Viva!'* The English soldiers shouted their own cry of 'Hurrah!', which had a much more martial and imposing tone.

The Portuguese troops were not engaged.

In the absence of orders and facing a menacing force of enemy cavalry, General Cole deployed his troops in line in the rear and formed a sharp angle with the right of the Spanish line. His battalions having been alerted to the risk of cavalry attacks from any direction, each regiment formed square two times with as much calm and regularity as they would have displayed in a review.

Whether due (as we believe) from some jealousy between General Latour-Maubourg and Marshal Soult or due to some other unknown reason, the 4,000 French cavalry, which covered the plain and could easily have enveloped our right, did little. The regiment of Lancers of the Vistula did charge three times, but was destroyed. Their last charge was against the Portuguese brigade of the 4th Division commanded by General Harvey, who ordered his front rank to kneel, waited for the lancers to reach pistol shot range and then delivered [a murderous volley as] a *coup de grace*.

When General Cole saw that the 2nd Division had replaced the Spaniards, he decided on his own initiative to attack the hill occupied by the enemy army, the possession of which would evidently decide the outcome of the day. In undertaking this attack without having received an order from the Marshal, and then taking on himself the responsibility for such a decisive movement, he acted with moral courage of which few English generals have given an example. He placed one Portuguese battalion in a square on the left of the Fusilier brigade. The rest of the Portuguese brigade advanced *en potence* and supported the attack of the British. Four English elite companies formed in square on the right of the Portuguese to cover their flank against the enemy's cavalry.

All this happened just at the moment when the Marshal, horrified by his losses and entirely despairing of victory, had begun to evacuate the village of Albuera and gave the first orders for retreat, which would have been very difficult to carry out given the existence of an enemy fortress and an unbridged river behind us and, above all, the superiority of the French cavalry.

When the Marshal saw the 4th Division marching forward and regained some hope of success, gave me the first and only order I received from him, which was to go to the rear and find a Spanish regiment which had not suffered much and lead it to support the attack being executed by the 4th Division. I executed the order and found a brigade of Walloon Guards. After I had shown the officer in command the way to proceed, I left him and rejoined the Fusilier brigade.

My general and all the staff are wounded besides almost all the commanding officers but, despite being thinned by a continual storm of shot and shell, the line continued to advance in good order and firing.

We had just retaken the three guns lost at the commencement of the action and I had just pointed out to a colonel a squadron of the enemy who were about to charge his grenadiers when, at the moment I was thinking about the strange caprice of destiny that had Frenchmen, Englishmen, Poles, Spaniards, Portuguese and even Swiss killing each other on this field, I was hit and knocked off my horse. It was almost the end of the affair, when the 2nd Division advanced in support of the attack of the 4th Division.

In the final analysis, it was the bravery of the soldiers and their superiority man for man that gave us the victory after this bloody combat.

If the French columns had marched forward and broken our line at the point where 2/3rds of our men were out of action, we would have lost. It is in such cases the individual courage counts. The French officers made every effort to keep their men under control, but the first ranks of their column threw themselves on those behind. They cried that it was butchery and were soon in disorderly flight towards the stream and the forest beyond.

Their superiority in cavalry, our immense loss, and the irresolution of the Marshal (who neglected to attack with the Portuguese) prevented us from pursuing and taking advantage of the terrific panic that had come over the enemy army.

Our loss was 7,000 killed and wounded, of which 4,000 were English. The Fusilier brigade lost 54 officers and 1,100 men out of 1,500. French losses were 1,000 prisoners, 3,000 killed and, if we are to believe intercepted letters at Seville, 5,000 wounded. Although Marshal Soult withdrew his army to Llerena, Marshal Beresford did not appreciate the extent of his success. He was worried about being attacked the next day and wrote the following to Lord Wellington: 'If I am attacked, I hope I shall not survive another day as dreadful as this one.'

Here now are the details which concern me: I never felt the shot that knocked me off my horse. I fell unconscious and stayed several minutes in that state; coming to, I could not see anything and everything seemed black to me. I felt blood flowing on my face then little by little my sight returned and I perceived my loyal horse who had stayed next to me rather than running off.

I tried to get up and remount him and I fell down several times before I was finally able to get into the saddle. But instead of going to the rear as I intended, people tell me they saw me covered with blood galloping to and fro over the field of battle until one of them got hold of my horse and led me to a surgeon who I knew. He sat me on the ground, asked me if I was wounded by a sabre cut, told me he did not believe my wound was dangerous and applied a bandage. He was an Englishman who I knew and who was very surprised to hear me responding in German to his questions. I was 10th person placed in a wagon with my domestics following it and I arrived that evening at Valverde where I took up residence in a house where I had lodged before. It was full of wounded but I threw myself fully clothed on a bed and slept profoundly until the morning when I got up and went downstairs, but since that moment 10 days have passed of which I have no recollection. They tell me that I ordered my groom to saddle my horse and but when I tried to mount, the general saw me and stopped me. I had not had anything to eat or drink for 40 hours. They took me to a house where two of my comrades on Cole's staff were lodged, one of whom had just had his arm amputated.

It was believed that the enemy cavalry would occupy Valverde so all the wounded able to be transported were moved to Elvas. I stayed behind with my two companions under the care of our skilful friend Guthrie, to whom it is certain I owe my life. In a case as severe as mine, the solicitous attentions of a friend are crucial. It is only a friend who would sacrifice the hours of his rest to care for me – after a battle the surgeons are so occupied that one cannot ask a stranger for more than one or two visits a day when constant treatment is indispensable. I have no doubt that I was hit by a piece of a howitzer shell. My hat covered with waxed cloth and attached by a chinstrap was neither shot off nor holed but instead there was a two-inch cut in the cloth as if it has been sliced by a razor. However, my head was cracked and dented as if it was a tin vase that had been struck against a hard surface.

The most astonishing thing is that from the moment I received the wound that I am describing I never felt any pain in my head. Because Guthrie did not believe I would recover otherwise, he wished to trepan my head, but I was so violent against it he left the operation to a later time when I would be calmer.

## 4. Blakeney Narrative

*Major Sir Edward Blakeney was the commander of the 2nd Battalion of the 7th Fusiliers. His recollections concerning the advance of the Fusilier Brigade are only known because they were quoted by others involved in trying to determine the exact sequence of events.*[41]

When we reached the part of the position allotted to us, the action in our front had been going on very severely. A fog and severe rain prevented our seeing actually what had occurred; but when it cleared up, which was in about ten minutes, we saw the French columns placed in echelon on our side of the hill, with the artillery, twenty-three pieces, above, and an echelon of cavalry on their left flank, covering the whole plain with their swords.

The Second Division of British Infantry was to our left and front, and had, just as we arrived, been most severely handled by the cannonade and Polish Lancers. A squadron of these Poles had moved close to us,

---

41    Blakeney to Wade, quoted in Wade, Letter to the Editor of the *United Service Magazine*, 19 March 1841, reproduced in Cole, G.L., *The Correspondence of Colonel Wade, Colonel Napier, Major General Sir H. Hardinge and General the Honourable Sir Lowry G. Cole* (London, 1841), p. 17.

when a British squadron charged, and drove them back. At the most critical moment. Sir Lowry Cole ordered the brigade to advance.

The word coming from the left, the 1st Battalion of the Royal Fusiliers moved first; my battalion, the 2nd Fusiliers, next; and the 23rd Welch Fusiliers on the right. We moved steadily towards the enemy, and very soon commenced firing. The men behaved most gloriously, never losing their ranks, and closing to their centre as casualties occurred.

From the quantity of smoke, I could perceive very little but what was immediately in my front. The first battalion closed with the right column of the French, and I moved on and closed with the second column, the 23rd with the third column. This appeared to me to be the position of the three battalions for a few minutes, when the French faced about at about thirty or forty yards from us. Our firing was most incessant; and we kept following the enemy until we reached the second hill, and the position they had previously occupied.

During the closest part of the action I saw the French officers endeavouring to deploy their columns, but all to no purpose; for as soon as the third of a company got out they immediately ran back, to be covered by the front of the column. Our loss was, of course, most severe; but the battalions never for an instant ceased advancing, although under artillery firing grape the whole time.

## 5. Cooper Narrative

*One of the best-known accounts of Albuera is the one found in the memoirs of Sergeant John Cooper of the 7th Fusiliers.[42] He provides key details of the formation used by the Fusilier Brigade and evidence from the English perspective that the French failure to deploy was a key reason for their defeat.*

May 16th, 1811.

To prevent us taking this fortress, a large army under Marshal Soult was assembled, and marched to relieve it. Therefore Marshal Sir William Beresford sent off the guns, stores, etc., to Elvas, and prepared to meet the enemy near the village of Albuera. Of the enemy's approach we had no idea or apprisal. Right about midnight on the 15th of May, we were suddenly ordered to march, weary and jaded as we were with being on picquet duty near the city walls for thirty-six hours.

After marching till daylight appeared, we halted and put off our greatcoats. Everyone was complaining of want of rest and sleep. Having marched a few miles further up a valley we heard distant sounds, and

---

42    Cooper, John S., *Rough Notes of Seven Campaigns in Portugal, Spain, France, and America, During the Years 1809–10–11* (London, 1914), pp. 63–8.

though they grew more frequent, yet we did not think that they were the noises of a battle field, as we were quite ignorant of any enemy being near. But so they proved, for in a few minutes the words, 'Light Infantry to front', 'Trail arms', 'Double quick', were given. We then knew what was astir. Being tired, we made a poor run up a steep hill in front; but on reaching its summit we saw the two armies engaged below, on a plain about three quarters of a mile distant.

The French army consisted of 22,000 infantry and 4,000 cavalry. Our army was composed of about 7,000 English, 2,000 Portuguese, and 16,000 Spaniards; but in these we did not place any confidence. Of cavalry, we had perhaps 1,200 or 1,400. I do not know the number of our guns, but I do remember that the French had more than twice as many.

We were now quite awake and roused in earnest. Towards the centre of the line we moved rapidly; then formed close column, and lay down in a storm of hail and rain waiting for orders.

During the blinding shower of hail, etc., the French, having crossed the river which ran between the two armies, made a furious onset on the Spanish right wing which was posted on a hill, and drove it in great confusion into a hollow.

In moving to the right, to regain the ground thus lost by the Spaniards, General Hill's [sic, should be Stewart's] right brigade suffered dreadfully. The carnage was awful on both sides, and the dead lay in rows where they had stood. What greatly contributed to the slaughter of our men was an attack made by a body of Polish lancers on Hill's right, before it got solidly formed. The day was now apparently lost, for large masses of the enemy had gained the highest part of the battle field, and were compactly ranged in three heavy columns, with numerous cavalry and artillery ready to roll up our whole line. The aspect of that hill covered with troops directly on our flank was no jest, as we had no reserve to bring up.

At this crisis, the words 'Fall in, Fusiliers' roused us; and we formed line. Six nine-pounders, supported by two or three squadrons of the 4th Dragoons, took the right. The 11th and 23rd Portuguese regiments, supported by three light companies, occupied the centre. The Fusilier brigade with some small detachments of the brigade left at Badajoz, stood on the left. Just in front of the centre were some squadrons of Spanish cavalry. The line in this order approached at quick step the steep position of the enemy, under a storm of shot, shell, and grape, which came crashing through our ranks.

At the same time the French cavalry made a charge at the Spanish horse in our front. Immediately a volley from us was poured into the mixed mass of French and Spaniards. This checked the French; but the Spanish heroes galloped round our left flank and we saw them no more.

Having arrived at the foot of the hill, we began to climb its slope with panting breath, while the roll and thunder of furious battle increased. Under the tremendous fire of the enemy our thin line staggers, and men are knocked about like skittles; but not a step backwards is taken. Here our Colonel and all the field-officers of the brigade fell killed or wounded, but no confusion ensued. The orders were, 'Close up'; 'Close in'; 'Fire away'; 'Forward'. This is done. We are close to the enemy's columns; they break and rush down the other side of the hill in the greatest mob-like confusion.

In a minute or two, our nine-pounders and light infantry gain the summit, and join in sending a shower of iron and lead into the broken mass. We followed down the slope firing and huzzaing, till recalled by the bugle. The enemy passed over the river in great disorder, and attacked us no more, but cannonading and skirmishing in the centre continued till night.

Thus ended the bloody struggle at Albuera, 16th of May, 1811. The enemy ought not to have been beaten, for they were greatly superior in all arms, besides having an advantageous position. To allow a line two deep without reserve, with few guns and cavalry, to drive them from a hill was positively shameful. Had those columns been deployed into line and properly led, they might have swept us from the hill side like chaff. But they did not.

Having returned to the top of the ridge we piled arms and looked about. What a scene! The dead and wounded lying all around. In some places the dead were in heaps. One of these was nearly three feet high, but I did not count the number in it.

When our regiment was mustered after the battle it numbered about eighty. As we went into fire 435 strong, we lost 355. The first battalion some hundreds stronger than ours lost 353. All the three colonels of our brigade fell on that hill side; viz., Colonel Sir William Myers, killed; Colonels Edward Blakeney and Ellis, wounded.

What was now to be done with the wounded that were so thickly strewed on every side? The town of Albuera had been totally unroofed and unfloored for firewood by the enemy, and there was no other town within several miles; besides, the rain was pouring down, and the poor sufferers were as numerous as the unhurt. To be short, the wounded that could not walk were carried in blankets to the bottom of the bloody hill, and laid among the wet grass. Whether they had any orderlies to wait on them, or how many lived or died, I can't tell.

But if they were ill off, our case was not enviable. We were wet, weary, and dirty; without food or shelter. Respecting the wounded, General Blake, the Spanish Commander, was asked to help us with them, but he refused to send any men to carry them off.

We lay down at night among the mire and dead men. I selected a tuft of rushes and coiled myself up like a dog, but sleep I could not, on account of hunger and cold. Once I looked up out of my wet blanket, and saw a poor wounded man stark naked, crawling about, I suppose for shelter. Who had stripped him, or whether he lived till morning, I know not.

Before daylight we were under arms, shivering with cold, and our teeth very unsteady; but the sun rose and began to warm us. Half a mile distant were the French, but neither they nor we showed any desire of renewing hostilities. A little rum was now served out, and our blood began to circulate a little quicker. We then rubbed up our arms and prepared for another brush; but nothing serious took place, except cavalry skirmishes on the plain before us. Towards evening the enemy retreated into a wood two miles off, and next day disappeared.

In this action the English and Portuguese lost between 4,000 and 5,000 in killed, wounded, and missing. The Spaniards suffered little. The enemy's loss was very great. Wellington arrived from the north of Portugal a few hours after the battle. Had he come sooner we should have had more confidence of victory. This may appear from the brief dialogue which took place between one Horsefall and myself, when marching to attack the dark columns on the hill. Turning to me, Horsefall drily said, 'Whore's ar Arthur?', meaning Wellington. I said, 'I don't know, I don't see him.' He rejoined, 'Aw wish he wor here.' So did I.

On the 19th, we left this bloody field, and encamped in the wood which the French had left. Here all the water we used had to be fetched two miles. Our next move was to Almendralejo.

## 6. Harrison Narrative

*Lieutenant John Christopher Harrison of the 23rd Fusiliers wrote a letter to his mother on 24 May that provides an interesting perspective on events of the day since he was originally assigned to guard his brigade's baggage before finagling permission to join his regiment before its famous advance.*[43]

---

43    Quoted in Glover, Michael, 'The Royal Welch Fusiliers at Albuera', *Journal of the Society for Army Historical Research*, Vol. LXVI, No. 267 (Autumn 1988), pp. 146–54.

. . . At about 11 o'clock at night on the 15th, Captain Orr of the 7th, who commanded the baggage of the brigade, received orders from Sir William Meyers to march to Valverde and endeavour to meet the brigade if possible at Albuera the next day, that if we did not leave the camp before 12 o'clock we might expect to be taken. This was pleasing intelligence on a dark night but you may be sure we took the hint and lost no time in making our departure. The whole of our troops evacuated the trenches about the same hour.

Daylight brought us in sight of Valverde where we halted but a short time to rest our men and animals, then waited on General Lumley who was on his way to join the army. He gave us instructions to proceed and cautioned us to be prepared for the enemy on the right as it was apprehended they were drawing round by Almendral. We had about 50 men under arms and after disposing of them to the best advantage and procuring a guide, we proceeded with our group. About half past eight our ears were saluted with the reports of two or three cannon shots, and nine o'clock brought us in sight of the army, which was formed in two lines on each side of the road on an immense plain and about a mile in our front. Here we joined the rest of the baggage of the army and I was not a little anxious to get rid of my troublesome office and join my regiment. Orr at first objected to my going as I was second senior and he wished to go himself. However, I soon got over this obstacle and we both went forward to ask the whereabouts of the brigade, which no one could give an account of. I discovered General Cole who we came up to and here I met with another obstacle for he would not hear at all of my leaving the baggage but after a few gentle remonstrances I soon overcame this, and by this time saw our division coming down the left and rear of the line in open column.

As soon as I saw Ellis, he desired me to go back and bring the drums up and all the spare hands I could collect in the baggage. I got back to the rear with all haste and left my horse with my servant and mule and moved forward with about 40 men of the brigade and joined as they were crossing the road. The action was now beginning and our riflemen attacked the enemy. As they were collecting a large force and seem to threaten to turn our right flank of our army, our division advanced in contiguous columns of battalions at quarter distance till within about musket shot of the French, when we closed and deployed on our first battalion company.

I should have told you previously to this, I solicited the Colonel for the command of the seventh battalion company as Captain Courtland was acting field officer. To this request he readily consented. In this situation, we remained some time and some Spanish cavalry were driven in, whom I am sorry to say figured shamefully. The French cavalry, who are now in great force and looked very formidable, elated with a little success over the Spaniards, advanced *au pas de charge* on our line but observing us so unshaken and so little dismayed at their fierce appearance, when within about one hundred yards, they wheeled about and we saluted their *'derrières'* with a smart fire. Their Infantry formation was covered by their field pieces which kept up a heavy fire with grapeshot and round shot on our line at a very short range. I am sorry to say some time elapsed before these noisy gentlemen were answered by our artillery on the left of our brigade. At this time the brigade on our left, the 3rd, 48th, and 66th were warmly engaged. Some cavalry arriving on our right to divert the attention of the enemy's cavalry, our brigade advanced at a steady pace reserving our fire and leaving the Portuguese brigade to join our second line.

The French infantry were formed on an eminence we had every disadvantage of the ground. They soon open their fire. We returned handsomely, came down to the charge and cheered. They faced about after a few paces and, others coming to their assistance, the contest soon became general and a most determined fire kept up on both sides, so near as to be almost muzzle to muzzle. They again drew us on by showing us their backs and we twice repeated our former treatment. This work lasted some time, then continually bringing up fresh regiment, our brigade being much broken by its loss, not above one third of our men were standing. Their infantry flanked our regiment on the left and were coming in our rear, their cavalry at the same time making a desperate charge on our right and rear and I assure you we had enough to do.

At this juncture I met with my reward for the day and the Portuguese brigade coming up, our people gradually retired from the scene they had supported with credit to themselves and honour to their country.

It was now time I was off the roster as well as many of my brave companions and my first enquiries were for one of the 'pestle and mortar' fraternity [a doctor] but without any hope of success. With the assistance of my sword, I hobbled about a half mile to the rear when I met our sergeant sutler who, with the feelings in foresight of an old soldier, had brought a horse for the relief of his comrades, and conveyed me about a half mile to the rear to where the baggage was then standing, where I was glad to lay down. It was now between one and two and commenced raining hard and never ceased the whole evening. The firing was all over before one o'clock. . . .

[I] slept pretty well on a little straw till morning when I proceeded to operate on myself and cut open my overalls. As no mark was through

I was afraid the ball had lodged in. It entered about three inches above the knee and luckily it passed through on the underside and lodged in the overalls under the knee where I found the gentleman myself and mean to keep it for a memento of the day. . . .

I should tell you of my rascally servant who left me all that 24 hours and lost my sword that I had taken such care to bring off the field. . . .

I had a close shave when we first went into action. A ball passed through the centre of my cap, taking the point of my hair and went through several folds in my pocket handkerchief which was in my cap.

I have attempted to give you some small idea of the battle of Albuera but you must recollect we can only speak as to what comes under our own immediate observation. I believe never was British bravery more conspicuous on this occasion and the French fought with more than their usual intrepidity. 16th of May will be a proud day for the Fusilier brigade. I understand everyone admits we saved the fate of the British army. Had we been brought into action sooner, the events might have been less disastrous to the brigade on our left. The 48th and 66th lost their colours and many men and had many men taken. The colours of the 3rd Buffs were re-taken by the first [*sic*, should be 7th] Fusiliers. I believe every soldier did his duty but there is not much doubt a great want of generalship was evinced throughout the whole affair, otherwise our success must have been more complete. . . .

Our regiment marched into the field about 600. Deduct the light infantry company, 60 men, not engaged, leaves us 540 out of which our loss was as follows (as correctly as Major Thomas could send it in on the 18th).

One captain, one second lieutenant, three sergeants, sixty rank-and-file killed; one lieutenant colonel, three captains, eight subalterns, ten sergeants, one drummer and two hundred fifty-seven rank-and-file wounded; one sergeant and thirteen rank-and-file missing. McDonald is dangerously wounded. Booker's right thumb and four fingers cut off by a sabre. McClellan, also wounded, fell into the hands of the enemy but I'm happy to say was recovered. They were not treated gently; a fellow not finding it an easy matter, forced McDonald's ring off his finger with his teeth. . . .

The Spaniards stripped poor [Captain Frederick] Montague and [2nd Lieutenant Revis] Hall of ours before they were dead. These are villains whose health and prosperity we have so often evoked in our sparkling glasses. I was glad to see so many of these plundering rascals get severe raps.

## 7. Hill Letter

*Captain John Hill, who commanded the light infantry company of the 1st Battalion 23rd Fusiliers in the action, wrote a letter to his mother soon after the battle.[44] From his position on the far right flank of the Allied army, he had a unique view of the attack of the Fusilier brigade.*

Albuera 22 May 1811

I wrote immediately after the last action to inform you that I had escaped unhurt. This, thank God, was necessary to quiet your apprehensions when not one half has had that good fortune. We had, previous to the 16th, gradually withdrawn our mortars and heavy cannon, anticipating some efforts would be made to relieve that place. Between 12 and one in the morning of the 16th, we marched from our trenches before Badajoz (in front of which I had been with my company as a covering party three previous days), and during the dark in which we decamped left four of our sentinels under the walls, whom we could not find among the corn. However, they have made good their retreat.

Three leagues from Badajoz, we joined the 2nd Division of the army which was at the moment engaged in a cannonade with the enemy. The men soon found our division on the right. The light companies were found on the right of the Portuguese in a hollow square; with this to cover its right, the line moved on to carry some heights on which the enemy had posted artillery, cavalry, and sharpshooters. As our line approached, their infantry crowned the heights in columns, afraid, as the prisoners informed me, to deploy in consequence of the superiority in cavalry we had manifested in the affair of Campo Mayor.

From the square on the right in which I was (which outflanked their infantry, but in return was outflanked by the enemy's cavalry), I conceived the depth of each of the columns was nine ranks. The distance of the enemy's second line or column (which you please) was about 60 yards, in their rear again some cavalry was found. Anxiously looking to the left to see how our regiment got on, we saw them gradually ascend the slope which brought them to a ridge commanded by another, still higher, which the enemy occupied, distant about 60 yards. Here a most destructive heavy fire of musketry was exchanged, the infantry mutually advancing; at last the enemy halted; our people continued advancing, and we had the satisfaction of seeing our regiment on the summit of the hills on which their two lines or columns had not been able to maintain themselves.

---

44    Hall, C.D., 'Albuera and Vittoria: Letters from Lieutenant Colonel J. Hill', *Journal of the Society of Army Historical Research*, Vol. LXVI, No. 268 (Winter 1988), pp. 193–8.

I have been speaking of our regiment in consequence of its being on the right of the Fusilier brigade, nearer to me and less covered with smoke. The other two Fusilier regiments were in line with them to the left, and at the same moment carried the height opposed to them. The Fusilier brigade, arrived on the height, were attacked in front by cavalry who, receiving the fire of all our companies, put themselves in order and prepared to charge, thinking the whole unloaded. The spurs were in the horse's sides, they were coming on, the Grenadiers then fired on them about 15 paces distant and the file fire recommenced from those who had first fired, when they went to the right about and galloped off. During this, some small parties of cavalry had got in our rear and took prisoners the wounded who were getting away from the fire.

On the left the British suffered most amazingly. I do not hesitate to say that at one moment I thought it would have been the most fatal to our arms. . . . The regular Spanish troops at this moment came up and took their places on the left which has been occupied by the British; their conduct was extremely good, their loss ⅔ of what they brought up to that point. One of the generals (I think Blake) had the whole of his attendants, one excepted (his Adjutant General) killed or wounded, and Blake himself had his horse shot under him. . . .

[I]t was nothing but the steady, determined, attack of the infantry on the right that saved the day. Had they been broken, we should have been annihilated. . . . The Portuguese behaved very well; a brigade of theirs was between us and the Fusilier battalions; their steadfastness, with so great a number of cavalry in their neighbourhood does them great credit.

## 8. Philipps Letter
*Lieutenant Grismond Philipps of the 23rd Fusiliers, provides additional testimony in a letter to his father that the cheering by the Fusiliers was a prominent accompaniment to their successful advance.*[45]

Albuera May 19, 1811

Dear Father,
I have only got time to inform you that the army under the command of General Beresford (to which our regiment was attached) has had a severe engagement with the French under the command of Soult in which they were entirely defeated with the loss of that 8,000 men killed and wounded, having left the latter in our hands.

---

45   Goodrich, Richard, 'Letters Home', *Waterloo Journal*, Vol. 21, No. 2 (August 1999), pp. 20–6, at 24.

I have escaped unhurt, thank God for it, as it is wonderful to me how I did. Our brigade consisting of the first and second Battalion of the 7th Regiment and our own [23rd Fusiliers] were ordered to charge a column of the enemy, which we did, and in the most gallant manner, we advanced to within about 20 paces of them without firing a shot. When our men gave three cheers and fired, the enemy broke in great confusion. We followed them, but were obliged to retreat as their cavalry was going to make a charge on us. . . .

[F]rom the fatigue I have undergone I have been obliged to borrow 50 dollars to buy a horse, and I have given a bill for the money which I hope you will have the goodness to accept.

I am dear father,

Your dutiful son,

G. Philipps

## 9. Guthrie's Narrative

*George Guthrie was a surgeon attached to the 4th Division who went on to have a distinguished medical career. The biographical article below, while not strictly speaking a memoir, contains unique details of the battle that can only have come from Guthrie himself. Guthrie wrote several medical treatises that contain numerous case studies of soldiers wounded at Albuera. These are beyond the scope of this volume, but illuminate the real human suffering that resulted from the battle.*[46]

At the battle of Albuera, . . . Mr. Guthrie was the principal medical officer, because he was the only staff officer on the field. . . .

It is contended by historians that Marshal Beresford had his army assembled under his orders at six o'clock on the morning of the fight, which did not begin until nine; and that he lost these three hours in doing nothing, instead of, during that time, moving his troops into the position he afterwards endeavoured, when too late, to place them in; by which neglect, they contend, he not only lost the lives of the best of his army, but his own reputation as a general. Strange to tell, the Marshal and his defenders submit to this imputation, rather than state a fact of the simplest kind, which would confound at once their adversaries. This fact is, the troops said to be there at six in the morning, and who ought to have been moved, were not there, and could not consequently be moved! Historians may be precise on these two points of time in future, if they please. The British troops on the ground were

---

46   'Biographical Sketch of G.J. Guthrie', *The Lancet*, Vol. 1 (London, 1850), pp. 76–736, at 730–2.

the 2nd Division, under Sir W. Stewart; Germans of the light division under General Alten and Sir Colin Halkett; and cavalry under Sir W. Lumley. The 4th Division of infantry, consisting at that time of one British brigade, one Portuguese, and some Spaniards, under Sir Lowry Cole, ought to have been there, but were not. The reason conveys a precept. The 4th Division raised the siege of Badajoz at one in the morning with the intention of joining the Marshal at Albuera, leaving the pickets in the trenches for the purpose of continuing the belief that the besieging force was present. Less than four hours of a night march, which is always very slow, should have brought them there at least by six in the morning.

An accident prevented it. The road forked about half way; the left-hand road leading to Albuera, the right towards Jurumenha, on the river Guadiana, and away from the field of battle. The assistant quarter-master general had placed two native guides at the fork to show the right road, instead of an English officer or non-commissioned officer, on whom confidence could be placed. The guides fell asleep, and gave no sign as the troops passed, who followed the wrong road for one hour before the mistake was discovered, when they had to countermarch for another, and thus arrived late on the field of battle; so late, that the first gun was fired by the German artillery when the head of the 4th Division was one mile distant from the nearest soldier under the orders of Marshal Beresford.

When the report of the first gun was heard, the 4th Division halted until closed up. The general commanding, and his staff, then rode forward to the guns, to join the Marshal, whilst Sir W. Myers, commanding the Fusilier brigade, brought them forward in close order, now prepared for everything. Mr. Guthrie who had ridden to the front with Sir Lowry Cole, placed himself a little to the left of the German guns, in order to see their practice, hoping that, being in a blue coat, and somewhat apart, he might be taken for a civilian, and not fired at in particular. Whilst engaged in estimating the number of the French manoeuvring below (at which it was afterwards said he was very expert), Dr. Stanford, surgeon 29th Regiment, came up to say, that, all other staff officers being absent, he was the principal on the field, and requested his permission to cut off the leg of one of the artillerymen just struck by a cannon-shot, from a French battery, which had halted, unlimbered, and returned the fire of the German guns, with the hope of distracting their attention. Mr. Guthrie desired a tourniquet to be applied, if necessary, and that the man should be left in a hut in sight, in the rear. This being done, Dr. Stanford returned, saying the man earnestly prayed that his leg might be cut off. Mr. Guthrie again refused, saying, 'These gentlemen below', pointing to the French, 'do not mean to make their serious attack here; it will be over there,' (pointing to some hills on the right) 'where you now see nothing, but of which, if the French get possession, we shall be killed or taken to a man. On those hills the two British divisions must win the battle. Leave not your regiment for an instant, or you will not see it again.' Dr. Stanford thought it harsh, shrugged his shoulders, and walked away, possibly descanting on the evils of a little brief authority.

In a few minutes the 2nd and 4th divisions were in march for the hills designated. They were too late, the French were before them and the contest was desperate. Dr. Stanford's regiment (the 29th) went in action 410, and came out 95! The Fusilier brigade, whose last charge decided the fate of the day, lost 1,050 out of 1,500. Four other regiments lost less, and one was reported as losing more. They were nearly all returned killed, although their bodies could not, in the hurry of making up a return, be found. It was, however, supposed by the English at Albuera, as it was afterwards by the French at Waterloo, that they must be killed, it not being possible that they could be taken. After a few days, however, they began to re-appear by twos and threes. They had been surprised when in open order by the Polish Lancers, who first rode over, and then carried them off, like a flock of sheep, pricking them a little by the way to make them go faster; an evil which arose from the delay in not taking up the right position in the early part of the morning. Those men who returned having been aided in their escape by the Spanish peasantry, obtained for themselves, rather irreverently, the appellation of 'the resurrection men'.

Future strategists and tacticians may bear in mind, if they please, a little circumstance of a rather ludicrous nature, which may have had some influence on the result of this memorable day. When Sir Lowry Cole raised the siege of Badajoz, by withdrawing the force under his command, he left the pickets in the trenches, in order to deceive the French Governor as long as possible, with orders to a staff officer to withdraw them soon after daylight; and before he thought the garrison could have time, on observing the smallness of their numbers, to come out and attack them. This gentleman – a worthy old Scotchman of the Celtic breed, and, like most of his countrymen, as brave as his sword – having other duties to perform, soon forgot the pickets; and in his anxiety to be in for what was supposed to be an impending fight, followed the troops. When nearly on the field of Albuera, he recollected he was to have brought off the pickets. The old gentleman – Randy Dandy, as he was affectionately called, for everybody liked him, who was rather bald, with reddish hair, a clear, florid complexion –

103

suddenly turned pale, big drops of sweat broke out on his forehead, when the recollection of the deserted pickets suddenly flashed across his mind. What was to be done! He rode up to Sir Lowry Cole, and manfully stated his forgetfulness. 'Go back, sir,' said the General, 'and do not let me see you again without the pickets.' Randy Dandy went off at a gallop, and slackened not his pace until he entered the trenches, where he found the pickets as quiet and as comfortable as possible. He withdrew them without molestation, although the distant firing could be distinctly heard. The French General would not believe in the absence of the rest of the besieging force; he did not suspect staff officers could be so forgetful, and remained perfectly quiet, the day being now well advanced, instead of marching out, as in all probability he would have done, if the trenches had been abandoned in the morning. He had in Badajoz a strong force of infantry, as well as of cavalry, whose sabres, as the Portuguese had found to their cost the day before, were sharp; and if he had appeared on the field of Albuera at even two o'clock in the afternoon of that day, with 1,600 infantry and 500 cavalry, few if any of the British army would have again seen Portugal!

Mr. Guthrie placed himself on the plain a little in the rear of the two British divisions of infantry with the cavalry on the right. It was impossible to keep out of the way of either shot or shell. Assistant-staff-surgeon Bolman was struck by one on the chest, which went through him. Rain came down in torrents; the lightning was more terrific than the flashes of the guns, the thunder louder; and what with the noise of the cannon, the shouts of the combatants, the cries and moans of the wounded, the outcry and exclamations of some flying Spaniards, and the darkness of the day, it might have been thought that all the fiends in Pandemonium were taking holiday. At three o'clock the fight was over, and Mr. Guthrie found three thousand wounded men at his feet, with four wagons only for their removal, and not an article for their relief, except such as might be contained in the panniers of the regimental surgeons; the nearest village of Valverde being seven miles off. The ignorance of the British nation of the fate of those who fall for its honour, as it is called, is inconceivable; it is only equalled by the utter carelessness of almost everyone on the subject; and the miseries the unfortunates who are badly wounded undergo, on most occasions, from a neglect which might generally be obviated, is a disgrace to, and a condemnation of the people who are desirous of being considered amongst the most humane and charitable in the world.

It is after a great battle that the work of the doctors begins. Tired, like everybody else, with the labours of the previous night and day, the dangers of which they are in great part exposed to, unless they absent themselves, they are then called upon to work in a way of which few people have any conception. Nine-tenths of the wounded, for the first three or four days, lie on the bare ground; the doctor has to kneel by the side of the wounded man; his back is bent until he cannot straighten himself; his mental and corporeal powers are equally strained to the utmost; and it is not surprising that under such circumstances, wanting almost everything, even food, the doctors should often think their own lives worth nothing. At the village of Valverde, where Mr. Guthrie stationed himself, and to which the worst cases of wounded were principally brought, the scene was dreadful. His iron constitution enabled him to set an example the few medical men who were present endeavoured to follow. From five in the morning until eleven at night their labours were incessant, under the most painful circumstances.

## 10. Narrative of Anonymous 27th Foot Private

*The author of this narrative was a member of General Kemmis's brigade of the 4th Division, and consequently did not arrive at Albuera until the morning of 17 May. His impressions of the aftermath of the battle are vivid and striking and the unique details he provides (including the statement that the Polish lancers pretended to be Spaniards) could only have come from comrades who were in the battle. The author has never been identified, although this account is sometimes attributed to a man called Emerson, who was the person who submitted the memoir to* The United Service Journal.[47]

We halted only a few hours at Elvas, and continuing our route, crossed the Guadiana at Jurumenha, and during our march, heard at intervals the deep rolling sounds of artillery in the direction of Albuera. Late on this evening we entered Olivenza, where we halted till about two o'clock next morning, and on setting out, met some of those who had been wounded early in the action we had heard the preceding day. Their accounts were vague and contradictory as to the probable issue of the contest they had left. In our progress we passed numerous groups of wounded, seated on mules or asses, and many straggling slowly forward on foot, or lying by the road, some of whom were already dead. Their numbers increased as we advanced, and fully testified that the battle had been one of the most sanguinary kind. . . .

About six o'clock, A.M., we came in sight of our troops on the field of battle at Albuera: the French were discerned near a wood, about a mile

---

47    *The United Service Journal and Naval and Military Magazine* (London, 1830), Part 1, pp. 287–94 and 415–22, at 419–22. The memoir was reprinted in Maxwell, W.H., *Peninsular Sketches; By Actors on the Scene* (2 vols., London, 1844). v. 2, pp. 205–42, at 232–42.

and a half in their front. We now advanced in subdivisions, at double distance, to make our numbers appear as formidable as possible, and arriving on the field, piled our arms, and were permitted to move about. With awful astonishment, we gazed on the terrific scene before us; a total suspension took place of that noisy gaiety so characteristic of Irish soldiers; the most obdurate or risible countenances sunk at once into a pensive sadness, and for some time speech was supplanted by an exchange of sorrowful looks, and significant nods. Before us lay the appalling sight of upwards of 6,000 men, dead, and mostly stark-naked, having, as we were informed, been stripped by the Spaniards, during the night; their bodies disfigured with dirt and clotted blood, and torn with the deadly gashes inflicted by the bullet, bayonet, sword, or lance, that had terminated their mortal existence. Those who had been killed outright appeared merely in the pallid sleep of death, while others, whose wounds had been less suddenly fatal, from the agonies of their last struggle, exhibited a fearful distortion of features. Near our arms was a small stream almost choked with bodies of the dead, and from the deep traces of blood on its miry margin, it was evident that many of them had crawled thither to allay their last thirst. The waters of this oozing stream were so deeply tinged, that it seemed actually to run blood. A few perches distant was a draw-well, about which were collected several hundreds of those severely wounded, who had crept or been carried thither. They were sitting, or lying, in the puddle, and each time the bucket reached the surface with its scanty supply, there was a clamorous and heart-rending confusion; the cries for water resounding in at least ten languages, while a kindness of feeling was visible in the manner this beverage was passed to each other.

Turning from this painful scene of tumultuous misery, we again strolled amongst the mangled dead. The bodies were seldom scattered about, as witnessed after former battles, but lying in rows or heaps; in several places whole subdivisions or sections appeared to have been prostrated by one tremendous charge or volley.

We here found the Fusilier and Portuguese brigades of our division, whom we had not seen since we went to Badajoz, where they had also been employed. They had arrived on the ground just before the action commenced, in which the former brigade was nearly annihilated. When we separated from them at Olivenza, the Fusiliers amounted to at least 2,250 men, and on their muster this day, only about 350 stood in their ranks. Before their going to Badajoz, 29 men of our regiment had been detached to this brigade, to assist as artificers during the siege of that fortress; of these only one now remained fit for service. The loss in several other British regiments was reported to have been equally severe; those of the 3rd, 31st, 48th, 57th, and 66th, were particularly mentioned, and the field before us presented ample proofs that those reports were but too true. All the survivors with whom we conversed were heartless and discontented. They complained bitterly that the army had been sacrificed by a series of blunders, especially in placing the Spaniards on the key of the position, and in not crediting that the Lancers, who had for a time been mistaken for Spaniards, were really French. In our inquiries amongst the Fusiliers, the following particulars were collected on the spot; but before proceeding to their relation, I shall notice the numbers of the contending armies, and relative situations to the bloody field.

The combined army was under the orders of Marshal Beresford, and amounted to nearly 28,000 men, forming in round numbers about the following proportion: 12,000 Spaniards, 8,000 Portuguese, some German artillery and riflemen, and the remainder British. Marshal Soult commanded the French forces; consisting of at least 25,000 veteran troops, about 4,000 of whom were cavalry, a species of force in which we were very defective. The enemy occupied exactly the same position as noticed on our advance thither; and our army the same ground as at this time. About half a mile in our front was a river, from which the ground towards us rose in a gentle swell, free from ditches or wood, except a few dwarfish shrubs. Near the extremity of our line on the right, the ground was more elevated, rising into a few knolls; and rather in front, on the left, was the ruinous village of Albuera, on the great road, leading to a bridge over the river. The only living creatures seen in Albuera at this time were an old man and a cat.

About eight o'clock on the morning of the 16th, the enemy began to move from the wood seen in front, which till that time had concealed their numbers. Soon after, several columns advanced towards the river, one of which immediately crossed on the right, and commenced a vigorous attack on the Spaniards, while others attempted to pass at fords and at the bridge. The Spaniards, consisting of the united corps of Generals Blake, Castaños, and Ballesteros, defended themselves with the utmost bravery, but were at length driven from their position, leaving behind them ample and indubitable proofs of the obstinate valour by which it had been maintained. From this post the enemy's artillery was now enabled to rake the field, and scattered death throughout our line. Before even attempting its recovery, it became necessary to change our front, and while executing this manoeuvre, a large body of French lancers, which had for some time been hovering about, dashed between the open divisions, and in the confusion that ensued, a dreadful havoc was made before they could be expelled.

Favoured by a tremendous shower of rain and hail, which had fallen early in the action, those lancers passed the river unobserved, and on the storm abating, they were seen in front within musket-shot of our lines, and reports were made that they were French, but not credited. From their being thus allowed to move quietly about, they evidently perceived that they were mistaken for friends, and kept in a compact body, waiting an opportunity to pounce upon us. At length, while our divisions were detached, in the act of deploying into line, they advanced in squadrons at full gallop, shouting in Spanish, 'Vivan los Ingleses', 'Vivan los amigos de España', and the next moment they were in our ranks, which were so completely surprised, that whole companies were destroyed without firing one shot.

The defeat of the enemy, the recovery of the heights that had been so fatally lost, and the other events of this memorable action being so well known, I omit their relation, and shall only observe, that my narrators gave their commander little credit for what has been since termed one of the most brilliant victories of the Peninsular war. Their complaints were loud and general, and always ended with some expression of deep regret for the absence of him whom we looked up to with unlimited confidence, whose presence gave us additional courage, and under whom we deemed ourselves invincible and certain of success, – need I add, that person was WELLINGTON.

From the heavy rain that had fallen the preceding day, and the trampling of men and horses, the field of battle was at this time a perfect puddle, without one dry or green spot on which we could repose or be seated. Wearied and chilled after our forced march, and wading through the sloughs, we kindled fires, and as fuel could not be had, the muskets lying about were thrown on promiscuously for that purpose. These arms made truly a crack fire, for several being charged immediately exploded, the balls whistling through the mud and casting it up in our faces. Alarmed at those salutes, we for some time examined if the guns were discharged, but tired of those researches, several again exploded, happily without doing any mischief.

On this night our situation was, if possible, more gloomy and uncomfortable than any we had yet experienced, war on every hand presenting one of his most horrid and terrific forms, while at the same time we laboured under the greatest privations. Neither provisions nor liquors could be had at any price, and the surrounding country was so wild and depopulated, as to bid defiance to all attempts to better our state, even by marauding. The only place of rest, if such it could be called, was sitting on our knapsacks in the mud, into which many occasionally dropped, overcome with sleep and fatigue, and remained for a time as insensible as the gory corpses on the field.

## 11. Von Wachholtz Diary

*Friedrich Ludwig von Wachholtz was a captain commanding one of the two rifle companies from the Duke of Brunswick Oels Corps that were attached to the 4th Division. His diary indicates that all the light infantry and rifle companies of the division were combined into a separate light battalion for the battle.*[48]

16th May, Thursday. [Lieutenant Carl von] Berner was in the trenches [in front of Badajoz] during the night, and we had just begun to deliver ourselves to some rest, when we suddenly got the order to march off in silence at 12 o'clock. Our camp was completely empty, the baggage also had already departed for Valverde, we only marched through it, turned left and arrived after a march of seven hours towards 7 a.m. at a point on the main road from Badajoz to Albuera one mile [a 'German' mile is 7.5 km] distant from the former, which in the darkness we should have reached easily without any risk within two hours. Now we continued, marching on the main road. About 8.30 a.m., we heard dull blows, which we soon recognised as cannon fire. Within a quarter of an hour we were already not far from the village Albuera, situated at the river of the same name. There were gentle, though not inconsiderable, heights on our side and on the other side, but the area in general was very flat and no object, not even a tree, was seen. The village was occupied by the two riflemen battalions of the German Legion, and close to them [were] several cannons, which already had begun to maintain a vivid fire with the enemy artillery. The enemy stood in columns on the slope, the river not far from his front. It was Soult, with about 25,000 men, including 4,000 men cavalry and 42 guns. We had about 30,000 men, but much less cavalry and 39 guns. Close to the village a wide stone bridge crossed the river, besides this, there were also fords in many places.

Our army stood in a distance of maybe 300 to 400 paces from the river, the left wing behind Albuera. With joy I saw long lines of Spanish troops; it was General Blake with his corps of 15,000 men, who departing from Cadiz, had landed in southern Portugal and come up here. Our situation however was not very good; it was

---

48  Wachholtz, H.L. von, 'Auf der Peninsula 1810 bis 1813. Kriegstagebuch des Generals Friedrich Ludwig v. Wachholtz, Beihefte zum Militär-Wochenblatt, Issue 8/9 (1907), pp. 259–326, at 270–5. Translation courtesy of Oliver Schmidt.

victory or destruction, because in the case that we were beaten, we faced a flat, plain ground, a superior cavalry of 4,000 men, an enemy fortress and the river Guadiana, over which no bridge could be built, for a distance of 3 miles [22.5 km] behind us. Also our baggage was close behind us.

Without halting, the light battalion was immediately moved forward, and our division passed behind the battle line of the 2nd and the Spanish divisions and formed on its right wing, with our light battalion on the extreme right in column, behind the grenadiers of the Portuguese brigade. This was because our right brigade [under General Kemmis] was still on the right bank of the Guadiana. Farther to the right of us were a few regiments of cavalry, at the most 1,000 men, and 9 guns, amongst them Sympher's brigade [battery]. Having reached this spot, all of a sudden it started to rain very heavily; we crept under low brushes and took whatever cover we could. In this moment I still believed that we would neither attack, nor be attacked. But after a quarter of an hour, the rain ceased, the sun came out. *We* [emphasis in original] formed a square of four ranks and slowly advanced in this formation. The arrival of a few [cannon] balls convinced us that the enemy had passed the river during the rain and taken possession of a few heights on this bank of the river, the evidence of this we soon saw for ourselves. Still we slowly continued to advance, having in front of us a few of our cannon and a strong column of enemy cavalry.

Suddenly this cavalry made an attack upon the few cannons, which quickly fell back to the Portuguese line. The latter opened its files with much order, let the guns pass, then closed again and received the cavalry with such good discipline, that it had to go back. This cavalry was the only enemy which we had directly in front of us during the rest of battle, and slowly moved in closed column here and there, without letting itself being disturbed, even less losing its countenance, by the fire of the artillery on our right wing, which was directed nearly exclusively on them. A few times I thought they would charge on us, but our cavalry at our side, which by the way did nothing at all, the artillery, and even our square, as I was told afterwards by some prisoners, forced them to keep a respectful distance. For us [*sic*] Englishmen, I was not afraid, we would have received them properly, but the more forward and much bigger part of our square consisted of Portuguese, who always could be kept in order and close formation only by much shouting.

That they were not really in a good place, was also proven by a cannon ball, which ricocheted diagonally through our square, taking in front the legs of a few men, passing right through the breast of the officer marching in the centre at the side of the flags, and then continuing on its way without further ado. Where in front the gap had been created by the wounded, they did not want to close up properly and believed all the time that the next cannon ball must hit directly on the same spot. However, the main part of the battle happened in the centre, which the enemy wanted to pierce in closed columns, and because this all happened on a hill to our left, we were eyewitnesses. I am not perfectly sure, but I presume our army was formed in two lines. The first (the 66th Regiment) was successfully penetrated by the enemy, and in this moment 800 Polish lancers in their grey greatcoats rushed ahead, cut down and took prisoner a great number of infantry and a brigade of artillery, which was commanded by Cleeves.

At first, we were not aware so much of this danger, because we thought they were Spanish cavalry which had permitted itself to be chased back, and cursed them in our hearts. But now our brigade approached [this cavalry] and received them firmly and with such a well-aimed fire, that they had to retreat as quickly as they had come and lost half of their prisoners and all captured artillery with the exception of one gun. On this, our brigade continued its victorious path, just up to 70 to 80 paces from the enemy columns, which still mostly were in closed order. Here it [the brigade] stopped, and now from both sides a terrible fire commenced, which might have continued this way for a little over half an hour. The whole ground behind our line was covered with bloody wounded men who were limping backwards, It was a gruesome beautiful scene, to see both lines so close one to the other, breathing fire at each other, and death with terrible roars raging amongst them. But even higher rose the beats of the fearfully and eagerly anticipating heart, when all of a sudden in our line a dull, then louder and louder and finally horrible 'Hurrah!' arose, and our brigade dashed with the bayonet onto the enemy column.

When the brigade was 15 paces away, their first ranks began to waver as the enemy saw the long bayonets wielded by strong Englishmen. Soon the others followed, and within two seconds, in the greatest swiftness and disorder, they took flight. And now we advanced for about another few hundred paces, and then stood firm, without thinking about further pursuit or exploitation of the victory, and only sent out the light companies behind them, up to near the river. In this, I with my company did not take part, to the great dissatisfaction of the latter, because for the case of unforeseen events, General Harvey ordered me to stay with his brigade. The enemy made good use of our indecision and slackness, quickly passed back over the river, and in no time had reformed in columns on the other bank, which individually

111

marched up the heights and covered their retreat with a numerous cavalry, some skirmishers and guns.

Not long after this, we took a position on the taken hills, and our brigade came to stand just on the spot where the bayonet attack had ravaged. We could see here all its results, because an area of about three and a half thousand square paces was covered with dead and wounded to such an extent, that they were seen every 10 paces heaped one over the other by dozens. A wounded enemy sergeant was lying close to me. I started a conversation with him, but without complaint and without showing sign of his pain which surely was stirring in his shattered bones, he only uttered with a bitter voice: 'Here the reward for twelve years of service.' The Englishmen on the other side filled the air with laments and wails, even though for them the first care was taken, to bring them forth in blankets and to bandage them. However, it seems that near the bridge the combat still continued, and we moved a bit closer to it, to be at hand. Actually, I was anticipating that the enemy would certainly make a second attack, perhaps during the night, and the slow withdrawal of the enemy columns confirmed me in this opinion. But after we had endured a hearty cold rain, the fire quite ceased and we went back to our hills to take a bivouac there.

It was a shame to see our brigade, originally one of the strongest ones, now diminished to such weakness. Brigadier Myers had received two severe wounds, Colonel Ellis of the 23rd and Colonel Blakeney of the 7th Regiment were also wounded. In all, the brigade had lost 12 officers and 1,200 men dead and wounded (one company formed up with 4 men!), but on the other hand it had the honour to have gained the victory all alone. We, the light companies, had done nearly nothing and therefore no losses. Also General Cole was wounded lightly, but his adjutant, Captain Roverea, had received a severe wound in the head.

I myself was not wounded, but the fatigues of the past days, the march of this morning, the battle, the rain which I had to suffer without a greatcoat, and finally the absence of the baggage, so that no refreshments could be obtained, exhausted me to such an extent, that I threw myself onto tussocks on the blood-covered and sodden ground, in the midst of dead and wounded, and rested quite comfortably.

I will mention here a few circumstances which I learned later but will give some idea of the lack of skill of our commander [Beresford], although we already had some notion of this from his behaviour at Campo Mayor. In the beginning, Marshal Beresford had no correct information at all about the enemy, and [displayed] a complete lack of judgment, because on the morning of the battle he had ordered the two light battalions, which were already positioned at Albuera, to cook in peace, and the artillery, to send out horses and mules for foraging. Both, however, did not act as ordered, which was very fortunate. A second proof of his incapacity as a commanding general, was the choice of our position, because even though we had plenty of time to calmly occupy those hills, which presented the best position . . . he did not do so and we had to retake them during the battle with heavy losses. If he had, we could have waited for the enemy to attack, which he was obliged to do if he wanted to attain his goal of relieving Badajoz. By the way, the fortress already had a dinner arranged for Soult, because the bold enemy had no doubt of his victory . . . .

But back to Marshal Beresford. During the battle, when the 2nd Division had been routed, he believed everything lost, he thought a [defensive] position had to be taken, and he gave the two light battalions in Albuera the order to retreat. These had already prepared all the walls and houses, stood safely behind them and together with some artillery repulsed with good effect the repeated efforts of some enemy columns to pass the bridge. But they had to obey the order and quit the village, which the enemy immediately occupied. They are barely out of the village and 100 paces away, when the Marshal thinks better of it and orders them to stay in it. Now they have to take back their village with the bayonet and lose some officers and about 70 men. Without these orders [they would have lost] perhaps not six.

Concerning the reproach that he did not exploit the victory properly, I don't want to judge about this. Given the heavy losses from the battle, it would have been very hard for us to pursue the enemy with energy, take the opposite heights and, in the presence of the superior [enemy] cavalry, turn their retreat into a complete rout, as some wanted. Maybe we even would have forfeited our victory. However, even if he [Beresford] is lacking in strength of mind, he certainly has physical strength, because, as I am told, he was just behind the centre when the lancers broke through and an officer came chasing towards him. He awaited the enemy cavalryman calmly, parried his lance thrust, and then pulled him from his saddle by hand and threw him to the ground.

Altogether, our (English) loss, dead and wounded, is calculated near 4,000. After a few little promenades through the lines of the dead, where I saw with bleeding heart the horrors of war in the highest degree, night approached. We remained on our spot, the cold increased, no tree or piece of wood was seen, there was no other expedient than

113

collecting the muskets which were lying around by thousands, smash off the butts and by this means maintain a fire. This happened, and during the whole night the whole army made fire only from these guns. Maybe this has never been seen before.

17th May. After a sad night, tormented by cold, hunger and exhaustion, finally the sun reappeared. At the side of the fires, actual heaps of musket locks, barrels etc. were seen lying around, the debris of the guns. We advanced to the right wing of the 2nd Division, to which we were to belong during Cole's illness [sic], and here we met the Spanish. There were many former Prussian officers there whom I knew: Major Grolman, a Count Dohna, a Lützow, also Schepeler and Oppen, the latter adjutant to General Blake. One of them wore openly the Pour le Mérite . . . .

18th May, Saturday. I had a walk with Oppen and Schepeler along the Spanish line; they were sometimes quite beautiful and well-clothed troops, especially the Walloon Guards.

## 12. Nooth Letter

*The letter below from Major Nooth of the 7th Fusiliers illustrates the sensitivity of the British to any loss of cannon or colours.*[49]

Camp, Albuera,
18th May 1811
To Major Pearson, commanding Fusilier brigade

Sir,
When the first battalion of the [7th] Fusiliers under my command drove the enemy from the heights they were desired to obtain the possession of, the guns which our artillery on the left had been obliged to abandon, together with the regimental colour of the Buffs, which fell into our hands, Sergeant Gough got possession of the colour, and I am requested by the regiment to say, if this is meant to be the subject of an official report to Field Marshal Beresford, that they do not wish to obtain, and will willingly forgo any credit to be acquired at the expense of brave soldiers who discharged their duty to the utmost.

I have etc. etc.

Mervin Nooth, Major, Commanding first Battalion [7th] Fusiliers

---

49    Nooth to Pearson, 18 May 1811, reproduced in Knight, C.R.B., *Historical Records of the Buffs East Kent Regiment (3rd Foot) 1704–1914, Part 1: 1704–1814* (London, 1953), pp. 352–3.

## 13. Anonymous 4th Division Officer Letter
*This anonymous letter is one of several that were published in English newspapers soon after news of the victory had arrived in England.*[50]

Camp Albuera
18 May 1811

In a hut constructed with the arms of our enemies and thatched with broom – seated on a knapsack, I write on a drumhead a few particulars of our sanguinary conflict, with the army of Soult, the day before yesterday – a day ever to be remembered with sensations of pain, pleasure and pride. On the 15th, our division, the 4th, was left to protect the trenches in front of Badajoz, while the battering train, etc., were removing to the safe side of [the] Guadiana. We had that day a smart brush with the garrison, which occasioned considerable loss to our brigade before the sally was checked.

We arrived next day in time to share the honours of a field contested with such heroism, that victory was long undecided. The Portuguese supported the attack under a destructive cannonade, and exposed to cavalry, for at least two hours, and the Spaniards with unusual firmness displaying instances of the truest bravery. The enemy at last broke like a rabble – and forfeited, by their promiscuous flight, the estimation in which we should otherwise have held them. Nothing but a deficiency of cavalry prevented us from completing their defeat. Our prisoners say, that they were prepared to meet the worst from the British, but that we should have taught the Portuguese to fight so well, quite astonished them.

## F. King's German Legion Accounts (Except Artillery)

### 1. Alten Narrative
*Major General Charles Alten commanded the 1st and 2nd Light Battalion of the King's German Legion at Albuera. For unknown reasons (which, however, may have had to do with the Napier-Beresford pamphlet wars), he authored and signed a very detailed statement concerning his actions during the battle.*[51] *The statement is dated Hanover, October 1833.*

The independent light brigade under my command, consisting of the 1st and 2nd Light Battalions K.G.L., and numbering 1,100 combatants,

---

50    *Aberdeen Journal*, 26 June 1811.
51    Portuguese Arquivos Nacionais, Torre do Tombo.

arrived on its ground in the immediate vicinity of Albuera in the evening of the 15th May 1811, where it bivouacked for the night in the rear of the village close to the houses, having pickets in front of the place posted along the margin of the river.

On the morning of the 16th the enemy directed his first attack against that part of the position which was occupied by my brigade. After the pickets had been called in, the former had been placed in the following manner: The part of the village nearest to the large stone bridge over the Albuera river was occupied by the 2nd Light Battalion, which with its skirmishers lined the mud walls enclosing the houses, and had advanced a party of their best marksman to a well, surrounded by a stone wall and situated in front about half way between the village and the bridge. The churchyard in the centre of the village was occupied by two companies of the 1st Light Battalion, the skirts of the village on the left and some garden walls facing towards the Albuera river (where it was crossed by a minor bridge) were occupied by two more companies of the 1st Light Battalion. The rest of that battalion, consisting of four companies, remained in reserve on its ground in the rear of the village.

The enemy's attacking force directed against my brigade, was composed of a column of infantry supported by artillery and a regiment of Lancers, the latter marching at some interval on the left. This cavalry advanced rapidly to the river and crossed it by fording the Albuera about 400 yards above the bridge out of the reach of our rifles and taking their right shoulders forward they continued their movement towards the right of the Allied position, partly opposed by the skirmishers of the British heavy brigade, but owing to the inequality of ground, we lost sight of them.

The enemy's infantry threw their skirmishes forward, cannonading at the same time the village of Albuera. The fire of their artillery was ably answered by a battery of the German Legion and, after the latter had been withdrawn to the right, by a Portuguese one sent to replace it. This cannonading and skirmishing having lasted for some time, a close column (apparently a brigade) advanced up to the bridge but owing to the well-directed fire of the 2nd Light Battalion and of its advanced marksmen, the latter repeatedly picking off the officers who led the enemy's columns, the enemy failed several times in forcing this passage. After different fruitless attempts and a heavy loss this column, however, succeeded in crossing the Albuera, partly by the bridge and partly by fording, and then without advancing to the attack of the

116

village, it took the right shoulder forward and continued its movement towards the right of the British position.

Meanwhile the engagement on the right had become very serious and doubtful for the Allies, and it was at this time of the day, that I received Marshal Beresford's order to get loose of the village with my brigade, with the ultimate view of taking up a position in the rear of it, covering the Valverde road. The brigade was withdrawn by detachments from the village in order to be formed out of musket shot behind the same, but, before it was actually formed and just about the time that the last detachments were in the act of quitting the village, the battle had been decided on the right in favour of the Allies and the Marshal's countermand arrived. Several companies of the 2nd Light Battalion, which were the nearest at hand, instantly faced about and retook the village, cheering and advancing in double quick time, without meeting any serious opposition. The enemy was found to have thrown only a very few straggling *tirailleurs* into the place, and even these were not met with, till the churchyard, situated in the centre of the village, had been passed.

The 1st Light Battalion in the meantime rapidly advanced on the right of the village, its left wing closely skirting the same, and then throwing a strong line of skirmishes forward. These became briskly engaged with the enemy who kept possession of the bridge and the broken ground on the margin of the Albuera river. The bridge during engagement was for some time retaken by part of our skirmishers making a dash at it, but these being unnecessarily exposed in so advanced a situation, they were recalled, however, without the enemy taking possession of the bridge during the remainder of the engagement. The firing having continued for a couple of hours, ceased altogether. The enemy then placed a small advance picket on the bridge, my brigade leaving the skirts of the village occupied by a strong picket which had its advanced post in the enclosure of the well situated in front.

The principal loss of the 1st Light Battalion took place after the evacuation of the village, and that of the 2nd Light Battalion before that event.

Casualties of the brigade was as follows: 1st Light Battalion – 4 rank-and-file killed, 4 officers, 3 sergeants and 55 rank and file wounded, 2 rank and file missing.

2nd Light Battalion – 1 officer and 3 rank-and-file killed, 1 officer, 3 sergeants and 28 rank and file wounded, 1 rank and file missing. For a Total of 104 men killed, wounded, or missing.

## 2. Lindau Narrative

*Friedrich Lindau was a soldier in the Second Light Battalion, KGL, who published a memoir of his military service in 1846.[52] His narrative serves as a reminder that the task of obtaining food is never far from a soldier's thoughts.*

One morning we received the order for departure; both are like battalions marched off at about midday and came by 10 o'clock in the evening to a large heath near Albuera. We lay down with our packs full, with our rifles to hand; towards morning we heard a great deal of noise and when it was daylight we saw we were on the left flank of a great army of English, Spanish, and Portuguese.

Near the village that lay in front of us stood a 25-foot high tower [most likely the church steeple] where we had an outpost. I sneaked into the village to look for provisions and noticed my brother standing on guard up on the tower; he asked me to bring him some wine. In a house in the village I found an old man who did not want to leave and he lamented that his wife had taken all the provisions with her. Other houses were quite empty; only in a stall did I find a sheep, which I took with me. When I again came near the tower my brother called to me that I should kill the sheep quickly, hurry back to my company and warn them that the enemy was advancing. I at once slit the throat of the sheep and let it lie by the tower so that my brother might remove it. I warned our commander of the proximity of the enemy and hurried back to the tower with the adjutant. From high up the tower he saw the enemy, but he came down quickly with my brother and ordered us to hurry to our companies and not to take the sheep with us since the enemy was already here. I nevertheless cut off a leg and hurried back; but scarcely had I tied it in my pack then our company advanced against the skirmishers.

We pushed forward through the village and occupied a field opposite; it was eight or nine-foot-high thistles, through which we moved quite unnoticed as far as a little river. On the other side of the river were enemy skirmishers who fired on us persistently; behind them were troops of the line and cavalry. We also fired continuously; for all that, the enemy pressed over the river many times, we drove them back from it again with fixed bayonets. Soon we heard strong fire from the whole line on our right and saw that the battle was in progress. We might have been fighting for about one and a half hours, in which

---

52    Lindau, F., *From a Waterloo Hero: The Reminiscences of Frederick Lindau* (J. Bogle, trans. & ed., A. Uffindell, ed.) (Barnsley, 2009), pp. 57–62. The first edition was *Erinnerungen eines Soldaten aus den Feldzügen der Königlich-deutschen Legion* (Hameln, Germany, 1846).

we lost many people, though the enemy even more, when we had to draw back because the Portuguese stationed behind us were to take our places. Here we came under fire from two sides, since the Portuguese took us for French and shot at us until our Colonel Halkett chased the Portuguese away and threatened the commander himself with a sabre; at this time a bullet tore away my piece of mutton, which I had bound to my pack some hours before, and another pierced my canteen.

We now marched through the ranks of the Portuguese and stationed ourselves behind the village, where we immediately received the command to take up our earlier position again since the Portuguese had yielded it to the French. We placed the bayonets on our rifles and with a 'Hurrah!' went into the village, which was already occupied by the French. They began to shoot at us, but fell back with such haste that on my own I chased 10 Frenchmen out of the ruins of a house and could only reach the last with my bayonet, which, as he jumped over a wall, I ran through his body. The French fell back over the river, we again took up our former position and the fighting continued until evening, during which the French constantly led fresh columns against us but none of them was in a position to dislodge us. However, the thistle field was in the end so shot to pieces that it was no longer able to protect us. Towards evening, the enemy, who were Alsatian and spoke German, called over to us that it had been plenty enough for the day, they wanted to cease fire; we might do the same. It became quiet on our flank apart from the rain that had not ceased all day and still constantly poured down in streams, and from the centre to the right of us we could hear all the time heavy fire and a cry of 'Hurrah!'

When we saw the watch fires at the French half an hour away we marched back to the camping place of the previous night. I had to stay as an outpost on a piece of ground to the left of the village; I found a soft place to lay down but the cold and the storm as well as a disgusting stench in my nostrils did not let me sleep the whole night. So I stole very stealthily into the village to look for food. Here I suddenly heard a low moan; I went towards it and recognised an officer of our battalion, Captain [Georg] Heise, who, with his face covered in blood, asked me in a faint voice to shoot him to death. I shuddered at such misery and comforted the man – of whom I was fond, for he was a true friend to the soldiers – with kindly words, that he should be patient, it would soon be better for him. Then I lay some hay under his head, hurry back to my outpost and lay down again. Next morning I realised that my soft camping place was a body that had been covered over with a little earth, and of which the feet still stuck out.

119

After we were detached from the outpost at noon we paid a visit to the battlefield. A mass of wounded from our side and the enemy lay there, infantry and cavalry, private soldiers and officers, among a multitude of dead. The day was very hot, the unfortunate men called out for a drink of water, which we fetched for them from the neighbouring stream and eased the agonies of the death throes since we could not comply with the wish of most them to be shot. Close by a wall was Captain Heise with a bullet through his head, already dead. [He in fact was still alive and was transported to Elvas, where he died on 10 June.] I was heartily thankful that I had been fortunate enough to come through, since death had been really close to me too, four times; apart from the shots already mentioned I had got a bullet through my shako and another through my coat tail.

Towards evening I left the battlefield; the cries were weaker, most of the wounded were already silent, and these two freezing nights might well have freed them from their dreadful agonies. We slept in camp under the open sky, while cold and hunger tormented us because by this time nothing had been supplied for two days. The Poles in our battalion had already cut pieces of meat for themselves from the dead horses and eaten it raw, loathsome fare to the rest of us; I was always too disgusted to eat it, although I enjoyed my food. At last, towards the end of the next day came a long awaited refreshment after we had spent three days quite without food and drink, working in the heat part of the time.

The next morning we crossed the river and arrived at the encampment abandoned by the French, but found nothing in the wood except a crowd of wounded and dead Frenchmen. We lit a fire but had no food, so I went with a comrade further into the wood to take in birds from their nests; we did not find any but were richly compensated another way. At a clearing in the woods two donkeys were grazing, one old and one young. At once we chased after the animals and succeeded in chasing the young donkey fast into a thicket; we were not allowed to shoot it. We slaughtered it at once, took the meat and turned back to camp, where our arrival brought about great rejoicing; we roasted the meat and in no time it was eaten, since many good friends turned up to enjoy the excellent donkey meat.

## G. Cavalry Accounts

### 1. Long's Letter to his Brother
*Colonel Robert Long started the day of battle as the commander of the British cavalry, but he was superseded by Major General William Lumley shortly*

*after the fighting commenced because Beresford wanted a commander who was senior to the two Spanish cavalry commanders in the field. Long took this action as a personal affront that he never forgave, and his animosity towards Beresford is evident in the letter he wrote to his brother.*[53]

Bivouac near Solano
About 2 Leagues from Almendralejo
22 May, 1811

Our situation does not permit me to enter into those details of our late interesting proceedings which led to the battle of Albuera on the 16th Inst, a battle which we ought to have lost, but which the unconquerable spirits of the troops secured to the fortunate commander. The fault committed by us was not occupying the proper position, and what indeed was the key of it. The French saw our error, took advantage of it, and we had to recover by deadly exertion the ground which if disputed originally as it ought to have been done, would have cost our enemies rivers of blood and saved our own. However, as it was, enough has been shed. Our loss amounts to more than 5,000 men, that of the enemy killed and wounded I would state as being very short of the mark if estimated at 7,000. We buried upwards of 2,500 in the field. An intercepted letter from one of the *état major* to Soult States that the amount of wounded with *his* column at 4,000, and wherever we have followed them, hundreds are abandoned, and their positions strewed [*sic*] with dead. We have followed, or rather kept them in sight only, ever since, and we hope this night to be at Almendralejo, as I just learned that they have abandoned Azeuchal. Had the whole army been put in motion to follow the victory I can have no hesitation in asserting the greater part of Soult's corps must have been destroyed, all his wounded and prisoners taken, his artillery and baggage and in short everything that constitutes an army. But it has been deemed more prudent to offer him the golden bridge to retreat by, and our troops have resumed the investment of Badajoz.

This cavalry was so much superior to ours both in quality and numbers that our services during the day of action were limited to keeping them in check, and counteracting their attempt to gain our flanks, and deprive the infantry of our support. We only came in contact with them, partially, twice, but our artillery made considerable havoc among them. I never, in any instance of my life, saw such a

53    McGuffie, T.H. (ed.), *Peninsular Cavalry General 1811–1813: The Correspondence of Lieutenant General Robert Ballard Long* (London, 1951), pp. 105–107.

scene of carnage in the same space of ground. The field of battle was a human slaughterhouse.

In consequence of the union of the Spanish cavalry, and to prevent disputes about rank, General Beresford directed Major General Lumley to take command of the whole cavalry, and, in my opinion, rather indelicately, permitted this command to be assumed after the action had commenced, and whilst I was manoeuvring the troops. This I can never forgive and thus fortune deprived me again of what I am free to think and hope might have been my hard-earned reward. Deeply hurt, I did not abate my zeal and endeavours to promote the Marshal's glory, and my perfect knowledge of the ground, which I had reconnoitred the night before, enabled me I believe to be of assistance to the officer who thus superseded me.

It is odd enough that the evening before the action I pointed out, to the Adjutant General the defect of our position as then taken up, and foretold the consequences; had I obeyed the orders I received in the morning to move with all the cavalry to the position intended for us in the rear of the British line, the consequences might have been fatal. The Quartermaster General [D'Urban] had himself marched off with one of the regiments and not half an hour afterwards down came a strong column of cavalry opposite the ground they had occupied, and endeavoured to force the passage of the river; which a portion of them actually accomplished, but were driven back by a charge of the 3rd Dragoon Guards, which regiment and the 13th [Light] Dragoons (foreseeing the danger) I had detained near the village of Albuera to counteract any such attempt. Had my advice been followed as to a further part of the disposition I think the fatal advantage taken of our infantry by the French cavalry would not have occurred. I pointed out the certainty of this happening, recommended a regiment to be placed in column on the very spot where it happened, and even placed Spanish corps in reserve there; but which corps, when the French attack upon our infantry by their cavalry took place, never moved one yard in advance to the assistance. The only difference in what afterwards happened between what General Lumley did and I should have done, was his not availing himself of a favourable opportunity to attack the enemy's cavalry during the retreat, and at a time when their infantry was flying in all directions. By shaking their covering force at such a moment we should have been put in a situation to cut off a great part of the runaways.

The events of the battle rested entirely on the cavalry preserving the ground. Had they been beaten, the infantry would have been annihilated. But tho' dreadfully weakened by separation on different points, our countenance was so firm and imposing, with the whole French force (upwards of 3,000) attempted, and appeared to wish, but they dared not carry into effect the duty of attacking us. But as I propose giving you in detail the whole of our proceedings on the first favourable opportunity I shall add no more at present to what the Gazette will make you acquainted with. I escaped unhurt. Captain Dean had a hard knock on the shoulder blade, which however being a grazing shot only incommoded him for the moment. He was riding by my side when it took place. I heard it strike him, and after a short exclamation he begged me to look and see if the shot had gone through him. At the first view of his coat, I really thought it had, but told him not, and sent him to the rear to have his wound dressed. In 10 minutes, to my other surprise, he returned to me all live and well, only a little sickened with the blow. . . .

Now, my dearest C., as I have been talking a great deal of myself and my thoughts in this letter, I beg what I have said may be confined to my belongings. I shall always speak the truth to them, both for and against myself. When I commit a fault I shall acknowledge; where I feel myself right in thought or action I shall declare it.

## 2. Long's Letter to Le Marchant

*Long wrote a second letter about the battle to another cavalry officer, Gaspard Le Marchant, then superintendent of the Royal Military Academy.[54] His remarks in this letter are even more critical of the dispositions made by Beresford and D'Urban. There is a sketch plan included with the letter that served as the basis for the modern interpretation of the plan that is included in this volume (see Illustrations).*

Villafranca 5 June 1811

Dear Le Marchant,
. . . Since that time events of considerable importance have taken place on this side [indecipherable words, possibly 'of the'] Tagus & the battle of Albuera forms a strong feature in the history of the campaign. I have every day to regret my own inability to use the pencil, & the absence of a skilful assistant who could furnish me with sketches of the ground to elucidate my remarks. I lament it the more after the present occasion because a sight of the ground with a delineation of the manner it was taken up to meet the impending storm, would

---

54    Long to Le Marchant, Le Marchant Papers Packet 13a, Item 8, Royal Military Academy, Sandhurst.

speak more forcibly than any language I could use, & would prove to you at once upon what a fragile foundation often rests the safety of armies & of nations. Had I not been a personal witness of the fact, I never could have believed it possible for a human being with his eyes in his head (brains were not wanted) to make so egregious a mistake as was committed at Albuera in the distribution & arrangement of the troops. The position of Albuera is naturally strong & excellent. The river deepens after passing the village & is no longer fordable, besides the cliffs which form its left bank boundary are most commanding & easy movement of the enemy in that direction is instantly seen, & can be most expeditiously counteracted.

The river towards its source becomes shallower, but the banks are steep and boggy offering only small fords in a few detached places & above where the junction of it with another small rivulet takes place a kind of ravine is formed which is a strong natural line of defence or obstacle, difficult to be surmounted in presence of an enemy. Considering the village of Albuera as the left point of *appui*, the position extends away to the right along a ridge of high commanding ground, exceedingly strong, & presenting by its salient and re-entering angles a perfectly natural line of fortifications. In the rear of these heights is a large plain, but intersected by a small rivulet or two which form a good protection against cavalry. This ground falls from the heights towards the point where the right of the troops was placed as marked in the adjoining figure, whence an almost interminable plain extends to the left towards Badajoz, & for 2 leagues, to the rear towards Valverde.

Faced [?] with this description of the ground, if intelligible, how would you or Jarry have occupied it? I will tell you how it was taken up by a British general, assisted by a Quarter Master General who was a favourite pupil at Wycombe. Vigil [*sic*]. The whole of the high ground which forms the position was abandoned – not occupied at all – but two lines of infantry were drawn up on the plain, without any *appui* to either wing, fronting Albuera, & parallel [*sic*] with the Badajoz road. The cavalry was directed to form in rear of the left of the line, where the British infantry was posted. It is true I never saw the British infantry, for the Spaniards were on the right & nearest to me, the former therefore might have been more *en potence* than in a direct line, but this is of no consequence. In this manner the key to the position was abandoned & those heights presented to the enemy for occupation, which, if possessed, flank and enfilade the position selected from right to left, whilst their rear is presented to the plain upon which, of course, the enemy's cavalry was to be expected to act. The scientific part of these arrangements being that exposed to your view and contemplation, I am to state occurrences as they actually took place. . . .

The enemy continued to advance occupying Almendral & Solano successively & about noon on the 15th May a heavy column of cavalry, with infantry & artillery marched down upon me at Santa Martha. As soon as their force was reconnoitred, I fell back upon Albuera, their advance skirmishing with my rear all the way. I passed the river, took up the ground as described in the sketch, the enemy occupied the wood in my front. At this time not a British infantry soldier, or Spaniard was there & had the enemy commenced immediately his attack, the position would have been carried that evening before the army could be collected. Having reconnoitred the ground, I waited anxiously to see it taken up as I expected it would have been, & I took the opportunity of pointing out to the Adjutant General the evident advantages of our situation, & my hope that they would not be overlooked. He returned to the Marshal [and] they both went over the ground. I was satisfied all would be right & I thought [?] more so when I rec'd an order to remain where I was 'till relieved by the Spaniards.

During the night the Spanish infantry arrived & also the British troops, & in the morning I beheld them, to my astonishment, arrayed as you see them in the sketch. I again reconnoitred the ground, & returned with a trembling heart to my post. There I met Col. D'Urban our QMG, who directed me to withdraw all the cavalry immediately & the guns, & take them to the rear of the British infantry, & he actually withdrew and marched off himself with the 4th Dragoons posted for the defence of the bridge & ford near the village. I [indecipherable word] again, said nothing, but having assembled the 13th [Light] Dragoons in rear of the 3rd Dragoon Guards there I determined to wait & detain them 'till I saw the ground I was about to relinquish occupied by these troops. Scarcely had half an hour elapsed when the enemy was observed in motion along the direct road to Albuera, apparently to force the passage of the bridge & ford near the village, whilst heavy columns of cavalry, infantry and artillery debouched from the wood on our right, & passed the river and ravine without opposition. Their infantry columns directed their march towards the heights, his cavalry circling round them into the plain in the rear & left.

I detached part of the 3rd DG to take up the ground where the 4th D had been withdrawn, & opened a heavy fire from the guns attached to my division which they answered. They formed their columns opposite the ford & pushed over three detachments of pikemen to cover the passage of the rest. They were as often beaten back again by the 3rd DG. Information of these movements having been communicated to

Head Quarters, I cannot describe what their feelings were. The 4th Dragoons were ordered back to me. The Spaniards began securing their flank as well as they could, but it was soon discovered that if the enemy gained and possessed the heights the day must be lost, and the prize was nearly in their hands. The British infantry was brought at a run from the left to the right, I kept the enemy in check with my guns as long as I could, at length their advance, & the movements of their cavalry obliged me to relinquish the heights & take up a defensive position in the plain, to check their cavalry & support the flanks, & cover the rear of the infantry thus menaced with attack.

The head of the British column had scarcely reached the first height on the right before they came in contact with the enemy. Their gallantry was irresistible, & their advance under a tremendous fire, progressive. Unfortunately, they uncovered their right flank in proportion as they gained ground, of which part of the enemy's cavalry took advantage, charged & routed them. I had foreseen this event, & pointed it out as likely to occur to both General Lumley & one of the Spanish generals. The former thought he had not sufficient British cavalry to spare a part of it to counteract such an intention, but the latter at my urgent request formed his regiments in 2 lines in the rear of the point threatened, but he did so at too great a distance to afford succour with the requisite expedition. I also placed 2 guns to cooperate, but the enemy cavalry became so soon mixed with our own people, they could not fire.

Another division of British infantry was brought up, recovered the ground lost & maintained their superiority. A second attempt of the enemy's cavalry was made of [two indecipherable words], likewise, in the same spot, but they threw back a few companies *en potence* & this, assisted by the charge of 2 squadrons of the 4th D detached for the purpose, & some Spaniards, secured them from the fate of their less fortunate predecessors. At length the success of our infantry on the left, & the firm attitude shown on the right, which kept in check an immensely superior cavalry, were crowned with perfect success by the complete rout & defeat of the enemy's infantry in all directions. Not a retreat but a flight, a *'sauve qui peut'* marked their return to the woods which gave them their shelter.

The loss on both sides has been enormous. That of the enemy would have been little short of the extermination of their whole army had it been followed up, & why it was not I cannot say, seeing that we have at the moment nearly 20,000 men whose services do not appear necessary in prosecuting the siege of Badajoz. . . .

I forgot to mention that the union of the Spanish cavalry obliged our chief to appoint a senior officer to command the whole & General

Lumley was selected for this duty, but not having arrived 'till an hour after the action of the 16th had commenced, he was permitted, I think rather indelicately, to supersede me on the *champ de bataille*. At that moment there was no necessity for this step, & the mortification might have been spared me. I shall never suffer personal feelings to interfere with the discharge of my duty, I therefore acted in second with as much zeal, as I would have shown if left to the sole responsibility for the cavalry movements of that day. . . .

The carnage at Albuera succeeded any thing I ever saw in my life in the same space of time & of ground. The theatre of action was a human slaughterhouse & the wounded most pitiably circumstanced – not a shrub or a tent to shelter them against torrents of rain, or a scorching sun exposed to which many of them remained stripped, some for 24, others for 48 hours in the spot where they fell, there being no means of transport to remove them. We bivouacked [indecipherable word] & the following night in the midst of this scene of butchery unheeding and unheeded! Lord bless you, I can say no more. Remember me to [indecipherable word].

Faithfully,
RL

## 3. Madden's Diary

*Charles Dudley Madden was a lieutenant in the English 4th Dragoons who kept a diary of his service in the Peninsula.[55] He provides some important details of the movements of the Allied cavalry during the day, as well as some interesting comments about the Polish lancers.*

May 15 – The French made their appearance on the heights above the town in the early part of the day. We retired to Albuera and encamped on the heights near the town with a small river in our front. In the course of the day the advanced guard of the enemy came in sight and continued to multiply in every part of the wood near our lines. In course of the evening our lines were formed on our position which was some high ground which formed near a crescent with the river in our front which was only fordable in a few places; the town was on the left of our lines, near which was a bridge over the river. In the front line was drawn up, on the left some Portuguese, in the centre a part of General Blake's Walloon infantry, next [to] them the 1st Division of British infantry commanded by General Stewart, then next [to]

---

55    'The Diary of Lt. Charles Madden, 4th Dragoons', *Royal United Service Institution Journal*, Vol. 58 (1914), pp. 516–19 (April).

them General Cole's division of British infantry. The second line was formed of the remainder of General Blake's, General Ballesteros and the Portuguese. Our army consisted of 10,000 British, 8,000 Portuguese, and 10,000 Spanish. We had three regiments of British cavalry, two of Portuguese, and about 900 Spanish cavalry. We had about 35 pieces of artillery. The French proved to have 21,000 infantry, 4,000 cavalry, and 52 pieces of artillery. Their army was commanded by Marshal Soult, next to him in command was Mortier. Their infantry kept themselves concealed under cover of a large wood.

May 16 – Early in the morning the enemy was discovered placing their army in order of battle, and showing every appearance of an intention of attacking us, particularly as they were seen bringing their artillery in front. At 8:00 o'clock a.m. they moved the whole of their army in front of our lines on the other side of the river and commenced their attack by attempting to pass a large column of cavalry across a ford near the centre of our lines. As the ford was narrow they could only pass over it with a small front. The 3rd Dragoon Guards were drawn up in front of the ford, and charged the head of the column, on which the enemy retired across the river; this attack seems to have been intended as a feint, as their serious attack was aimed at our right.

They advanced against that point in three immense columns, with about 3,000 cavalry on their left flank, so as to turn our right. They came on with such rapidity that they had gained the height our first division was to have been formed upon, before it had been completely formed, and began to pour down on us like an immense torrent.

At this instance nothing but British steadiness and bravery could stand. The 1st brigade of the 2nd Division, consisting of the 3rd, 48th and 66th, formed up, and after several tremendous volleys on both sides the British charged them at the point of the bayonet. The French being strongly supported stood firm, and a more awful scene was never witnessed. It was a near perfect carnage on both sides, bayonet against bayonet for near half an hour. As the brigade which at that time was principally engaged had pushed rapidly forward, they were a considerable distance in front of their support, which the enemy seeing, they moved a large column down on either flank, and surrounded them. At the same time a large body of cavalry commenced a charge on them, as they began to retire, and cut them down in all directions. The whole brigade, 3rd, 48th and 66th became prisoners when the right wing of the 4th Dragoons got orders to charge their cavalry, which they obliged to retire leaving a great number of the prisoners. The enemy continued to push for the columns to the interval where the gate stood.

When a part of General Cole's division came up, a tremendous cannonade, and fire of small arms, continued for several hours, in some instances at 10 paces asunder; each party charged with the greatest bravery, and the day was for a length of time bearing an awful unfavourable appearance. Had their cavalry, which was three to one of ours, charged round our right flank, which they might have done, and so came in our rear, the day was lost. They attempted it, but was checked by a brigade of horse artillery, which mowed them down in six and ten at a time; however, had they pushed forward we could have shown them no opposition.

After a determined contest for about four hours, in which all our infantry was engaged, with most of the Spanish and Portuguese, the enemy began to give way, when an immense cannonade was opened on them as they descended the hill, and they retired in considerable confusion. Had we a sufficient body of cavalry to charge them as they fell back, they must have been entirely cut up, but as the attack still continued on our left, we were obliged to keep a large portion of our cavalry to keep in check a column which menaced that part, and seemed determined to force the bridge. I was stationed near the bridge with the left wing of my regiment, and a squadron and a half of the 13th [Light Dragoons], to cover some guns and defend the ford against a column of cavalry in our front. We had a brigade of Portuguese cavalry in our rear as our support. The enemy moved forward with the intention of attacking us, on which we advanced near the ford, when an immense fire of artillery was opened on us, every shot told; however, our advances had the effect of checking their cavalry.

We remained for five hours exposed to a heavy fire of artillery and musketry. We had nine guns playing from the church over the bridge which did great execution. We also had near us a brigade of German riflemen. The uproar and confusion was dreadful, each party cheered when they came to the charge, and every inch that was gain could easily be discovered on which side it went by the immense shout of the parties engaged. They were like an immense body of water ebbing and flowing. Had a man time to reflect, one's situation must have been dreadful, but each man had his point to watch, which took up his whole attention. Wretched objects in all shapes and descriptions were to be seen in every direction, some creeping on their hands and knees, with both there like shut off, and others in equally a distressing situation.

What made our situation more critical, three-fourths of our army were composed of Spaniards and Portuguese, the former of whom were greatly deficient in discipline, and from frequent defeats by the French had an utter dread of them. However, Providence inspired all

129

our united force with steadiness and courage; both the Portuguese and Spaniards endeavoured to follow the glorious example of the British troops. Our loss was dreadful. In one division, which consisted of 4,000 men, we had killed, wounded, and prisoners 2,990, the two first in command killed, and an equal proportion of officers; our whole loss out of about 8,000 or 9,000 British amounted to 4,000, with 2,000 Spanish and Portuguese. The French were supposed to have lost between 7,000 and 8,000 men, with two generals killed and three wounded. We had in the charge of the right wing of the 4th [Dragoons] two captains and one lieutenant taken, and one captain and one lieutenant severely wounded, with a great proportion of men and horses killed and wounded. In the left wing three men dangerously wounded, one having his thigh shot off, with eight or nine horses killed.

The charge of our right wing was made against a brigade of Polish cavalry, very large men, well mounted; the front rank armed with long spears, with flags on them, which they flourish about, so as to frighten our horses and then either pulled our men off their horses or ran them through. They were perfect barbarians, and gave no Quarter when they could possibly avoid. However, they confess to have lost 300 men. A sharp skirmish continued until night.

The whole army kept in their lines close by their arms. A more dismal sight was never witnessed; the baggage to the whole army was leagues in the rear and not a man had a dry stitch on them, as it rained with a cold wind and sleet most part of the day. The hill we lay on had not a twig to make a fire with; and the ground was ankle deep in mud. The dead and wounded lay in heaps through our lines, as all lay exactly on the spot we fought on; in the groans and screeches of the wretched, few of whom had been removed, made it an awful scene, together with a prospect of the engagement being renewed at daylight, or an attack under the cover of night. Much was to be dreaded, as we had a most experienced general (Soult) to guard against, who had an utter contempt of the Spaniards, who formed one-third of our army.

May 17 – The morning for several hours was very foggy and dark, so that we could not discover the enemy's intention; this was an interesting time, the whole army stood to their arms, every moment expecting a renewal of the engagement, and the morning was so cold, with sleet and rain, that we could scarcely sit on our horses. However, as it cleared up we could discover a column of the enemy moving towards our left, as if either inclined to attack that point, or move off. The cavalry, consisting of about 4,000, continued drawn up in the course of the day; deserters came in, who gave information that the enemy had commenced their retreat towards Seville. I rode over the field of battle, where lay between 5,000 and 6,000 dead and wounded, most of whom were completely naked. In some places they lay so thick a person could have supposed they had been collected for the purpose of being buried. The wounded met one's eyes entreating assistance, many of whom lay covered with mud and wet for 10 hours without their wounds being dressed. British officers lay mortally wounded, in many instances stripped of their clothes for hours before they were dead. This piece of inhumanity was to be attributed to the Spaniards who plundered the whole of the night after the battle, without respect to rank or persons. The different attitudes of the dead could not fail striking a man's eyes. The British universally lay with their arms in a position of charging, and the countenances of both parties, even in death, bespoke a fixed determination to conquer or fall. On an average, two-thirds of the British officers were either killed, wounded, or prisoners. The Buffs, which went in 600 strong, could only muster 40. The 48th and 66th about the same. The two latter lost their colours. The enemy failed in raising the siege of Badajoz.

## 4. Somerset Letter

*Lord Edward Somerset was a lieutenant colonel of the 4th Dragoons. His letter dated 3 June 1811 to his brother, the Duke of Beaufort, gives some details of the experience of his regiment during the battle.*[56]

. . . I did not join the regiment till the morning after the battle and therefore shall not pretend to relate the particulars, which you will read in the public dispatches. But it is evident that nothing but the obstinate intrepidity of a British soldier could have repulsed the enemy. Soult was confident of success and made his attacks in the most furious manner. His great superiority in cavalry gave him a great advantage and had at one time nearly decided the day in his favour. My regiment was very much exposed during the whole time and two squadrons made a very gallant charge against a body of cavalry composed of Poles that were armed with long spears having a flag at the tip. This charge did a great service and kept their cavalry in check whilst affording our infantry time to rally. In the attack we experienced some loss – Captains Phillips and Spedding and Lieutenant Wildman were taken prisoners, Spedding been thrown from his horse, the other two having theirs killed. Wildman was also badly wounded. Captain Holme and

---

56    Edward Somerset to the Duke of Beaufort (his brother), 3 June 1811, Badminton Archives, England.

Lieutenant Chantry, the adjutant, were also wounded and Holme's horse was killed. Our loss altogether was one sergeant and 22 men killed and wounded and 20 horses. Captain Dalbiac's charger was likewise killed. I am happy to say that both Spedding and Wildman have since made their escape from the enemy, and what is singular is, that of 700 or 800 prisoners lost that day at least 600 have got away and re-joined the army.

## 5. Bennett Narrative

*Thomas Bennett, a trooper in the 13th Light Dragoons, was not heavily engaged in the battle, but had an interesting observation concerning the way in which the French suffered the bulk of their casualties.*[57]

The immense loss sustained by the French chiefly took place when the Allies regained the height from which the Spaniards had previously been driven. In forcing the enemy into the low ground towards the rivulet, the carnage caused by our musketry and shrapnel shells was a mess. I was an eyewitness to the whole ranks of the enemy mown down like hay.

## 6. Lumley Narrative

*Major General Sir William Lumley was reassigned from command of an infantry brigade to command of the Allied cavalry early in the morning of the 16th. He did not leave a contemporaneous account of his services on the day, but provided some information to Beresford in his pamphlet war with Napier.*[58]

Frequently, as time and circumstances would permit, I scanned with no small anxiety the whole line of infantry on those hotly and effectively contested, and most important heights, the key of our position; but, to the best of my recollection, was not aware of the advance of the two brigades (the Fusiliers and Harvey's), until they had passed my left flank. They then came under my eye; and, as D'Urban states, the rain and smoke having at that time cleared away, I saw them, as one body, moving to engage; and, although they had become so oblique, relative to the point where I stood, that I could not well speak to the actual distance between the two, there did not appear any improper chasm or distance. Just about this period also it was that D'Urban came up to me, and upon my asking him how

---

57    Fortescue, John, *Following the Drum* (Edinburgh, 1931). p. 89.
58    Beresford, W., *Refutation of Napier's Justification of his Third Volume* (London, 1834), pp. 225–6.

matters were going on upon the left and elsewhere, and his giving me a hasty detail of facts, he finished with saying, 'The great object is to make that Portuguese brigade cling well to the hill: I have just been with them for that purpose.' And well and bravely, to my mind, did they obey his instructions.

## 7. Light Letter

*Lieutenant William Light of the 4th Dragoons was the British liaison officer to the Spanish cavalry. His letter describing the attack of the Spanish cavalry after the destruction of Colborne's brigade is quoted in Napier's history of the war.*[59]

After our brigade of infantry, first engaged, were repulsed, I was desired by General D'Urban to tell the Count de Penne-Villemur to charge the lancers, and we all started, as I thought, to do things well; but when within a few paces of the enemy the whole pulled up, and there was no getting them further; and in a few moments after I was left alone to run the gauntlet as well as I could.

## H. Artillery Accounts

## 1. Dickson Letter

*Major Alexander Dickson was an English artillery officer who commanded the Portuguese artillery at the battle, operating independently of the English and German artillery commanded by Major Hartmann. A five-volume set of his correspondence was published from 1905 to 1908, but it lacks Dickson's letter about Albuera, which was not published until 2001.*[60] *Dickson states emphatically that he was ordered to retreat, although the order was quickly countermanded. Unfortunately, the sketch accompanying the letter has been lost.*

Elvas
May 22, 1811

My Dear Sir,
In my last letter dated the 8th inst., I informed you that the investment of the city was completed, and I continued getting up my heavy artillery. . . .

---

59   Napier, William F.P., *History of the War in the Peninsula and in the South of France from the Year 1807 to the Year 1814* (6 vols., London, 1828–31), v. 3, p. 640.

60   Vigors, Desmond, 'The Battle of Albuera – Dickson's Missing Letter of May 22', *The Journal of the Royal Artillery*, Spring 2001, No. 1 (Vol. CXXVII), pp. 43–5.

About the same time General Cole's division joined us on the morning of the 15th [*sic*, should be 16th], which was a little after 8 o'clock, the enemy first showed himself in force, a regiment of cavalry had been seen in the wood the night before but no infantry. I enclose rough recollection of the battle as the thing appeared to me; of course, there are many faults but on the whole I think I will give a tolerable just idea of the leading particulars.

Our army is represented in the situation it stood, when the French infantry began to move to the attack. The Spaniards in all were, I believe, about 12,000 men. They had some cavalry which I know charged during the action, but I do not know the exact situation where they were drawn up.

The wood through which the enemy advanced is pretty thick, and for a considerable time prevented us from discovering their intentions.

Albuera is a small village, nearly in ruins, with the exception of the church, and without inhabitants. The first appearance of the enemy with the advance of seven or eight squadrons of cavalry, some light infantry, and a troop of horse artillery from the wood, towards the bridge of Albuera by the Seville road. They drove in our pickets on that side and formed in the plain commencing a fire of artillery towards the village, which was answered by some of my guns and those of the German artillery against their cavalry. At this moment I thought it was only reconnaissance but soon afterwards a strong column of infantry was discovered advancing by the same road towards the bridge, and a brigade of General Stewart's division was sent to the village in consequence to support Baron Alten.

Soon afterwards another column was discovered moving through the wood to their left, apparently with a view of turning our flank, and the column approaching the bridge, having halted and beginning to return, proved that their effort would be directed on our right. The British brigade of Stewart's marched from the village to the right, as also did the remainder of the same division, and Cole's drew up *en potence* to meet them in case they should turn us. When the grand French column of infantry, supported by a strong corps of cavalry was marching over the height No. 4 a thick shower of rain came on which much favoured their approach, and during which they passed the river and advanced upon and came around the heights No. 1. Stewart's arrived and formed on No. 1 and partly on No. 2 but they had hardly completed their formation when the attack began and the right brigade, being charged by a strong body of cavalry, gave way and three of the regiments were nearly cut to pieces, losing five colours, viz., the 3rd, the 2nd of the 48th and the 2nd of the 66th regiments.

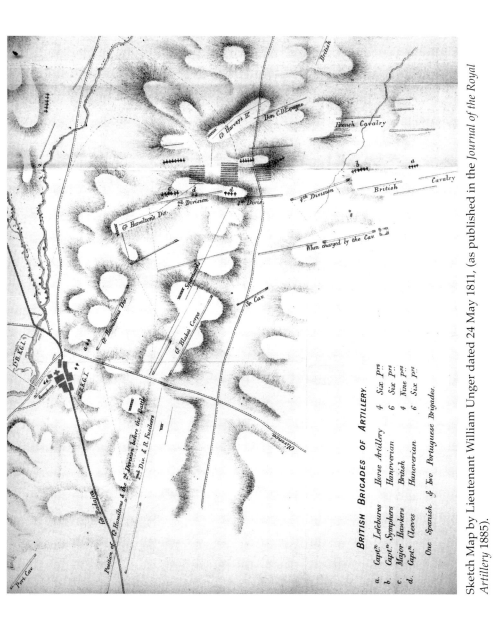

BRITISH BRIGADES OF ARTILLERY.

a. Capt.ᵗⁿ Lefebure    Horse Artillery    4  Six Pʳˢ
b. Capt.ᵗⁿ Symphers    Hanoverian        6  Six Pʳˢ
c. Major Hawkers       British           4  Nine Pʳˢ
d. Capt.ᵗⁿ Cleeves     Hanoverian        6  Six Pʳˢ

One Spanish & Two Portuguese Brigades.

Sketch Map by Lieutenant William Unger dated 24 May 1811, (as published in the *Journal of the Royal Artillery* 1885).

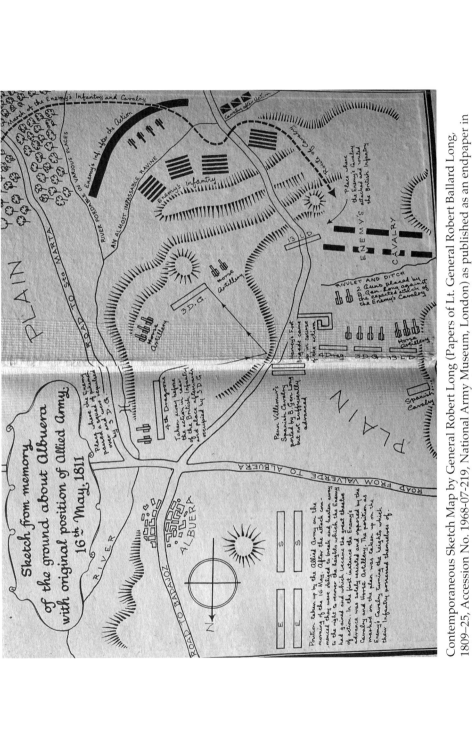

Contemporaneous Sketch Map by General Robert Long (Papers of Lt. General Robert Ballard Long, 1809–25, Accession No. 1968-07-219, National Army Museum, London) as published as an endpaper in T. H. McGuffie, *Peninsular Cavalry General 1811–1813* (London, 1951).

Spanish Order of Battle and Key to Spanish Map dated 11 June 1811. (Antonio Burriel, *Batalla de la Albuera* (Cadiz, 1811))

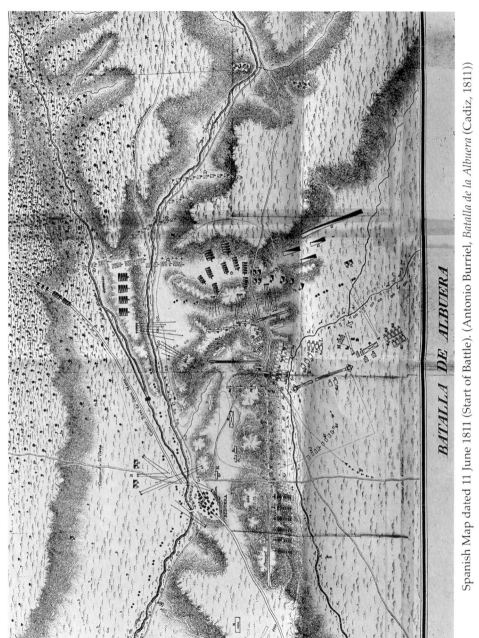

BATALLA DE ALBUERA

Spanish Map dated 11 June 1811 (Start of Battle). (Antonio Burriel, *Batalla de la Albuera* (Cadiz, 1811))

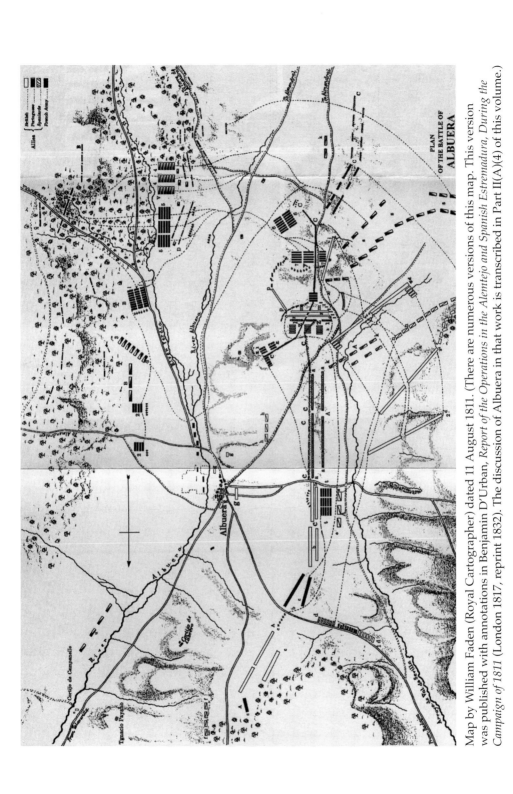

Map by William Faden (Royal Cartographer) dated 11 August 1811. (There are numerous versions of this map. This version was published with annotations in Benjamin D'Urban, *Report of the Operations in the Alentejo and Spanish Estremadura, During the Campaign of 1811* (London 1817, reprint 1832). The discussion of Albuera in that work is transcribed in Part II(A)(4) of this volume.)

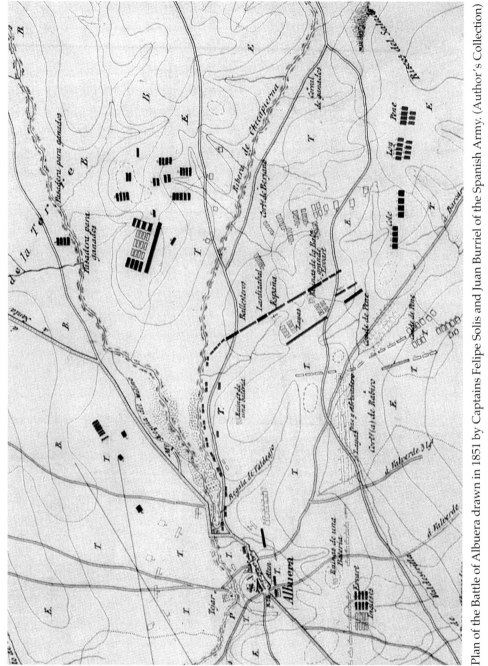

Plan of the Battle of Albuera drawn in 1851 by Captains Felipe Solis and Juan Burriel of the Spanish Army. (Author's Collection)

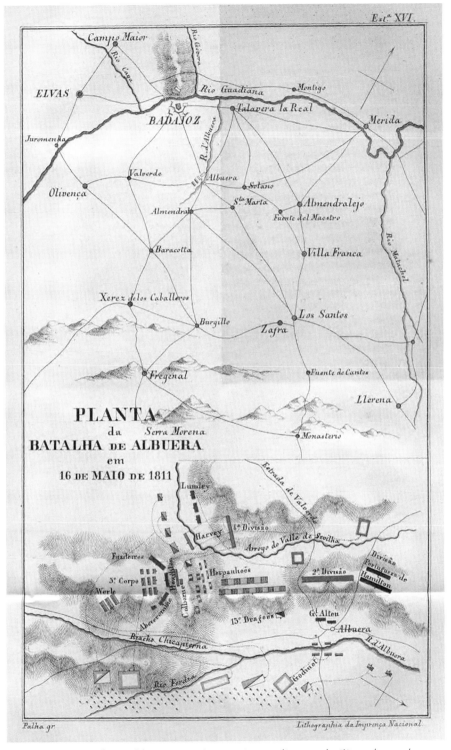

Portuguese Map. (https://www.napoleon-series.org/images/military/maps/
Portuguese/albuera.jpg)

Watercolor Panorama of the Battle (Anne S. K. Brown Military Collection, Brown University, Providence, RI (https://repository.library.brown.edu/studio/item/bdr:249588/)). The annotations on this panorama have been transcribed as Account II(J)(5) in this volume.

Captain Cleeve's brigade of six-pounders was on the hill No. 1, and in consequence fell into the enemy hands but it was all afterwards retaken except the howitzer which was carried off by them. The enemy then formed and attacked hill No. 2 and pressed the troops on it very hard, the centre brigade of Stewart's being just giving way when General Cole's division came up to their support. Indeed as far as I could observe the enemy had actually got to the top of hill No. 2, nor did General Cole succeed in driving them off these hills without having a most obstinate contest, every inch of ground being disputed. At length British prowess prevailed, and the enemy gave way in their turn and were driven down with great slaughter, nor did they rally much until they had passed the rivulet when they retired into the woods. Nor could we pursue, our cavalry being so inferior. The left brigade of Stewart's commanded by Colonel Abercromby was very instrumental in saving the day, having made a most vigorous and successful charge on the enemy.

Marshal Beresford himself for a moment thought he was defeated, as I received an order to retreat with my artillery towards Valverde and Baron Alten, absolutely by order quit the village for a moment. All this was, however, soon countermanded and rectified.

When the attack became certain, Hamilton's [division] moved to hill No. 3 but it was very little if it all engaged. We suffered considerably from the fire of the enemy's guns, of which I think they had about 45 or 50, whereas we had only 32.[61] The cannonade on both sides was tremendous during the whole business, and probably [only] in a few battles were more casualties by cannon shot in this.

My six-pounder brigade was on hill No. 3 and my nine-pounder brigade defended the village, which the enemy's light troops pressed hard on, and absolutely got possession of when we fell back by order, but they were immediately driven from it again. They were, however, able to keep possession of the bridge.

I was well satisfied with my own brigades. Hawker was part of the time on No. 2 and his brigade, by my own observation, did great executions. I heard General Cole speak very handsomely of Sympher, and Cleeve's guns, I am told, were served until the enemy was amongst them, when retreat was impossible, for their cavalry absolutely came round the hill. Of the horse artillery I know nothing, except being told that one gun was for a short time taken but was absolutely afterwards recovered.

---

61    In a letter to Beresford dated 25 July 1833, Dickson clarified that the allies had a total of 38 guns in the battle, but he undercounted the Spanish artillery by two guns, so the real total was 40. Portuguese Arquivo Nacional, Torre do Tombo.

Major Hartman commanded the British and German artillery as Colonel Framingham had not arrived. He has since joined the army.

On hills 1 and 2 everyone declared they have never seen such a field; in the space, I think, of from 1,000 to 1,200 yards there were certainly not less than 6,000 dead and wounded, French, English, Spanish and Portuguese. The Spanish, as far as I could see, behaved very well. A Portuguese brigade, commanded by Colonel Harvey in General Cole's division, behaved with the greatest gallantry and coolness, but our dear bought victory was certainly decided by the Fusilier brigade in the same division. If the enemy had attacked early in the morning before General Cole came up we must certainly have been beaten.

The loss on our side, including Spaniards, I should judge 5,500 in killed, wounded and missing, and of the British only I don't think it much under 4,000. The fact is the Spanish once in line could not be moved, I mean could not manoeuvre, and the Marshal was obliged to use the British that knew how to move, or else our flank must have been completely turned, hence the heavy loss they have sustained. I think the French must have lost at least 7,000 men. They remained quiet in the wood all next day, and the day after retreated, and were pursued by our cavalry and light troops. On the 19th it being certain they were in full retreat, General Hamilton's division reinvested Badajoz, and I was ordered to proceed to Elvas to make again preparation for the siege.

## 2. Dickson Recollection
*Dickson added some additional details to his original story about Beresford's order of retreat in a letter written in the context of the pamphlet wars between Napier and Beresford in the 1830s.[62]*

The Portuguese artillery under my command (12 guns) attached to General Hamilton's division was posted on favourable ground about 750 or 800 yards from the bridge, at least 700 yards south-west of the village of Albuera, their fire bore effectually on the bridge and the road from it to the bridge, I received my orders to take up this position from Lord Beresford when the enemy threatened their main attack at the bridge. At a certain period of the day, I should judge it to have been about the time the 4th Division moved to attack, I received a verbal order in English from Don Jose Luiz De Souza (now Conde de Villa Real, and aide-de-camp of Lord Beresford) to retire by the Valverde road or upon the Valverde road, I am not sure which; to this I strongly

---

62    Quoted in Napier, William, *A Letter to General Lord Viscount Beresford* (London, 1834), p. 32.

expressed words of doubt, and he then rode off towards Albuera; as, however, I could see no reason for falling back and the infantry my guns belonged to being at hand, I continued in action, and though I believe I limbered up once or twice previous to the receipt of this message and moved a little to improve my position, I never did so to retire. Soon after Don Jose left me, seeing Lord Beresford and some of his staff to my right, I rode across to satisfy myself that I was acting correctly, but perceiving that the French were giving away I did not mention the order I received and as soon as Lord Beresford saw me, he asked what state my guns were in, and then ordered me to proceed as quickly as I could with my nine-pounders to the right, which I did in time to bring them into action against the retiring masses of the enemy. The foregoing is the substance of an explanation given to Lord Beresford which he lately requested.

## 3. Hartmann Narrative

*Major Julius Hartmann was a Hanoverian artillery officer who commanded the British and KGL artillery at the battle. His command was independent of that of Major Dickson, commanding the Portuguese artillery. His recollections appear in an article he wrote for a German military periodical in which he refers to himself in the third person.*[63]

. . . The weather in the early morning of 16th May was fair and clear, but became dark and foggy towards 7 o'clock, which changed, when the sun rose higher, to alternating sunshine and isolated, sometimes dense, sometimes fine, showers of rain, which darkened everything.

A bit before 7 o'clock the enemy suddenly very rapidly advanced with several lines of cavalry, a few batteries of artillery and, under their cover, with one closed column of infantry towards the bridge of Albuera, and began to fire at the town and at the lines which appeared behind it on the heights. Against this movement, the battery of the 2nd Division, under Captain Cleeves, and the brigade of the right wing of this division were taken forward. However, it was improbable that the enemy could have the serious intention to occupy the strong defile of the river, especially because a bit below [north of the bridge], the left bank appears more and more high and steep and the river itself is cut in much deeper. . . . Therefore one assumed immediately that this attack was only intended to hide an undertaking towards the Allied

---

63 Hartmann, G.J., 'Kriegsoperationen des rechten Flügels der englisch-portugiesischen Armee von der Mitte des Monats März bis Ende Mai 1811, und die Schlacht von Albuera am 16ten Mai 1811', *Hannoversches Militairisches Journal*, Zweites Heft [2nd issue] (Hannover, 1831), pp. 91–126, at 107–15. Translation courtesy of Oliver Schmidt.

right wing. This was confirmed quickly by the fact that the greatest part of this cavalry which had advanced from the forest, moved up the river, as if they were looking for places to cross the watercourse in masses. At the same time, the fire of the skirmishers on the right wing constantly increased, even though the movements could not yet be observed. But shortly afterwards, several densely packed enemy columns appeared on the heights between the forest and the river Albuera. They advanced straight on to the line of hills in front of the Allied right wing, and by pressing against it obliquely, showed the intention to overwhelm and the sweep up the position from this side. Therefore, the cavalry brigade, which up to now had observed the enemy between the town and that range of hills, moved completely towards the right wing, and as it, due to the great superiority of the enemy cavalry, did not want to expose itself, it took a position drawn back obliquely to the left.

At the same time, the 2nd Division was ordered to face right and march off to meet the enemy on the heavily threatened right wing. The brigade of its own right wing had already, as mentioned before, advanced towards Albuera and therefore had a way which was a bit shorter, or it might perhaps have received the order for this movement a bit earlier, as Marshal Beresford was just near to it, anyway, it was far ahead of the other two brigades. Four guns of the division marched at its head in order to reach the right flank as quickly as possible, the other two followed the brigade.

Meanwhile the columns of the enemy had crossed the river Albuera and ascended the area in front of the line of hills, over which the Spanish light infantry slowly retreated.

Just in this moment of the combat, one of the aforementioned rain showers started, and darkened the air to such a degree that one could see hardly a few hundred paces ahead. The four guns of the 2nd Division had reached the extreme slope of the hill and fired on the advancing enemy columns. Under this protection, the first brigade of the 2nd Division began to deploy in line, and advanced in battalions, as soon as they were formed, towards the enemy.

The latter had already come very close to the highest point of the range of hills with his columns, and taking advantage of the darkness of the air, a Polish lancer regiment (*le premier régiment de la Vistule*) and some hussars had passed on behind the columns and swarmed onto the flank and rear of the 3rd infantry regiment (the Buffs), which formed the right wing. In this way, they also attacked the other regiments. The former [the 3rd] was thrown into disorder, as it did not have time to form a square. A disordered flight took place between the guns and the artillerymen could limber up only the guns at the left. Drivers and horses were wounded and killed in great number, and the commander of the battery (Captain Cleeves) and two subaltern officers fell wounded into enemy captivity. Through the presence of mind of some NCOs and artillerymen, 3 guns were immediately rescued, the other fell for the moment into enemy hands. The lancers and hussars swarmed in such a manner through the midst of the troops that the Marshal and his suite came into great danger, and he and some of his entourage even got entangled in fighting with them.

In the meantime the middle brigade [Hoghton's] of the 2nd Division had formed and advanced in line with determined steps; the brigade of the other wing [Abercromby's] followed *en echelon* on the left side. A 9-pounder battery (Major Hawker) was taken ahead and followed this line at the right. The 4th Division, which was only two brigades, an English and a Portuguese, strong (because the one of the right wing had to remain before Badajoz), was also ordered to the right wing and soon after advanced in line, until it had reached a position of the same height with the 2nd Division, but below the slope of the hills. The Portuguese division, Hamilton, moved into the space between Albuera and the 2nd Division, keeping its artillery with it. The Portuguese 9-pounder battery was placed to the right of the bridge on the height, in order to defend it, a 6-pounder battery left of the town. A weak brigade of Portuguese cavalry observed the river below Albuera.

During the time, the enemy had constantly continued to advance in three big masses, and thus had missed the right moment to deploy in line, as he could not perceive our orders and movements behind the hills. [Hartmann footnote: The author has seen only three big masses, supported by a reserve following it. Others, also eye witnesses, claim there were more. It is possible. However, at such occasions, it is advisable to stick to one's own perception. Be it as it shall be! These masses could not be deployed.] Therefore, his strong columns were now taken from three sides, and all efforts to advance further or only to deploy in line, failed through the fierce and near musketry of the English infantry. After the English brigade of the 4th Division had then executed a wheeling towards the deep left flank of the columns, it continued to advance irresistibly, protected by the fire of the 9-pounder battery (Major Hawker), and the enemy was forced, after a most pertinacious and bloody combat, to draw back his thinned masses behind the river Albuera.

During this attack, the enemy cavalry had undertaken several attempts to unsettle the Portuguese brigade of the 4th Division, which had stayed in line. This would have enabled them to renew their

139

attacks against the right wing of the English infantry on the horizontal ground on top. But the steadiness of this brigade (under the English brigadier Harvey), the crossing fire of three [sic, even though in the following footnote he names but two] artillery batteries [Hartmann footnote: The English 9-pounder battery of the horse artillery and the 6-pounder battery of captain Sympher of the English-German Legion.] and the position of the English cavalry foiled all their efforts to achieve this purpose, and so in the end they saw themselves forced to make, together with their retreating infantry, a retreat over the river Albuera.

The combat on the Allied right wing, in front of and near the town, in the meantime had not been less violent. The enemy repeatedly undertook determined attacks on the bridge, which however remained without success, until the troops received an order to cover the retreat towards Valverde. The commanding general had given this order in a moment, where the result of the fight for the plain on the hills might have seemed doubtful to him. Major General von Alten as well as the commander of the Portuguese artillery, Colonel Dickson, received this order, in consequence of which the town and the bridge were evacuated and immediately occupied by the enemy. Soon after the retaking was urgently ordered, in which the braveness of the troops succeeded with great sacrifice and much spilling of blood. However, the bridge could not be retaken completely.

A fierce cannonade, under the cover of which the enemy retreated with the greatest part of his forces into the forest and also brought the lightly wounded there, ended the battle, which had lasted only three or four hours.

The loss on both sides was immense and due to lack of means of transport, the heavily wounded had to lie on the battlefield under the open sky during the following nights. The village of Albuera did not offer any shelter except the church, since the village itself had been previously burned. The wounded of the Allies were partly brought with cavalry horses to Valverde on 18th, after the complete retreat of the enemy. Of the enemy wounded which had been left on the battlefield, those who were still alive were brought on 18th into the church of Albuera. It is said these were close to 800 men. When the enemy retreated, he left a part of the prisoners and wounded of the Allies back in the forest. The loss of the English-Portuguese army was given as 4,500 men dead, wounded and missing, the loss of the Spanish, who had remained in the second line during the most fierce part of the battle, as 1,500 men. The loss of the French army is assessed at 9,000 men, which doesn't seem to be too high an estimate, if one considers the murderous effect of the cannon and musketry fire in such close distances, as they took place between the fighting troops during the decisive part of the battle.

Of the three guns which were lost in the beginning, the enemy had only been able to carry off one howitzer, the limber of which still had its horse team. Two cannons were retaken during the attack of the 2nd Brigade of the 2nd Division.

After the end of the battle, the Spanish took the position of the English troops, and these united their ranks, which had become very thin, below the range of hills, on the right wing. Both armies, during the 17th of May, remained in their opposing positions, which they had taken after the combat.

## 4. Cleeves Letter

*Captain Andrew Cleeves was the commander of the 2nd artillery company of the King's German Legion that accompanied Stewart's division in its advance and was also overrun by French cavalry. Four days after the battle, he composed a written explanation of the loss of one of his guns.*[64]

To Major Hartmann
Camp near Albuera
May 20, 1811

Sir,

According to your request, to explain the loss of the howitzer in the battle of the 16th instant, I have the honour to state as follows:

The enemy began the battle with a pretty heavy cannonade on our left, which the battery of artillery under my command opposed. The action getting warm on our centre and right, the first brigade of General Stewart's division (Colonel Colborne's) was ordered to the scene of action with four guns of my battery, to the right of the head of the column, and the remaining two following the rear. Getting near the enemy, I formed line, and came to action on the top of the hill, about 80 or 90 yards distance from the enemy's column (which I imagine was just going to deploy) to cover the formation of our infantry, which formed in the rear of my guns, making the hill nearly the centre of this front.

The left of our line discharged a volley of musketry and charged the enemy, but were repulsed; the right did the same and would have been successful, had not, in this critical moment, our soldiers descried

---

64    Reprinted in Beamish, North Ludlow, *History of the King's German Legion* (reprint London, 1993), pp. 385–6. This officer's name is given as 'Cleves' in the Army List for 1811.

the enemy's cavalry, which tried, *ventre à terre*, to turn out right flank, and our line gave way.

I had then no other chance left to cover our soldiers and save the guns (the men ran through our intervals, which prevented our limbering up) but to stand firm, and to fight our ground. We prevented the cavalry from breaking our centre; but finding no opposition on our right, they turned us, and cut and piked the gunners of the right division down. The left division limbered up, and both guns would have been saved; but the shaft horses of the right gun were wounded, and came down, and the leading driver of the left gun got shot from his horse. Corporal Henry Fincke had presence of mind enough to quit his horse, to replace the driver, and then gallop boldly through the enemy's cavalry; his own horse, which ran alongside of him, secured him from the enemy's cuts and saved the gun, which I immediately made join the fight again. At this moment I was made prisoner, but had the good luck to escape unhurt.

Two guns were nearly immediately retaken; but the howitzer was carried off. Lieutenant Blumenbach was taken and wounded with the left division; Lieutenant Thiele and myself were taken with the right; the former badly wounded by the Polish lancers.

I have the honour to remain, sir,

Andrew Cleeves,

Captain, King's German artillery

## 5. Unger Narrative

*Second Lieutenant William Unger of the King's German Legion artillery drew up a sketch map of the battle on 24 May. The current location of the sketch is unknown, but a printed map based on the sketch was published in 1885 and is reproduced in this volume (see Illustrations).*[65] *The map provides some unique details of the ground close to the village and is the only source that shows KGL light infantry posted on the French side of the Albuera River.*

Azeuchal May 24th, 1811

When the 4th Division, and the Spanish corps under Don Carlos D'España, on the said morning at about 9 o'clock, arrived near Albuera, the French (who were advancing on the road leading to Santa Marta and Solana) had already attacked the village and bridge of Albuera. A brigade of horse artillery, supported by cavalry and light infantry,

---

65    Unger, William, 'Description of the Plan of the Battle of La Albuera, Fought by the Allied Forces against the French, on the 16th May, 1811', *Journal of the Royal Artillery*, Vol. XIII (1885), pp. 126–7.

was drawn up about 600 yards in front of the bridge, and opened up on the troops defending the bridge and village. The light 6-Pr. [pounder] brigade, German Artillery, of the 2nd Division, was posted on the right of Albuera with a few cavalry; the light division, G.L. [German Legion], in the village, having at both bridges some riflemen a little in front.

The 2nd Division of infantry and General Hamilton's division were drawn up in line. On the heights above Albuera the Spanish corps of General Blake on the right.

As the Brigade [of] 9-Prs. [pounders] was placed on the commanding spot within 700 yards of the place, and the French marched down a body direct to the village, I presume a grand attack was expected on those heights; but at the same time their largest forces marched to their left on the roads pointed out in the plan; part of their cavalry crossed the small rivers a little above the bridge, moving up the valley.

Many of our troops were immediately ordered to march to the right; heavy rain came on, which prevented us for some time to perceive the disposition of the enemy. Our cavalry and some Spanish troops were still skirmishing with the French advanced guards, till a brigade of the 2nd Division arrived on the right. Major General Cole, commanding the 4th Division, deployed on the right of the Spaniards but had their right thrown back. Colonel Colborne being ahead of the column of the 2nd Division, advanced with the brigade, and four guns G.A. [German artillery], formed across the hill within 90 or 100 yards of the enemy.

The French had already possession of the favourable heights opposite, where they had placed 2 brigades of artillery. They likewise advanced with their columns, with cavalry on their flanks.

The right brigade of the 2nd Division charged them immediately with the bayonet; when, that very instant, a Polish regiment of cavalry (pikemen) wheeled round, fell in [the] rear of [the] brigade, sabred down many of the infantry and artillerymen, took one howitzer, two guns, and near 700 prisoners; the remainder of the brigade were lying dead and wounded on the spot.

The centre brigade of the 2nd Division then came up with two guns, put a stop to the rapid advance of the French, who charged at the same time with a regiment of cavalry. Brigadier General Harvey's brigade of Portuguese infantry then went off after receiving a volley.

Then the left brigade of the 2nd Division, who was then in line, supported by four 9-Prs., R.A. [Royal Artillery], and the whole of British cavalry, with four guns, R.H.A. [Royal Horse Artillery], on the flank, advanced in line, charged the enemy at different times with the bayonet (particularly the left brigade of the 2nd Division and the Fusiliers of the 4th), drove them from all the ground they had gained,

143

recovered two of the guns the enemy had taken, and threw the enemy's lines in disorder and flight.

The French cavalry, much superior to ours in numbers, retired in good order, covering the retreat of the infantry from being cut up by our cavalry.

The enemy made a stand on the right bank of the river, which was fordable, but was soon dislodged by our light infantry and artillery. They left a rear guard of about 4,000 or 5,000 infantry, with a brigade of artillery and cavalry on the hill between the two rivers, and retired into the wood. 6,000 dead were lying on the field of battle. Our loss in killed is estimated to amount to 5,000, and that of the French 9,000 or 10,000.

A new position then was taken by Marshal Sir William Carr Beresford, marked with light colours on the plan.

On the 17th the enemy moved off their wounded, baggage, stores, etc., and on the 18th, in the morning, the rear guard consisting of almost all the cavalry, followed on the road leading to Solano, pursued by our cavalry and light infantry.

William Unger, lieutenant, German artillery

## 6. Whinyates Letter

*Second Captain Edward Charles Whinyates served with Captain Lefebvre's battery of Horse artillery, which was under the orders of General Lumley. His account of the battle in a letter to a family member confirms that the battery was missing two guns and that one of the remaining four was briefly captured by the French cavalry.[66]*

In Bivouac, near Solano,
20th and 22nd in May, 1811

My Dear Uncle,
The battle which was fought near Albuera on the 16th Inst, was the most sanguinary and awful combat that has been fought in the Peninsula. The actors in the field of Talavera give the pre-eminence in horror to the battle of Albuera. On the 13th of May the cavalry, with our troop of horse artillery, which occupied Villa Franca fell back by Almendralejo to Santa Marta. On the 15th we retired to Albuera, where we were joined by more Portuguese cavalry in Baron Alten's brigade of sharpshooters. Here we learned that the army was marching to occupy a position near the village of Albuera, which stands within 300 yards

---

66    Whinyates, F.T., *Whinyates Family Records* (3 vols., privately printed, 1894), v. 2, pp. 230–3.

of a stream flowing from the direction of Almendralejo and Torre and falling into the Guadiana close to Talavera-Real. This rivulet flows through a valley from 1,200 to 1,600 yards broad, found it on either side by rising ground of inconsiderable altitude and of easy acclivity. There is a stone bridge in Albuera, and close by, one of the many fords which everywhere traverse the streamlet.

Our riflemen were posted in the village and on the banks of the stream, while the cavalry with our four horse artillery guns [Whinyates Footnote: The two guns left in Lisbon had not yet joined.] *appuyed* their left on Albuera and extended in an almost parallel direction to the stream. The first line of infantry were more than a half a mile in rear of us upon the rising ground near the Valverde road. In their rear was an extensive plain, and to the right some high ground sloping gradually to the river and intersected by two transverse valleys or ravines. On these last mentioned heights the battle was fought.

About seven o'clock on the morning of the 16th, massive columns of French infantry and artillery, which had been concealed in a wood on the opposite side of the river, advanced by the Santa Marta Road and made a very sharp attack on the bridge. This attack was a feint; and when it appeared that the attention of the cavalry and our four guns was engaged in the defence of this point, the enemy moved heavy columns to our right with the intention of turning that flank. The heights, which became the chief scene of action, were occupied by some small corps of Spaniards, but when the design of the enemy was fully ascertained our infantry made a counter-defensive movement in that direction. The French soon brought up some heavy guns and formed their troops under cover of some rising ground which was at right angles to our first position into the rivulet upon which Albuera stands. To meet this movement the Spanish infantry was formed on the first of the transverse heights, whilst our cavalry and horse artillery moved into the small plain on their right and thus prolonged the alignment. The French attack now formed on the rising ground in front of these troops.

At this instant, Colonel Colborne's brigade, at the head of the 2nd Division, moved up at a double from the rear, and though having but time to form three of the four regiments yet it instantly passed on to charge the French advance, which was in line, supported by heavy columns. The French line instantly gave way, and the brave but mad handful of men, away from support and running to certain destruction, pushed on, and got on the flank of the columns. At this moment more French troops arrived, and a fire of infantry and artillery, the heaviest and most murderous perhaps that was ever witnessed, commenced.

145

The bugle sounded for Colborne's brigade to retire; they obeyed. Instantly they were charged by the lancemen who, issuing from the body of the columns, galloped in from the playing against their left flank. This was a most awful moment; the fortune of the day seemed lost.

The Fusilier brigade (7th and 23rd), who supported, were almost destroyed; but at last, the regular advance of Cole's division, the steadiness of the Portuguese, and the good countenance of the Walloon Guards turned the victory; the enemy gave way, and were successfully driven from the heights with immense loss. The advance and charge of the 2nd Division against such masses of infantry, and such superiority of numbers, was glorious, but it has been almost the annihilation of some regiments. Soult, however, though beaten, and most decisively so, carried off trophies. Three regiments lost their colours, or more truly, the regiments being extinct the colours remained in the hands of the enemy. We lost, also, one of the German artillery howitzers, the brigade [Whinyates Footnote: Now termed a battery.] having suffered in killed, wounded and prisoners, forty-five men. I am quite well and jolly, and did not get a scratch, although one of my guns was for a moment in the hands of the enemy, and it lost some horses and men.

The next day, the 17th, both armies remained quiet, and at night the French retreated by the Solano road having sent their baggage and many sick by that of Santa Marta. Two French generals are dead, and Soult with others are said to be wounded. The enemy abandoned three hundred sick in Almendralejo. It appears that the strength of the enemy was about 30,000; 22,000 were in the principal attack on the right flank, and 4,000 at the bridge. The accounts of our prisoners, who hourly escape, and those of the French deserters all state the enemy's loss as enormous, and go so far as to say it amounts to 10,000 men. I feel convinced it must be 7,000 or 8,000, if not more. The French yielded the field to us in great confusion; and, had we not suffered in the vital part of our forces – had the Spaniards been a manoeuvring army – the French would have been annihilated. I just learned our infantry are coming up. We shall march in five minutes. I write in great confusion, and if I have not puzzled you it is not my fault.

Very affectionately yours,
E.C. Whinyates

# I. Portuguese Accounts

## 1. Loureiro Letter

*José Jorge Loureiro served as an aide to General Archibald Campbell, commander of a brigade composed of the 4th and 10th Portuguese Line regiments. His letter to his father describing the battle was probably preserved because later in life he served as the prime minister of Portugal.[67]*

Badajoz, 20 May

My Dear Father,

My last letter, dated the 17th of this month, from the battlefield of Albuera, assured you that I am alive. But then, my haste, the circumstances, work and fatigue allowed me just enough time to tell you that I had survived and that the battle had gone in our favour; now that I have time and none of the those obstacles are in my way, I will give you a brief description of the battle, as I saw it.

There has never been a more glorious day for the three nations as 16 May, nor has there been a worst day for humanity on the peninsula as that day. Humanity suffered the most terrible massacre imaginable between two small armies for the glory of our cause.

We all thought we would retreat to another place, closer to the Guadiana, and that we would wait there for another English division that was marching to join us; but the opposite occurred, and on 15th we marched to Albuera.

Although the French had already arrived, we were still able to take possession of the village. Our armies were separated from each other by a small creek. Our position could be surrounded on all sides; our camp wasn't fortified at all, for the creek could be crossed at many places and cavalry could manoeuvre freely everywhere. But we had to position ourselves in between that place and Badajoz, and there was no better position.

At around 7 o'clock, the firing started on the whole of the right flank, for the French wanted to destroy it. At that point the English division moved to the rear of the Spaniards to support them. As it turned out, my brigade and another English one made up the left flank, to defend the village of Laura.

At around 2 o'clock, the French broke through the Spanish line. It was then that the English brigade attacked with bayonets in support of the Spaniards, causing the French to flee immediately. The English

---

67    *Revista Militar*, Vol. 55 (1903), pp. 364–6. Translation courtesy of Simone Meiseles.

advanced more than they should have and were unable to thwart a regiment of cavalry lancers who were attacking them, and nearly the whole brigade was killed or taken prisoner. The other brigades, however, pursued the enemy as they were fleeing, slaughtering them mercilessly.

While all this was happening on the right flank, the left did not rest. The French attacked the village as well, which as I said, we defended. My regiment advanced in support of the rifleman and suffered terribly heavy cannon fire and so many bullets and bombs flew right by me but I consider myself very fortunate to have escaped with my life; for a while I felt like I was the target. Finally, around 5 o'clock it was almost all over for the right flank; the French were soundly and shamefully defeated.

The English soldiers, most of them have been through many battles, said they've never witnessed a massacre such as this one before.

I went to the battlefield to see for myself, and it was an awful, unsettling sight. There were dead everywhere, so many that the horses could barely find trails to pick their way around them.

Finally, on the 17th, both armies were in the same spot as they were before the battle started, and on the 18th, the French fled on the high road to Seville.

Affectionate greetings to all, your humble and loving son,

J.J. Loureiro

## 2. Correia de Mello Narrative

*Major José Correia de Mello of the 11th Portuguese Line kept a journal of his services which includes an entry for Albuera.*[68]

When dawn came we were only one league away from the city of Badajoz, because of the time wasted from having lost our road and from having to bring along our artillery. General Cole ordered his division to speed up the march along the road through Albuera to Seville, and I was ordered to go with two companies to lead the artillery. This assignment brought me to the vicinity of the enemy and less than three leagues from Badajoz we began to hear the roar of very violent firing. The general was ordered to form his division as a reserve on the height to the right of the line, and a Spanish brigade was with us.

---

68   Quoted in Chaby, Claudio de, *Excerptos Historicos e Collecção de Documentos Relativos a Guerra Denominada da Peninsula – Parte Terceira: Guerra da Peninsular* (Lisbon, 1863), Pt. 3, pp. 396–7. Translation courtesy of Joao Centeno and Antonio Millan.

Combat was raging when our General Cole was ordered to deploy the brigade in line forming a square on the right with the 1st Battalion of the 11th Line, the one that I commanded, and we began to march forward with all the regularity and appearance of a veteran troop, which caused the two thousand enemy cavalrymen and some battalions of enemy grenadiers in the vicinity to keep a respectful distance. Our right flank was protected by some English cavalry and artillery. I saw an aide-de-camp approach the square to inquire about its circumstances. . . . In accordance with the circumstances of the action, we continued to advance on the enemy, who, finally, hesitant and discouraged, retreated, still suffering the effects of a well-aimed volley fired when the cavalry attacked the left brigade, which inflicted a lot of loss.

In my view, two things decided the action: first, the calm manner in which my brigade resisted the enemy cavalry, and second, the fire discipline of the soldiers who showed the greatest firmness even after discharging their muskets.

We finally took the height of Albuera, making the enemy retreat in disorder across the small river below; and then we took up the positions we are now occupying.

It is quite natural for the French to boast of having won, in spite of losing the battlefield and ten thousand men, because they captured eight hundred of our men and three flags, as well as a howitzer. They lost five generals, of which one was killed.

General Blake and other Spaniards distinguished themselves greatly and set the best example for their troops.

### 3. Peacocke Memoir

*Thomas Peacocke was an English officer who fought at Albuera as a captain in the 23rd Portuguese Line, which was part of General Harvey's brigade of the 4th Division. The National Army Museum, London, has a microfilm copy of his manuscript memoirs.[69]*

In the night we received orders to march in the direction of Albuera and join the division assembling at that point, to oppose the *corps d'armée* under Marshal Soult (Duke of Dalmatia) which had advanced from Seville and was destined to raise the siege of Badajoz. We marched all night and reached our ground between 8 and 9 o'clock the following morning.

---

69     NAM, 27 September 1982.

16th of May 1811 – Battle of Albuera. The particulars of this glorious and hard-fought action have been fully detailed in the *London Gazette*. . . . Marshal Beresford had been left in command of the camp before Badajoz, and charged with the operations of the siege; his instructions from Lord Willington gave him an option to fight a battle if he thought proper but with such injunctions to <u>hazard nothing</u> that one knows not whether most to admire the nerve which determined him to meet the ablest of Napoleon's generals, or the ability he displayed in his dispositions for the contest. The quartermaster general of the Portuguese army, Sir Benjamin D'Urban, had a principal share in these arrangements; he acted as chief of the staff to the Allied forces, under the Marshal's orders, and by his splendid talents, essentially contributed to the success of this arduous day; his rapid *coup d'oeil* embracing the local features of the ground, secured every advantage as the opportunity arose, and his services on this occasion will long be remembered by those who witnessed the brilliant display of them during one of the severest conflicts fought in the Peninsula. Marshal Soult is said to have declared that the morale of the *corps d'armée* under his command received a wound in the bloodstained field of Albuera from which it never afterwards had been able to recover!

Our brigade major having fallen early in the action, the brigadier general requested me to take his place during the remainder of it, which gave me an opportunity of seeing more of the battle than I could have done at the head of my infantry in the line. The night was cold and rainy; we slept in the field for which we had so obstinately contended, surrounded by the dead and dying, and the following morning exhibited a scene of human suffering such as I shall not easily forget. The lofty Soult, foiled in the avowed object of his advance from Seville, was compelled to retrace his steps with the crippled remnants of his corps and retire before the victorious columns of the Anglo-Portuguese army. Marshal Beresford harassed his retreat and followed him as far as circumstances allowed when he resumed his operation against Badajoz.

## 4. Harvey Narrative

*Brigadier General William Harvey, commander of the Portuguese Brigade attached to the 4th Division, wrote up some details of the battle the day after the event, but these are known only through an excerpt quoted by William Napier in one of the pamphlets he wrote in his extended pamphlet war with Marshal Beresford.[70]*

---

70    Napier, William, *Letter to General Lord Viscount Beresford* (London, 1934) p. 31.

The 23rd [Portuguese Line] and one battalion of the 7th Fusiliers were in line. The other battalion at quarter distance, forming square at every halt to cover the right, which the cavalry continued to menace. Major General Lumley, with the British cavalry, was also in column of half squadrons in rear of our right and moved with us, being too weak to advance against the enemy's cavalry.

## J. Miscellaneous Accounts

### 1. Stanhope Narrative

*James Stanhope was not present at Albuera, but he merits inclusion in this volume because his journal entry for 17 March 1812 provides a very early primary source for a relatively famous quote about Soult's view of English soldiers that appears in many secondary sources without attribution.[71] The authenticity of the quote is enhanced by the fact that Stanhope gives the quote in (somewhat fractured) French, but it is still unclear how the words attributed to Soult would have become known to Stanhope.*

March 17, 1812 . . . rode with General D'Urban over the ground of Albuera; he being the Q.M.G. to Beresford of course defends him for his movements on that day and his testimony is a valuable one as he is one of the most sensible men in the army and equally loved & esteemed by all who have the happiness of his acquaintance.

The pros & cons of this action are about as follows. He [Beresford] was obliged to fight, some say he is reproached with having placed the Spaniards in the most exposed spot, but of course the French would have attacked them had they been anywhere else. Blake was so slow in executing every movement that they were hardly in line in time. Then he ought (they say) to have entrenched himself, or not have fought. Now what struck me on passing the ground was that adopting a hill behind the village as the spot for a reserve with the line *appui* [in support] on the village & the right entrenched, it would have been much stronger & had the Marshal instead of showing his line on the crest of the hill, kept most of it in masses behind it so as to have been able to move to any spot, the French could not have selected the Spaniards; for we lost our men in retaking what they lost, not from want of courage, but of conduct. But in answer to this it is said that

---

71    Stanhope, James, *Eyewitness to the Peninsular War and the Battle of Waterloo: The Letters and Journals of Lieutenant Colonel The Honourable James Hamilton Stanhope 1803 to 1825, Recording His Service with Sir John Moore, Sir Thomas Graham and the Duke of Wellington* (Glover, Gareth (ed.)) (Barnsley, 2010), p. 73.

the Spaniards were immovable & if put in a mass would never have been deployed.

It is impossible not to admire the able conduct of General Lumley who could keep his cavalry from being defeated, so outnumbered as they were.

The French left 2,200 dead on the hill. Soult said, '*Ces bastardes Anglais ne savant pas quand ils sont battus.*' ['These English bastards don't know when they are beaten.'][72]

## 2. Fitzroy Somerset Letter

*Fitzroy Somerset was Military Secretary to the Duke of Wellington. His thoughts on the battle and Beresford's generalship expressed in a letter dated 23 May undoubtedly reflect the views held by the Duke and his staff at that time.*[73]

Elvas May 23d 1811

My Dear Brother,

You will hear by the time you receive this of the very severe action which was fought on the 16th at Albuera by Beresford's corps and the Spanish troops under Castaños and Blake. It appears that Soult collected all the force that was disposable in the vicinity of Seville & marched on the 10th to that place with the intention of raising the siege of Badajoz. His force has not been accurately stated but I should conceive from all accounts that it amounted to at least 25,000 men, & a large force of cavalry. Albuera is on the high road from Seville to Badajoz, & the high ground behind it covers the roads leading to the latter place & to Valverde, Olivenza, etc. Beresford took up this position on the night of the 15th but did not actually occupy the important points until the moment of the advance of the enemy to the attack. For the account of the action itself, I must refer you to the dispatch of the Marshal, from which I fear you will not be able clearly to understand how the affair really stood. You will be glad however to learn that the Spaniards

---

72    A longer, more polished version of this quotation is found in many books and articles, including *The United Service Magazine* (1842), Part 1, p. 150: 'Marshal Soult is stated to have observed, "There is no beating these troops, in spite of their Generals; I always thought them bad soldiers, but now I am sure of it; for I turned their right, and penetrated their centre: they were completely beaten; the day was mine, and yet they did not know it, and would not run."'

73    Fitzroy Somerset to the Duke of Beaufort (his brother), 23 May 1811, Badminton Archives, England.

behaved with the greatest bravery though they wanted the *mobilité* of disciplined troops. However, it is a great point to get them to fight.

Beresford does not appear to have managed the battle with much skill or I think our own loss would not have been so severe, but the superiority of the British troops was never more clearly evinced, for although they fell in ranks entire, still they were not to be repulsed and at length succeeded in driving the French back. Besides the dreadful loss we have sustained, which exceeds 4,000 British, there are other circumstances attending this victory which will be looked upon with an evil eye by the British public. At the moment that Colborne's brigade consisting of the Buffs, 2nd Batt. 48th, 66th and 31st regts were charging the French infantry they were attacked in the rear by the Polish cavalry, who literally swept the three first regts away, & carried with them the colours of the 48th and 66th. This may not signify, but we are too apt to regard an eagle as a trophy, to expect that Bonaparte will pass lightly over this misfortune and I should fear the ill-minded people at home would join in the cry against these unfortunate regiments which are literally destroyed with the exception of a few men, who were saved by a gallant and successful charge of the 4th Dragoons commanded by [Lieutenant] Col. Leighton. We also lost a howitzer. Sir William Myers and Col Duckworth are much regretted, as they were most promising officers.

### 3. Charles Stewart Letter

*In 1811, Charles Stewart, who later changed his name to Charles Vane and received the title of Lord Londonderry, was Wellington's adjutant general and had accompanied his general to meet with Beresford after the battle. The letter he wrote to his older half-brother, Robert Stewart (Lord Castlereagh), on 22 May is an important source for many points relating to Beresford's behaviour during the day since Stewart would have been present during discussions between the Marshal and Wellington.[74] The sketch map mentioned in the letter could not be located.*

Headquarters, Elvas May 22nd 1811

. . . When we came to Elvas more accurate particulars were known and soon after Colonel Arbuthnot arrived from the Marshal's headquarters at Albuera with the details. In endeavouring to give you particulars, you must make allowance for my receiving them from many channels,

---

[74]     Stewart to Ct., 22 May 1811, Durham Records Office, Letters of Lord Londonderry, D/ LO/C 18/62.

and not having been an eyewitness and having had the sole advantage of traversing the bloody field and seeing the ground where this hard-fought contest happened. The gallantry of our troops never underwent so severe a trial. The loss of British, which exceeds for the numbers engaged anything that was ever heard of, was suffered while maintaining or rather securing ground without a retrograde step having been made by British troops. Indeed, we are hardly permitted to exult in the victory and the most [indecipherable word] ambition had rather it should not have been fought than won at the expense of such a mass of <u>invaluable</u> men.

The village of Albuera is situated on the road from Badajoz to Seville. [There are] some undulating heights on this side of it and two small streams that run parallel with them afford in this part of the country the best position that an army can take up having for its object the covering of an advance from Seville towards Badajoz. Marshal Beresford having determined on occupying this ground moved his army there on the 14th and 15th but the enemy arrived at the place nearly as soon as him and Beresford's cavalry, which had been sent forward to Almendralejo to reconnoitre, were driven back in haste, Soult pushing on with rapidity his superior squadrons. He had moved from Seville on the 10th and by forced marches of at least six leagues a day, bivouacked his army in a large wood on the further side of the Albuera stream which Beresford actually intended to take up with his people on the night of the 15th but was thus precluded.

I am conscious in anything I even confidentially say to you how easy it is to find fault or discover errors and how difficult it is in managing such a machine as an army, that everything should be done as it ought. Therefore, with this caution, I shall not hesitate to give you my fair opinion as the position and the accounts I have received strike me. Beresford on the evening of the 15th seems not to have attempted to take up the ground in the manner which might have rendered it very formidable. But like a Spanish army and officers, as the high road leads from Albuera to Badajoz, he places his army across it as if this alone could stop the foe. From this period to the commencement of the action his right seems to have been placed where his left should have been and by the continued struggle to secure high ground on the right which the enemy early availed themselves of, all our calamitous loss was sustained whereas if the right hills had been strongly occupied, which (more especially as it was our line of communication with Valverde, the only way we had to retreat) became doubly necessary, the victory might have been gained with a very slight comparative loss. In fact, the right was the key of the position, and this does not seem to have been perceived until the enemy were actually in possession of it.

As [indecipherable word] crisis [indecipherable word], you may well imagine that the fate of the army hung up on a thread after repeated efforts had failed to recover the high ground and the carnage of British had been immense, for if that flank had been destroyed and turned, there was no chance of retreat – the whole British force either *hors de combat* or so diminished a brigade could scarce be produced, the Portuguese and Spaniards must have yielded to the general dismay that must have been the result. Providence, however, for the sake of mankind decreed it otherwise and the advantages which human foresight has not enabled Beresford to avail himself out in the first instance seem to have been reserved to be realised by the inextinguishable, unexampled and (I may say) incomprehensible valour of British soldiers.

The Spaniards under Blake, in number about 12,000, occupied the right in good order of battle, Stewart's division of infantry the centre and the Portuguese under Hamilton the left, Cole's division being in reserve. The British effective firelocks in the field, exclusive of General Kemmis's brigade which did not arrive from Badajoz in time to be an action, could not exceed 7,500 firelocks. The Portuguese amounted to 10 or 11,000 men. In the range of height before alluded to there were three principal ones and a fourth on the right rather advanced. Neither this nor the one on the left next to it were occupied. The whole range however forms a glacis to the rivulet or stream and towards the rear there is likewise an undulating slope which certainly offers excellent ground to conceal the movement of troops behind, so that had the strong hillocks been occupied by batteries and some slight defences thrown up in the night, the columns might have been moveable under their protection to any part of the position but no measures of precaution or previous preparation seem to have been adopted.

The Spaniards were formed in two lines between the two hills on the left. The right of Stewart's division was on the left height immediately above the village of Albuera. This commands not only the village but the bridge over the rivulet over which the high road to Seville leads. Still more to the left of the village and on this side of it is high strong ground bounded by the stream which here gets larger and deeper so that the most obvious point of attack clearly appears to be the height. The enemy advancing with all their cavalry at nine in the morning and supported by two large columns of infantry moved towards the bridge and threatened the left of the position but, under cover of the cavalry and favoured by thick weather, they rapidly changed their attack to our right and soon possessed themselves the most projecting Heights and the one adjoining which became now the great object of contest. The Spaniards had been driven back, but it seems to be agreed they retrograded without precipitation or disorder.

But as Beresford found them unwieldy and difficult if not impossible to manoeuvre, he passed Stewart's division through the Spaniards to the right and my gallant friend William Stewart deploying his first brigade in line from column moved up the hill against the column to the enemy. The Buffs, 66th, 48th (2nd Battalion) and 31st formed this brigade under Lieutenant Colonel Colborne. Their advance was fine and their fire well directed but before they could arrive near enough to charge, the enemy's cavalry broke in round their right. A wing of the Buffs was endeavoured to be thrown back, but this regiment in the disorder it occasioned fell back on the next brigade of the division under Hoghton while it was advancing in column to deploy and threw it into momentary disorder. The greatest part of the first brigade under Colborne was now either mowed down by the enemy's grape and fire from the heights or cut up by the cavalry and lance men. The Buffs were nearly destroyed. The 66th and 48th the same and the 31st suffered severely, though from being on the left less than the others.

General Hoghton's brigade now came on and he gallantly fell, cheering them to the charge having three balls pierce his body. The 57th, 48th (1st Battalion) and 29th formed this brigade. The 57th under Inglis performed miracles and Way with the 29th was equally conspicuous. Both are wounded but doing well (the latter will not lose his arm). Notwithstanding, however, all the gallantry of these troops and of the third brigade of the division, consisting of the 28th, 34th and 39th under Colonel Abercromby, the enemy maintained their post and we at this period had lost a brigade of guns and eight stand of colours of the Buffs, 66th, 48th and 57th regiments.

General Cole's division now came in for their glory. The Marshal seeing where the danger accumulated had first moved Cole to form *en potence* on the right but now ordered him down to carry this formidable height. The Fusilier brigade headed by Sir William Myers, although they lost their gallant leader and out of 1,100 men left 700 killed and wounded on the field, ultimately forced the enemy to abandon his hold and aided by Colonel Abercromby's brigade, and the Portuguese brigade under Colonel Harvey who repelled the renewed attacks of the enemy cavalry, they re-took all the guns but one howitzer and three out of the eight stands of colours were regained. General Cole was wounded slightly and most of his staff. My friend William Stewart had two slight contusions, but did not leave the field.

When the enemy once gave way on the height, they withdrew in tolerable order across the rivulet and took up for the night the ground they had advanced from. While their main effort was going on the right, they also attempted carrying the village and the left but the Portuguese troops and General Alten's brigade of light troops which lined the walls of the village prevented their making any impression. They kept some cavalry on this side which was observed by the 13th Light Dragoons and the Portuguese brigade under Colonel Otway.

The large force of the enemy's cavalry, however, in addition to what made havoc in our infantry, kept hovering around the right, and our heavy brigade under General Lumley was judiciously moved always as they moved to oppose them and thus kept in check a force which, if it had been permitted, would have penetrated round into the rear of our troops and might have proved most fatal. Our artillery was well served and I believed heretofore it was impossible for men to exert themselves as the British soldiers did on this memorable day.

It is in vain for me, not having had the good fortune to have been present, to attempt detailing all the instances of heroism and good conduct I hear of, but the 57th and 31st were very conspicuous, the former on ascending the hill stood their ground against a column of Grenadiers. However, the enemy's fire thinned their ranks, these regiments never broke, and at the conclusion of the action the dead and wounded were in two distinct lines where they had nobly stood their ground. The 31st (which we must [?] feel most deeply involved in) fought with perfect order, deployed, charged, and resisted cavalry, and gave every proof of perfect infantry. It is asserted [?] immediately after the action that in a very small space there were of friends and foe 7,000 bodies of killed and wounded on the ground and laying so thick that the artillery in advancing at the close of the action was obliged to pass over them deaf to their cries and turning their eyes from the brave fellows that were laid thus prostrate in the dust.

Beresford exposed himself at the point of contest considerably. In some instances, he drew the Spanish officers from the ranks and made them lead on their men. He was charged by a Polish pikeman whom he grappled by the neck and threw him out of his saddle, whence he was bayonetted by the infantry. A lieutenant of the Polish heroes upset and discomfited the whole Portuguese staff. He charged one, knocked another down with the butt of his pike, overset a third and in short the deputy quartermaster, who had neither the nerve nor the force of the Marshal, had great difficulty in dispatching him. They swear he bit the ground and was a very devil. . . .

157

You have now a long but not, I hope, altogether uninteresting detail account but it is not written by a spectator. [indecipherable word] [indecipherable word] I refer you to those more accurate and better accounts that will be received in England. By this opportunity, I should only add that I see a great deal before us and it depends on the support we have from home and the policy that guides the councils whether we shall ultimately succeed or fail in the great effort we are making.

The enemy's loss is said to be three generals killed (Werlé, Pépin and some others) and three wounded. It is added Soult had a contusion. 7,000 are estimated as killed and wounded. The prisoners state having so many generals *hors de combat* they were at a loss relative to orders, there being no one to give or receive them in the divisions or brigades. They also declare that if their columns had deployed they would have beat us and I believe there is some reason in this assertion.

I enclose a rough sketch from Dashwood only drawn from a slight view of the ground but it may give a general idea however inaccurate it may be.

I annex now a copy of the return of killed and wounded.

God bless you. Ever your most devoted br.

Charles Stewart

[P.S.] As I have no time to write at length to my dear father, pray send him this. It may amuse him.

## 4. Beresford Letter to Stewart

*Given the comments made in the preceding letter from Stewart to Castlereagh, it is intriguing to discover that Beresford considered Charles Stewart to be a good friend to him.*[75]

Almendralejo May 25, 1811

My Dear Stewart,

When I saw you at Albuera I had a great deal to say to you but you know how we were interrupted and had not an opportunity of again renewing our conversation. I was then not very well and in spite of the good fortune I had had, was very much out of spirits from the conviction of having acted unwisely in risking so immensely as would have been the consequence of misfortune. However, Lord Wellington's usual kindness and assurances have a little tranquilised

---

75    Beresford to Stewart, 25 May 1811, Durham Records Office, Letters of Lord Londonderry, D/ LO/C 18/63.

me on that head and I have only ever to regret our great loss, which also at that time much weighed upon my mind. I hope, however, as the result has been as much as I looked to, the retreat of the enemy and the abandonment on his part of Badajoz, that in England the risk I run not being known and as the consequences will be considerable, that there the loss will be considered without much ill-natured comment.

I expect shortly to see you and will then fully explain everything to you and my reasons for, whilst my desire was against risking a battle, which if unfortunate on our part I saw plainly would overturn everything that Lord Wellington had, by his great talents and enterprise and patience joined, been so long in acquiring. However, I will leave this subject till we meet, and to you I will not conceal anything on this subject as I know I can communicate all my reasons in confidence and in that friendship which I am so desirous of maintaining with you. . . .

In the meantime, believe me most sincerely

Beresford

## 5. Legend for Battlefield Panorama

*The watercolour panorama of the battlefield reproduced in the Illustrations section of this book was apparently painted by a British participant while events were still fresh in his mind.[76] The panorama shows the battlefield from the perspective of an observer near the village and features manuscript annotations added by the artist to explain the scenes depicted that add some fascinating details of the action.*

1. Alphabetical Manuscript Annotations
    A. Hill of Santa Marta
    B. Wood of Albuera from whence the French made their attack
    C. River Albuera – it runs down the ??? from all that black line of wood at the foot of the hills to the right hand ???
    D. French Infantry
    E. Col. Colbourn's [*sic*] brigade attacked by the Polish pikemen
    F. Gl. Horton's [*sic*]
    G. Genl. Cole's Reserve
    H. Spanish Infantry
    I. French Cavalry
    J. Count Penne-Villemur's Spanish cavalry, they charged at this moment, not very effectually not regularly altho they behaved

---

76   The panorama is in the Anne S.K. Brown Military Collection, Brown University, Providence, RI, USA. A high-resolution copy of the panorama can be viewed at
     https://repository.library.brown.edu/studio/item/bdr:249588/.

well, but in retiring to reform, Gen. Houghton's brigade mistaking their irregular uniforms for the French, poured in two vollies and killed a large proportion

L. English cavalry

M. Two squadrons of the 4th D[ragoo]ns which charged

N. Spanish cavalry

O. English guns

P. Baron Alton's [sic] division of the G. Legion

2. Other Manuscript Annotations
 – You will observe that the French cavalry by outflanking us wanted to get into the Valverde road and cut off our retreat to the Guadiana. See Dispatch.
 – A heavy shower of rain drifting from this quarter
 – Long stream [?] of prisoners, wounded, baggage, mule carts, led horses, etc. going to the rear and cutting towards the Valverde road
 – Wounded carried on men's backs, or in their arms, prisoners. B. Alton's [sic] men dressed like the Rifle Corps, French prisoners were in blue or grey.

## 6. British Casualty Report

Return of killed, wounded, and missing, of the corps of the army under the command of Lieutenant General Viscount Wellington, KB, under the immediate orders of Marshal Sir William Carr Beresford, KB, in the battle with the French army commanded by Marshal Soult, at Albuera, on the 16th of May, 1811.[77]

General Staff – 1 killed; 7 wounded.

Royal British Artillery – 3 rank and file, 9 horses killed; 1 captain, 10 rank and file, 10 horses wounded; 1 rank and file, 1 horse missing.

Royal German Artillery – 24 horses killed; 1 lieutenant, 16 rank and file, wounded; 1 trumpeter, 29 rank and file, 10 horses missing.

3rd Dragoon Guards – 1 lieutenant, 9 rank and file, 9 horses, killed; 9 rank and file, 6 horses wounded; 1 rank and file, 4 horses missing.

4th Dragoons – 1 sergeant, 2 rank and file, 11 horses, killed; 1 captain, 1 lieutenant, 1 staff, 1 sergeant, 1 trumpeter, 15 rank and file, 10 horses, wounded; 2 captains, 2 rank and file, 2 horses missing.

13th Light Dragoons – 1 horse killed; 1 rank and file wounded.

1st Battalion, 3d Foot, or Buffs – 1 captain, 1 lieutenant, 2 ensigns, 4 sergeants, 208 rank and file, killed; 4 captains, 9 lieutenants, 1 ensign,

---

77    *London Gazette Extraordinary*, 3 June 1811.

11 sergeants, 1 drummer, 222 rank and file, wounded; 2 lieutenants, 15 sergeants, 1 drummer, 161 rank and file missing.

1st Battalion, 7th Royal Fusiliers – 2 sergeants, 63 rank and file, killed; 1 lieutenant colonel, 3 captains, 11 lieutenants, 14 sergeants, 263 rank and file, wounded

2nd Battalion, 7th Fusiliers – 1 captain, 1 lieutenant, 1 sergeant, 46 rank and file, killed; 1 major, 3 captains, 9 lieutenants, 1 staff, 16 sergeants, 1 drummer, 269 rank and file, wounded.

1st Battalion, 23d Royal Welsh Fusiliers, 1 captain, 1 ensign, 1 sergeant, 73 rank and file killed; 1 lieutenant colonel, 2 captains, 4 lieutenants, 3 ensigns, 1 staff, 12 sergeants, 1 drummer, 232 rank and file, wounded; 1 sergeant, 5 rank and file missing.

3rd Battalion, 27th Foot – 3 rank and file, killed; 5 rank and file wounded.

2nd Battalion, 28th Foot – 1 drummer, 26 rank and file, killed; 2 captains, 3 lieutenants, 1 ensign, 8 Sergeants, 123 rank and file, wounded.

29th Foot – 1 captain, 1 lieutenant, 3 ensigns, 2 Sergeants, 73 rank and file, killed; 1 lieutenant colonel, 1 major, 3 captains, 4 lieutenants, 3 ensigns, 1 staff, 12 sergeants, 220 rank and file, wounded; 11 rank and file, missing.

2nd Battalion, 31st Foot – 2 sergeants, 1 drummer, 26 rank and file, killed; 2 captains, 2 lieutenants, 2 ensigns, 4 sergeants, 115 rank and file, wounded.

2nd Battalion, 34th Foot – 1 captain, 1 lieutenant, 1 ensign, 3 sergeants, 27 rank and file, killed; 2 captains, 2 lieutenants, 6 sergeants, 85 rank and file, wounded.

2nd Battalion, 39th Foot – 1 lieutenant, 14 rank and file, killed; 1 captain, 2 lieutenants, 1 ensign, 4 sergeants, 72 rank and file, wounded; 2 rank and file, missing.

1st Battalion, 40th Foot – 3 rank and file killed; 8 rank and file, wounded.

1st Battalion, 48th Foot – 1 lieutenant-colonel, 2 lieutenants, 6 Sergeants, 58 rank and file, killed; 5 captains, 7 lieutenants, 1 ensign, 1 staff, 9 sergeants, 1 drummer, 183 rank and file, wounded; 6 rank and file, missing.

2nd Battalion, 48th Foot – 3 lieutenants, 1 ensign, 4 sergeants, 40 rank and file, killed; 4 captains, 4 lieutenants, 2 ensigns, 3 sergeants, 1 drummer, 82 rank and file wounded; 1 major, 2 captains, 5 lieutenants, 1 ensign, 8 sergeants, 7 drummers, 175 rank and file, missing.

1st Battalion, 57th Foot – 1 major, 1 captain, 3 Sergeants, 1 drummer, 83 rank and file, killed; 1 lieutenant colonel, 1 major, 6 captains, 11 lieutenants, 2 ensigns, 11 sergeants, 3 drummers, 304 rank and file, wounded.

5th Battalion, 60th Foot – 1 sergeant, 1 rank and file, killed: 1 lieutenant, 2 Sergeants, 16 rank and file, wounded.

2nd Battalion, 66th Foot – 1 captain, 1 lieutenant, 1 ensign, 1 sergeant, l drummer, 50 rank and file, killed; 1 captain, 8 lieutenants, 3 ensigns, 13 sergeants, 91 rank and file, wounded; 4 sergeants, 1 drummer, 96 rank and file, missing.

97th Foot – 1 rank and file wounded.

1st Light Battalion, King's German Legion – 4 rank and file, killed; 1 major, 1 captain, 1 lieutenant, 1 ensign, 1 staff, 3 sergeants, 55 rank and file, wounded; 2 rank and file, missing.

2d Light Battalion, King's German Legion – l Lieutenant, 3 rank and file, killed; 1 captain, 3 sergeants, 28 rank and file, wounded; 1 rank and file, missing.

Total British loss – 1 general staff, 1 lieutenant colonel, 1 major, 7 captains, 13 lieutenants, 9 ensigns, 31 sergeants, 4 drummers, 815 rank and file, 54 horses, killed; 7 general staff, 4 lieutenant colonels, 4 majors, 43 captains, 81 lieutenants, 20 ensigns, 6 staff, 132 sergeants, 9 drummers, 2,426 rank and file, 26 horses, wounded; 1 major, 4 captains, 8 lieutenants, 1 ensign, 28 Sergeants, 10 drummers, 492 rank and file, 17 horses, missing.

Total Portuguese loss – 1 general staff, 1 staff, 2 sergeants, 98 rank and file, 9 horses, killed; 1 general staff, 1 lieutenant colonel, 1 major, 5 captains, 5 lieutenants, 2 ensigns, 1 staff, 14 Sergeants, 1 drummer, 230 rank and file, 9 horses, wounded; 1 drummer, 25 rank and file, missing.

General total – 2 general staff, 1 lieutenant colonel, 1 major, 7 captains, 13 lieutenants, 9 ensigns, 1 staff, 33 sergeants, 4 drummers, 913 rank and file, 63 horses, killed; 8 general staff, 5 lieutenant colonels, 5 majors, 48 captains, 86 lieutenants, 22 ensigns, 7 staff, 146 sergeants, 10 drummers, 2,656 rank and file, 35 horses, wounded; 1 major, 4 captains, 1 lieutenant, 1 ensign, 28 sergeants, 11 drummers, 517 rank and file, 17 horses, missing.

(Signed) CHARLES STEWART, Major General and Adjutant General.

# PART III
# SPANISH ACCOUNTS

## 1. Castaños's Dispatch

*Spanish Captain General Francisco Xavier Castaños was the senior Spanish commander in Extremadura, but he commanded the smallest force in terms of numbers. His generous decision to cede direction of the Allied army to Marshal Beresford is recounted in a dispatch he wrote to the president of the Junta of Extremadura, which also emphasises the admirable cooperation between all the Allied troops on 16 May.[1]*

Field of battle
La Albuera
19th of May 1811

Most Excellent Sir,
Great battles which by their consequences become memorable, cannot be described so as to represent faithfully, all the glorious days that have been achieved, and to render justice to the gallant soldiers. The mountains and plains of La Albuera, have become the theatre of honour, by one of the most bloody battles fought since the commencement of the war; they will be remembered with admiration by posterity, as in the short space of seven hours, being covered with the bodies of more than 8,000 warriors, killed and wounded on both sides, from whose blood luxuriant laurels will spring, to crown with glory the Anglo-Portuguese and Spanish arms.

It is not an easy task, nor does it become me to give you all the details of a battle so gloriously contested, as it may be important in its

---

1    The dispatch was published in Cadiz in the *Gaceta Extraordinaria de la Regencia* on 24 May 1811. An English translation was published in several English newspapers in June. All translations of texts originally in Spanish are by Mark S. Thompson. For additional publications by Mr Thompson on Albuera and other similar subjects, see https://marksthompson.weebly.com/my-publications.html.

results – perhaps some of its most promised advantages are already felt, and before the arrival of this dispatch, it will not be a matter of surprise if Cadiz should reap the first fruit of this memorable victory, some particulars of which I am now about to detail to your Excellency. I wrote to your Excellency on the 26 April last, that the Guadiana having overflowed its banks, the bridge which had been constructed in front of Jerumenha, had been carried away, and thereby the communication between this part of Extremadura and Portugal cut off, and consequently preventing my intended interview with Lord Wellington at Elvas.

Under these circumstances, his Lordship addressed me by letter, in which he communicated his ideas upon the plan of operation to be pursued in Extremadura, all of which were consistent with my own, except in one respect, which related to me personally. His Lordship recommended as a principle to govern in all cases where the Allied armies were united that the chief command should be exercised by the general highest in military rank and seniority; this principle of course would have put me in charge, but I considered that I ought not to accept the command, and proposed what I deemed more proper, which was that the general who brought the largest force into the field should command in chief, the others to be considered as auxiliaries. This proposition was accepted, as Your Excellency can see from the attached copies of my letter to Lord Wellington and his response to me.

I immediately sent a copy of Lord Wellington's letter to General Blake, who agreed with my proposition and with the plans of military operations, the consequence of which was that command was given to the illustrious and distinguished Marshal Beresford, and the result of the glorious battle of La Albuera proves how much he merited this position.

On the first intelligence of Marshal Soult's march upon Extremadura, General Blake ordered his troops to unite with the Allied army. This movement was made with such exactness with the plan agreed upon, that the very minutes would appear to have been calculated, for all the forces were concentrated by 11 o'clock on the night before to the battle, without Marshal Soult having the slightest intimation of it, but expected when he made the attack, that he would be opposed by only a part of the Allied army. What is even more remarkable is that the junction was effected on the heights of La Albuera, the very position marked out by Lord Wellington to give battle.

Here were united on the 16th the generals, officers and soldiers of three nations, among which prevailed the utmost harmony and sentiment, and union of action; with no other rivalry than the honourable desire of excelling in glorious deeds of arms. All were gratified, and each alike shared in the triumph of this glorious day, and no one has occasion to borrow the laurels of another.

Marshal Soult, with an army somewhat inferior to ours in infantry, but greatly superior in cavalry and artillery, did not delay a moment his intended attack. He commenced it by marching against our position near La Albuera, which was the centre of our line, but this was soon discovered to be a feint, and that his object was to gain our right flank, where the Spanish troops were posted, attacking it most impetuously with the greater part of his force, and by extending his flanks several times, he endeavoured to gain our rear; but our second line, and the corps of reserve, judiciously posted, repaired instantly to our assistance while the battle became more bloody and obstinate. The enemy became furious, repeated his attacks, constantly sending fresh troops; but he was always steadily opposed, and for seven hours every man stood his ground, notwithstanding the intrepidity and impetuosity of his Polish cavalry, and the formidable fire of his numerous and heavy artillery, from which there was a continual thunder during the whole engagement. At length at 2:30 p.m. the enemy was compelled to give way on all sides, bravely fighting as he retreated; he was charged and pursued to the woods and heights, in which he took post at night, leaving the field of battle strewed [sic] with dead bodies, and an immense number of wounded. The rain which fell heavily during the battle, caused rivers of blood to flow down the sides of the heights, and presented a most horrid spectacle of war.

The loss of the enemy, according to a moderate estimate which has since been confirmed by deserters, fell little short of 7,000 killed, wounded and prisoners; among the killed is General Werlé, who fell in the field, and General Pépin, who died of his wounds last night; Generals Gazan, Brix [sic] [Brayer?] and another were wounded. Our loss has been considerable, though less than that of the enemy.

General Blake always at the head of his troops, in the midst of danger, was hit by a musket ball which grazed his left arm, without doing him the least injury, and thus his valuable life is preserved for his country; he set a noble example to the officers under him, who strove to imitate his coolness and intrepidity, by pressing into the foremost ranks during the whole action.

Although I was an eyewitness to the glorious deeds performed in that obstinate battle I cannot particularise, where all the generals, officers and soldiers, conducted themselves with the most heroic bravery and coolness. The good order, exactness, and speed of their manoeuvres, which were performed with a silence seldom observed

165

on such occasions, have been the admiration of all. The generals commanding divisions, without waiting for the main bodies, led their advance into battle, everyone repaired to his post with alacrity and defended it with valour.

Soult, without even getting sight of Badajoz, was obliged to retreat before daylight, by Villalba and Almendralejo, leaving in the woods, where he had encamped, a great number who had died of their wounds during the night, and 200 that were so badly wounded that they could not be removed, and sent, as a great number of his other wounded had been to the neighbouring towns. He is pursued and observed by the cavalry and advance under General Lardizábal and some battalions of English light troops.

These are the circumstances which I have considered it my duty to communicate to Your Excellency, relative to the battle of La Albuera, the excellent dispositions of which were directed by Marshal Beresford, united with General Blake, and crowned with a glorious victory, which promises results of the highest important. God preserve, etc. etc.

## 2. Burriel's Account
*A full set of official Spanish after-action reports for General Joaquín Blake's 4th Army Expeditionary Corps was assembled and published shortly after the battle by Adjutant General Antonio Burriel, acting as Blake's chief of staff.*[2] *The longest narrative was apparently drafted by Burriel himself.*

Account of the Battle of Albuera
Won over the French commanded by Soult on the 16th of May 1811, by the allied Spanish, English and Portuguese army.

Badajoz was the only town in Extremadura where there were French at the beginning of May 1811. This fortress was left to its own defence, and already under siege by the Allied army, when the expeditionary force (made up of troops from the Fourth Army), entered the province, under the command of Lieutenant General Joaquín Blake, a member of the Regency Council, who had disembarked on the 18th of the previous month in the district of Niebla, and had crossed the mountains avoiding the French army at Seville, which had advanced a division into Guillena and Gerena. The roughness of the terrain prevented the bringing up of artillery.

On the 10th, the headquarters was situated in Monasterio on the royal road, with the division of Lieutenant General Francisco Ballesteros,

---

2     Burriel, Antonio, *Batalla de la Albuhera* (Cadiz, 1811). Translations courtesy of Mark Thompson.

which was part of this force. The other divisions were occupying Fregenal, Xerez de los Caballeros and Burguillos, with the greater part of the cavalry in Fuente de Cantos, and some in Montemolín, having left the remainder in Fregenal.

The enemy had regrouped in Seville, leaving Gerena and Guillena. On the 7th and 8th, the cavalry patrols from Monasterio advanced to within two leagues of Seville along the causeway. The road from Llerena to Seville via Cazalla was occupied by some enemy troops.

In the meantime the Allied army commenced the siege of Badajoz, on the 4th they attacked the fort [invested the south side of the Guadiana], and on the 8th, entrenchment began.

The infantry of the Fifth Army was also involved in the siege with the exception of a small force that had other duties, and the cavalry led by the Count de Penne occupied Llerena.

On the same day, the 10th, the commander-in-chief in Monasterio heard news that Soult had left Seville that morning with all the forces that he had been able to gather. The news was confirmed in the afternoon, and the troops that were near Cazalla with Latour-Maubourg also moved in consequence, forcing the Count de Penne to leave Llerena.

Immediately, the General ordered the troops that were stationed at Monasterio to withdraw to Xerez and Burguillos, and for the cavalry to retreat along the royal road.

In the following days all of the infantry changed their positions and moved slowly from Fregenal, Xerez and Burguillos to Salvaleón, Salvatierra and Barcarrota. The cavalry maintained its position on the royal road within sight of the enemy.

Marshal Beresford and Captain General Francisco Xavier Castaños moved on the 13th to Valverde de Leganes, where on the next day the commander-in-chief of the expeditionary force [Blake] joined them and the three generals conferred together.

Having received information that the enemy was continuing its march and was near to Santa Marta, all the troops of the combined army set out on the morning of the 15th to meet up at Albuera, in accordance with the plan agreed among the generals.

The infantry divisions which were stationed in Salvatierra, Salvaleón and Barcarrota met up in the afternoon at the headquarters in Almendral; from that point the three columns followed the same road to Albuera, marching with speed and with all imaginable order.

The French, who that morning were in Santa Marta, advanced a force of five hundred cavalry and six hundred infantry along the Almendral road in order to discover the position of the troops which they may have known or supposed to be somewhere nearby. They reached Nogales and went as far as Torre del Almendral, a village a quarter of a league away from Almendral. The [Spanish] horse grenadiers were posted in front of it with the first battalion of Volontarios de Cataluña (from the Fifth Army) under the command of the Colonel of grenadiers, José Rich, and both gallantly repulsed the reconnaissance, which the enemy did not succeed in completing, nor did it inform them of our strength, position or movement. The columns continued their march undisturbed without the necessity for other troops to take part in the action.

The army of Marshal Beresford marched the same day to Albuera, having suspended work on the siege of Badajoz, and having withdrawn the artillery, except for a brigade of infantry that was stationed to the right of the Guadiana river.

The Spanish cavalry with the English and the Portuguese continued on the same day, the 15th, their retreat from Santa Marta to Albuera, followed by the enemy, which remained half a league away from the position.

The expeditionary force met up with the army led by Marshal Beresford that night. At dawn an English division was due to arrive commanded by General Cole and another from the Fifth Army under Brigadier General Carlos España, with six artillery pieces from the same, as soon as they were able to put this into effect.

Soult, who had led his army on the 10th to Ronquillo from Seville, marched forth with his army to Monasterio on the 11th, no doubt with the intention of allowing no time for the troops there to withdraw. He then marched in the direction of Llerena and gathered together the corps, which, on the orders of Latour-Maubourg, had come there via Cazalla.

His successive movements up to the 14th gave an indication that at times he was thinking of taking the road through Almendralejo and Merida. His cavalry met ours on the royal road before Fuente de Cantos, from there it went on to Villafranca and Villalba, leaving that road. As mentioned above, on the 14th he directed all his troops to Santa Marta, where his advance guard entered on the morning of the 15th. The remaining divisions arrived during the course of the day. Soult had joined the fifth corps of the army, which had been commanded by Mortier until a short time before, with all that he could get from the first corps led by Victor, with the garrisons of the kingdoms of Cordoba and Jaen, and with the fourth corps under the command of Sebastiani; which, along with other troops, consisted of four squadrons of Polish lancers (first regiment) and four from the 20th and 21st French dragoons. The extraordinary diversity with which deserters and informers talked concerning the strength, stems from the fact that it was founded from several nationalities and came together in an instant: but through information received after the battle, it became known that there were from twenty-five to thirty thousand men, including four to five thousand cavalry, with thirty to thirty-six artillery pieces, some of them twelve-pound guns.

The small town of Albuera, of which only the walls remained, is situated on the royal road from Seville to Badajoz, four leagues away from this place, three away from Olivenza, two away from Valverde de Leganes, nine from Merida, five from La Solana and three from Santa Marta, another town on the royal road. By the side of the town runs the stream of the Albuera, over which is a new bridge thirty yards further up than the town, which is part of the causeway; another bridge stands down parallel to it which is old and in poor repair. This river is formed by the meeting of the Nogales river and the Chicapierna stream, which takes place some forty yards further up than the new bridge. The Chicapierna stream and the Nogales river are not obstacles to progress. Cavalry and infantry can cross at most points, however there is sometimes the need for the artillery to go to certain places to cross.

The terrain on both banks is level and open with a gentle slope towards the river and the stream. On the right bank there is a holm oak forest through the middle of which the royal road to Santa Marta passes, without coming out into the open until a short distance before the river. This wood is closer to the river at the southern end and this is from where the enemy launched its main attack. On the left bank of the Nogales and the Chicapierna stream there is not even the slightest obstacle or tree. The terrain rises steadily and gently to just a gunshot and a half away from the river, at which point the waters of the springs run into the small stream of Valdesevilla which flows at the foot of the slope. All these slightly raised areas of land form a slope which cannot be seen and whose highest point is to the rear of the town on the road to Valverde de Leganes, and that from there it stretches out in a north-south direction. The position, which the Allied army occupied at dawn on the 16th, was in this same north-south direction.

The column of Colonel Rich marched that night from Torre del Almendral, and at dawn they joined the army. The cavalry of Brigadier Loy, moved during the night in order to protect the column.

The divisions, which, on reaching those fields during the night, had remained in two lines fairly close to the river, aligned themselves with part of the English advance guard or light troops, by order of the English Quarter-Master-General, regrouped at dawn in the new position.

The troops of the expeditionary force were to the right in two lines; the first was composed of Mariscal de Campo José de Lardizábal's division holding the right, in which were stationed to the rear, two battalions in closed ranks [columns] separated from the troops in front. To the left of these troops was the division of Lieutenant General Francisco Ballesteros, which reached to the Valverde road. The division of Mariscal de Campo José de Zayas was placed in the second line and was two hundred paces or a little more from the first line.

The cavalry of the expeditionary force occupied the ground to the right of the infantry in two lines. It was under the command of Brigadier General Casimiro Loy and the second line was led by Lieutenant Colonel José Marrón; and under the orders of the Count de Penne-Villemur and the second line was under the command of the Lieutenant Colonel Antolin Reguilon. The cavalry faced the two small hills, which were the extremity of the slope in that area, from which the right flank of the infantry was a long gunshot away. The bloodiest scene of the battle was on these two low hills, as will be seen later.

The infantry took this position stretching out horizontally behind the line of battle and carrying out this movement with the usual banners and guides with the greatest precision. The highest part of the slope hid the troops from the view of the enemy from the wood and the Santa Marta road.

The army of Marshal Beresford, made up of English and Portuguese, had its left flank on the Valverde road, and stretched out its right flank perpendicularly to the road in a line forming a continuation of the first Spanish line. The position was occupied by light English troops. The artillery of the English and Portuguese were situated near to Albuera on the road to Valverde.

The English cavalry advanced and was close to the Chicapierna stream, from which position it later withdrew when the enemy crossed the stream on the right flank. The Portuguese cavalry was stationed to the left of the line.

With the Allied army stationed in these positions, Captain General Francisco Xavier Castaños, commander of the Fifth Army, arrived with his headquarters, and an infantry division under the command of Brigadier Carlos España and six pieces of field artillery. At the same time the English division under the command of General Cole arrived. A battalion of España's brigade was stationed to the right of General Zayas, with the Spanish artillery, the rest were situated on the left.

After the sun had come out, some enemy cavalry was discovered to be in the wood near the royal road. Then, for a long time nothing happened, so there was doubt as to whether the enemy army would approach. Some infantry was then discovered, and it was soon realised that the enemy was coming in force, hiding itself in the woods.

A column of four hundred horse and four or five infantry battalions with six artillery pieces followed the royal road. These battalions and the cavalry deployed almost in front of the new bridge over the Albuera, and the artillery started a bombardment. More troops were then to be seen coming out of the holm oak forest, although their direction could not be determined for certain, and they increased the artillery fire.

In the meantime, the artillery of the Allied army had advanced up to the bridge in order to reply to the enemy's manoeuvres and the first line marched forward to occupy the crests of the hills, showing itself to the enemy forces.

These [the French] continued to appear to be attacking the centre, and they continued their artillery fire. Some English artillery pieces advanced a little on our right with two battalions of General Lardizábal's division, because, as the enemy forces were moving to their left, they were posing a threat on that side.

It was after half past eight in the morning when the general in chief received several warnings that the enemy was attacking its forces on the right of the Allied army. These warnings increased, coming from officers of the general staff, which were accurate when saying that the enemy was advancing.

Therefore, the troops received orders to march towards the French [advancing] on the right. Two battalions of Spanish guards, the Irlanda regiment and the Voluntarios de Navarra (belonging to the Fifth Army) moved from the second line to the front line in order to cover the right flank. The two Spanish [Guards] battalions spread in a hammer shape and rested their left flank on the right side of the line. The other two battalions formed a column in the rear. The six pieces of artillery of the Fifth Army were placed with these battalions.

All the battalions, under the command of General Zayas and the commander of the brigade, Brigadier Juan de la Cruz Mourgeón, marched in this way towards the front in order to occupy the right side of the hills where all the Allied army was situated.

The English troops, which, with two battalions from the division of General Lardizábal, had gone ahead when the action started and had arrived at the stream, passed through the new front when the general position was changed, together with the skirmishers and were placed to the right of the cavalry where they remained almost until the end.

171

The rest of General Lardizábal's division also marched forward in order to get to the same place. Two battalions from Ballesteros's division also marched in support of General Zayas, another two stayed in place, facing the brook of the Albuera, and later the rest of the division with their general followed the movements towards the right, with the other troops.

The other two battalions, from Zayas's division which was part of the second line in the first position, changed the front line and took position in the second line, in the new position under the command of the Brigadier Ramón Polo; commander of this section [brigade]. The battalions led by General España, which were situated on the left, moved in the same direction and finished this manoeuvre by moving to the first line on the right of the battalions under the command of General Zayas. The first battalion of Walloon Guards marched towards the bridge to reinforce the battalions and the English infantry that were there, and to support the artillery.

The English and Portuguese cavalry kept their advanced position close to the Chicapierna stream in front of the infantry. The enemy infantry advanced strongly so the Allies had to retreat on the right of the line. The division led by the Count de Penne advanced to support this movement. At the same time the division [of cavalry] led by Brigadier Loy moved forward on their right, threatening the left side of the enemy artillery and holding infantry there in order to keep the enemy back. All the cavalry was then under the command of the English General Lumley, who moved to the right of the new position of the infantry.

When the troops that marched on the right reached the top of the hill, they discovered the enemy. A terrible fire of artillery then took place.

The French, who resisted the attack at the front with some troops and cannons, sent the majority of their forces through the woods against the right wing of the Allied army in order to surround them and attack them from behind.

The advantage the enemy sought was, not only to attack through the flank and from behind, but also to cut off the road to the mountains and, if they were lucky, the roads to Valverde and Olivenza. The enemy passed by the Nogales river and the Chicapierna stream; the cavalry occupied the left, the artillery the centre and the columns of infantry the right, on whose flank marched a battalion of skirmishers, covering and protecting the movement.

The enemy, after passing the rivers, had to change the front line to their right, to surround what they thought was the Allied troops. This was, in fact, a new line, ready for battle, thanks to the precise orders [given by the Spanish] and the speed with which the generals and troops executed them.

The skirmishers from the Guards and Irlanda [regiments] came into contact with the French and opened fire on their skirmishers and cavalry, but soon stopped in order to attack them with bayonets, forcing them to retreat to the main body of their army.

Then the French decided to advance their troops. The battalions led by Zayas were immediately ordered to fire on them. General Lardizábal marched in column, deployed his front line in battle in the same alignment and started firing. General Ballesteros made the same manoeuvre on the left, keeping two battalions to the rear and firing at everything in sight. He soon attacked the enemy columns on their right flank, stopping them and forcing them to cease fire.

The fire of artillery and muskets was lethal due to it being close range but the admirable perseverance of the troops put an end to this first attack. Consequently the French suffered serious losses in their first reserves.

Because of the calmness and accuracy with which the battalions marched and fought under the orders of their generals, who corrected them with the flags and guides at the front; the strength and distinguished valour with which they resisted and forced the French retreat and their discipline and good manoeuvres, created great hope of success on this day.

The order and steadiness could be felt everywhere and the commander-in-chief's orders were understood and carried out with the precision and the speed of a practised exercise.

When the battle started, the English troops were already moving. General Stewart, with some of his battalions, occupied the right side of the battalions under the command of General Zayas and crossed the line through open spaces. Other English battalions fell in between the second line. The English artillery moved into the new line and directed its fire at the main attacking force and the streams.

Portuguese troops remained in reserve and the firing continued in the area around the village and along the stream. Once the French had recovered from this first attack, they tried to attack again, encouraged by the arrival of new troops sent to help and by the continuous fire of their large artillery. This artillery was always very close, so the battalions in the second line [also] suffered great losses.

Suddenly, it started to rain heavily and westerly winds blew causing many problems with respect to the hardest parts of the combat, but regardless of this the battle continued with vigour. The right of the infantry, which was formed by some English battalions and led by

General Stewart, was attacked by four squadrons of lancers. The musket fire and a charge from the second line of the cavalry (from the Fifth Army) led by Lieutenant Colonel Antolin Reguilon and from the squadrons from the front line, led by Count de Penne, with two English squadrons on its right, however repelled and disordered the enemy's cavalry and infantry. This incident did not affect the rest of the line, which remained with all possible steadiness and so was the case for the second line. All this put the steadiness of the troops to the test.

Thirty or forty Polish lancers from the cavalry that had just attacked, tried to gain access from the right between the first and the second lines. Many of them were successful in their attempt. Others arrived later and were fired on as they moved from one part to another, then some English battalions of the second line, believing that the first line was completely destroyed, opened fire on both. This [fire] was in the direction of where the commander-in-chief of the expeditionary forces was; but the fire stopped immediately: some soldiers on the first line opened fire, in their rear on the lancers, killed some and took prisoner the commanding officer. Everything took place in a few moments but this brief and critical event influenced neither the steadiness of the troops nor their ability to fire at the enemy, who renewed the attack but this time more forcefully.

General Stewart was shot twice and Brigadier Carlos España was injured by a lance but neither retreated. General Cole was much more seriously injured.

Meanwhile, the enemy artillery that was situated close to the stream kept firing continuously at the cavalry. The Allied army did not cease firing either.

They approached the enemy and musket fire broke across his line; they brought some skirmishers and Polish lancers against our line. The enemy hoped to gain some success from this unexpected manoeuvre.

The Allied army did not lose its inexplicable courage and kept the ground that it had won. Here the struggle was very bloody. For two hours or more, both armies fought blindly in order to achieve the victory. As soon as the enemy was defeated, they attacked again after their reserves which were positioned behind them, on the top of the hill, joined them.

The cavalry on the right, formed on the plain, and supported by the English and Portuguese infantry, manoeuvred in front of the enemy and thereby imposed caution. The division of the Fifth Army had already defeated the squadrons that attacked General Stewart's division and with two English squadrons were under the enemy's fire and suffered calmly whilst covering the infantry flank.

174

Another battalion of General Zayas's division moved from the second line to the vicinity of the village and the banks of the river in order to relieve the ones that had gone there before to support the artillery. The skirmishers and the English corps fired at anyone who tried to attack. The skirmishers of the regiment of Campo Mayor also followed upstream.

It was still raining and also windy and the smoke bothered the soldiers. However, there was no doubt about their victory because of their fire and strength. They marched under the orders and followed the example of their generals against the advancing French. They fired at close range and forced them to retreat leaving the ground covered with dead bodies and injured soldiers, so much that it seemed that they were crossing a line of men at rest.

The [French] infantry, confused and disordered, took refuge with their powerful reserve. The artillery covered the stream while the cavalry retreated and crossed it, followed by the Allied troops.

At the moment of the victory, in this final period of the action, the first line of this second position was formed by the brigade led by General Stewart, the regiments of Rey, Zamora and the light infantry of Voluntarios de Navarra, a company of sappers and a detachment of the company of guides which belonged to the Fifth Army; the Irlanda regiment, the second and fourth battalions of Spanish Guards with General Zayas; the Murcia and Canarias regiments and the second battalion, Leon [regiment] with General Lardizábal and an English battalion of infantry. On General Ballesteros's left, there was the light battalion of Voluntarios de Barbastro; the first battalion of Voluntarios de Cataluña (belonging to the Fifth Army) and the Pravia regiment and on the left of all this, two English battalions and the artillery that was placed in the line.

Some soldiers from the battalion of Voluntarios de Campo Mayor were still positioned near the stream. Soldiers in skirmish formation marched towards the bridge with the Ciudad Rodrigo regiment, while some English light infantry and some pieces of artillery provided support from the immediate vicinity of the village.

The second line was formed by the Imperiales de Toledo regiment, the Voluntarios de Patria, the Legion Extrangera, and another battalion of the Walloon Guards belonging to General Zayas's division, which had originally been stationed by the bridge in front of the Ciudad Rodrigo regiment. Battalions of the Infiesto and Cangas de Tineo regiments were in line formation in echelon immediately in the rear of the first line formed by the Irlanda regiment and the Spanish Guards;

175

the Castropol and Lena regiments were in the first line of the original position, facing the stream.

The cavalry was on the right of the lines and on its left an English and Portuguese division was ready to engage on the command of General Cole.

Five Portuguese squadrons were stationed beyond the village on the left of the original position, where they stood the whole day observing and threatening the enemy squadrons formed in front of the village; and four other English ones defended the stream in front of the position that was occupied at dawn by Spanish troops.

When the enemy retreated, the troops advanced towards the Chicapierna stream; the cavalry passed over charging the enemy, which because of its numbers and skilful manoeuvres, was able to make an orderly withdrawal, covering its infantry and artillery. The Allied cavalry arrived at the stream and the Spanish carried out manoeuvres around the French left in order to force them to withdraw. Some pieces of artillery situated near the stream fired on the enemy reserve and its cavalry, and another piece maintained the fire against the skirmishers, and supported by some advanced corps, maintained the fire against the French who were trying to reform.

The troops in the second line advanced towards the stream; a Portuguese division took the right of this position.

The fire from cannons and infantry continued until after three in the afternoon when the rain was at its worst.

Protected by their cavalry and artillery, the enemy attempted to re-group at the edge of the woods behind the streams.

The Allied army formed two lines occupying the original position on the hill that they had taken in the morning, but also further on the right where the struggle had been more intense.

The enemy quickly removed the injured soldiers who had walked back or had been carried away from the battlefield during the struggle, taking advantage of the time given by those who had not been injured: for this reason they held the same position; but they were forced to leave two hundred wounded in their bivouac when the rest of their infantry and artillery retreated on the morning of the 18th. The cavalry covered the retreat, which since daybreak had placed itself in front of Albuera, at the edge of the wood on the road to La Corte de Peleas and La Solana.

Then the cavalry also moved threatening the enemy. The Brigadier Count de Penne passed the streams with his division and placed himself on the left flank after having marched as if to attack them, thus forcing them to change their position. Brigadier Loy's division

176

supported this manoeuvre and the English and Portuguese marched to support them, standing on the left.

The losses of enemy troops was considerable, as the fire they suffered in the different attacks was from very close quarters, as it had never happened before. According to prisoners' and deserters' reports there were more than seven thousand dead and injured men. Some of these reports exaggerated losses to a great extent. General Werlé died on the battlefield. General Pépin died during the night, Brigadier Maransin was seriously injured and died the following day, General Gazan, chief of staff of the French army, and General Brayer were wounded, together with huge loses of men of all ranks. The losses suffered by the Allied army were also considerable, but smaller in comparison to the enemy.

The cavalry followed the French, maintaining fire against their supporting skirmishers and capturing some prisoners. The division commanded by General Lardizábal followed and took position in the wood by the road to Santa Marta, where they were bivouacked until the morning of the 19th.

Two English light battalions advanced to contact the cavalry and the same day the divisions of the expeditionary forces and of the infantry of the Fifth Army advanced towards the villages on the west side of the Royal Road, on the enemy's flank.

In the two previous days, the troops suffered great difficulties in the bivouacs because the continuous rain had produced plenty of mud, it felt like November instead of May.

There was no wood, but their happiness was increased by their victory and some provisions which their constant sobriety saw as sufficient; these made them ignore the difficulties. The soldiers from the three nations congratulated each other everywhere sharing drinks and making clear in all the possible ways the security of their trust.

Antonio Burriel
Adjutant General

## 3. Lardizábal's Account

*From Burriel's published compilation of reports.*

Your Excellency: At seven o'clock on the morning of the 16th, the enemy appeared at the edge of the woods in front of the Albuera where the Royal Road leads to Badajoz. The enemy had three squadrons of cavalry and around three thousand infantry with three pieces of artillery on their right, indicating that the attack would be to our left. Following this movement we prepared ourselves to receive it, my vanguard

177

division occupied the right of the line, followed by the third division led by Lieutenant General Francisco Ballesteros. At the same time, a column and several skirmishers who were crossing the little stream that divided the two armies, turned up on our right flank. Carrying out your orders they positioned themselves for battle over the crest of the hill, and under the orders of Field Marshal José de Zayas, the second and fourth battalions of Spanish Guards, with the Irlanda regiment from my division moved to the right.

Finally, as the enemy appeared in several columns revealing little clarity concerning their strategic plans, I formed the battalions into columns with the front on the right in order to avoid being flanked and enable quick access to all areas. At this very moment the heavy enemy artillery fire and the advance of three columns with their respective reserves, eight hundred Polish lancers and the dragoons that covered their left, left no doubt of the real attack.

The division started the battle quickly with two Spanish pieces of artillery on the right, which were stationed on the guards battalions' left. This movement was followed by the third division. The heaviest fire of artillery and muskets was started here in both lines. Both sides and centre were attacked at once with the greatest of courage; they [the French] were repelled for a while and had to stop firing. The enemy were reinforced and again returned to the fray with bravery, and despite the hail of bullets, one of the most difficult operations was carried out in this battle. The English troops came to replace us, in order for us to resupply with cartridges and to give some rest to our soldiers, as we had been more than two hours suffering the most lethal fire. A change in the two lines was carried out with the silence and order of a holy service. They sustained the fire for half an hour with their characteristic perseverance and bravery, and we, passing through their empty spaces, occupied the front line at the moment when the enemy gave their third charge with all the possible strength, desperately, making the final effort to break our line through the centre.

When I realised their strategy, I chose to meet them with the always brave regiments of Murcia, Canarias and Leon, led with the greatest courage by their very honourable leaders and with the third division on their left, we charged at each other with the firm mutual intention of destroying one another. The death of General Werlé, who led the enemy column, the taking of the Polish standard by the Murcia regiment and the huge number of losses that they suffered in the assault, all combined to cause their immediate flight. Keeping within reach of them I followed them with the same three regiments and a small English battalion that was on my left. However, I had to halt because all the enemy cavalry was on my right and they could easily surround us. The battalion of Campo Mayor and the skirmishers of the division, under the command of the Lieutenant Colonel Lorenzo Calvo, guarded part of the English artillery as Your Excellency ordered, and fought the whole day with their well-known perseverance and courage.

I think, Your Excellency, that I do not risk anything when I state that never before has infantry fought so close to the enemy, with so much enthusiasm, for such a long time and with so much strength and tenacity. It would be an offence to single out anyone as solely responsible, commanders, officers and soldiers achieved the victory and all in general were covered by the most lasting glory.

## 4. Account of Ballesteros
*From Burriel's published compilation of reports.*

In answer to your official letter in which you asked me what actions the division under my command carried out in the battle of Albuera on 16th of this month, I must say to Your Excellency that my division was stationed resting on a parallel line to the stream having their left side on the road to Valverde and the right in the vanguard. The enemy columns were already in movement and the attack was declared on the right, the regiments of Cangas and Infiesto moved to support the part of the fourth division that occupied the attacked point. The first battalion of Cataluña and the regiments of Barbastro and Pravia with the vanguard passed to form on the left of this point and the regiments of Castropol and Lena stayed as the reserve in front of the first position.

When the enemy was to the left of our new line, which was held in strength, I attacked the enemy columns with the forces of my division that I had on my left and with some of the vanguard on the right flank stopped their fire. But once these forces had rallied and a new charge was given, it was necessary to withdraw from this position which was occupied again by the first English line, and although this was held with the greatest of courage, the attack was too severe, so I renewed the attack with the same troops with bayonets on the flank at the same place as before and resisted the enemy despite the terrible fire. The English and the Spanish troops that were in that place protected this movement. From this moment onwards, the enemy retired to the stream in a disorderly manner, pursued by the soldiers of the whole line who were supported by the regiment of Castropol who had marched there with this objective. The struggle being over, my division occupied its original position once more including the regiment of Castropol and the skirmishers.

The courage and bravery of all the officers and troops under my command and in particular the troops that followed me in the charges, have fulfilled their duties in such an admirable way that I cannot praise any of them in particular, however, I believe it is my duty to commend the following; commander of the Barbastro regiment, Brigadier Francisco Merino; commander of the first battalion of Cataluña, Colonel Dionisio Vives; Colonels of Infiesto, Càngas, Castropol, and Pravia, Diego Clark, Guillermo Livezay, Pedro Gastelù and Luis Diaz, who has died as a result of his wounds; commander of Lena, Jayme Butler who was wounded; Adjutant General of the General Staff and the second adjutant Felipe Montes and Miguel Aulestia who were injured, the first one slightly hurt and the second one seriously; first and second adjutants of the same corps, Emeterio Velarde and Martin de Párraga, both dead on the battlefield and whose losses have been extremely painful for me because the first one, leaving aside his good qualities, did say in his last moments, 'It is not important if I die, if the victory is ours,' and the second for being an admirable officer. I also commend Captain of engineers, Pedro Aguago and my Aides-de camp on the battlefield, Captains Manuel Guerrero and Rafael Saravia, and with the same rank, Antonio Arron, Manuel Granados, Geronimo Valdés, Juan Millana and Juan Manuel Peon, all these officers lost eleven horses in action.

## 5. Account of Zayas
*From Burriel's published compilation of reports.*

Your Excellency: on the dawn of the 16th, the fourth division under my command was on the field of Albuera deployed in battle and formed in the second line of the vanguard. At seven, the enemy appeared and following the orders given by Your Excellency, the fourth battalion of Spanish Royal Guards was stationed on the right flank of the line; the second battalion carried out the same movement and the regiments of Irlanda and Navarra remained as reserve for both, formed in closed column: the artillery of the Fifth Army under the command of José Miranda stationed in the open space between the two first battalions.

At half past eight, the enemy, who had appeared near the river Albuera, threatening the village, left no doubt about their plans of attacking our right. Then under new orders from Your Excellency, I marched to a small hill on the way to the position we occupied. The troops carried out this movement with the highest order and precision.

When we arrived at the front, a terrible fire of artillery began from both sides. The fortitude with which the soldiers endured the attack was a premonition of the heroic courage that they were going to show. The light infantry of the Guards fired bravely against the enemy skirmishers of cavalry and infantry, reinforced by the first company of skirmishers from the Irlanda regiment under the command of their intrepid commander, Lieutenant Colonel Ramon Velasco. They ceased firing and marched boldly against the enemy, who were forced to withdraw in a shameful way.

But the enemy recovered and then forced our skirmishers to retreat to gain the support of their battalions: this movement caused the enemy to advance faster until within reach of musket shot. Then the fourth battalion of the Spanish Royal Guards opened fire under their officers' commands, displaying an incomparable courage and perseverance in this battle; the second battalion did not lose any time carrying out the same action; and the Irlanda regiment passed to the right, which was our weakest point. The clash was so terrible and stubborn that only men very determined to win were able to persevere; but at last, the French, fierce soldiers, instruments of tyranny, could not resist the Spanish courage.

In order to make up for their disgraceful performance, they tried a new charge, which was carried out with courage by the Polish lancer squadrons, to which the second battalion of Guards and the Irlanda regiment opposed with fire and bayonets. The enemy was defeated: but not without serious losses for us. Having failed in their attempts, the enemy repeated their attacks of infantry many times and always with bayonets; only the fourth battalion of Guards, similar to the three hundred Spartans, was immovable at its post: the second battalion forced by the enemy's superiority and the disadvantage of the land had to concede some steps but without turning their heads, in order to emphasise their discipline and courage, only a brief moment was enough to recover and attack the enemy again. The Irlanda [regiment] were also in good spirits and the last charge that they carried out against the enemy with bayonets, having lost fifteen officers was very well executed in our opinion. The regiment of Voluntarios de Navarra preserved the good standing of its ancient name.

The sappers always accompanied the artillery and acted with firmness. The rest of the fourth division under the command of Brigadier Ramón Polo, commander of the second section [brigade], did not waste their time; and although they were not in the hottest point of the action, they did their best, distracting and disrupting the enemy forces, and suffering with steadiness the fire of artillery to which they were subjected all the time: the forces of skirmishers distinguished themselves, especially in the vicinity of the village and in the defence of the river.

It is remarkable and I must express with satisfaction to Your Excellency that during the action the infantry were not intimidated by the enemy cavalry and attacked them without regard to the terrain or their numbers.

If I do not restrict the report of this memorable battle to the movements of my division, I would tell Your Excellency with enthusiasm about the English troops' intrepidity and courage, who fought and manoeuvred on our right.

When everyone has tried more than is expected, it is very difficult to identify the most distinguished: however it is my duty to declare to Your Excellency that Brigadier Juan de la Cruz Mourgeón, commander of the first section [brigade] of my division, contributed with his example to the maintenance of the order, discipline and bravery with which the troops fought and to him I am extremely grateful.

The chief of the General Staff [of the 4th Division], Marquis de la Roca, did not carry out his actions with less interest, going at the appropriate moments to the most risky points and consequently fulfilling my expectations.

Worthy of recommendation are Brigadier Juan Urbina and Colonel Diego Ulloa, commanders of the second and fourth battalions of the Spanish Royal Guards, the first one is seriously wounded sharing the same [bad?] luck as his brother Joaquín.

Upon my conscience, Your Excellency, there is neither an officer or individual from the three battalions that having had the luck of being at the main point of the attack, should not be mentioned, so the nation with its gratitude could reward their enormous efforts that contributed to the success in such a memorable day; but as this is not possible, I enclose to Your Excellency, the list of wounded officers and the recommendations made by some of the chiefs of the forces about some of their soldiers.

I do not want to talk to Your Excellency about the officers that came with me personally, but I would be doing something unfair if I did not mention Lieutenant Colonel Bertoldo Schepeler's scrupulous honour and gallantry, and the activity and assistance of Josè de Eceta and the enthusiastic efforts of my aides, Captains Julian Zurita, Juan de la Hera and Ramón de Sentmanat, the first one having died some hours after being wounded, the second one being seriously injured and the third one having had his horse killed.

182

## 6. Account of de España
*From Burriel's published compilation of reports.*

I have the honour of informing Your Excellency that the first division of infantry of the Fifth Army, whose command was given to me by the commander-in-chief, met up with the Allied army on the eighth of this month (being in front of Badajoz), joined the division under the command of General Guillermo Estuwuz and took part in the digging of trenches until the 13th, when the army advanced from in front of Badajoz to Albuera in order to stop the French army. The division stood together with the division of the English General, Jaime [*sic* Lowry] Cole, occupying the posts from the left of the parallel of the Cerro del Vinto to the Guadiana river.

On the afternoon of the 15th, the enemy came out in order to displace the troops that remained in the front of the place: the division took position on the left of the hill but only the light companies were deployed as the enemy went in again.

That same day I received the order from Your Excellency to follow the movement of General Cole's division and as this division had started to march at twelve o'clock in the evening of the 15th/16th, I followed in the same direction and at seven in the morning of the 16th we arrived in the vicinity of Albuera, where the Allied army was already formed in order of battle.

I was appointed by the commander-in-chief to the division led by General Zayas who ordered me to position the light infantry battalion from Navarra on the right of the line to support the artillery and the Guards battalions, and the Zamora regiment on the left of the second line; the first battalion of Voluntarios de Cataluña that had not joined the division because it was detached with the cavalry at the army's vanguard, was placed by the commander-in-chief's orders in the division led by Lieutenant General Francisco Ballesteros. When the struggle became widespread and the enemy tried to force and break our army's right wing with some desperate attacks, the Guards battalions and the Zamora regiment were ordered by the commander-in-chief to form a new front at a perpendicular front to the right of the two lines of the army, this manoeuvre together with the Spanish and Allied troops' courage stopped and resisted the enemy's fury. These two regiments accompanied by sappers and a detachment of guides began firing against the cavalry, forcing their retreat. The first battalion from Cataluña charged the enemy with Lieutenant General Ballesteros's division, with the characteristic courage of this respectable corps; and its honourable commander, Colonel Francisco Dionisio Vives, [they] acquired new honour due to the army's appreciation of his bravery and talents.

I must mention to Your Excellency in order to be just, the courage and zeal of divisional staff officer, Colonel Estanislao Sánchez Salvador (from whom I have received a lot of support on this occasion). I must also praise the good behaviour of sergeant major of the regiment of Zamora, Pascual Ollogui; Captain of the regiment, José Quintanilla and Lieutenant José Villaroel; also Captain of the King's regiment, Martin Muñoz and commander of the light infantry company of the King's regiment, Captain Hermosilla; commander of the company of sappers, and Lieutenant of the detachment of guides, Clemente Grimas: I must also say to Your Excellency that the sergeant major and the provisional commander of the Voluntarios de Navarra did what they could to carry out completely all their duties.

On this occasion the staff officers, Aguado and Otelun have received new responsibilities as was recommended by Your Excellency; and in general, the troops' behaviour gives us hope that with good discipline and methodical training, the soldiers of the army will honourably maintain the old reputation of the veteran corps which remains as the strongest force today.

## 7. Account of Loy
*From Burriel's published compilation of reports.*

Following your orders requesting information concerning the movements of the division of cavalry that was under my command in the glorious battle of the 16th May, I must say: that after the enemy appeared, I moved to support the right flank of the infantry, advancing upon it, and forming my two lines, which position I kept by manoeuvring and with my skirmishers' support, despite the fact that I had all the enemy cavalry in my front and that the cavalry that was supposed to support me had retreated. When the enemy artillery started to fire upon my lines, I received orders from the general of the cavalry to fall back to the English lines; which I carried out by positioning us on the right; and once I was joined to the Allied cavalry, I followed their movements of attack until forcing the enemy cavalry to retreat to the bank of the river, then the advance was halted and we kept our positions.

The valour, calmness and enthusiasm in fighting was evident in all the officers of the staff, corps, commanders and officers; and in all the individuals of the division, which is why I recommend all of them to Your Excellency's benevolence.

## 8. Account of Penne-Villemure
*From Burriel's published compilation of reports.*

Your Excellency: In order to give a clearer idea about the movements that the Spanish cavalry carried out in the battle of Albuera, it is necessary to remember that the enemy's position was as follows:

The right was set on the Royal Road, its left was spread out through the woods along the small river Albuera which separated the two armies; the centre and the left were covered by quite large gulleys and a number of hills that were in front of the position that the majority of the enemy occupied and on these hills they had positioned the strongest units of their cavalry. To pass from this position to the Spanish one, a large gulley had to be crossed: the enemy knowing well that their position was unattackable, they left a reserve in this natural fortress: on the morning of the day of the battle the enemy started carrying out a false attack, while their cavalry crossed the stream that separated us, it being their intention to go round the town of Albuera with their cavalry on the heights to our right, cutting us off from our withdrawal.

The English cavalry had been in front of the Allied infantry since the day before of the battle, their left close to the town: in the first attack against Albuera, orders were given to the Spanish cavalry to position themselves behind the infantry from the same nation in order to support it. The English cavalry stayed in its post at that time; but when the enemy cavalry was going around to the left, I received orders to detach some of the Spanish cavalry in order to meet the enemy on their left: as the cavalry from the Fourth Army was positioned on our right and thus closer to the enemy's left, I detached Brigadier Casimiro Loy to this area, and with the cavalry from the Fifth Army, I marched to support the English.

The Fourth Army detached skirmishers and other light troops in order to face the enemy ones; but there being a greater number, I ordered them to fall back to the bottom of the hill.

During this time the English cavalry took the decision of marching to form on the plain on the right of Albuera where the heaviest part of the struggle was already taking place, due to the fact that there was a gulley which separated it from the plain which was occupied by the enemy cavalry after having moved to their left. The Fifth Army positioned itself on the English cavalry's left; but some time later it received orders to march to the position that the first line of English infantry occupied on the hill to protect this infantry from all the enemy cavalry's attacks; but as the Spanish were so close to the batteries that the enemy had placed on the hills, I must say and all the army has been witness to it, that we were situated in the most lively part of the action alongside two other English squadrons that were also sent to that area. I have never seen a troop suffer with more bravery and endurance from such immediate danger. The cavalry of the Fifth Army was formed in two lines, the first was formed in line and the second, led by Lieutenant Colonel Antolin Reguilon of the Algarbe [Algarve] Regiment, in column of squadrons, being closer to the infantry. I suddenly saw some kind of disorder among the English infantry which was on the first height, disorder caused by a charge of two columns of French infantry with the Polish lancers at their centre who breached the ranks of the English infantry, taking three pieces of cannons and making prisoners of war the artillery men that manned them, of whom sixteen were set free later in Almendralejo and taken to Merida by a detachment from the Cruzada squadron.

Due to this order of events, I sent Lieutenant Colonel Antolin Reguilon with the second line to attack the enemy cavalry's flank, and he subsequently carried it out with so much precision, that the lancers became disordered and were forced to withdraw hurriedly, suffering many losses. With my first line, I turned a quarter to the left, and marched to support the second line that was mixed with the enemy. The English squadrons also advanced. This movement of the Spanish cavalry gave time for our second infantry line to advance, and to cause disorder among the enemy. The two lines of Spanish cavalry not only had to suffer the enemy's artillery fire but also a fusillade made at short range by a line of English infantry that was in the reserve on our right flank, who mistook us for French men as we are a troop without a regular uniform, but all these disgraceful accidents could not disturb this cavalry's good dispositions. Re-establishing the order at this point and the lost [artillery] pieces being recaptured by the line that had just charged, I realised in time that the enemy cavalry wanted to recover their losses, charging the two English regiments of Heavy Dragoons. At this very moment I advanced at full gallop with part of the cavalry of the Fifth Army on the left of the two regiments, and addressing General Lumley, the Allied army's commanding [cavalry] general, I signalled to him that it was the right moment to destroy the enemy's cavalry, already almost defeated and threatened by an infantry line. In this very moment I was ordered to march and surround the enemy cavalry, while the English charged in the front. I carried out the order given to me with all happiness possible, forcing with this movement, all the enemy cavalry to retreat, taking some prisoners detached on the right, that marched towards La Torre in order to cover that flank. Some of their cavalry escaped but were followed by the English. In these circumstances and facing the enemy cavalry that had crossed the stream again to take possession of the heights of the Albuera; I noticed that the enemy wanted to detach two hundred men from their cavalry in order to take the road to La Torre and to Almendral. As my position was very close, I foiled their attempt with a detachment that forced theirs to retreat; and during the evening I fell back onto the main body of the army, after having established our chain of advanced posts in the same position I occupied during the day.

## 9. Account of Miranda

*From Burriel's published compilation of reports.*

At seven o'clock in the morning of the 16th, I arrived with the artillery under my command to the field of Albuera, and as ordered by Joaquín Blake, the artillery took a firing position behind the first line, with two battalions of Spanish Royal Guards and a company of sappers. From this position they marched to occupy the height on the right threatened by the enemy, and from there they fired on the enemy's batteries, supported by the skirmishers of the light battalion of Campo Mayor. A box of munitions was destroyed on a limber by an enemy's shell; this accident caused us to stop firing for a while, because it caused disorder among the livestock.

Next, General Zayas ordered two, four-pound pieces to be positioned on the left flank of the battalion of Spanish Guards, that covered the left of our first position; our firing continued, and the enemy answered this with a battery of eight-pounders, deployed for this objective, and with the rest of their pieces they supported their columns of attack which effectively charged the position, in particular the lancers, forcing us to support the artillery that defended our troops, who received them at point-blank range. The enemy having already been repulsed by the English charge and the strong and constant fire from our line, we fired on them with the section of heavy calibre artillery under my command, and this section stayed within the enemy's sight supported by the regiment of Murcia until the action concluded.

Lieutenant, Joaquín Moscoso died by a cannonball; Antonio Arderius injured by a musket bullet; one dead corporal; six injured artillery men, three of them by a cannon ball; three dead mules and seven injured.

## 10. Blake Letter, 26 June 1811
*From Burriel's published compilation of reports.*

Your Excellency,

The desire for accuracy has obliged me to delay the report of the Battle of Albuera; but the one I now enclose to Your Excellency, made by the General Staff has, as I see it, all the precision which such a remarkable event demands, which must go down in history, not through a poetic description which, being exaggerated, would detract from the true merit of these valiant defenders of our country, but rather as a plain and simple narrative, which bears the respectable character of truth and can at all times instruct those devoted military men, who enjoy studying such operations in detail. In addition to comparing the divisional commanders' reports and drawing up the field plan, extensive enquiries have been undertaken concerning the several movements and events that occurred, correcting them all in agreement with the same commanders.

General Castaños, having the same interest in accuracy, and justifiably believing that this would be better met by bringing all the information together, ordered the field officers of the Fifth Army to send their reports to me.

These, along with those of the expeditionary corps under my command, are by way of an appendix to the general account, so as not to deprive the corps and certain individuals of the praise of which they are worthy.

And since the names of the officers who are under my command are not going to appear in any of the reports, it would be a great injustice if I did not make honourable and distinguished mention of them, that is to say: of the Adjutant General, carrying out the functions of chief of the General Staff, Antonio Burriel; of the first Adjutants, Antonio Ramón del Valle and Juan Blake; the second Adjutants, José Sanchez Boado and Luis de Landaburu; and of my aides de camp, Sebastian de Llano, Càrlos Oppen and Pedro Muzo, all of whom confirmed by carrying out beautifully important and hazardous assignments throughout the battle, their well-founded reputation for courage, intelligence and zeal, and no less worthy of my esteem is the Commander of my Guard, Tomas Valiente; the Quartermaster General, Luis Elexaburu; and the Captain of Engineers, Francisco Ramirez, who also accompanied me during the battle:

God save Your Excellency for many years.

Nogales, 26th June 1811.

Joaquín Blake.

P.S. Even though I have proposed to myself to make no particular mention except for few officers under my immediate command who are part of my military family, leaving the praise of others to their respective leaders, it is impossible not to mention the ardour and enthusiasm which Lieutenant General Gabriel Mendizábal showed when involved in events of the highest risk in order to encourage his troops and to help to defeat the enemy, even though he had no specific command in that battle and was simply following his well-known patriotic impulses. His actions were by no means modest when taking on the roles as general, adjutant or as a simple volunteer: he only sought to make a contribution, and he did this with the utmost efficiency in encouraging the soldiers and the officers by his exhortations and the example set by his bravery, going sometimes on his own initiative, and at other times by my order, wherever the struggle appeared most dangerous or uncertain.

## 11. Individuals Mentioned by Burriel
*From Burriel's published compilation of reports.*

REPORT OF THE OFFICICERS AND SOLDIERS THAT FOUGHT IN THE BATTLE OF THE 16TH AND ARE RECOMMENDED BY THE CORPS CHIEFS

<u>2nd battalion of Royal Spanish Guards</u>

| | | |
|---|---|---|
| With rank of Lieutenant | Sergeant Serafin Grau | |
| 2nd Sergeants of grenadiers | José Lloret | |
| | Jacinto Pradas | |
| | Jose Membrilla | wounded |
| 2nd Sergeants | Eugenio Heredia | wounded |
| | Blas Negro | |
| 2nd Sergeant with rank of Second Lt | Juan de Cantos | |
| 1st Corporals | Manuel Guerra | |
| | Victoriano Muñoz | wounded (seriously) |
| Grenadier | Juan Pastor * | |

*When this soldier left the high ground where his company had been fighting, a Polish soldier stabbed him with a lance, piercing his overcoat. Stepping aside, the soldier aimed at the Pole, and shot down his horse.

## 4th Battalion of Royal Spanish Guards

| | |
|---|---|
| 1st assistant | Nicolas Melgarejo |
| 2nd assistant | Miguel Laci |
| Sergeant with rank of Second Lieutenant | Nicolas Sanchez |
| Ditto of Grenadiers | Florentin Ferrer |
| Ditto | Pedro del Real |
| 2nd Corporal | Juan Muñoz |
| | Antonio Iglesias |
| | Mauricio de Vela |
| Grenadiers | Juan Gamero |
| | Pedro Rodriguez |
| | Diego Sobrino |

## Irlanda Regiment

| | |
|---|---|
| Captain | Joaquín Tortosa |
| | Francisco Velasco |
| Captain with rank of Lieutenant Colonel | Miguel Noguera |
| Lieutenant with rank of Captain | Pedro Santana |
| Second in command | Antonio Martin |
| Second Lieutenant | Francisco Rodriguez |
| 1st Sergeant with rank of 2nd Lieutenant. | Càrlos Nolari |
| 1st Sergeant | Antonio Sayago |
| 2nd Sergeant | Pedro Carrasco |
| | Vicente José |
| | Pablo Pleter |
| Corporal of grenadiers | José Mela |
| Grenadier | Andres Vizuer |

La Torre, 23 May 1811. This is a copy of the originals that the corps have given to us. The Marques de la Roca. – Approved. Zayas.

## 12. Schepeler's Account

*Andreas Daniel Berthold von Schepeler, a native of the Westphalia region of Germany who had served in the Prussian army in 1806, was one of a number of foreigners who had come to Spain to continue fighting against Napoleon after their own countries had been defeated by the French. He arrived in Spain in 1810 and obtained a staff appointment with the rank of colonel, and served in that capacity at Albuera. He remained in Spain after the fall of Napoleon and included a comprehensive account of the battle when he wrote a history of the war.[3] Following his main text is a long note, which contains his personal recollections of the battle. This was originally written in the third person, but has been changed to the first person voice for the sake of clarity.*

On the 14th, the three generals conferred at Valverde. On the 15th, Beresford led his army to Albuera, and Blake's corps arrived there that night, after a forced march. When the infantry crossed that evening at Almendral, the cavalry had already skirmished in the vicinity. They arrived at midnight at the position and, a rather singular thing, marched through the middle of the British cavalry bivouacs without anyone challenging them by shouting: 'Who goes there!'

The Albuera stream, which runs south to north-east from the village of the same name to its junction with the Guadiana, resembles a small river due to its increasing depth and width. The village is located on the left bank, which, from the village to the Guadiana, is visibly well higher than the right – this left part of our position was quite strong. In front of the village is a narrow, old bridge and 200 *toises* above is another, rather wide, of stone and, 200 paces further, another stream joins the Albuera, which makes the bottom somewhat marshy. Further still above the village, the Albuera stream is fordable almost everywhere. Here, the left bank looks like the right bank but the terrain is even gentler and consists of very undulating hills, so that the right wing [of the Allies] did not have a natural anchor point because the ground rises continually as it extends [south] towards Almendral. On the other side [the right bank], and along the stream mentioned above, there is a chain of heights covered by woods that slopes gently down to the stream. The Santa Marta road runs through these woods then

---

3  von Schepeler, Andreas Daniel Berthold, *Histoire de la Révolution d'Espagne et de Portugal ainsi que de la Guerre Qui en Résulta* (3 volumes, Liege, 1831), v. 3, pp. 266–77.

across a large open plain opposite the village of Albuera, somewhat distant below the small river.

On the morning of the 16th, the Allied army was on the right and left of Albuera in two lines. On the right flank, Ballesteros was in the first line with Zayas and Lardizábal in the second line, while the English division of Stewart was in the centre and the Portuguese of General Hamilton were on the left flank. A brigade of the latter, together with Cole's division (and also España's brigade), both just arriving from Badajoz, and the Portuguese brigade of Harvey, formed the second line of the centre and the left flank, which went down to the left of the village, which was occupied by the light brigade (German) of Alten. The cavalry under General Lumley were extended on the right of the Spanish on the heights above the Albuera stream.

The Spanish numbered 12,000 bayonets, the English and Portuguese 13,500, and the cavalry 2,000 horses. There were 32 pieces of artillery. The second line was on the highest line of hills, behind which lies the start of the Rivillas brook, which joins the Guadiana close to Badajoz.

The morning was foggy with a dark sky that threatened coming rain. After daybreak, enemy cavalry troops skirmished with our picquets on the other side of the Albuera, eventually pushing them back to our side and, at 8 o'clock, two regiments of dragoons under General Briche appeared in the plain accompanied by a light [horse] artillery battery. General Godinot followed with some infantry and made as if to attack the village. A Spanish battery on the height near the village church engaged the French and this cannon fire began the bloody day.

Castaños, Beresford and Blake were gathered with their generals and staffs on a height next to the village between the first and the second lines where, while eating, they kept an eye on the movements of the nearby enemy. [See Note at the end of this account.] The general opinion was that the attention of the enemy was focused on our right flank even though it seemed reckless to attack there since, in the event of a defeat, they could be cut off from the road to Andalusia. And, indeed, Soult's bold plan was to crush the right wing of the Allies, to cut them off from Valverde, and throw them back on Badajoz and into the Guadiana.

While Briche and Godinot threatened Albuera, Girard with two divisions of the 5th Corps, followed by the reserve under General Werlé, marched south from the Santa Marta road and descended the wooded slopes near the brook close to the heights on right bank of the Albuera, whose reverse slopes were also covered by bushy woods.

The enemy cavalry were already descending the slope [to the stream] at the moment when Beresford ordered Zayas's division and part of that of General Cole to form a new line of troops perpendicular to the first line. But the enemy crossed the Albuera, and Zayas was sent towards a dominant hill some 1,100 paces south of the end of the original right flank and also south of the new south-facing position. The second division (Lardizábal) followed him.

It was none too soon to occupy this new position because French skirmishers were already close. Latour-Maubourg's cavalry, preceding the enemy infantry and covering its left flank, had already occupied a rise, distant by 400 paces from the other, with horse artillery, which Lumley had abandoned in order to extend the new perpendicular line past the start of the Rivillas brook on the right and prevent the right from being outflanked.

Zayas was still occupied deploying his troops and his two cannons were just getting into position when, on the hill opposite, the leading elements of the enemy infantry appeared, and heavier artillery replaced the light pieces that had followed the cavalry, which now moved left towards the Valverde road. The second division accompanied this change of position by Zayas and Ballesteros formed the extreme left wing of the new position. In this position, stretching 1,200 paces from the Albuera stream, the troops were formed in two lines with small intervals between units. Part of Blake's first two divisions occupied the former position of Ballesteros, and a single battalion was posted behind the left flank of that general on a height which was near to the marshy ground mentioned above.

This new position was perpendicular to the previous front of the army and supported the left wing still arrayed along the Albuera stream; the village itself remained occupied by Alten. Hamilton advanced with his Portuguese into the previous first line to dispute the passage of the river by Godinot, with support from the Spanish battalions in their rear. This part of the previous position was now the elbow of the new position and prevented the left wing from being outflanked; Otway's Portuguese cavalry brigade was also here. Stewart's division marched in columns behind the hill occupied by Zayas. Cole, who had been previously positioned with the second line of English and Portuguese, now moved further to the right and partly in the valley of the Rivillas, to form a line between Stewart and the cavalry, which constantly manoeuvred to avoid being outflanked by the enemy on the extreme right.

In short, the two armies marched to their positions to do battle, the loss of which threatened the Allies with complete destruction. An earlier and faster change of position would have left the army in a strong position on the heights between the Albuera and the Rivillas, curtailed the turning movement of the enemy, and not left so much of the outcome of the battle to fate and fortune.

However, before the new line of battle was completely formed, the enemy advanced, in columns, quickly down the hill where his batteries were positioned and towards the Spanish. The [Spanish] field guns were soon reduced to silence, an ammunition cart exploded and the enemy battery bombarded the waiting battalions. One on the right (led there by España from his division) wavered and was replaced by the Irlanda regiment of Zaya's division. The fire of the Spanish battalions stopped some of the French masses on the left but, nevertheless, others pressed on resolutely across the gap between the two hills when, at the same moment, the first brigade of General Stewart's division, in columns of half-companies, advanced beyond the right of Zayas against the enemy battery. It soon reached the left flank of the French attackers, wheeled to the left and pushed them back to the foot of the height with the bayonet. As the enemy fell back, two regiments of hussars and the Polish lancers charged the rear of the English line and dispersed the whole brigade.[4] A battery, almost 800 prisoners (including their brave Colonel Colborne), and three colours[5] were taken by the French. Only the last battalion was able to retire in time to the hill [occupied by the Spanish troops]. The failure of the Spaniards to advance in line with the English in fact enabled them to preserve this important position.

The enemy [cavalry], drunk with victory, began to shout, 'Now we only have to deal with the Gavachos (Spanish)!' and, charging straight ahead at the gallop and in disorder, passed between the first and second Allied lines. The English in the rear line fired at them and some of the shots struck the Spanish troops in the front line. Nevertheless, they held firm and only a few riders in the interval were able to escape.

The masses of French troops in front reformed and attacked again with their reserve, and some other battalions formed up on the left

---

4     Schepeler Note – After the battle I found a soldier of this brigade fatally wounded and lying on his stomach only twenty paces from the place where the enemy battery had been. On asking if he still lived, the Englishman answered 'Yes, but who won the battle?' I answered 'Us' and he asked: 'Who is this "us"?' 'English and Spanish,' I replied. 'Ah well, well' sighed this hero for the last time. Not far from Albuera was a French officer, half-raised on his left arm, and I saw reflected in his truly handsome face both the pain of a leg wounded by a cannon ball and the pain of his first defeat. 'You are seriously wounded,' I said to him, and a simple 'Yes, Sir' was his answer. When some Portuguese, whom I called, picked him up, he said seriously 'I thank you very much, Sir' but not another word, not another complaint passed his lips.

5     Schepeler Note – The French say six, which would be all those accompanying the three regiments but nevertheless, I did myself, [later] see one flying and another torn and, if I am not mistaken, they took only three.

opposite to the English and Portuguese in the previously mentioned line formed to the right of the hill. An English brigade replaced that of España, close to Zayas.

The murderous combat now became an extended battle fought, on the side of the Allies, in the traditional way in line.

When Colborne advanced, two English guns[6] had taken position on the hill but were soon after replaced by two Spanish, which enfiladed the enemy advancing on the right in line but their officer and almost all of the gunners were killed. The head of a dense enemy column then appeared on the bloody hill and pushed back a battalion. Zayas's troops had expended all their ammunition. The 4th battalion of the [Spanish Royal] Guards, on the left, had not been relieved and men began to search the pockets of dead for additional cartridges. When this expedient ceased to provide more ammunition, the Guards nevertheless held firm in the face of a destructive fire. An English brigade (Houghton's) assembled in the second line and then took over the Spanish position but the English were nearly obliged to use force to move the Guards battalion out of the way.

On the left flank were two battalions from Ballesteros's division, formed by platoons, that had been forced together by the enemy fire, but the general was nevertheless able to hold them in their position until they were relieved.[7] Some English battalions were prevented from making a bayonet charge against the wavering enemy opposite them due to the fear of enemy cavalry coupled with the absence of friendly cavalry in the centre. After having fired all their cartridges, they were withdrawn in good order to the rear and lay down on the ground behind a gentle slope, quietly awaiting the end of the battle.

Harvey's Portuguese brigade, on the extreme right flank, while waiting, had repulsed a cavalry attack, and then the entire line of the Allies advanced against the French. In front of Albuera village, there was lively skirmishing with the enemy who had penetrated to the houses at the outskirts but the passage of the bridge was bloodily disputed, including by some battalions moved from the main line. Thus the battle ebbed and flowed from the right side of the hill, where they exchanged volleys at fifteen paces, to the Albuera stream, with neither side gaining a decisive advantage.

---

6     Schepeler Note – Those were commanded by Lieutenant Scharnhorst, currently a Prussian major and son of the famous General Scharnhorst, to whom Prussia owes so much for its restoration.

7     Schepeler Note – Don Emeterio Velarde, general staff officer, fell from his horse, mortally wounded. He gave his service papers to a friend to save them and expired with these words: 'I die, content, for my fatherland.'

The French, almost all in massive columns [*masses*] which allowed only the front ranks to fire, suffered horribly. General Pépin fell, mortally wounded; Generals Gazan, Maransin and Brayer were wounded and, when Werlé led forward the last part of the reserve, he received a mortal wound.

The mass of French troops still held firm on the crest of the hill and opposite an English regiment whose right flank had bent back in a definite hook, when Zayas led the Spanish back up on to the hill. The brave force advanced in close order, with shouldered arms, through the narrow open gap. When the Spaniards were just ten paces away, the enemy turned suddenly to flee. At the same moment, a Portuguese light battalion ran onto the right of the hill and into the left flank of the French mass, which caused it to spiral to the rear. Those in the rear ranks of the mass, suffering from fire without the possibility of resistance, folded under the pressure and those on the flanks also melted away, following the first fugitives, resulting in a complete rout and dispersion. In a complete change from the situation only hours earlier, there were now only retreating troops from the hill to the river and the three French reserve battalions and one reserve battery stemmed the tide for only a short time. All the French fled across the Albuera. The left flank, fearing that they would be cut off, hastily followed the right, while the cavalry covered their retirement.

If only the centre of the Allies had advanced quickly, there is no doubt that the enemy army would have been completely split into two parts. However, there was not even a squadron of cavalry there as the sudden victory had been a surprise and the battalions on the right of the hill, still insufficiently supplied with ammunition, advanced slowly and with pauses. A new attack made by Godinot against Albuera village drew only slight attention and was too insignificant to obtain a victory for an already beaten army. This defeated army started to rally on the heights on the other side of the Albuera, where its artillery was concentrated to protect it, but nevertheless, in spite of the efforts of the officers, it took a while before some battalions reformed. Only a few companies of Allied riflemen advanced towards the small river and Latour-Maubourg's cavalry, concentrated into dense masses at each of the two passages across the Albuera and in great danger, owed its survival to General Lumley. He carefully formed his troops into a line on the height and fired some artillery into the enemy troops but he did not send even a single battalion to fire a full volley into the hard-pressed horsemen. He should have dared to do more because there would certainly have been greater disorder with each advance towards the retreating mass; since the infantry had obtained a victory, the cavalry should have completed it. Instead, Lumley (and Beresford) followed the example of Sackville at the battle of Minden in the Seven Years War and built the French a 'bridge of gold' allowing the defeated enemy to escape without real pursuit.

The day had started rainy and a violent downpour fell when the English brigade [of Colborne] advanced but, nevertheless, the violent thunder of the battle, which lasted until three o'clock in the afternoon, caused the clouds to disappear and produced a clear sky. However, the clouds re-appeared at dusk and the night was damp and cold. The Allied army remained on the hills of battle without firewood and the wet brush, even when supplemented with the wood from the butts of thousands of abandoned muskets, provided only weak fires. But who could describe the suffering of the Allied casualties . . . and their number was great! The Spaniards had approximately 2,000 dead and wounded, the Portuguese 389, and the English 3,616 with 600 taken prisoner. The remainder of the prisoners taken in the rout of Colborne's brigade had escaped in the fight, and the enemy had taken away only a single gun. The battalions of Zayas's division on the hill, hardly 1,500 men strong at the outset, alone counted 900 dead and wounded. Myers's English brigade had 1,000 casualties, and that of General Hoghton, which advanced with 1,500 bayonets, had lost 1,050. These two English commanders died gloriously at the head of their brigades. Beresford himself had been attacked behind the second line by a lancer who was killed by one of the Marshal's dragoon orderlies. Lieutenant Colonel Oppen (who came to Spain with the author) knocked another lancer off his horse. Brigadier de España then ran up courageously to kill this defenceless enemy but the noble German would not permit it.

Soult lost 8,000 men, and there were many French wounded and taken prisoner. The slaughter of these 15,000 men took place for the most part between the two hills on which the opponents had faced each other; in the space of 100 yards, the ground was covered with heaps of dead and grievously wounded men. The enemy wounded must have feared the vengeance of the Spaniards for they all implored the protection of Allied officers, particularly the English. The writers of this nation proudly recount such facts, as proof of the generosity of their warriors, whose conduct was not animated by the need for revenge. And why would they have had any such need? The French were not devastating England; but it is difficult to believe that English soldiers would have behaved so charitably in their own land, where love of country was not a small thing among the people. Surprising thing! Where the French casualties lay thickest (where the Vth Corps columns had fought), some Germans cried out to the author in their native tongue, asking him for protection against the Spaniards; despite the fact that he wore a Spanish uniform, though with a white plume. Did the instinct of self-preservation, increased by the pain of wounds, cause them to speak their native language, or did some lucky chance give these unfortunates the knowledge that there were Germans among the Spaniards? As night advanced, Soult withdrew his army behind the stream to the wooded heights. He deliberated with the generals whether a new battle should be fought: however, the danger seemed too great. On the 17th, the two armies remained in line of battle until the afternoon; for each awaited an attack.

Note –

The battle of Albuera has been described as inaccurately by the French as by the English. The former do not do justice to the latter and the latter, in their turn, refuse it to the Spanish. I write this to tell, not out of vanity, what I saw and heard because combats and battles are largely won by chance, and each soldier present does what he can. I was attached to General Zayas and was eating breakfast at a time when most staff telescopes were pointed to the front and to the left. Recalling the boldness of Soult from 1799 in Switzerland, I believed there would be an attack against the right flank and, watching the wooded heights in that direction, I soon saw the flash of bayonets in columns. My involuntary exclamation, 'That's where they are coming from, that is where they are going to attack!' made all heads turn that way, and Blake ordered me to gallop towards the hill on the right. At the same time the creation of an 'elbow' for the line [a new line at right angles to the original line] was ordered. On arriving at the hill, I saw the head of the [French] columns descending on the other side of the Albuera, returned at the gallop and made that report but Zayas was already advancing.

I then met Marshal Beresford, led him up the hill, showed him the columns in the distance and said: 'The French are supported by cavalry and so for a successful attack on their battery and the hill that might split the French forces, it would be good if we also had some squadrons in the centre.' The Marshal replied that there was already some cavalry in that position. After the battle, I learned that Penne[-Villemur] and his cavalry had been on the far end on the right of the hill but had withdrawn closer to Lumley because they had been under heavy fire.

When Colborne's English brigade advanced, I went looking for Beresford to point out the danger [of their exposed flank]. Along the way, I met Castaños who told me to continue to seek out the Marshal. However, I could not find Beresford and instead warned some of the officers of the column about the enemy cavalry and returned close to Zayas. This general had remained firm on the hill without moving forward and we soon saw the English dispersed. A lance thrust, aimed from behind at my side, revealed to me that enemy riders had penetrated [between the lines] at the gallop. Beresford's report says 'The Spanish had lost the hill.' From the beginning to the end of the battle, I was at this point from which one overlooked the two lines.

A little later, I had again led the Irlanda regiment forward with its colour. That unit shifted a little to the right, suffered heavy casualties and was replaced by another battalion; the guards on the left remained immovable. When the English came up to relieve them, I suddenly found myself in front of a British battalion, led by a general and Cruz-Murgeon, and went forward, waving my hat and shouting 'Hurrah!' to them. As the fighting died down, Zayas placed himself in front of the left wing of the guards (now in the second line), which, because of the English battalion, bent a little backwards. I led them to the right and found myself, by chance, the first person all alone in a French column; my unexpected survival in this situation was miraculous. As the enemy fled, I galloped towards the closest Portuguese (on the right), to prompt them to advance up the hill of the enemy and, once again later, to advance against the cavalry at the Albuera. Each time they gave me the answer that they had no orders to do so. When an order finally arrived (to tell the truth, a little too late), they advanced defensively. I led some Spanish troops, re-supplied with cartridges, against the right flank of the cavalry, which had passed the small river, and immediately saw that an advance by even a few battalions would have had a great success at this juncture, and even more brilliant results would have followed if the attack would have been joined by some cavalry. We were so little familiar with victory that we were surprised by the smile of fortune and were satisfied just to drive the enemy away.

On the 19th, I in vain asked his superiors (and also General Alava, who had come south with Wellington) for a company of light infantry to attempt to free some of the English prisoners while they were travelling through the mountains [to Seville]; they laughed at the request. For the English who read this book, I will add again here that a staff officer or English general was seriously wounded beside me and fell from his horse and that, on my right, another was wounded. There was also a senior officer who, on the morning of the 17th, visited us because he wanted to identify the [Spanish] battalion that, he said, only reluctantly allowed his unit to replace them. The position held by the 4th battalion of Guards was clearly marked by two lines of dead and seriously wounded, as was that of an English battalion which had fought to the left of and somewhat above the guards.

It is only to record for the Spanish their share of the victory that I wrote this long note.

## 13. Lützow's Account

*The biography of Prussian General Carl von Grolman, who was present at Albuera as a member of the Spanish army, contains an account of Albuera. His biographer states that the account is based on unpublished information from Captain Leo von Lützow, another Prussian who was a company commander in the Spanish Legión Extrangera, along with material from von Schepeler and Burriel.[8] The narrative below has been edited to remove portions obviously attributable to the latter two sources.*

... The combat between the advance guard division of Lardizábal and the French developed very quickly and was very intense. The latter had without great difficulties and in spite of some attacks by the Spanish cavalry, passed through the shallow river Albuera and [had] deployed into battle line in a right angle to it. General Lardizábal had occupied the first knoll in front of the slope of the heights, while the French deployed in a depression which was situated behind it, and on a second knoll.

General Blake thought the advance guard division was not strong enough on its own, and he therefore sent as reinforcements the two battalions of the Spanish guards (the 2nd and the 4th) as well as the regiment Irlanda from the division of Zayas, while he ordered the division of Ballesteros to occupy the height which was to the left of the one occupied by General Lardizábal.

When the English division of General Stewart arrived, he ordered it to take position as second line behind the advance guard division.

On the height which in the beginning had been occupied by Lardizábal and the complete division of Zayas, only the Imperiales de Toledo and Legion Extrangera had remained, to serve as a reserve. The height was higher than all the others, and from it an excellent overview of the whole battlefield was possible. ...

When General Ballesteros had reached the same level with Lardizábal, General Blake ordered the general attack. This was executed immediately and with great energy, but repulsed by the French.

---

8    Conrady, E. Von, *Leben und Wirken des Generals der Infanterie und kommandirenden Generlas des V. Armeekorps Carl von Grolman. Erster Theil. Von 1777 bis 1813* (Berlin, 1894), pp. 247–54. Translation courtesy of Oliver Schmidt.

The rain, which blew into the face of the Spanish, worked much in favour of the French.

Two regiments of hussars fell onto the retreating Spanish troops and overran everything. The battalions of the Stewart's division, which meanwhile had formed a second line behind Lardizábal, fired calmly at the enemy cavalry and intended to advance to attack the following French columns, but in this moment some Polish lancer squadrons, which in the rain had ridden unnoticed around the wing, threw themselves at their rear and flanks, and caused disorder and confusion also to them. Here, the enemy cavalry took several guns and howitzers and made many prisoners. Marshal Beresford was also nearly taken prisoner because at one moment behind the brigade he was attacked by a lancer and only saved with difficulty by his orderly. The lancers and hussars . . . raced up to the height where the Imperiales de Toledo and Legion Extrangera stood, who received them with a heavy fire, without moving. The Spanish cavalry, which had stood to the right of General Stewart's division and was still completely in good order, hurled itself on the hussars and lancers, which by the fire and the long attack had fully lost their formations. The enemy horsemen made a turnabout, rushed in frantic rout through their own infantry and brought the advancing columns into disorder. This moment was used by the Allies and thus the battle won.

General Hamilton with his division, which had just arrived to the right of Stewart's, attacked the French columns in their right flank, General Stewart, who had quickly rallied his division, advanced in the front, and General Zayas advanced nearly in the same moment on the left flank with Imperiales de Toledo and Legion Extrangera in compact columns with shouldered arms. . . . The two forces were only 10 paces apart, when they [the enemy] turned back and fled.

Everywhere, the advance was successful and decisive. The enemy retreated in disorder. When the English cavalry and the division of General Cole began to advance from the Arroyo de Valdesevilla, the retreat turned into a frantic rout in spite of the resistance of the French cavalry. The French cavalry covered the retreat a bit against the English cavalry under General Lumley, then it also retreated slowly over the stream and marched obliquely to the left, while the reserve, which consisted of newly formed troops of King Joseph Bonaparte, advanced up to the stream.

General Godinot, who until now had done little to molest General Alten, who was occupying the village Albuera, tried with an attack to divert Allied attention and relieve pressure on the retreat over the stream.

A very lucky circumstance for the French was that there was no cavalry in the centre, which could have taken up the pursuit of the enemy and turn the rout into destruction. Also, Marshal Beresford and the generals were too surprised by winning the battle thought to be lost, to be able to think of an energetic pursuit. They contented themselves to form up on the heights close to the stream those Spanish troops which still were in the best order (Imperiales de Toledo, Legion Extrangera and Ciudad Rodrigo) along with the Portuguese division and some artillery as well, and have them observe the retreat of the enemy. The skirmishers stood at the bank of the stream.

It was now 2 p.m., and the weather had become quite clear. . . . In this position a bivouac was taken during the night. The latter was cold and wet, and to maintain the fires, on the hills without wood, no other material was found than a few wet shrubs and the stocks of a few thousand muskets which were lying dispersed on the battlefield. . . .

The Legion Extrangera had only a loss of 19 men. . . . For its good behaviour during the battle, the Legion had received much praise amongst the Spanish. Grolman was promoted to lieutenant colonel and received the cross of honour. The latter was also given to Captains von Lützow and Count Dohna.

# PART IV
# FRENCH ACCOUNTS

## A. Command and Staff Accounts

### 1. Soult's Published Report
*The official French account of Albuera, dated Solano, 21 May, was published in* Le Moniteur Universel *on 13 June 1811. (An English translation of the document appeared in* The Times *of London on 21 June, a circumstance that underscores the routine contact between the two countries that continued despite Napoleon's Continental System.) According to this account, Soult was unaware that Blake's Spanish troops had arrived at Albuera until after the battle had started, and the realisation that he was significantly outnumbered caused him to abort his attack.*

My Lord,

I left Seville during the night of the 9th-10th, as my report of the 9th informed you. On the 12th I joined the division commanded by General Latour-Maubourg between Fuente Cantos and Bienvenida. On the 14th, I took up a position at Villa Franca and Almendralejo; on the 15th [I was] at Santa Marta and Villalba; my cavalry was advanced to Albuera where I learned that the enemy's army was gathering. The various Spanish, Portuguese and English corps, having arrived from Cadiz and Lisbon, and even an English brigade withdrawn from Sicily, were threatening Andalusia. My advance had freed this province and the enemy had recalled all his corps to concentrate them at Albuera. On the 15th, therefore, we found ourselves in the presence of the army of the enemy, and I resolved not to lose a moment, and to engage in battle.

The enemy's position was a favourable one; it was situated at the junction of the routes leading to Badajoz and to Jurumenha by way of Valverde and Olivenza; but Blake's Spanish division had not yet joined the rest, and although knowing that if I postponed action I could expect to get reinforcements, and that I only had 4 brigades of infantry totaling 15,000 men with 3,000 horses, only 18,000 men in all, I judged it expedient to attack on the right in order to prevent Blake and his 9,000 Spaniards from joining the rest, and to threaten their line of communication; moreover, the nature of the ground made this the most advantageous point of attack. I knew that General Beresford, who commanded the opposing army, had two divisions of English infantry amounting to 10,000 men, 8,000 Portuguese and 3,000 Spanish commanded by Castaños, with 3,000 cavalry, making 24,000 men in all; but I never doubted that I would succeed.

Division General Latour-Maubourg commanded all the cavalry and Division General Ruty, the artillery. Division General Girard commanded the first two brigades, some 7,000 men. Brigade Generals Werlé and Godinot each commanded another brigade.

General Godinot was ordered to feign an attack on the village of Albuera with his brigade and 5 squadrons under the orders of Brigade General Briche; while the rest of the army under my command assaulted the enemy's right, which was immediately outflanked by our cavalry. General Latour-Maubourg manoeuvred with audacity and skill; he sought in vain to force the enemy cavalry into combat, but the latter constantly avoided engagement. General Girard with his two brigades marched at the *pas de charge* and took the enemy's position. This was occupied by a Spanish division and an English brigade, who fell back after a fairly stubborn resistance, and were hotly pursued. The battlefield was covered with their dead, and we took considerable numbers of prisoners.

The second line of the enemy then advanced and considerably outflanked ours. When I arrived on the high ground, I was surprised to see such a large number of [enemy] troops and, shortly thereafter, I learned from a Spanish prisoner that Blake had arrived with 9,000 men, and had joined at 3 a.m. in the morning. The contest was no longer equal. The enemy had more than 30,000 men, whilst I only had 18,000. I decided I could no longer pursue my plan of attack, and ordered that we should hold the position we had taken from the enemy.

However, the enemy line soon approached ours, and the fighting then became most terrible. General Latour-Maubourg ordered a charge by the 2nd Hussars, the 1st Lancers of the Vistula, and the 4th and 20th Dragoons which was executed with such skill and bravery that three English infantry brigades [regiments?] were entirely destroyed. Six cannon, 1,000 prisoners and 6 colours (those of the 3rd, 48th and 66th English regiments) fell into our hands. The enemy left us the position we had taken from him, and did not dare to attack again. The firing lasted until 4 p.m. in the afternoon, when it finally finished.

Generals Werlé and Pépin were killed. Generals Maransin and Brayer were wounded. Colonel Praefke of the 28th Light Infantry was killed, along with Battalion Commanders Astruc and Camus, of the 64th [Line] and 28th [Light] regiments. Our loss in dead and wounded amounts to 2,800 men. The enemy did not capture any of our men except for 200 or 300 wounded who fell behind the enemy lines.

The enemy lost three generals killed, two English and one Spanish, and two generals wounded. 1,000 English were taken prisoner (some escaped but today we counted 800); 1,100 Spanish were also taken. All the information I have received up to now indicates that the loss of the enemy in dead and wounded amounts to 5,000 English, 2,000 Spanish and 700 to 800 Portuguese. This gives losses of 9,000 men for the whole enemy army, a loss triple our own. Our troops covered themselves with glory. The cavalry made the most beautiful charges and was particularly distinguished. The artillery maintained its reputation. I constantly had 40 guns firing in battery [*en batterie*], pouring death upon the enemy lines. The English lost one man in two.

On the 17th, we held our position. 5,000 men from Elvas joined the enemy army. I continued to hold the battlefield, and on the 18th, at daybreak, I made a flanking move on Solano. I ordered General Gazan to conduct my English and Spanish prisoners and my wounded to Seville with a suitable escort. As soon as I knew this had been done, I manoeuvred to join up with the other forces, and to complete the defeat of the enemy.

I cannot finish this report without mentioning to Your Highness in particular the services rendered me by General Gazan, my chief of staff; General Latour-Maubourg equally merits mention for his good services, and General Ruty for the manner in which he directed the artillery. I must also mention Generals Godinot, Bron, Briche, Bouvier des Eclaz, and Vielande; adjutant commandant Mocquery, my deputy chief of staff, General Bourgeat and Colonel Berge, of the artillery; Colonel Konopka of the Vistula lancers; Colonel Vinot of the 2nd Hussars, and Colonel Farine of the 4th Dragoons. I must also mention several other commanders and officers of all ranks who distinguished themselves especially; but all the individual reports have not reached me and I am obliged therefore to mention them in another report.

I must praise in particular the officers of the staff and my aides de camp, most of whom had horses killed under them and several who were wounded. I will have the honour in the future of sending Your

Highness a list of the officers whom I believe merit the favour of His Imperial and Royal Majesty.

I have the honour to be, with respect to Your Serene Highness, your very humble and very obedient servant,

Marshal, Duke of Dalmatia, Commanding General of the Army of the South

Solano, 21 May, 1811

## 2. Soult's Unpublished Report

*The unpublished version of Soult's report in the French Army Archives tells a different story from the published report in one very important regard.[1] In it, Soult admits that he was aware of the arrival of Blake's force before he began his attack, but goes on to state that his plan of attack against the Spanish flank would have inevitably succeeded but for a crucial mistake made by his generals. The mistake is not explicitly identified, but the report implies that it was the failure of Girard to deploy his troops into line. No information has been found concerning the circumstances under which the unpublished report was transformed into the published version, but one can suspect that the Emperor played some role in the revision.*

Report of His Excellency Marshal Duke of Dalmatia to His Serene Highness the Prince of Neufchatel, Major General

Solano, May 18, 1811

Since my departure from Seville, I haven't had the time to write to Your Serene Highness.; constantly I have been on the move and a great affair has taken place; I could not even before this moment give an account of its result.

I left Seville at ten o'clock on the night of the 9th to the 10th, as my report of the 9th informed you. On the 12th, I joined between Fuente Cantos and Bienvenida the column of the Vth Corps commanded by General Latour-Maubourg. On the 13th, the column commanded by General Bron, which had set out from Cordova, arrived and I mustered all my troops at Bienvenida. On the 14th, I took a position at Villa Franca and Almendralejo; on the 15th at Santa Marta and Villalba; the cavalry was pushed on close to Albuera, where the enemy army was gathering. On the 16th, I gave battle to the enemies. It pains me to have to report to Your Highness that the goal I set for myself has not been fulfilled and that many brave men have succumbed in the field of honour.

---

1      Soult to Berthier, 18 May 1811, *Service Historique de la Défense, Chateau de Vincennes, Paris*, File C8* 147*.

The position occupied by the enemy was advantageous; it was at the junction of the roads which lead to Badajoz, and to Jurumenha by Valverde and Olivenza. After having reconnoitred the position, I determined to attack their right flank so as to make the enemy fear for their line of communication, which ran in that direction, and, moreover, to have the advantage of the high ground sloping down towards them. I had the hope of attacking one day before the Spanish troops coming from Cadiz and led by Blake could join with the English and Portuguese troops under the orders of General Beresford; but this juncture had already taken place during the night which preceded the battle, and I had to fight a larger force than I expected the enemy to have at the start of the action.

I will admit, however, that despite this disadvantage, I would infallibly have won a decisive success had it not been for a fault which was committed in the engagement and at the very moment when a great advantage had just been obtained.

Division General Latour-Maubourg commanded all the cavalry, and General Ruty commanded the artillery. The infantry was formed into four divisions. I gave command of the two divisions of the Vth Corps to Division General Girard; General Godinot commanded the first reserve division and General Werlé commanded the second.

General Godinot was ordered to feign an attack on the village of Albuera with the 16th Light and one battalion of the 51st Line, supported by five squadrons under the orders of General Briche, while with the rest of the army under my command assaulted the right of the enemy, which was immediately outflanked by our cavalry; Latour-Maubourg manoeuvred with skill and audacity. He sought in vain to force the enemy cavalry into combat; the latter constantly avoided engagement and allowed the first lines of its infantry to be crushed. General Girard with the two divisions of the Vth Corps (forming altogether eight thousand combatants) was ordered to form up in front of the cavalry in the first position of the enemy which had been taken, to change direction to the right and attack as soon as he would be able with his lines deployed. Werlé's division, which I had reinforced with the 55th Line, followed immediately to support it.

The first movement was executed with enthusiasm and precision; an English division [brigade] was immediately overthrown and a charge that Division General Latour-Maubourg directed against it by the 2nd Hussars, 1st Lancers of the Vistula, and the 4th and 20th Dragoons completed its destruction. A thousand prisoners and six flags of the 3rd, 48th, and 66th English regiments remained in our hands. The rest of the division [brigade] was lying dead on the battlefield; seven pieces of artillery were also captured. The general rout of the enemy would have followed from this success if the first line had thereupon been deployed and had presented to the enemy a front equal to his own, but there was hesitation and the first line was forced to endure an unequal fire fight with the second English line which, in moving forward, immediately overwhelmed our attack columns on both flanks. The reserve division, which I brought forward, engaged at that instant, and checked that enemy advance. General Latour-Maubourg also manoeuvred on their right; but the damage was already done. With most officers killed or wounded, the infantry had to reform on the first position, which had been taken at the beginning of the action. The enemy made no move to attack it; the firing continued until four o'clock in the afternoon, and then, judging it useless to consume more ammunition, I put an end to it; the cavalry took position to the left of the infantry.

General Godinot perfectly fulfilled his objective in attacking the village of La Albuera. He had seized the bridge and was only waiting to see the attack from the left more advanced before he advanced to the village and moved with General Briche's cavalry against the enemy's left, it is unfortunate that this movement which was to complete the victory did not take place.

The loss of the enemy is very considerable; those of the English are no less than four to five thousand men, of whom more than fifteen hundred have been killed, and a thousand are prisoners; only eight hundred men of the latter, including twenty-five officers, could be taken away, the others were wounded who could not be moved. The rest of the casualties were wounded. The British also lost six flags and a howitzer, which was the only captured artillery piece that we have been able to bring off due to a lack of horses. Two of their generals are said to have been killed. The loss of the Spaniards is at least two thousand. The Portuguese also had casualties. The enemy had four thousand cavalry in line, including eighteen hundred English, eight hundred Portuguese and the rest Spaniards; eleven thousand English infantry, five thousand Portuguese, and fourteen thousand Spaniards; all the artillery, made up of thirty-two or thirty-six guns, was English. The former were commanded by General Beresford, and the latter by Generals Castaños, Blake and Ballesteros. All the troops which were in front of Badajoz had been withdrawn; all the artillery had been transferred to the right bank of the Guadiana, and all the reports assure us that the English were expecting a reinforcement of five thousand men, part of which actually arrived.

Our loss is unfortunately also considerable; General Werlé was killed at the head of the division as he charged the enemy. General Pépin was mortally wounded and died the next day in our camp. General Maransin was seriously wounded; he is not yet out of danger. Division General Gazan, Chief of General Staff, was wounded in the arm. General Brayer had a broken leg. Colonel Praefke of the 28th Light was killed. Colonels Schwitter of the 55th Line, Quiot of the 100th and Berge of the artillery were wounded. Several battalion commanders are wounded; Messrs. Astruc, of the 64th and Camus of the 28th Light are dead. Many officers of various ranks were also put out of action. The number of soldiers killed or wounded is almost four thousand all inclusive. The enemy captured only our dead or the dying; I sent our wounded and the prisoners of war to Seville.

On the 17th, I held my position, even that which had been taken from the enemy at the beginning of the battle. The enemies held theirs. On the 18th, I moved the army to Solano in broad daylight, where I took up a position. The enemy, who, on seeing my preparations, had believed I was launching a new attack, and had accordingly prepared for battle, seemed to want to march his whole army in pursuit of me when he realised what I was doing, but after an hour his troops halted, and he sent only a few squadrons which followed the cavalry from a distance.

I have no news from Division General Comte d'Erlon. The fortress of Badajoz is still strongly resisting and has caused losses to the enemy in several sorties; if provisions hold out until the arrival of the reinforcements which I have requested, this important place will be preserved. In the meantime I will manoeuvre according to the circumstances and I will face the enemies.

All the troops showed great valour. Those who, towards the end of the action, broke, are impatient to find the opportunity to make people forget this fault. But I owe praise to the cavalry and the artillery. All infantry regiments should be listed, although some did not support each other; Division General Gazan, Chief of the General Staff, deserves special mention for the dedication he has shown; General Latour-Maubourg also deserved it by his good disposition as well as General Ruty, on the subject of artillery; similar praise must be made of General Godinot.

I will also mention Generals Bron, Briche, Bouvier des Eclaz and Veilande; adjutant commandant Moquery, deputy chief of staff, General Bourgeat of the artillery, Colonel Konopka of the first of the Lancers of the Vistula, Colonel Vinot of the 2nd Hussars, Colonel Farine of the 4th Dragoons, Battalion Chief Gheneser, commanding the

16th Light. I should cite several other chiefs and officers of all ranks, who have particularly distinguished themselves, but the reports of the divisions not having yet reached me, I am obliged to postpone until another report to mention what they have done.

I owe special praise to the staff officers and my aides-de-camp, for the good service they have shown and their devotion; most of them were dismounted and several are wounded. Squadron Chief Tholosé, my aide-de-camp, and Captain Desperandieu, aide-de-camp to General Gazan, Hadry, chief of staff of Girard's division, Duroc, aide-de-camp to Gazan; Captain Laffite who was acting as aide-de-camp to me, Mon. Fabreguette, who was temporarily attached to General Werlé as aide-de-camp, Ingaldo and Chabouri, staff officers, and Michel, lieutenant adjutant, are in the latter case; Squadron Chief Malkewski of Your Highness's Staff, who served near me during the action, behaved perfectly.

I have the honour to renew the request for the rank of Division General in favour of General Godinot and that of Brigade General for Colonels Schwitter of the 55th, Quiot of the 100th Regiment, Rignoux of the 103rd and Moquery, deputy commander of my general staff.

I present Division General Gazan as worthy of the favours of His Majesty and I solicit for him the rank of Grand Cordon of the Legion of Honour that His Majesty had deigned to make him hope for.

Several requests for promotion must also be made in favour of other officers, but I do not have their statements at this time; shortly I shall have the honour of sending such a petition to Your Highness asking you to be good enough to have His Majesty the Emperor fill the vacant posts.

### 3. Lapène's Account

*Captain Édouard Lapène, a young artillery officer attached to the staff of the Vth Corps, wrote a history of the 1811 campaign that includes the following account of Albuera.[2] According to Lapène, the key mistake of the French during the battle occurred when General Girard came to the mistaken conclusion that the Allies were retreating and led his division to the attack without deploying in order to speed up his pursuit of the enemy, but he also faults General Godinot for insufficiently pressing his attack on the village.*

On the evening of the 15th, the Marshal was six leagues from Badajoz, at Santa-Marta; the French army was also assembled there. Half of

---

2      Lapène, É., *Conquête de l'Andalousie, Campagne de 1810 et 1811 dans le Midi de l'Espagne* (Paris, 1823), pp. 149–76.

General Werlé's brigade had remained two leagues further back at Villalba, charged with fortifying the castle of that name, a work of Moorish construction. This post, which had been designated to serve as a field hospital, was organised by the general and given a garrison formed of detachments of the 58th of the line and some mountain guns. Uncertain, moreover, for part of the day, as to whether Beresford had taken a blocking position, the Marshal was even inclined to believe that the enemy would hasten to avoid a decisive battle and recross the Guadiana. These thoughts about the intentions of the Allies were corrected by information from General Briche, commanding our light cavalry vanguard – he reported encountering enemy posts two leagues from Santa-Marta, on the road of Badajoz, and that they had fallen back before him. Informed of this discovery, the Marshal rushed to the scene himself, and made sure that the Anglo-Portuguese army was in position on the plateau above Albuera, halfway from Santa-Marta to Badajoz.

Back in Santa-Marta, the Marshal received important intelligence from his scouts on the situation of the enemy army; all agree that the latter, already augmented by the troops of General Castaños to a strength of 30,000 combatants, will be reinforced two days later on the 17th by a corps of 10,000 Spaniards, brought by Blake from the frontiers of Murcia, and recently landed at the mouth of the Guadiana, a development that will leave us opposed by 40,000 men. In light of this information, the Marshal decides to make his effort to save Badajoz by giving battle the next day before the arrival of Blake and his junction with Beresford; to, and to attempt at any cost to extricate Badajoz. The French, it is true, will have only 18,000 bayonets and 4,000 horses in this decisive struggle; but the troops are full of ardour and accustomed to victory. This confidence is transmitted quickly from the Marshal to the leaders who know his intentions: General Girard even demands the honour of being the first to attack with the Vth Corps, which has just been placed under his command.

The French army sets off in the night, and marches on Albuera by the royal road to Badajoz. General Werlé also receives the order to leave Villalba, and to join the line of march. Having arrived at daybreak at the edge of the wood in front of Santa-Marta, the high ground at this point, but then sloping gently to the foot of the enemy's positions, allows us to look down upon his formidable army from a distance. The enemy, placed above and behind the Albuera stream, had its left leaning against the village of that name, entirely abandoned since the beginning of the campaign by its inhabitants. The centre and the right extended over a vast plateau adjacent to the village, somewhat steep on the side of Santa-Marta, but level towards Olivenza and Badajoz. The flanks were protected, to the right, by uneven ground; on the left, by the meanderings of the stream which flows from south to north, and falls into the Guadiana a few leagues from the village. Cannon defended the approaches to this strong position. A battery established on the right of the hamlet, which seemed to us to be served by Spaniards, covered the bridge to be crossed, and the rising road which had to be followed to climb the height and capture Albuera. The Allies were ranged in two lines: the English and the Portuguese occupied the centre and the right, where there were also Spaniards; but the bulk of these, supported by some British troops, guarded the village on the left.

No sooner had this army and the dispositions of its leaders caught our eye than a silent agitation began spreading through our ranks: an indication that the prospect of this long-awaited combat has produced a sudden effect. A small number, still guided by old prejudices, regard with some disdain this army which has been committed for two years to avoiding battle, and is always ready to fall back prudently into the interior of Portugal. But most of us, troubled by the details of the recent affair of March 5 [the Battle of Barrosa], and the memory of the murderous action of Talavera, are not ashamed to admit that the French are finally going to fight worthy opponents and, to tell the truth, the imposing aspect of the English double line and its obvious larger size compared to our small number, made it clear that we were facing an unequal fight. Comforted, however, by the memory of past victories, and the last brilliant successes in Extremadura and Andalusia, our soldiers are confident, and ready to attack the Allies with their accustomed vigour. Moreover, there was no longer any doubt that Blake's column had joined the enemy army during the night, and that the enemy, having lifted the siege of Badajoz, had gathered all its forces at Albuera: a significant circumstance which could not fail to have a singular influence on the results of the campaign, whatever the outcome of the battle we are going to fight.

The Marshal, unable because of the weakness of his army to attack the enemy at multiple points, determines to concentrate his forces on one point to achieve a crushing result: he chooses for this purpose the extreme right of the Allies. The Marshal expects that, if their right is overthrown, the enemy must fall back on the left of their position, and unmask the road to Olivenza, the best one for their retreat. If we can block this road, the Allied army risks being completely cut off and thrown back on Badajoz, at the mercy of the garrison which, having gained freedom of manoeuvre by the lifting of the blockade, will undoubtedly fall on the rear of the enemy, and infallibly complete his defeat. The arrangements made for this purpose were as described below.

General Godinot, on our right, receives the order to march briskly on the village of Albuera and to seize it, or at least to oblige the enemy, by threatening this position, to weaken his right flank to bring help to his left. The troops of the Vth Corps, united under the orders of General Girard, and directed by the Marshal in person, will then advance against and overwhelm the weakened right of the enemy. General Latour-Maubourg, supporting the attack with 3,500 horsemen, will also advance on the right, ready to exploit any disorder if General Girard manages to break through. General Werlé's brigade, formed on its arrival on the ground in the rear of the Vth Corps, facing the point where the most important operations will take place, will also support the attack and replace the troops engaged if necessary, and will itself be supported in turn by the battalion of combined grenadiers under the orders of Colonel Varé. The artillery is all assembled under the direct orders of General Ruty and ready to bombard the wing of the enemy army chosen to be the target of all our efforts. Only one battery, served by mounted artillerymen, remains at the disposal of General Godinot.

This battery, which, on the morning of the 16th, had begun the action, was on the extreme right of the French army to support the movements of General Briche. Briche's light cavalry, posted the night before in front of the Allies, had harassed at daybreak their pickets posted in front of the Albuera stream. General Briche had even succeeded, after several advantageous charges, in driving back these posts across the bridge. Also in the morning, however, the 2nd and 10th Hussars under the orders of Colonel Vinot were detached to join the cavalry of General Latour-Maubourg on the left, so General Briche had only two regiments, the 10th and 21st Chasseurs à Cheval, to guard General Godinot's right flank and support his attack.

The orders once given all along the line, Godinot, whose movements were supposed to set up the operations of General Girard, directs the heaviest fire of his artillery on the village, with the intention of destroying the enemy batteries guarding its approaches. Our cannon, well served and aimed with accuracy, obtain some of these results, and the moment seems favourable to bring our right forward, and to close with the enemy; but General Godinot, instead of making a decisive attack with his troops, persists with an inopportune stubbornness in trying to cross the Albuera by the main bridge which is exposed to the enemy artillery, and thereby loses precious moments since the river could have been forded to the right or to the left without danger. Despite these unfortunate steps taken already at the start of the action, and the resulting delay in the attack which could directly determine the success of the day, the French marched confidently against the village, under a murderous fire from the Spanish artillery established near the church; the 16th Light finally enters Albuera, and after great sacrifices, seizes the first houses of the hamlet.

Just as Godinot's column was getting ready to cross the stream and then advance on Albuera, General Girard on the other flank, having just arrived on the battlefield, receives the order to execute the flanking movement against the enemy's right. This young general, proud to take the main part in the action at the head of the brave soldiers of the Vth Corps, directs his two divisions, which he has formed in compact columns by battalions [colonnes serrées par bataillons], towards the designated point of attack. The troops march with assurance and their weapons in the position of support arms; they cross the stream under the fire of the enemy, climb the escarpment above where the enemy is positioned, and attack with the greatest vigour the right flank of the Allies. Keenly alarmed by this sudden attack, Sir William Beresford immediately caused his first line to abandon the high ground closest to the stream. This retrograde movement causes some visible disorder in the enemy ranks.

This manoeuvre of the enemy, the object of which is to put his right in a more defensible position in the rear, having his centre for support, appears to most of our generals, including the Marshal himself, to be the start of the enemy's retreat. As a result of this view of the situation, the Marshal immediately orders Colonel Konopka, of the 1st Vistula Lancers, seconded by the 20th Dragoons, and Colonel Vinot, at the head of the 2nd and 10th Hussars, to fall on the right of the Allies and turn the retreat into a rout. The dark and cloudy state of the atmosphere allows our squadrons to approach almost with impunity, and favours after their aggression: they rush at the English bayonets with admirable dash and courage. The first enemy line is broken; 1,000 men are enveloped, lay down their arms, and surrender as prisoners of war; 6 pieces of cannon, whose murderous discharges did not slow down the vigour of our horsemen for a moment, were taken, and the gunners died at their posts. Carried away by their boiling ardour, some lancers penetrate to the second line, and even on the rear of the enemy camp, and several find death there; but almost all of the four regiments, after this brilliant feat of arms, reformed behind, and prepared to charge again.

These early successes seem to portend the brightest outcome since the day had begun auspiciously. One sees the enemy's right, in its second position, forming hastily into squares in front of the cavalry of General Latour-Maubourg, who, according to the order received, will overrun this flank, part of which has already been overthrown in the first charge. The hope of a speedy victory grows in our ranks, and if the attack led by General Godinot, on the left on the village, is pushed forward with vigour, following the instructions of the general-in-chief, perhaps the enemy, in spite of its superiority of numbers, will be definitively forced to retreat.

While the right of the Allies was being vigorously attacked by our squadrons, General Godinot had just, it is true, occupied the lower part of the village of Albuera. His brigade, composed of the 16th Light and 51st Line, held the enemy left in check and skirmished vigorously. But it was not clear whether this deadly skirmishing was all that was required at this moment or whether, following the order of the Marshal, we should attack more vigorously with bayonets, even at the risk of not entirely succeeding, in order to fix the attention of the enemy on his left, or even, if possible, to force the enemy back and turn the flank entirely? Ultimately, none of these results was achieved; either the orders given had been misunderstood, or the large number of enemies around the village prevented their execution. The operations on our right were finally limited to disputing the possession of Albuera with the Allies, and to bombarding them with our artillery. Our columns could not in their turn defend themselves from the murderous discharges of the battery placed next to the church, while we sought to maintain ourselves in the village. This battery was no less devastating to General Briche's chasseurs, which were forced, during the greater part of the action, to remain motionless on the right of the Godinot brigade, to prevent the enemy from taking advantage of his numerical superiority, and throw troops on this flank of our line. The movements of our right column consequently did not influence what was happening on the left. The Marshal was not long in noticing the lack of success on the right; but there is no time to remedy this, and the success of the day now rests on the operations of General Girard.

Girard, after crossing the stream at the head of the Vth Corps, formed in a compact column [*ployé en colonne serrée*], forces the Allies to abandon their first position to him and continues to advance in the same order still firmly convinced that the manoeuvres of the right and centre of the enemy line were undoubtedly the start of a retreat. General Girard supposes that it is crucial to launch an immediate pursuit of the enemy in order to achieve a complete rout of their troops. This unfortunate, strongly held belief, shared by the whole army including the Marshal, causes General Girard to proceed without stopping to deploy his columns as the enemy, driven from his first position, withdraws his right, manoeuvring on his centre. In short, General Girard commits the fatal mistake of pushing forward the Vth Corps, still in compact columns, and attacking the enemy in that formation.

Beresford, who, after the check suffered by his right, believed for a moment that the battle was lost, had nevertheless advanced his second line; at the moment that concerns us, three reserve brigades are also brought forward to support his right in its new position, and nearly the entire enemy army is engaged. This numerical superiority, and the mistakes already made by the French due to Girard's aggressive approach, gave the Allies an incalculable advantage, which they do not fail to seize. They calmly begin a continuous and well-directed two-rank fire. No shot is wasted against our tightly packed column, which can only respond with the insufficient and sporadic fire of its first two ranks. Except for those first two ranks, our soldiers fall defenceless to the right and the left, and those who survive become seriously demoralised. Our officers vainly attempt to rally the troops by their example. The first victim of the fault committed is General Pépin, who falls with a mortal wound; Generals Maransin and Brayer, belonging as well as the first division of the Vth Corps, are carried away dying; General Gazan, the chief of staff, is himself wounded.

General Girard is in the middle of the danger; in this critical position, he wants to deploy his troops into line and, immediately after, execute a general movement from his left to the right; but this passage of lines [passage de lignes], which requires space and calm, cannot be accomplished under such heavy fire. Colonel Praefke, of the 28th Light, the first regiment in the column, is mortally wounded, as are all his superior officers. Demoralisation is at its height; and the soldiers of this corps, which has already lost 600 men, regard themselves as victims who are being sacrificed. In this situation, the most desperate in which a troop, once so courageous, has ever found itself, results in some obvious wavering, which soon becomes a disorderly retreat. The 103rd Line, placed immediately behind the 28th Light in the column, and then, in turn, all the other regiments of General Girard's corps, successively exposed to the same dangers and the same losses, are forced to yield to the superior numbers of the enemy and to the superiority of their volleys after useless efforts to hold their ground. These troops soon form one confused mass which falls back pell-mell, and do not stop their retreat until they reach the first position of the morning on the other side of the stream. This stream, the banks of which have been muddied by the earlier crossing of troops and artillery, still presents an obstacle and leaves our regiments exposed to enemy fire during their retreat.

The Marshal, having thrown himself and his staff into the middle of the fray, ordered the immediate advance of Werlé's brigade, which forms the reserve: he hopes, with the help of this reinforcement, to restore the morale of the troops engaged, and to turn the tide of the battle. General Werlé confidently joins the combat at the head of the 12th Light and 58th Line. However, these regiments, barely arrived on the ground and being in the act of deploying, find themselves pressed by the troops of General Girard, who, already repulsed, suddenly fall back on them. They pass through the ranks of the reserve, and throw them into confusion. Werlé's brigade is nevertheless able to make a stand and to stop the Allies for a while. Despite the confusion, the reserve is soon able to move from defence to offence and launches an attack to regain the position which was taken at the beginning of the day. The resulting terrible struggle, equally fatal to both parties, does not end in victory for us. General Werlé is killed; his brigade, devastated by considerable losses and demoralised by the retreat of the Vth Corps, falls back in turn; but this retreat is more orderly even though there is a shortage of senior officers and the two battalions manoeuvre in isolation.

The enemy's right, swelled with all their reserves, advances rapidly. No longer opposed by our infantry, the enemy's objective is to prevent us from having time to reorganise our forces, regain composure and so possibly begin the action again. Placed in the front line after the retreat of the infantry, the French artillery, commanded entirely by General Ruty at this point, redoubled its efforts to hold its ground and restore balance to the struggle despite its isolated position. Our cannon, served with as much skill as activity, produces the most terrible effects. Despite the enemy's determination to retake the lost ground, they are stopped by the cannonballs and the volleys of grapeshot which rain down on their ranks and wreak havoc! The battlefield is furrowed in all directions by our projectiles, and their ricochets reach even the most distant reserves. A Spanish regiment, placed well in the rear, although being inactive for the duration of the fight, is itself almost destroyed by our fire. Eventually, the guns inflict so many casualties that the march of the Allies is slowed down; and we see them stepping over or trampling on heaps of corpses to continue their movements. This enormous destruction, without a doubt one of the most horrible that has taken place in the peninsula, only lasted less than two hours, between eleven o'clock in the morning and one o'clock in the afternoon.

General Latour-Maubourg's cavalry had wanted to take a direct part in the action, but later charges made by the lancers and the hussars could not duplicate their earlier success, and the attempts made by our dragoons and our chasseurs to break through the enemy's right in its second position were also unsuccessful. These troops, however, were an imposing presence throughout the battle and deserve great praise for preventing the enemy from overrunning our left when the infantry retreated. The English cavalry, 2,000 men strong, avoids combat with ours, and we force the enemy squadrons to move cautiously out of reach by preparing to charge at the first sign of an offensive movement by them. In the end, however, both cavalry forces suffer considerable losses. On our side, Latour-Maubourg's division, placed within range of the enemy on our right, suffered from the English artillery; but it was absolutely necessary for them to hold that exposed position for the slightest retrograde or even lateral movement could have allowed Sir William Beresford to throw troops into the interval which separated Generals Girard and Godinot, a manoeuvre that might have assured him complete success.

There were no longer intact columns of French infantry on the left of our line, and the skirmishers, who remained in small numbers between the batteries, only weakly protected our cannon. The officers and gunners thus find themselves exposed to a cloud of enemy skirmishers; the number of our artillerymen put out of action is consequently considerable; even ammunition begins to run out; it therefore finally became necessary to end this extraordinary combat of cannon against infantry and definitively abandon the field of battle. This movement is executed in good order; firing in echelons, our guns rejoin their respective divisions, which have already rallied behind the stream in the position they had in the morning, protected by a reserve battery of 12 guns, advantageously positioned by Colonel Bouchu.

General Godinot still held the lower part of Albuera, which had been taken, lost and then retaken from the enemy: this was the only outstanding result obtained by this general during the day. The 16th Light continued to defend itself with vigour in the village, against the Portuguese and the Spaniards who were emboldened by the success of their right; however, the Marshal gave General Godinot the order to abandon the village in order to bring all his troops back to the position occupied in the morning on the other side of the stream. Godinot immediately relayed the order to the colonel of the 16th Light, who at first seemed reluctant to comply, but after a further period of courageous resistance the colonel reluctantly obeyed the order, which had been repeated three times.

The battalion of combined grenadiers under the orders of Colonel Varé, placed in the centre of the line and serving with a portion of the cavalry to link the two wings of the army, had not been engaged.

In the middle of the action, the battalion was approached by part of the 88th Line, which had just been thrown into disorder, and it was feared that this battalion might be unsettled by this development; but these elite troops were in no way shaken, and only began to retreat when the Marshal gave them the order. This movement closely follows the evacuation of Albuera, and the crossing of the bridge by the troops of General Godinot. The exchange of gunfire does not take long to slow down and ceases entirely at 3 o'clock in the afternoon; the troops are from this moment occupying the same ground as in the morning, and the forward sentries are placed on the banks of the of the Albuera stream, which separates the two armies.

## 4. Anonymous Criticism

*This next document is almost certainly <u>not</u> a first-hand account of the battle, but earns a place in this volume because Professor Charles Oman notably relied on it to reach his well-publicised conclusion that, contrary to all the other relevant evidence presented in this book, Girard's Vth Corps advanced against the Spanish troops at Albuera in a 'mixed' order of battle and not in column formation. Oman explained in volume 4 of his* A History of the Peninsular War:[3]

I had long sought for an exact description of his array, of which the French historians and Soult's dispatch only say that it was a *colonne serrée de bataillons*. At last I found the required information in the Paris archives[1] in the shape of an anonymous criticism on Soult's operations, drawn up (apparently for Napoleon's eye) by some officer who had been set to write a report on the causes of the loss of the battle.

This document says that

the line of attack was formed by a brigade in column of attack [i.e. a column formed of four battalions in column of double companies, one battalion behind the other]. To the right and left the front line was in a mixed formation, that is to say, on each side of the central column was a battalion deployed in line, and on each of the two outer sides of the deployed battalions was a battalion or a regiment in column, so that at each end the line was composed of a column ready to form square, in case the hostile cavalry should try to fall upon one of our flanks – which was hardly likely, since our own cavalry was immensely superior to it in number.

---

3    Oman, Charles W., *A History of the Peninsular War* (7 vols., Oxford, 1902–30), vol. 4 (1911), pp. 379–80.

Oman's Note No. 1 – 'Those at the War Ministry not the *Archives Nationales.'*

*Even assuming that Oman is correct that this undated document was written soon after the battle, his interpretation is problematic because it is based on a fundamental and inexplicable mistranslation of the key portion of the document. As the full document in the French military archives makes clear, the excerpt that Oman focused on describes the formation that the author believes the French <u>should have</u> adopted, not the one they actually used, so the document in fact supports the contrary conclusion that the Vth Corps advanced in massed columns, which is the unanimous conclusion of all relevant French sources.*[4]

The Battle of Albuera

The battle of Albuera, which was fought to relieve the siege of Badajoz being conducted by the combined [English-Portuguese] army, should have had a very advantageous result except for the faulty manoeuvres of the French army. If the commanding general had had the type of military insight [*coup d'oeil militaire*] so useful for an army commander, the battle would have been won. He should not have left his massed troops without the opportunity to deploy and he would have recognised more quickly that the enemy line was very long relative to the size of the enemy force and in consequence was not very strong at any one point.

By attacking vigorously at one point he would have pierced the enemy line and would have been able to crush one of the wings before the other wing (which was half in the village of Albuera and half outside of it) was able to make a change in front to cover the centre where the principal attack should have taken place.

He should have known how to take advantage from his considerable artillery and from his cavalry, which was superior to that of the enemy. To the contrary, the infantry was crushed without being able to deploy. The artillery hindered its movements and the infantry hindered the movements of the artillery. The cavalry placed on the left flank checked that of the enemy but was not able to make headway without help from the infantry, and it was these defective dispositions which forced the French army, in spite of its valour, to abandon in disorder the field of battle.

Project of the Battle

The enemy army had its right extending towards the mountains of Feria and its left extending beyond the village of Albuera which

---

4    *Service Historique de la Défense, Chateau de Vincennes*, Paris File C$^8$ 72.

formed a strong point for the line. In front of this position there was a stream which did not constitute a serious obstacle and beyond which the French army formed in masses by regiment in lieu of forming in the following manner [emphasis added] [*se forma en masse par régiment au lieu de se former de la manière suivante*]:

On one line, having meanwhile a division in reserve, the regiments of which were formed in two ranks and in battle formation, in order to deceive the enemy and make it seem that there was a second line, which was not the case but which would have made the troops feel supported and would have provided a rally point in the case of disorder, experience having shown the impossibility of rallying troops actively under fire.

The heavy artillery (the army had ten 12-pounder cannons) should have targeted the village and several battalions should have made a convincing feint there to occupy the enemy and induce them to move more troops from the left to guard the village. The howitzers should also have done great damage to the troops of the enemy massed in the village.

The line of attack should have had a brigade formed in an attack column in the centre supported on its left and its right by the rest of the line in mixed order, that is to say with the battalions of the regiments deployed and in column, in such a manner that there was a column at each end of the line ready to form square if the enemy cavalry turned one of our flanks. However, such a circumstance was unlikely since our cavalry was superior in numbers and has been placed on the left flank to check that of the enemy. Several platoons of cavalry were posted on the right at skirmishers.

In the centre in front of the reserve, the regiment of Polish Lancers was destined to support the centre column when it broke through the enemy line.

The light artillery should have been posted in the intervals of each brigade directing all their fire on the centre of the enemy line, with several pieces supporting the cavalry on the extreme left.

The whole line should have advanced at a charging pace, halting only if necessary to respond if the fire of the enemy, which occupied the small hills, hindered our troops. The Polish Lancers with the reserve artillery should have followed the movement of the line.

Once the enemy line was broken (as effectively it was after our first charge), our cavalry on the left being very superior to that of the enemy should have changed direction to the left and turned the right of the enemy which, being composed in part of Spaniards, would have been overthrown.

The reserve seeing the success of this movement should have formed itself into columns on the right to stop the change in front which the enemy would have undoubtedly made to envelop our line. The heavy artillery firing on the village as described above would change direction and direct its fire to take the enemy from the Frank during each movement circumstance that would have prodigiously hindered and maybe even prevented its execution.

The enemy army would have retreated in disorder on the road to Olivenza and, since they would have had no way of crossing the Guadiana, our pursuit would have taken many prisoners. Even though it was very small, the Garrison of Badajoz would have meanwhile made a sortie and completed the demoralisation of the enemy.

There is no doubt that if [emphasis added] this plan had been followed in any way, the Allied army would have been destroyed given that our first attack had already routed them and given us 2,000 prisoners.

But the columns did not have large enough intervals to deploy easily and trying to deploy took a prodigious amount of time during which the enemy could not fail to overwhelm us with his fire. The enemy also profited from this fault in that our ranks became disordered as our men were knocked down without being able to respond in kind since only the heads of column were able to fire on the enemy. They [the French officers] tried to rally the regiments under fire, which was an impracticable thing to do, and the attempt only served to further frighten the soldiers who, above all, could see that there was no reserve.

The same stream that was crossed a short time earlier by the army with such success was re-crossed in a horrifying disorder with the artillery alone supporting the retreat and holding off the enemy, who did not dare to cross the stream themselves.

## B. Vth Corps Accounts

### 1. Girard's Account
*Unfortunately, the whereabouts of General Jean-Baptiste Girard's full report to Marshal Soult, concerning the actions of the Vth Corps, is currently unknown. However, there a summary of, and some translated excerpts from, the report in the catalogue for a collection of Napoleonic documents assembled by John Sainsbury in the nineteenth century.[5]*

---

5    Gerard [sic], Report to Marshal Soult, 16 May 1811, in Sainsbury, John, *The Napoleon Museum* (London, 1845), p. 481.

[The report] [s]tates that, conformably to his [Soult's] request, he [Girard] sends, with his report of the proceedings of the 16th instant, a list of the applications for promotion, and for enrolment among those officers of the Legion of Honour who have been particularly distinguished; also a list of casualties, and a memorial respecting the filling up with the vacant places, soliciting also his kind support of the application. This document, which is of great length, details most fully all the circumstances relating to the sanguinary battle. It commences by stating that on the 16th May, at break of day, the two divisions march upon Albuera; the combined army had assembled there during the night. It was formed of three lines behind the town. The first column was flanked on the right by a battalion of light troops, which, although engaged with the enemy, attacked vigorously and overthrew the English. Having gained the first eminence, we advanced at the charge to take possession of the second, which was defended by several columns of English, and supported on the right by a battery of four field pieces. A heavy fire suddenly opened, which soon became terrible. The French troops, however, continued to advance, when some other columns unexpectedly appeared, and attacked their first line, which having betrayed some hesitation, the second line then advanced, and rushing on the enemy, threw them into disorder and captured the field pieces. The Polish lancers, at the same time, executed a brilliant charge, made a great number of prisoners, captured six standards. The French then ascended the heights some sharpshooters had gained, and Girard's aide-de-camp was mortally wounded. The lancers at this juncture made a retrograde movement, and fresh columns advanced. The shock was terrible, the battle became desperate. They were fighting at only eight paces distant from each other. The troops were for a moment *pêle-mêle*, the colonel of the 100th Regiment received a thrust from a bayonet; fresh troops replaced those that had fallen, and the English were at the same time manoeuvring upon their flanks, etc.

A long list of the killed and wounded follows, and also of those for whom favours and decorations were solicited.

## 2. D'Héralde Narrative

*Jean-Baptiste D'Héralde was a veteran surgeon who had served at the battles of Austerlitz, Jena, Eylau and Friedland, so he had an interesting basis for comparison between those famous actions and the battle of Albuera. His manuscript memoirs, which were not published until 2002, contain a remarkably detailed account of the battle.[6]*

---

6    D'Héralde, Jean-Baptiste, *Mémoires d'une Chirurgien de la Grande Armée* (Paris, 2002), pp. 153–63.

The French army, 16,000 infantry strong, with 3,500 cavalry under the command of General Latour-Maubourg, and 33 guns, commanded by General Ruty and Colonel Bouchu, left Santa Marta on May 16, at seven o'clock in the morning. It advanced on a single road, the main road from Seville to Badajoz. One full league from the town, the dragoons and one company of artillery left the road to march towards our left and skirt the wood through which we passed on our way to Albuera.

The enemy army, 20,000 English, 12,000 Portuguese and 10,000 Spaniards strong, was placed in three lines on the Albuera plateau. It was commanded by General William Beresford, assisted by Generals Blake and Castaños. This army, which covered the siege of Badajoz, had established its centre in the town of Albuera. This village was traversed by the main road which leads to Badajoz. The Portuguese had established themselves on the Allied left facing us, extending their lines in that direction and thus covering the road to Talavera del Real. We saw the red coats in the village near the church located in front of the village to the right of the road; their lines, which extended to their right, were formed in front of and over the road to Olivenza and the bridge of Jurumenha. The Spaniards were in the rear and centre. Two small streams, one or two feet deep, with more or less steep banks, flowed from the right of the village, at the bottom of the high ground occupied by the English. These streams met near the main road and passed under a single bridge located 400 paces from the first houses of the town, thereafter forming only one stream on the left, covering the front of the Portuguese lines. These streams seemed placed there like a wide ditch defending the approaches to the plateau where the enemy was positioned.

At 10 o'clock in the morning we advanced through the woods, on the main road from Santa-Marta to Albuera. The English, who were a league from us, did not try to defend them. The infantry of the Vth Corps, under the orders of Girard, made a long halt there, as if they no longer needed to fight to reach Badajoz. Those who had some provisions ate them. The general himself with all his staff and some officers breakfasted in this wood. Suddenly we heard the rumble of the English cannon firing on our light cavalry which preceded us. Everyone says with surprise: 'The English are in Albuera!'

While the Vth Corps was making its long halt, the Reserve Division, with the 12th Light at its head, passed on the main road by order of the Marshal to form the vanguard of our small army. General Girard, who still feared that the enemy would not wait for him or that someone else would have the advantage of firing the first shot, asked the Marshal to let him lead the vanguard. Soult, who could refuse nothing to Girard, halted the march of the Reserve Division and the 34th and 40th Line, under the orders of General Brayer, took the lead of our small army. The 64th and 88th Line, commanded by Colonel Veilande, followed that movement, as well as the 21st and 28th Light, and the 100th and 103 Line, the division formerly commanded by General Gazan but now commanded by General Pépin. General Maransin commanded the second brigade there. The Reserve Division followed with the Werlé brigade in the lead (12th light and 58th line) and the other brigade (16th light and 51st line). A battalion of combined grenadiers of the 1st Corps, commanded by Colonel Varé, brought up the rear.

At noon, the 1st Brigade, headed by General Girard and his staff, emerged from the wood. The 27th Mounted Chasseurs was in line to the right of the road with a portion of the 21st Chasseurs. The Polish Lancers, the 2nd and 10th Hussars were on the left. We could see the enemy and Albuera ahead of us at close cannon range. The dragoons were to our extreme left, but far further from us than the enemy. General Girard ordered: 'head of column to the left'. We were at the edge of the woods at long artillery range. We don't shoot. After marching in columns by platoons along the edge of the wood, behind our light cavalry, General Girard ordered: 'right in line'. The 2nd Brigade arrived and formed into columns by divisions behind the 1st. Pépin's division followed the movement to line up on the left of the 1st Division; which took a long time and allowed the enemy to count us.

At the same time, the Polish lancers and the 2nd and 10th Hussars followed by our voltigeurs crossed the two small streams in front of us under the fire of three pieces of English cannon, in a battery a little way in front of the church. The English cavalry, seeing this movement, moved forward to charge the Poles disorganised from the crossing of the streams. The latter couched their lances and prepared to receive the enemy. The English turned and retreated behind their infantry lines. Our light cavalry followed them quickly along the plateau to our left, which brought them closer to our dragoons and placed them between the dragoons and the right of the English infantry. The voltigeurs of the 34th and 40th, commanded by Battalion Chief Pupersaque of the 40th, covered the Brayer brigade which crossed the streams using two shallow fords that General Girard had reconnoitred.

Having crossed the streams, General Brayer received the order to march straight to the road from Albuera to Olivenza and to overturn the enemy line from there.

'We will not worry about the village of Albuera,' General Girard assured, 'the Reserve Division will take care of it.'

This impetuous leader already believed the enemy in retreat and thought to cut him off from the road of Olivenza. His chief of staff, the brave Monsieur Hudry, wished to forbid me to have my medical equipment unloaded.

'Follow the division,' he said to Military Commissary Herry [Mery]. 'Headquarters ambulances will dress our first wounded.'

The 2nd Brigade joined us, formed in columns by division [*colonnes par division*], and in this order of battle it followed behind the 1st Brigade and formed the second line. Colonel [*sic*] Veilande, who commanded the 2nd Brigade, was a consummate tactician who had the full confidence of General Girard. We marched forward under the fire of the English cannon. Both streams had already been crossed by 5th Corps infantry. The 2nd Division, in columns, made its move to line up to the left of the 1st, but this move took far too long. This delay, which had the most disastrous consequences, could easily have been avoided by having the whole of the Vth Corps arrive by the same route as the dragoons on the left of the wood.

Our artillery, which at first had put some guns in battery on a small mound to the left of the road, behind the two streams, now sought a ford to cross them. At this time, it was 1 o'clock in the afternoon, a rain mixed with hail, hitting our faces, increased the difficulties that our infantry, already wet to their knees, were experiencing in climbing to the high ground. The line of our voltigeurs had already reached the top but could not advance any further. The English were in line of battle only 15 paces away. The 34th and 40th Line regiments arrived on the plateau with Generals Brayer and Girard. Their drums signalled the charge and the fierce cry 'Forward!' was heard. Despite its murderous fire, the first English line was reached and overthrown. The first line began to flee towards the second line which was advancing to its support. The Polish Lancers and the 2nd and 10th Hussars which were past the enemy right charged around their flank and the fine English regiment (known as the Buffs) was taken prisoner. Three pieces of artillery, three flags and 1,200 English prisoners were the trophies of this first charge. It was barely two o'clock.

The infantry of the 1st Brigade continued its forward progress and charged the English second line. The cries of 'With the bayonet!' were heard. The 2nd Brigade, in columns by division, marched behind the 1st and was of no help to it, although the 2nd Brigade lost many men from the volleys of English troops who had left the village and attacked it on its right flank. The march of these four regiments [of the 2nd Brigade] had been so rapid that they did not yet have a single piece of artillery to support them. Since our cannon could not climb directly to the plateau they ascended by means of a long flanking movement on the left.

The Spanish artillery, placed behind and to the right of the town, blasted the ranks of the 1st Division, whose position was most critical. General Brayer had his left leg broken by a gunshot. His aide-de-camp Carlier was killed. General Girard's horse was killed; he himself was injured. His first aide-de-camp [Duroc-]Mesclops was mortally wounded, as was his engineer officer, Captain Andouan [Andoucaud]. Chief of Staff Hudry had his horse killed. Those already killed or mortally wounded included two Battalion Chiefs of the 40th line, Bonneau [Gaspard-Bonnot] and Supersaque [Supersac], the grenadier Captains Lamare [Delamarre] of the 40th, Combarieux [Combarlieu] of the 34th, and Dautrement and Leconte of the 88th, Second Lieutenant Hapecher [Hubscher] (nephew of Marshal Lefebvre) of the 88th, the brave Lauran [Lorrain] of the 64th, officer of the Legion of Honour, and grenadier Captain Chevaillon [Chevailleau] of the same regiment.

Meanwhile, General Werlé with the 1st Reserve Brigade had already crossed the streams. He marched at the head of the 12th Light, which mounted the plateau in compact columns by division [*colonnes serrées par division*], followed by the 58th Line. The 1,200 English prisoners who were descending from the high ground at the same time caused much disorder in this column. Everyone wanted to have a prisoner and talk to him; this circumstance caused the officers and soldiers to believe the battle was already won.

During this time, the second English line is approaching ours. A murderous fire of two ranks starts at 150 paces from us; we have no artillery pieces to support Girard's division, which was taken in front by the English second line and on its right flank by the English who were coming out of the village with increasing fire every moment. A large number of dead and wounded thins our ranks. The position was no longer tenable.

Marshal Soult, who remained at the edge of the wood, with the 51st Line and the battalion of Combined Grenadiers, the only reserve covering the road and our wagons and baggage, must have believed the battle won on seeing the 1,200 English prisoners descend from the plateau, together with reports of three captured cannons and three captured flags which they had hastened to present to him; this impression is confirmed by the fact that he could no longer see a single man from the Vth Corps. Soult arrived at a gallop on the plateau with his chief of staff at 2:30 p.m., when our first line was making its retrograde movement. The second line (the 64th and 88th Line) in columns by division, did not have time to deploy. Veilande, who was in command, had just had his horse killed under him. They were faced by the second English line and attacked on the right flank by the fire of troops leaving Albuera. Heavy artillery fire increased the confusion.

The remnants of these four regiments withdrew slowly but in the greatest disorder, supported only by their skirmishers. General Werlé, arriving at the head of the 12th Light in a compact column [*colonne serrée*], was able to cover the retreating troops and halt the enemy advance by charging them vigorously. He threw the enemy back into the village and took possession of some buildings, but at the first shock this general was killed. A large part of his troops were already out of action. The colonel of the 12th Light had his horse killed under him. The enemy's firepower and the flight of the troops of the Vth Corps frightened the survivors. They broke up and withdrew in disorder despite the exhortations of the brave Colonel Dulong, who remained alone near the dead general.

Division General Gazan, Soult's chief of staff, sought to rally our second line, which he knew well since he had commanded these troops for a long time. His efforts succeeded for a moment, but soon he was wounded himself. Brigade General Pépin who commanded this division (2nd of the Vth Corps) was killed [actually, mortally wounded]. General Maransin, who succeeded him in this command, fell with a bullet through his body.

Marshal Soult himself tried to restore order by shouting: 'Halt!' but his command was not heeded. I saw him, close to me, descend from the plateau, stop a drummer and give the order to beat the signal for a retreat. Several drummers repeated it; all withdrew, not in flight, but in pell-mell disorder. Our left alone did not move. The 28th Light, supported by three pieces of light artillery from the dragoon division, kept up and received a furious fusillade. Its brave leader, Colonel Praefke, was mortally wounded and fell in front of his regiment. He pulled himself into a sitting position and ordered his men to stand their ground. His three battalion chiefs and the three most senior captains were killed. Aide-Major Latouche, giving aid to one of them, had a bullet through his chest. All the men of this regiment, faithful to the commands of their expiring colonel, remained in line firing by ranks and did not move. Captain Jacques Jean, the eighth chief of the day, commanded under the orders of the colonel.

The fates or luck that wins the battle abandoned us at Albuera, May 16, 1811. There, for the first time, I saw most of the fine troops of the Vth Corps show their cartridge boxes to the enemy. Almost all our soldiers retreated.

Our artillery, seeing the retreat of the infantry, made a flank march to regain the ford the guns had used in the morning. However, a howitzer that had entered the ford to cross the streams overturned and stopped the retreating infantry. 'Form battery, Form battery,' cried Colonel Bouchu. Fifteen guns were put into line. Where? In some low ground from which they could no longer retreat. Despair rather than fate placed them there; but those who commanded them and the brave men who served the guns wanted to sell them dearly to the enemy. To sell? That's the word! Never was a moment more pathetic. All the generals of the Vth Corps were killed, wounded, or dismounted. Marshal Soult, on horseback, descended from the plateau in our midst. He shouted to the retreating soldiers: 'Where are you going? Turn about face, no one is chasing you!'

He was mistaken or wanted to deceive them. The officers shouted, 'Halt!' Everyone repeated this word but no one stopped. I said that except for the 28th Light still fighting on our left, facing the enemy along with our squadrons of dragoons, and the 16th Light on the high road on the right near the town, everyone had retreated in the greatest disorder, not fleeing, I repeat, but pell-mell.

Our guns were soon unmasked by this retreat. They remained in line in front of the two streams, at the bottom of the plateau, in perfect order, as if on a firing range. Part of the infantry abandoned them and crossed the streams.

At this moment the English en masse in several compact columns [*colonnes serrées*] charged down from the plateau. Quickly their column heads reached the bottom and trampled on our unfortunate wounded whose plaintive cries were drowned out by the mournful notes of English bugles sounding the charge. Our blood had flowed, and the enemy followed its tracks like hungry wolves. In a moment theirs would flow as well!

Our gunners began to sweep the field with rapid fire. The sound of the cannon excited our soldiers. All stopped, looking for their eagles as rally points! The brave men who carried them had not crossed the streams; they had remained behind our guns, which already covered them with a cloud of smoke. The eagle of the 103rd Line, carried by a voltigeur from the 88th, was positioned next to that of the latter regiment. The eagle bearer lieutenant of the 103rd had had his leg broken by a shell. Almost all our remaining officers, having grabbed muskets, were seen surrounding these eagles and preparing to resist the charging enemy. Our grapeshot, launched by 15 cannons, thinned the ranks of their compact columns, but did not slow down their march. Those spared by the storm of metal finally reached the guns.

Twice these proud islanders came to touch the bronze which vomited death. They were mowed down by the hail of iron launched by our artillerymen and despite their efforts and their audacity, they could not seize a single one of our guns. In less than ten minutes, 7,000 English were killed or wounded at the foot of this same plateau which they had so brilliantly defended.

Alas, several of our own wounded were also killed by the fire of our guns. Finally, we heard the English bugles sounding recall instead of the charge; the English moved quickly up the slope of the plateau, no doubt fearing to be charged by our dragoons who were approaching the fray.

At this time, 3:30 p.m., the firing ceased and almost instantly the drums of the Vth Corps beat 'Au Champs' as ordered by Marshal Soult, who was maintaining the line that had been established in front of the two small streams. He praises the 28th Light and its old Colonel Praefke [born 1758] who, lying on the ground in front of his regiment, asked him if he could be carried away. Soult, telling him yes, assures the soldiers that we will attack the enemy that very evening and each one remains at his post. The old colonel is carried to the edge of the wood and dies there.

I regret not knowing the name of a brave lieutenant of light artillery, carrying a telescope and wearing a busby, who, wounded by two shots, refused to receive my treatment. He was everywhere, inspiring his comrades. A third blow laid him dead. His comrades paid him the honours of burial by digging a pit for him in front of the mouth of their guns, in front of the two streams, and saluted him with two cannon shots.

At 4 o'clock, everything was calm. We could see, on the right of the town, the English who were working to erect entrenchments in front of the church in the very place where we had taken their three pieces of cannon.

We spent the night of the 16th to 17th at the edge of the wood. Our first line and the artillery had by nightfall re-crossed the streams. Our guns were positioned on the road and to the right and to the left. The Marshal remained in the bivouac to the left of the road with the Polish lancers and our medical personnel. General Girard and his staff had also established themselves on the left of the road where the right of the Vth Corps was. I had put the body of his first aide-de-camp in a caisson.

The night was rainy. Oh, what a night! We can well imagine that despite all our zeal and our eagerness, it was impossible for us to dress this mass of wounded before nightfall. Those who were able to walk or who had horses, after receiving our care, took the road to Santa Marta without orders, where they were no safer. The greatest number and all whose wounds made it impossible for them to move were laid down here or there where chance had placed them. All spent the night in the bivouac, exposed to a cold rain without any food or drink. Our rapacious supply personnel had nothing to give to these unfortunates. Our whole little army and the 1,000 English prisoners received nothing.

On the 17th at dawn, the rain continued. Our drums beat 'La Diane'. The two armies were positioned at close range to each other without firing a shot.

At 11 a.m. the Combined Grenadiers of the 1st Corps with 4,000 of our wounded and the greater part of the English taken on the 16th left for Seville. General Maransin was carried by the English. This column was under the orders of General Gazan, himself having his arm injured by a bullet.

We slept again the night of the 17th to the 18th on the same ground. The 16th Light was still beside the bridge. We saw the English in Albuera demolishing the houses in order to use the wood to prepare the soup.

On the 18th at 3 a.m., our wagons and caissons approached the stream to the right of the road. Several thought that we were going to attack at this point. But no, this forward movement was just a way to access a side road to the right of the main road and begin our retreat to the village of La Solana, a full two leagues from Albuera.

Although I was the Chief Surgeon of Girard's division, at four in the morning I knew nothing of this movement and at 6 a.m. I was still loading the wounded on to caissons and artillery pieces of the rear guard at close range from the Portuguese posts. We even left several of our wounded in the woods who, not being informed of this movement and not knowing the road to the right, remained in their bivouac. They were taken by the enemy who, only at midday, sent strong patrols there.

One sees that this terrible combat, in which the French and the English showed great valour, was without result. It is true that we saved Badajoz momentarily, but Badajoz was not worth the brave men we lost there! Never did the Emperor engage in such a bloody battle with such a small force. Our attack was lively, daring even, but without elegance. Our attack lacked an overall plan. Our retrograde movement made the enemy believe for a moment that our centre was routed. Nothing less than the courage of the fine troops of the Vth Corps was needed to rally at such a difficult moment and fight afterwards one against three! This is true heroism!

In summary, the fight of Albuera was a butchery where we threw in our brave soldiers like mastiffs in an arena. The impetuous General Girard believed that he was going to sink an army of 45,000 men with his 16 small battalions, and he could have succeeded if General Godinot had seized Albuera; which was very difficult because the Marshal was having him attack a nearly impregnable position.

A skilful general, Latour-Maubourg remained in line with his dragoons, unable to charge the enemy sheltered by the houses of the village. As at the Gebora, he would have charged at the head of his men if the English had left Albuera.

If we had methodically engaged our fine artillery, which saved us, it would have crushed the Allied army which, having very little to oppose it, would have had to give in. But to attack the English as we did was to take the bull by the horns.

We had 400 or 500 horsemen more than the enemy, a fine and good cavalry, much more artillery and two-thirds less infantry. The Marshal had complete freedom of manoeuvre and nothing forced him to attack a position so advantageous to the English army which was protected in Albuera from the attacks of our cavalry and the fire of our artillery.

Honour to the English general for having chosen a position so well and honour to the brave men who fought there so valiantly, to the 28th Light and to its old colonel, to the Polish lancers who carried off a flag, to the 2nd and 10th of Hussars, to Colonel Bouchu and to his artillery, which saved us.

. . . all these great battles were much less deadly for the soldiers and officers of the Vth Corps than this battle of Albuera where more than a third of our infantry was put out of action. Out of 18,000 men, 7,000 were killed or wounded. It is horrifying! Of 383 officers of all ranks put out of action, 164 were killed: among this number, two brigadier generals (Pépin, commanding the 2nd Division of the 5th Corps, and General Werlé), two colonels, ten battalion chiefs, all captains of grenadiers. To use General Girard's expression: the brave officers who were killed there were the soul of his division.

Monsieur de Sommariva, Italian, captain in the 10th Hussars, was among the number of dead. Military surgery also had the honour of shedding its blood in this fight – 15 surgeons were injured in it and three died of their wounds. The losses of the English, Portuguese and Spaniards were more considerable than ours, according to the reports of the inhabitants and the English themselves. They had 9,000 men disabled, but many more dead than us. It is easy to imagine it because of the fire of our artillery which struck down their columns, while our losses were the result of musketry.

Forty days later, I revisited this field of carnage. I have traversed it several times with General Girard, another time with my brother and his comrades from the army of Portugal. Large pits dug by the English were filled with the heads of corpses they had burned. Two large pits had not been covered. We could judge their depth by the earth that was around. You could see these half-burned heads, piled on top of each other. There were over 1,200 in each pit. It was horrifying. Indeed, the English used to burn all the dead after a battle; the arms, legs, and trunks were consumed, but the heads did not burn. They made large pits where they threw them with any bones that had escaped the flames.

We also travelled through the town of Albuera, which is only a long line of little houses placed to the right and to the left of the main road from Seville to Badajoz. There was no longer a single inhabitant. The church and a large number of the houses were without roofs. The fountain still flowed with crystal waters. But let's leave this field of horror where the remains of so many of the brave rest in peace and follow our retreat to La Solana.

Having arrived at La Solana, we took position there. Marshal Soult, still seeing a large number of wounded who could not be transported without the help of artillery (since the 4,000 who had left with General Gazan had used all the means of transport available) and thinking that he might need his artillery to from time to time, ordered that the most seriously wounded, even those who could not walk, should be taken immediately to Almendralejo, a pretty little rich town three leagues from La Solana and four from Villafranca. A surgeon and a hospital orderly would be designated to remain prisoners with them in the event that we should leave the position (which was certain). 280 wounded from various units were taken there by wagons and on artillery pieces during the days of the 18th, 19th and 20th in the morning. All our wounded were placed in a large convent at the entrance to the town, on the right as you arrive from Villafranca. They were placed under the responsibility of the local authorities, and our cavalry left the town on the morning of the 20th.

Aide-de-camp Mesclop, from Bergerac, carried by the English, died on the stretcher which served as his bed, in a barrack in La Solana, on the 19th. This brave young man said to me 20 minutes before his death: 'What a blow for my poor mother!' Generals Girard and Bouvier des Eclaz, and Captain Gilibert of the 26th Dragoons, came to visit him. He consoled them and said to them: 'I am happier than my brave Colonel Chamorin, I am dying among my comrades!' Grenadiers of the 34th Line gave him the last honours. He was buried in the cemetery of La Solana.

At the same time, on the evening of the 19th, at 4 o'clock p.m., the cannon fired on a strong patrol of English cavalry coming out of the wood of Albuera. The 27th Mounted Chasseurs had a slight engagement in which one of the squadron leaders, Monsieur de Bourbon-Busset, fell from his horse and was taken prisoner.

## 3. Girard Anecdote

*After Girard was defeated at Arroyo de Molinos in October 1811, he expressed some views on his relationship with Soult to Surgeon D'Héralde.*[7]

Marshal Soult will be delighted to find me in trouble since he has already accused me of having manoeuvred badly at Albuera. If at that battle, like at . . . Ocaña, I had overthrown the enemy, he would have taken the credit. And he certainly would have been victorious at Albuera if he hadn't taken fright and had attacked the enemy boldly at the head of his reserves.

## 4. Maransin's Account

*General Jean Pierre Maransin was inspired to write an account of his own experiences at Albuera when he read Captain Lapène's book and concluded that it did not do justice to the actions of his division. Maransin's 1823 work 'Observations Adressées à Mon. le Capitaine Lapène pour la Rectification de quelques Erreurs et Inexactitudes concernant le 5me Corps . . .' can be found in the Musée Pyrénéen but is more easily accessible via the text of a modern biography of the general.*[8] *Although the document was written by Maransin, he refers to himself in the third person.*

The passage of the Albuera had taken place with all the haste of courage impatient to fight; in some places the depth of the ford and the difficulties of the escarpment on the opposite bank had delayed the march of the Vth Corps, the head of which continued moving in a line parallel to the enemy's order of battle.

The regiments successively resumed the same order for the formation of sections, platoons [*peletons*] and divisions; this movement continued in the same direction, with a view to carrying the Vth Corps to the right of the enemy line and to supporting the movement which the body of cavalry commanded by General Latour-Maubourg was making to out-flank it.

---

7    D'Héralde, Jean-Baptiste, *Mémoires d'une Chirurgien de la Grande Armée* (Paris, 2002) p. 174.

8    Cambon, Jean, *Jean-Pierre Maransin, General de Division, Baron de l'Empire 1770–1828* (Tarbes, France, 1991), pp. 82–4.

Having arrived at the point of attack, the Vth Corps changes direction by turning the column head to the right; Girard's division marches towards the enemy in attack columns [*colonnes d'attaque*], the second division following behind at 150 paces in attack column by battalion [*colonne d'attaque par bataillon*].

During this strategic manoeuvre to approach the enemy, an unexpected event, which may have greatly influenced the beginning of the battle, prevented us for a quarter of an hour from taking a single step. The event was a violent downpour of rain accompanied by extremely strong winds that forced our men to turn their backs to the storm. Favoured by this furious storm, the enemy had advanced his lines, a movement that was hidden from General Girard by a few irregularities in the terrain, so the division which he commanded was surprised by the first fire of the enemy's front line and replied with only a few shots. Within 10 minutes, the 40th Line began to fall back and the other regiments of the division also began to give way; the haste and disorder of this retreat were such that the troops of the various battalions and regiments found themselves intermingled.

It was feared that this disorder would prevent the second division under General Maransin, who had just taken command following the wounding of General Pépin, from taking the place of the first division by a passage of the lines and that, even if the manoeuvre was successful, the second division would be unable to resist the advance of the victorious enemy.

Already General Maransin had had two horses killed under him, but fortunately for the honour of the French army, he had not yet received the blow which was to strike him down! Placing himself in the centre of the line, he ordered the carabiniers of the 28th Light regiment who were near him to fix bayonets and encouraged them with a short resounding speech that inspired cheers from the men, a good omen of victory.

Girard's division had just retired through the intervals of the second division and already the enemy was approaching. Maransin orders a charge and leads it at the head of the 28th Light carabiniers. The French fire at almost point-blank range and stop the enemy advance, covering the battlefield with English dead.

The defeat of the English is complete. The same troops that had routed Girard's division in such great disorder are routed in turn without making the slightest resistance and are obliged to rally behind the second English line.

There now ensued at close range on the edge of an undulation of ground a tremendous combat between the English second line and

General Maransin's division, with the 28th Light infantry still in front. This was possibly the fiercest, most stubborn and deadliest combat that there had been in the course of the war.

Unfortunately, after having repulsed the English front line and forced the second to fall back, the bullet destined for him traversed General Maransin's body and put an end to his battle, so to speak. But his actions had given the reserve time to form and take up a position to continue the fight on an even basis.

It is not out of place to accompany the account of this battle with some reflections. The elements sometimes disturb the most perfect dispositions of an army, and at the same time favour the movement of the enemy army; the uneven ground, by concealing certain manoeuvres, further increases the disorder and causes one of the parties to be surprised.

The intrepid General Girard, carried away by the imprudence of his bravery, finds himself too close to the enemy and his division cannot complete a single volley, his retreat on the second division is made in such great disorder that the troops belonging to different battalions were mingled.

If the movement of this division had involved both the second line, or if it had exercised a disastrous influence on its morale, the battle would have ended the moment it had begun, because the troops and the reserve which followed the Vth Corps were not formed and they arrived only very slowly and disjointedly, and the enemy would not have faced any obstacle.

If the bullet which pierced General Maransin had come an hour earlier, the victory would have belonged to the enemy, and in any case, the disasters of the French army would have been incalculable.

## 5. Perrin de Solliers Narrative

*Another piece of evidence confirming the problematic nature of the formation adopted by the Vth Corps is provided by 2nd Lieutenant Perrin de Solliers of the 21st Light, a regiment in General Pépin's brigade.[9] His recollection appears in a book review he wrote in a French military periodical.*

Two historical examples of offensive movements executed in columns, which had diametrically opposite results, are cited by the author. One of them is the battle of Albuera fought on May 16, 1811. We will stop

---

9    Perrin de Solliers, Review of Examen Raisonné des Propriétés des Trois Armes . . . by M. Okouneff, *Le Spectateur Militaire*, Vol. 13 (July 1832), pp. 353–71, at 364–6.

here for a moment, because the blood of the writer of this article flowed for the first time for the honour and the glory of France in that battle.

There is no doubt that the infantry was called upon in that unfortunate affair to assault a numerically superior enemy in an advantageous position without adequate support. The other arms should have acted simultaneously, and supported the offensive movement. The violation of this principle was the cause of the failure experienced by the French army in this circumstance. The attack was carried out with great vigour, but they made the mistake of advancing in columns against an intact, deployed enemy line of infantry whose morale had not been shaken in any way. The French battalions, formed in close columns by division [*en colonnes serrées par division*], advanced at a charge, relying only on their audacity and their impulsive force. They soon found themselves under the fiercest fire. All the general and senior officers who were on horseback were put out of action after a few minutes, as well as a large number of junior officers. This unfortunate circumstance left the troops to themselves; a moment of wavering and a fatal hesitation followed. The head of each column, crushed by an ever-increasing musket fire, was forced to halt within pistol shot of the enemy line. Deprived of their officers, these battalions still managed to deploy without command and still had enough tenacity of purpose to expend almost all their ammunition. They only withdrew when they found themselves overwhelmed by a converging movement of the enemy forces. The regiment in which the writer of this article then served, two battalions strong, and numbering about 1,600 men under arms, had, in less than 20 minutes, 500 men and 21 officers killed or wounded.

All these circumstances can only enhance the glory of the Polish lancers, who were part of the French army. Judiciously engaged at the beginning of the action, they did all that could be expected of brave soldiers. If their brilliant charge did not have a decisive result, it is because there was not enough follow-up to turn it into anything more than an isolated triumph. I still have a vivid and emotional recollection of the daring Captain Kognoska [Konopka], brother of the chief of the Polish regiment, arriving at a gallop in front of the front of the French attack columns of the second line, and proudly displaying to them an English flag he had just captured, an action that inspired repeated cries of 'Vive l'Empereur!' from thousands of men. Honour be given to this brave man and his brave comrades!

## 6. Lavaux Narrative

*Lavaux is the only French infantryman to leave an account of the battle. His narrative does not add much detail to the story, but indicates that the French army was acutely aware of being outnumbered and that they shared the view that casualties were horrendous.*[10]

In the month of May, we left Seville once again to go and defeat the English who were coming to seize Badajoz. A great battle took place three leagues from the city, which was one of the bloodiest that was fought in Spain. We were not favoured with the victory for the English outnumbered us five to one. I believe that there was never a more deadly battle. The ground was strewn with dead bodies, as many on one side as on the other. We were obliged to retire to the rear. The English also left the battlefield but, seeing that we had abandoned it, they returned to take possession of it and removed all the wounded.

## 7. Vivien Narrative

*Captain Jean Vivien of the 55th Line was not present himself at Albuera but he served in the regiment for many years and had a close relationship with the unit commander, Colonel Schwitter. The colonel was apparently the source for the description of Albuera in the short biography of Schwitter that is embedded in Vivien's memoirs.*[11]

The Battle of Albuera, fought on May 16, 1811, by Marshal Duke of Dalmatia against Marshal Beresford, commanding the Anglo-Portuguese army which covered the blockade of Badajoz, which was begun under such happy auspices and terminated by a retreat on Seville, put Colonel Schwiter in a position to display his military talents, his composure, his personal bravery, and to show how he understood the duty of a regimental commander. Until nine o'clock in the morning, his regiment had been only modestly engaged, but when a movement of hesitation, followed by a hasty retreat, appeared in the Vth Corps, under the orders of General Girard, a movement which compromised the position of the 55th regiment, Colonel Schwiter, passing in front of the front of his regiment, harangued his men in the following manner:

> Even the bravest soldiers are not exempt from fear that can lead to serious disorders unless they heed their officers. We are about to be

---

10    Lavaux, F., *Mémoires de François Lavaux, Sergent au 103e de Ligne (1793–1814)* (Alfred Darimon, ed.) (Paris, nd), pp. 289–90.

11    Vivien, Jean-Stanislas, *Souvenirs de Ma Vie Militaire 1792–1822* (Paris, 1907), pp. 259–61.

attacked by the approaching strong English column. Soldiers – If you keep the utmost calm and obey my every order, I promise you that we will prevail however many the enemies we face.

A few minutes later, the English column rushed on the regiment, without doing it the honour to deploy, but it was received by a few shots of grapeshot and by a fire from two rows fed so well that it was forced to make a change of direction to the left, the colonel skilfully took advantage to form his regiment into close columns by division in each battalion, and to follow the forced retreat of the army. The loss suffered by the regiment had been inconsiderable, because the front of the enemy column and its flankers were far from presenting an extent similar to our line of battle; but that of the Anglo-Portuguese must have been immense, because they were received firmly and shot point-blank. During the action, the colonel was shot through his right leg; but since, at that difficult moment, he judged his presence to be indispensable, he had not spoken of it. Wounded at ten o'clock in the morning, it was only in the evening, when he dismounted from his horse, that he was able to bandage the wound, which was serious enough to cause him to be confined to his apartment in Seville for almost two months.

## C. Cavalry Accounts

### 1. Latour-Maubourg's Report
*The lengthiest surviving official French document other than Marshal Soult's dispatch is General Marie-Victor-Nicolas de Latour-Maubourg's report to the Marshal.[12] This document provides valuable details concerning the actions of the French cavalry during the battle, but does not explain how the French cavalry failed to overcome the resistance of the numerically inferior Allied mounted troops.*

Usagre, 27 May, 1811

To Marshal Soult, Commanding General,
I have the honour to forward to Your Excellency the report of the 16th inst. relative to the cavalry under my orders.
    At 7 o'clock in the morning on the 16th, immediately after Your Excellency gave me orders to march upon the enemy, I ordered the regiment of lancers of the Vistula supported by the 4th regiment of Dragoons to the nearest ford above the bridge of La Albuera and they

---

12    Latour-Maubourg, M.-V.-N. de, Report to Marshal Soult, Usagre, 27 May 1811, Add. Ms. 37425, ff. 65–9, British Library, London.

crossed under a heavy fire. The English cavalry wished to oppose the crossing, but were driven back with much vigour by Colonel Konopka, whose regiment killed many English troopers and took some prisoners.

The rest of the cavalry crossed at a ford about three quarters of a mile above the one I have just mentioned, and the regiments assembled between the two fords, exposed to the enemy's fire. The two regiments of Mounted Chasseurs, the 21st and 27th, together with some artillery, were posted under the orders of General Briche to the right of the bridge, to screen the enemy, which was present in force by the village of La Albuera and upon the heights which command it.

After having assembled the 2nd and 10th regiments of Hussars, the 4th, 20th, 26th, 14th, 17th and 27th Dragoons, and the 4th Mounted Chasseurs in the service of His Christian Majesty, I placed them in column, the several regiments being en echelon, and at a full interval from each other [en colonne par régiment et par echelons, et a distance entière]. The column was established in front of the heights about midway from the village of La Albuera, which the enemy was beginning to occupy. The position gave the cavalry a good position from which to move against the right of the enemy, whose cavalry was positioned reasonably far to the right and rear of their infantry.

The ten pieces of artillery attached to the cavalry were placed on two rises with flat summits [plateaux] in front of it. The fire of the artillery must have done considerable mischief to the enemy, who also had a considerable battery on another piece of high ground with a flat summit opposite to mine. The cavalry was exposed for more than two hours to the fire of this artillery, which was very lively and sustained, and lost many men. It was necessary, however, to maintain that position to keep the enemy in check and to give the infantry time to come up.

As soon as the skirmishers of the infantry arrived, I gave orders to the 2nd regiment of Hussars and to the regiment of Polish lancers to support them. The flat rise on which the infantry was to take position was carried and the 2nd and 10th Hussars and the lancers of the Vistula Legion charged the English infantry with complete success and in a manner that reflects the greatest honour upon those regiments. Your Excellency having immediately afterwards ordered them to another point, they made several other charges upon the infantry during the day in which they (especially the lancers) have lost many men.

The artillery followed the movement and took post on the flat rise from which the enemy had just been driven.

I had brought the two brigades of Dragoons commanded by Generals Bron and Bouvier des Eclaz towards the enemy's right flank to keep it in check as the action was becoming more general. I thought there would be an engagement of cavalry, but that of the enemy, placed in the rear of a considerable line of infantry and behind a ravine, held its position and offered me no opportunity of attacking it except at a real disadvantage due to the nature of the ground.

I received successively from Your Excellency the order to use the right-hand cavalry regiments to support the infantry on the flat rise and then the order to have the cavalry return to its original position to keep the enemy right in check. The 4th and 20th regiments of Dragoons charged the enemy's infantry as soon as they arrived at the flat rise, but their attack was not fully pressed home due to the nature of the ground and the density of the enemy's column. Nevertheless, the lead elements of these regiments sabred some English outside of their ranks and made some prisoners, but lost many men.

Soon after the infantry retreated, the cavalry, which I had positioned to protect that movement, also slowly retired, but it did not cross the ravine formed by the brook until the infantry and artillery had passed over.

The cavalry then took up a position upon the high ground that commanded the ravine.

While this was happening, the 21st and 27th regiments of Chasseurs crossed the river by the ford near the village of Albuera, in order to support the infantry that was attacking the village. They were occupied until nightfall in checking various attempts made by the enemy's cavalry to cross the brook. These two regiments have suffered a considerable loss, and General Briche highly praises the bravery and good behaviour of these units and their commanders, the Colonel Duke D'Arenberg and Squadron Chief Miller.

I must also to inform Your Excellency of the great praise due to the two brigades of Dragoons commanded by Generals Bron and Bouvier des Eclaz. The 26th Dragoons belonging to the brigade of General des Eclaz would have supported and continued the charge, had not insurmountable obstacles prevented the charge of the 4th & 20th Dragoons from being carried out.

The behaviour of the cavalry was perfect during the more than four hours that it was in position and manoeuvring under the enemy's fire. Generals Bron and Bouvier des Eclaz, Colonel Farine commanding the 4th Dragoons and Colonel Lallemand the 27th, Major Haubersard and Dejean commanding the 17th and 20th Dragoons, Squadron Chiefs Hardy and Lafite commanding the 14th and 26th Dragoons, Colonel Konopka commanding the Polish Lancers; Colonels Vinot and Laval commanding the 2nd & 10th regiments of Hussars, and Colonel Foirin of the 4th Regiment of Spanish Mounted Chasseurs have, along with all the officers and men of these regiments, given new proofs of their zeal and devotion. The regiment of Lancers took a thousand English prisoners and captured five English colours, the 10th Hussars took one flag and the 2nd Hussars took a mortar.

I have the honour to remit to Your Excellency the attached statement of the losses of the cavalry in men and horses, together with the list of services and petitions for promotion in the army or in the Legion of Honour, in favour of those soldiers of all ranks who particularly distinguished themselves.

The cavalry has to regret the loss of several officers of merit who were killed:
Captain Burel, 2nd Hussars
Lt. Sommariva, 10th Hussars
Captain Beau, 4th Dragoons
Second Lts. Beausse and Noel, 4th Dragoons
Captain D'Escretous, 20th Dragoons
Second Lt. Michelet, 20th Dragoons
Lt. D'Elzée, 26th Dragoons
Second Lts. Mayewski and Radlowski, Vistula Legion Lancers

All the regiments had many officers wounded and I have the honour to submit a list of those casualties to your Excellency. You will notice on the list:

Captains Cussy and Poitier, 2nd Hussars
Captain L'Eveque, 10th Hussars
Captain Masse, 21st Chasseurs
Captain Knoll, 27th Chasseurs
Squadron Chief Baillot, 4th Dragoons
Squadron Chief D'Oldenel, 20th Dragoons
Captain Taffin, 20th Dragoons
Lt. Ganderax, 14th Dragoons
Captain Berkheim, 17th Dragoons
Lt. Saguez, 27th Dragoons
Second Lt. Mateillet, 27th Dragoons
Squadron Chief Huppet, Vistula Legion Lancers
Captains Konopka and Leczinski, Vistula Legion Lancers

There are also an infinite number of others whose names Your Excellency will also find on the list.

I ought also to attest to the gallant conduct of my aide-de-camp and of the officers of the staff of the division of cavalry. Of the latter, M. Valguarnera, Squadron Chief, and M. Romanski, Captain, have been wounded, the former seriously.

I should also mention my picket composed of Dragoons from the 1, 2, 4, 9, 14 and 26th regts. They charged with the Polish Lancers in the first charge on the English infantry. Lt. Gaudelet of the 2nd Dragoons, the commander of the detachment, was killed; he was an officer full of merit. Four dragoons were seriously wounded.

I have the honour of recommending to Your Excellency the petitions I have forwarded in favour of officers and soldiers of all ranks.

Please accept, Your Excellency, the gift of my profound respect.

## 2. Kierzkowski's Memoir

*Captain Jakub Kierzkowski was an aide-de-camp to General Latour-Maubourg who gives more details of the charge of the Polish lancers.*[13] *This is the only source that suggests that Marshal Marmont was coordinating his plans with Marshal Soult at the time of the battle.*

Shortly afterwards the English under Wellington [*sic*] came up and imposed a blockade on Badajoz for good, attempting to approach the fortress using those same trenches and tunnels that we had made use of and which it had proved impossible to destroy in time. Marshal Soult hurried forwards to drive the English from Badajoz, gathering 22,000 troops and taking Zafra and Santa Marta, a mile from Albuera, where the English had already taken up their positions.

Marshal Marmont, with his corps, continued his march to assist us at Albuera, but Marshal Soult did not wait for Marmont before engaging in battle. It started with great fury. Throughout, I was placed at the disposal of General Latour-Maubourg, who commanded the cavalry. Once the army was deployed, with some regiments remaining in reserve, he sent me to Colonel Konopka in order to place his regiment to the left of the 10th Hussars. I immediately conveyed orders to Colonel Konopka to trot forwards, and wanted to go back to the general in order to report to him that Konopka was advancing. However, the colonel requested that I take him to the specific position, which I did before galloping back to General Latour-Maubourg with news that the regiment was now in position.

---

13    Kierzkowski, Jakub, *Pamiętniki J.F. Kierzkowskiego* (Warsaw, 1903). Translation by Marek Tadeusz Lalowski courtesy of Jonathan North. See more of this document at https://www.jpnorth.co.uk/historical-research/poles-during-the-napoleonic-era/two-lancers-at-albuera/.

The British artillery was now starting to hit the French cavalry, and their infantry was bravely advancing with the bayonet against their French counterparts. The left wing of the French infantry began to yield, whilst the French right pushed back against the English. Just then, General Latour sent me to Colonel Konopka, who was not then present with the regiment, ordering that one squadron of lancers charge the rear of the English infantry at the canter. The commander of Kostanecki's squadron fell on the British infantry, and took the entire battalion prisoner along with their standard and four cannon. The British sent a squadron of hussars against the Polish lancers, but they did not dare attack, seeing a fresh squadron of the lancers moving up in support.

The cannonade grew more intense, a round shot glancing under my horse, smashing my stirrup and wounding my leg. My horse collapsed and trapped my leg and I could not pull it out or get free from the horse until a captain of the 10th Hussars had me pulled out and so, soaked in my horse's blood, I mounted a mare taken from a killed hussar. Unfortunately she had been wounded between her ears with a pistol shot, and so I did not ride very far because she soon collapsed and died. Despite the oppressive heat, I managed to drag myself back to the road to Seville, where I found my servants and spare horses. I changed my uniform, kept one boot on one leg, and wore a slipper on the other, and mounted another of my horses.

Evening was coming, Marmont had not arrived and the army remained on the battlefield. It was not until the third day that Marshal Soult, lacking food for the army, was forced to fall back on Seville, and on Marmont's corps at Traxico. The English lost a lot of people at Albuera, especially from their cavalry. The Polish cavalry defeated their cavalry in each attack, because the English horses feared the pennons of Polish lances, so their horses always turned and fled, and the Poles stabbed them from behind. Many of the English complained about the conduct of the Polish lancers as they deployed their lances effectively when in pursuit.

### 3. Wojciechowski's Memoir

*This memoir by Kajetan Wojciechowski is the clearest account of the exploits of the Vistula Legion lancers in the battle.*[14]

---

14    Wojciechowski, K., *Pamiętniki moje w Hiszpanii* (Warsaw, 1845). Translation by Marek Tadeusz Lalowski courtesy of Jonathan North. See more of this document at https://www.jpnorth.co.uk/historical-research/poles-during-the-napoleonic-era/two-lancers-at-albuera/.

On the afternoon of 15 May 1811 we came across a huge, dense forest, through which the dragoons advanced as skirmishers whilst we pushed along the road through the middle. On the other side of the forest we saw the village of Albuera, on the right bank of the river of the same name, and with the bridge leading to it. Beyond the river the hills stretched towards a vast range of rocky mountains, and we observed that large numbers of infantry, dark masses of cavalry and artillery and a chain of outposts and pickets had been drawn up waiting. Then the sun began to set, and we, having established our camp, lit our fires. Of all the evils endured by the cavalry the very worst is when the horses are tired of riding and starving of hunger. I was just contemplating such sad realities, staring at the fire, when the order came to be ready at dawn for an inspection by our commanders. Having eaten a piece of rotten meat with my comrades and having drunk a glass of brandy, I fell asleep calmly.

At dawn on 16 May, the trumpets sounded the reveille; I jumped up and was already at the head of my brave boys, when I heard the command: 'Platoons, prepare to advance, by the right, walk.' While we were parading around the Marshal [Soult] as he stood in the centre, the sun began to rise. Our colonel [Jan Konopka] shouted: 'Flankers, forward!' Riding past him, I heard the command: 'Lances upright, advance to the left of the bridge, swim the river, attack the enemy!' Our platoons were moving off at a gallop, and I stopped for a while, listening in case of further orders. Then the colonel shouted at me in French, 'Are you deaf?' In a flash, I turned my chestnut horse around and was first to throw myself into the river. Near the bridge we saw some enemy engineers.

On the far bank of the river I formed up the platoon which had followed me, whilst [Peter] Rogojski did the same. We were then attacked by a squadron of London [sic] dragoons and routed them. Two other squadrons came up against us, and we started to withdraw in good order seeing Captain Leszczyński behind us at the head of two platoons of flankers and the regiment attempting to form on the right side of the river. So we turned and hit the English again and the two squadrons that had tried to follow us were crushed. It was only when overwhelming force came up against us that we began to encounter difficulties. Each of us began to fight with a few dragoons, and this uneven duel continued for quite some time when our artillery took up position and began to hit the English. Seeing how many of their corpses begin to litter the battlefield, the enemy dragoons yielded and withdrew.

Seemingly abandoned, and having fought in a protracted melee against overwhelming enemy, I asked Sergeant Rogojski: 'Peter, have you anything to drink here?' He grabbed his flask, took a sip, and handed it over to me. Just then, as I was drinking, a cannon ball flew between us, having been poorly aimed by our gunners, missing us by a hair's breadth.

The English saw that no one had arrived to assist us, so they attacked us for a third time. When we noticed that our supporting troops had fallen back and the regiment on the right side of the river was no longer visible, I called on Rogojski to cross the river immediately and open fire from the other bank. To our misfortune, the horse being ridden by the corporal from Rogojski's platoon slipped on the muddy ground by the river bank, and held them up for some time. Meanwhile, surrounded by attacking Englishmen, and having lost 14 men from my platoon, and with a sabre in my hand we retraced our steps and throwing ourselves into the river, were glad to reach the other bank.

On that side of the river Piotr Skrobicki, a regimental adjutant, suddenly appeared informing us that he brought orders to cross for a third time, but we did not listen to him. The commander of our squadron [Telesfor] Kostanecki rode up after him and said: 'And so, is this the authentic gentry of Poland: waving sabres, cheating death, and ignoring orders?' Having explained to him that we had not yet received any orders, we then followed him until I saw that my horse was lame in the leg. A good creature, which, despite being injured, saved my life. As we trotted along the river to the place our regiment had initially been positioned, we caught sight of a naked corpse. It was our poor [NCO] Jagielski, the first bullet fired had hit him, and thus he found the death he had himself foretold.

We lost Captain Leszczyński in this sad expedition; hit by a bullet, he died few days later and was buried in Llerena.

Having rejoined the regiment, we found the Spaniards, Portuguese and English under the command of Marshal Beresford drawn up in combat formation and ready for the battle. The enemy army rested its left wing on the village of Albuera, stretching its line along some heights which ran from Santa Martha and which began rather steeply before dipping as they neared Olivenza and Badajoz. At the foot of this position was a small river Albuera. The right wing was occupied by the English, whilst the Portuguese and Spanish took up positions in the centre and on the left.

Marshal Soult, having studied the enemy position, concluded that it would be impossible to attack all along the line with his meager forces. He therefore elected not to divide his forces, but decided instead to launch attacks against selected points. General Godinot was ordered to seize the village of Albuera, firmly held by the Spaniards [*sic*], whilst the Vth Corps, commanded by General Girard, was to attack the English, or the enemy's right. General Latour-Maubourg with 3,700 cavalry men was detailed to support him and, after overrunning the enemy positions, to pursue the routed Englishmen. All these manoeuvres were supposed to take place under the cover of the French artillery commanded by General Ruty. A light artillery battery was left however to General Godinot and it was this battery which opened the battle in the morning of May 16th.

General Godinot crossed the river and opened heavy fire on the village of Albuera while General Girard struck the enemy's right with determination and energy and forced the English into a slow and orderly retreat towards the middle of their position, which they sought to strengthen by this movement. Having seen their manoeuvre, Marshal Soult ordered our regiment to attack them in their flank. We set off in preparation for this attack, but we had a wide ravine to cross, and so had to then form up in sight of the enemy's line before finally striking them in squadron formation. Having scattered three English infantry regiments, we took 1,000 prisoners and six guns, and after repulsing an attack by the London Dragoon Regiment, we returned to our former position.

Meanwhile, General Godinot was still engaged against Albuera, and had not managed to drive the Spaniards [*sic*] from the village; General Girard, however, stormed the British position with bayonets fixed. This initial success was very costly, for we had two generals killed, and three wounded, and there were battalions in which not a single officer remained. After this first attack, Vth Corps was on the point of rolling over the second and third enemy lines but lacked the strength to do it and therefore our infantry, quitting the positions they had just occupied, began to withdraw slowly, with the English following them. Then General Ruty, having concentrated all the artillery, opened a murderous fire, which, over the course of several hours, caused a great deal of damage in the enemy ranks. General Godinot retreated from Albuera and Marshal Beresford, having noticed the hesitation in our ranks, wanted to throw all of his infantry against us in order to decide the fate of the battle.

It was then that Marshal Soult appeared in front of our regiment and shouted: 'Colonel! Save the honour of France!' So Konopka ordered an attack, we fell on the enemy, whom we stopped in their tracks for some time, winning time for General Latour-Maubourg to move forward and frustrate their intention to do us harm. The English in their reports, described the battle of Albuera, and mentioned our regiment: 'The Poles started the battle, continued it and concluded it with the greatest glory.'

Later our colonel was promoted to the rank of general. We received 11 crosses of the Legion of Honour for our regiment, and I finally received one too for the loss of 3 horses killed under me, and my scabbard cut and the wound from a musket shot which I also received. We lost five officers killed and 11 wounded in our regiment and 200 soldiers wounded and killed at Albuera.

## 4. Gougeat Memoir

*Louis-Antoine Gougeat was a simple trooper in the 20th Dragoons who served as an orderly to Captain Comte de Marcy. It is surprising to learn that Gougeat took no part in the combat, but instead merely looked after his officer's extra mounts.*[15] *His memoir provides a rare glimpse into the relationship between officers and enlisted men in Napoleon's armies.*

That same day, which was May 15, 1811, around 10 a.m., we saw several columns of cavalry descending like us from the mountains and crossing the fields of Extremadura. Arriving at a large village, which we passed without stopping, we were informed that a division of infantry and a large artillery park preceded us. Everything announced that a large concentration of troops was preparing for battle.

At two o'clock in the afternoon, the vanguard, commanded by Captain de Marcy, encountered a detachment of English cavalry and charged it vigorously. The regiment, which had remained in observation, resumed its march in order to support, if necessary, its vanguard. I was returning at this moment with several other dragoons from the drudgery of forage detail and as we were walking, trying to follow the direction our comrades had taken, I met Adjutant Major Crispiesse, who took me with him to his 'lodging'. What he called so were trees that were designated to each company at the place where they were to camp. I hitched my horses to those allocated to me and waited for my captain, who did not return with the regiment until nightfall. After he was sure that the horses had had their supply of fodder, he said to me: 'I am suffering from fatigue and hunger, but it is quite useless for me to send you a fetch of food from my comrades; they are no better supplied than I.' And he was already wrapping himself in his cloak to go to sleep. I then approached and,

---

15    Gougeat, Louis-Antoine, 'Mémoires d'un Cavalier d'Ordonnance du 20e Dragons (1810–1813)', Carnet de la Sabretache 1901, pp. 321–44 and 400–22 at pp. 334–7.

presenting him with the general's haversack, I told him under what circumstances it had come into my possession. He laughed heartily at the adventure and sent me to fetch Captain Pommereuil who, fortunately, was camping quite close to us and whom I soon found, thanks to the light of the bivouac fires. The two friends dined together, singing my praises. When they had finished, Captain Pommereuil shook my hand warmly: 'Brave Louis,' he said to me (that is how he treated me since the Ventosa affair), you saved my life; I will never forget you.' As for my captain, I don't know why but he did not say a word to me.

On May 16, before day broke, the calls of reveille rang out throughout the French camp. We could also hear the trumpets of the English army. Soon great rumours arose from everywhere announcing an impending clash of the two armies. The trumpets sounded the call 'to Horse!', and instantly my captain arrived. As I was bridling his horse, he asked me for the bottle of brandy. As he handed it back, he shook my hand and said, 'It's going to be hot today; there are many who, tonight, will no longer need anything.' And unfastening his money belt, he handed it to me, adding: 'Ah! My poor Louis, this may be the last moment we spend together. If the English break my back, this will be for you. Farewell!' And he galloped off to put himself at the head of his company. I was moved more than I can say.

The regiment resumed the path it had travelled the day before. Already the cannon thundered from all sides.

Emerging from a small wood, we saw the English army deployed on the hillsides in front and to the right of the village of Albuera. Beyond the wood and at the entrance to the plain which extended below the village and the positions of the enemy army, flowed the little river of the Albuera, over which there was only one bridge. Our cavalry crossed it at a ford which was below the bridge. As I arrived at this place, the sergeant major of my company shouted to me: 'You are going to have the captain's horses killed, withdraw!' The noise of cannon and musketry was so intense that I did not hear this warning. At this moment the light cavalry arrived, among which I distinguished a superb regiment of Polish lancers; it marched on the right of the English positions while the dragoon divisions marched on the left; the infantry and artillery established themselves in the centre. Soon the troops in the centre executed several forward movements which made me lose sight of them. I stopped on a hill on the right, from where I saw the regiments of dragoons making successive furious charges on the English infantry. I was trying to figure out the progress of the battle, which still seemed to me very indecisive, when suddenly

I saw, at my feet, a battalion of French infantry fighting alone against a mass of English cavalry and stopping it dead in its tracks with lowered bayonets.

I came back to the little river. Already the bridge and the ford were encumbered with men and horses and were no longer passable. Seeing this, I walked along the stream. The bullets and cannonballs falling around me and striking the trees were also causing a few casualties here and there. I looked frequently towards the ridge over which I had seen the dragoons disappear; I could only make out thick billows of smoke. The clouds thickened and a fine rain began to fall. Having finally found a convenient passage, I crossed the Albuera and entered the small wood of which I have already spoken and which was still being struck by quite a few cannonballs. I found there a battalion of infantry whose officers anxiously asked me for news; I told them what I had just seen. I was placed close to the path leading to the field hospital where the wounded were passing; the spectacle presented by the interminable procession of these unfortunates was heartbreaking.

In the afternoon, the weather having cleared up and the smoke dissipated, we could better see the movements of the two armies. I was still looking towards the side where I supposed the dragoons were fighting, but the distance did not allow me to make out what was going on there; my concern grew. Looking back around me, I saw a horseman appearing to be in great pain and heading towards the field hospital; it was an officer of my regiment named Monsieur Darenne who was injured. I ran to meet him and helped him get off his horse. A surgeon thinks his injury was not serious. Monsieur Darenne reassures me a little about my captain, whom he left in good health when he left the battlefield.

Around 4 to 5 o'clock, having heard no more from my regiment, I went in search of it. The cannonade and musketry died down; the battle seemed to be coming to an end. As I passed through the places I had walked in the morning, my heart sank at the sight of the many dead and wounded lying on the ground. When I arrived at the positions occupied by the dragoons, combat had completely ceased. I found my comrades in a pitiful state: they were defeated and broken with fatigue; their faces, blackened by gunpowder smoke, were unrecognisable. I had, however, the satisfaction of learning that my captain was safe and sound; he was shown to me, at a distance, lying in his cloak. While he rested, I gave his horse a few handfuls of barley; the poor beast, dying of hunger, was eating the branches of the bush to which it was tied. A stone's throw from me, foot soldiers were cutting up a dead horse and carrying off hindquarters to eat. My captain, having heard me talking, called out to me. He was sad and worried. Of the food I offered him, he only accepted a small piece of bread, which he ate slowly and silently, after which he went back to sleep.

During the night a muffled noise was heard in both camps, the cause of which we could not guess. At daybreak, the sergeant major in command of my company came to bring my captain the order to go and take command of the service detachment accompanying General La Tour-Maubourg. Monsieur de Marcy left immediately, advising me not to leave the regiment. When day broke, it was seen that the two armies had retired: the infantry and the artillery had recrossed the river, the cavalry alone remained on the ground which it had conquered. The cavalry in turn retreated into the little wood, which we found crowded with wounded. We transported all these wounded on our horses to the village of Los Santos and deposited them in a field surrounded by walls.

## 5. Bremond d'Ars letter

*Théophile de Bremond d'Ars was a second lieutenant in the 21st Regiment of Mounted Chasseurs. As described in a letter to his father, he was wounded in the battle and recalled that the duration of the battle was longest for the units charged with the threatening of the village of Albuera.*[16]

Llerena
May 24, 1811

I have been here since yesterday, after having taken part, on the 16th of this month, in the battle of Albuera. I was wounded by a shot in the left arm. Fortunately, the bullet went through and did not hit my elbow joint. But the wound nevertheless gives me great pain and my arm is very swollen. However, I believe that it will not be serious.

The battle was fought four leagues from Badajoz against the English, Spanish and Portuguese armies far superior to ours. It was a very bloody affair, which started at 7 o'clock in the morning and did not end until 6 o'clock in the evening.

Although I am not quite comfortable, I am resting at the moment. I had first thought of going to Seville to recuperate, but I prefer not to go far from the regiment. Villedon who had remained in Olivenza is a prisoner in England. Mr. de la Pommeraye, officer with the 2nd Hussars and who was, in his youth, in pension at Bourguignon, in

---

16    The letter appears in Bremond d'Ars, Anatole de, *Historique de 21e Regiment de Chasseurs à Cheval* (Paris, 1903), pp. 250–2.

Saintes, is also prisoner; but he is with the Spaniards. I was very close to him, so I was very angry to know he was taken. He knew my brother Josias well.

My letter will not be very long today, my dear father, because I am suffering a little. I therefore conclude by assuring you once again of all my attachment and embracing you with all my heart.

P.S. Leon Delaage's regiment was also at the battle; but I think he was near Seville. I haven't had a chance to find out yet.

*Bremond d'Ars added another detail about Albuera in a second letter, dated 16 August.*

I had forgotten to mention to you at the time that at the bloody Battle of Albuera against the English, the unfortunate Poijeux, my former orderly, had been killed by a cannonball next to me at the moment when I was hurt. I very much regretted his loss, although I had a little to complain about. He had been with me for four years. I now have a fat German from Flanders, a good man who was in my service almost two years ago. It was he who has replaced poor Poijeux.

## D. Artillery Accounts

### 1. Pernet Narrative
*Captain Pernet was an artillery officer acting as ADC to General Bourgeat and his memoirs are quoted extensively in a biography of that general (even though his first name is never given).[17] His account of the battle highlights the important role played by the French artillery in preventing a more disastrous outcome.*

After having had the breaches we had made in the fortress of Badajoz hastily repaired, having had our batteries and our trenches filled, having supplied the place with supplies and having left a garrison and having evacuated Olivenza, Campo-Mayor and Albuquerque, our army returned to Seville. Shortly afterwards, the united Spaniards, Portuguese and English advanced in force, resumed Extremadura, and invested the place of Badajoz. Our army marched again for Extremadura through Monasterio and Constantina. We met the enemy army on the heights of Albuera on May 16, 1811. We formed our attack columns. Marshal Soult ordered me to lead a battery of 6 guns to

---

17      Rey, Jules & Remy, Emile, *Le General Baron Bourgeat, 1760–1820* (Grenoble, 1898), pp. 99–101.

the cavalry commanded by General Latour-Maubourg, which formed the left of our line of battle and which was threatened by the enemy's right wing. I engaged in a lively cannonade with the enemy; during this time our infantry advanced in close columns and deployed in line of battle; the fusillade and the cannonade became general all along the line. We drove an English regiment to our left and took two cannon from it, which I sent immediately to our park. While I was busy at my battery and bringing together the two pieces that the English had just abandoned us, their cavalry charged us sharply, came up to my battery driving back before it a regiment of our hussars to the point of crossing swords with the enemy. General Latour-Maubourg, seeing the danger of our position, ordered his dragoons to charge the flank of the English cavalry, which, fearing to be cut off, retired again, a circumstance that allowed us to disengage. My battery having been reunited with its division, following the orders of the Marshal, I rejoined my general and I received a slight wound from a bullet in the left shoulder. The enemy, who was much superior to us in number, marched on us, caused some disorder in one of our regiments, which had not been able to deploy properly and which withdrew with great difficulty; our whole line felt the effects and retreated.

My general ordered Colonel Bouchu, his chief of staff, to put himself at the head of the artillery reserve, made up of 12 guns. We advanced on the field of battle, and our division batteries joined us; our infantry retired in order behind our artillery battle line and continued to retreat. Whenever the enemy showed up to pursue us, we thundered it with our artillery. We thus made our retreat in stages, continuing our fire. Our troops were driven back to the Albuera stream, which was very deep and had steep banks and so could only be crossed by a small number of fords which were established there. While our artillery thus protected the retreat with continuous and well-directed fire, our infantry crossed the stream by fords and reformed in line behind, on the heights, opposite those of Albuera, occupied by the enemy army. Our artillery also arrived there successively without losing either cannons or caissons. Several times General Latour-Maubourg told us to withdraw with our artillery, because the infantry did not remain to protect us, and if the enemy came to attack us strongly, he himself feared that he could not protect us effectively.

During that day, we suffered fairly heavy losses, and although the battlefield was left to the enemy, they suffered greater losses than ours. Fortunately, our artillery was able to courageously and intelligently support the retreat of the French army, which had behind it an almost insurmountable obstacle, except for the fords.

Each army thus remained in position throughout the night, the next day and the following night, without exchanging a single shot. We limited ourselves to making reconnaissance, treating our wounded and bury our dead. Our army left its position during this second night and we reached Zafra by daylight. After a few hours of rest, our army corps divided in two columns; one headed for Monasterio and the other for Constantina and we returned to Seville.

## E. Miscellaneous Accounts

### 1. Lamare Narrative

*Captain Jean-Baptiste-Hippolyte Lamare was an engineer officer assigned to the garrison of Badajoz who wrote an account of all the sieges of the southern border fortresses in 1811 and 1812.[18] He provides some details of the actions of the garrison while the battle was being fought and makes the case that the battle was indeed a French success in the greater strategic context of the effort to control the southern invasion route between Portugal and Spain.*

On the morning of the 15th, the besiegers had withdrawn all their artillery, and only a few troops still occupied the main points of attack; nevertheless, as we had not had any news from the outside, everything that happened under our eyes was still shrouded in mystery. To put an end to this state of affairs, the governor resolved to make a sortie in order to reconnoitre the enemy position, to try to take some prisoners to obtain information about the situation of the belligerent armies and, at the same time, to destroy some of the enemy siege work.

Consequently, four companies of infantry, 50 cavalrymen, two pieces of cannon and 100 men of the Engineer corps, under the command of Battalion Chief Marquet and Captain Gillet, left at noon by the Porte de la Trinidad, and advanced as far as the battery, whence they flushed out the trench guards. The cavalry under the command of Captain Sommervogel, which had sortied by the Talavera road, encountered a Portuguese post. This was charged impetuously and defeated completely, with the result that two Portuguese officers and seven soldiers were brought back as prisoners. In the meanwhile, the column completely demolished the battery it had seized and brought back to town the materials which the enemy had been forced to abandon there. After two hours, which was the time needed to destroy the battery, the enemy assembled about 1,200 men

---

18      Col. L***, *Relation des sièges et défenses d'Olivença, de Badajoz et de Campo-Mayor, en 1811 et 1812, par les troupes françaises de l'armée du Midi en Espagne* (Paris, 1825). Although the author is identified in the book only by the first letter of his last name, there is no doubt he was Lamare.

and prepared to attack us; but as the governor had accomplished his designs, he caused our troops to fall back behind the lunette, and leaving us with the loss of only four men wounded.

Captain Sommervogel and Sergeant Schoen, of the 2nd Hussars, distinguished themselves particularly. The enemy suffered a loss of more than 50 men, sabred by the cavalry.

We learned from the prisoners that the French Army of the South was approaching the town and that the Allies were preparing for a battle.

On the 16th, there were no more enemies left in front of the town, but we were still in the same uncertainty about the course of events since no definite news had reached us; however, it was urgent to take advantage of this moment of respite to destroy the works of the besiegers. As soon as day broke, all the available troops, followed by 200 civilian residents and all the means of transport that could be mustered, turned to this task with extreme ardour. While the garrison was diligently carrying out this work, a battle was going on at Albuera, not far from the walls of the town, but we did not have the slightest inkling of that because the sound of 80 pieces of cannon and 60,000 combatants was diverted by a north-westerly wind and could not be heard at Badajoz; a profound silence had succeeded the tumult of the siege, and the troops occupied with the destruction of the trenches patiently awaited future developments favourable to their wishes.

The Battle of Albuera was perhaps the bloodiest action of the Peninsular War, where 22,000 French, commanded by Marshal Soult, clashed with 38,000 Allies; the losses were considerable on both sides and amounted to more than 14,000 men; possession of the field of battle was the only advantage which the Allies derived from a clash whose greatest violence lasted hardly more than two hours and a half, and which the English, with their eternal presumption, qualified as a brilliant victory. The events which followed proved how disastrous the results of this pretended victory were to them; in fact, the object of the French advance had been to raise the siege of Badajoz, in order to give time to the army of Portugal to unite with that of the South, in order to drive the Allies out of Extremadura; this object having been attained, it is evident that this battle, which cost humanity so dear, was advantageous only to the French. We will not stop to report the details which are beyond the scope of this work and which, moreover, have already been described with great clarity and precision by artillery Captain Lapène, an eyewitness.

The days of May 17 and 18 were again employed in demolishing the works of the besiegers, and this effort was so successful that on the morning of the 19th there were no longer any traces of the siege left. Thus ended this siege, undertaken with sufficient forces, but badly directed, and which would probably have had only fruitless results, even if the Allies would not have been forced to raise it in order to face Marshal Soult.

## 2. Official French Casualty Return, 15 July 1811

*This document in File C⁸ 356 of the French Service Historique de la Defense at Vincennes is based on returns from various divisions and is certified by Adjutant Commandant Mocquery, assistant chief of staff to General Gazan. The numbers below are the ones in the archival document, but it appears that the compiler made some mistakes of addition because not all the row and column totals are correct.*

Vth Corps

| Unit/ Service | Officers Killed | Soldiers Killed | Officers Left on Field/ Prisoners | Soldiers Left on Field/ Prisoners | Officers Wounded | Soldiers Wounded | Total |
|---|---|---|---|---|---|---|---|
| Command and Staff | 5 | – | – | – | 8 | – | 13 |
| 34th Line | 4 | 104 | – | – | 13 | 298 | 419 |
| 40th Line | 4 | 35 | 1 | 73 | 9 | 226 | 348 |
| 64th Line | 5 | 99 | – | 168 | 18 | 361 | 651 |
| 88th Line | – | – | 6 | 141 | 5 | 253 | 405 |
| 21st Light | 3 | 61 | 2 | 24 | 11 | 154 | 255 |
| 100th Line | 4 | 50 | 2 | 51 | 8 | 152 | 267 |
| 28th Light | 7 | 53 | 1 | 112 | 10 | 313 | 496 |
| 103rd Line | 4 | 48 | 3 | 74 | 10 | 148 | 287 |
| Total | 31 | 450 | 15 | 643 | 84 | 1,905 | 3,128 |

Reserve

| Unit | Officers Killed | Soldiers Killed | Officers Left on Field/ Prisoners | Soldiers Left on Field/ Prisoners | Officers Wounded | Soldiers Wounded | Total |
|---|---|---|---|---|---|---|---|
| 12th Light | 3 | 108 | 1 | 132 | 14 | 511 | 769 |
| 16th Light | 2 | 39 | – | 12 | 7 | 321 | 381 |
| 51st Line | – | 2 | – | – | – | 1 | 3 |
| 55th Line | 4 | 68 | – | 38 | 6 | 235 | 351 |
| 58th Line | 6 | 23 | 2 | 24 | 15 | 258 | 328 |
| Total | 15 | 240 | 3 | 206 | 42 | 1,326 | 1,832 |

## Cavalry

| Unit | Officers Killed | Soldiers Killed | Officers Left on Field/ Prisoners | Soldiers Left on Field/ Prisoners | Officers Wounded | Soldiers Wounded | Total |
|---|---|---|---|---|---|---|---|
| 2nd Hussars | 1 | 4 | – | 8 | 3 | 57 | 73 |
| 10th Hussars | 1 | 3 | – | 3 | 4 | 21 | 32 |
| 21st Chasseurs | – | 3 | – | – | 3 | 19 | 25 |
| 27th Chasseurs | – | 7 | 1 | 5 | 2 | 11 | 26 |
| 4th Dragoons | 3 | 27 | – | 1 | 1 | 38 | 70 |
| 20th Dragoons | 1 | 6 | 1 | 4 | 3 | 10 | 25 |
| 14th Dragoons | – | 6 | – | – | 1 | 17 | 24 |
| 17th Dragoons | – | 12 | – | 1 | 3 | 29 | 45 |
| 26th Dragoons | 1 | 5 | – | 1 | 2 | 12 | 21 |
| 27th Dragoons | – | 2 | – | 3 | 3 | 11 | 19 |
| 1st Lancers | 1 | 41 | 1 | – | 9 | 78 | 130 |
| 4th Spanish Ch. | – | 2 | – | – | – | 4 | 6 |
| Total | 8 | 118 | 3 | 26 | 34 | 307 | 496 |
| Horse Casualties | | 420 killed | | | | 239 wounded | 659 |

## Artillery

| Unit | Officers Killed | Soldiers Killed | Officers Left on Field/ Prisoners | Soldiers Left on Field/ Prisoners | Officers Wounded | Soldiers Wounded | Total |
|---|---|---|---|---|---|---|---|
| Artillery | 1 | 19 | – | – | 3 | 72 | 95 |
| Horse Casualties | | 82 killed | | | | 81 wounded | 163 |

Combined Grenadiers

| Unit | Officers Killed | Soldiers Killed | Officers Left on Field/ Prisoners | Soldiers Left on Field/ Prisoners | Officers Killed and Wounded | Soldiers Killed and Wounded | Total |
|---|---|---|---|---|---|---|---|
| Combined Grenadiers | – | – | – | – | 10 | 362 | 372 |

Recapitulation

| Unit | Officers Killed | Soldiers Killed | Officers Left on Field/ Prisoners | Soldiers Left on Field/ Prisoners | Officers Wounded | Soldiers Wounded | Total |
|---|---|---|---|---|---|---|---|
| Command and Staff | 5 | – | – | – | 8 | – | 13 |
| Vth Corps | 31 | 450 | 15 | 643 | 84 | 1,905 | 3,128 |
| Reserve | 15 | 240 | 3 | 206 | 42 | 1,326 | 1,832 |
| Cavalry | 8 | 118 | 3 | 26 | 34 | 307 | 496 |
| Artillery | 1 | 19 | – | – | 3 | 72 | 95 |
| Total | 60 | 827 | 21 | 875 | 171 | 3,610 | 5,564 |
| Combined Grenadiers | | | | | | | 372 |
| Grand Total | | | | | | | 5,936 |
| Total Horse Casualties | | 502 killed | | | | 320 wounded | 822 |

## 3. Soult Comment on Casualties
*Soult followed up his official reports on the battle with a more informal letter to Berthier dated 4 June 1811 which includes some interesting remarks that indicate that the number of French wounded was actually 5,800, including 200 wounded who became prisoners on the field of battle, and not 3,600 as stated in the official casualty return. Some of the discrepancy between the two numbers could be accounted for by the return of lightly wounded men to duty between the date of the battle and the July date of the official return.*

*The location of the original letter is unknown, but a summary with excerpts can be found in the catalogue of the Sainsbury Collection of Napoleonic documents.*[19]

The Marshal's letter, with documents enclosed, affords much interesting detail respecting *'cette sanglante affaire'*. It recommends strongly the General of Division Gazan, and others for promotion or admission into the Legion of Honour; also the names of officers proposed to take the place of those who had fallen in the field, [and includes] a statement of the numbers who had perished in the fight, and a list of the English prisoners. (The officers are named, but the noncommissioned officers and privates are only numerically noticed.) Speaking of the disasters of the battle, which he emphatically designates 'a bloody affair', he observes:

> the Emperor will remark with pain the great number of soldiers who have unfortunately fallen in the field of honour at Albuera. Of the wounded, 4,500 have arrived at Seville; 600 remain with their regiments; 500, who could not be moved, are under treatment in the commune of Extremadura; the rest remain on the field – the enemy, I think, has made 200 prisoners. The loss of so many valorous soldiers is to be deplored; but the regret is lessened by the enemy having lost from 7,000 to 8,000 men, of which 4,500 are English.

The English prisoners, by the schedule taken in bivouac before Albuera, May 17, enclosed in the Marshal's letter, amount, officers and men, to 816. He [Soult] speaks, at this date, June 4, of their having been escorted to Seville, but that several of the officers had escaped on the road. The English lost six flags on this occasion. Annexed is a statement of favours sought to be conferred by the Emperor on the Marshal's staff officers. This document has the autographed decisions of Napoleon, confirmed by his decree, August 6, 1811.

---

19    Napoleon. Decisions and Signature on Marshal Soult's, Duke of Dalmatia, long autograph letter to the Major General Prince Berthie, relative the battle of Albuera. Dated Llerma, June 4th, 1811. Sainsbury, John, *The Napoleon Museum* (London, 1845), p. 483.

# ALPHABETICAL LIST OF EYEWITNESSES

Alten, Charles – British Major General
Anonymous Artist – Battlefield Panorama
Anonymous Officer – 2nd Battalion, 48th Foot
Anonymous Officer – British 4th Division
Anonymous Officer – French Staff
Anonymous Private – 3rd Foot
Anonymous Private – 27th Foot
Ballesteros, Francisco – Spanish Lieutenant General
Bayley, Charles – Lieutenant, 31st Foot
Bennett, William – Trooper, 13th Light Dragoons
Beresford, William – Portuguese Field Marshal, commander-in-chief
    of the Allied army
Blake, Joaquín – Lieutenant General, commander of the Spanish 4th
    Army Expeditionary Corps
Blakeney, Edward – Lieutenant Colonel, 7th Fusiliers
Broke, Charles – Major, 4th Division Staff
Brooke, William – Major, 2nd Battalion, 48th Foot
Burriel, Antonio – Chief of Staff, Spanish 4th Army Expeditionary Corps
Castaños, Francisco Xavier – Captain General of the Spanish 5th Army
Clarke, John – Lieutenant, 66th Foot
Cleeves, Andrew – Captain, KGL Artillery
Close, Edward – Lieutenant, 2nd Battalion, 48th Foot
Colborne, John – Lieutenant Colonel, 66th Foot and commander of the
    1st Brigade, 2nd Division
Cooper, John Spencer – Sergeant, 7th Fusiliers
Correia de Mello, José – Major, 11th Portuguese Line
Crompton, George – Lieutenant, 66th Foot
Dickens, S. – Lieutenant, 34th Foot
Dickson, Alexander – Major, Commander of Portuguese Artillery
Dobbin, Robert – Lieutenant, 66th Foot

261

España, Carlos d' – Brigadier, Spanish 5th Army

Girdlestone, James – Captain, 31st Foot

Gordon, Arthur – Captain, 3rd Foot (Buffs)

Gougeat, Louis-Antoine – Trooper, 20th Dragoons

Guthrie, George – British Surgeon

Hamilton, Thomas – Ensign, 29th Foot

Hardinge, Henry – Deputy Quartermaster General, Portuguese Army

Harrison, John Christopher – Lieutenant, 23rd Fusiliers

Hartmann, Julius – Major, KGL, commanding British and KGL Artillery

Héralde, Jean-Baptiste d' – French Surgeon

Hill, John – Lieutenant, 23rd Fusiliers

Hobhouse, Benjamin – Lieutenant, 57th Foot

Inglis, William – Lieutenant Colonel, 57th Foot

Lamare, Jean-Baptiste-Hippolyte – Engineer Captain, Garrison of Badajoz

Lapène, Édouard – Captain, Vth Corps Staff

Lardizábal, Jose de – Mariscal de Campo, Spanish 4th Army Expeditionary Corps

Latour-Maubourg, Count Marie-Victor-Nicolas de – Division General commanding the French cavalry

Lavaux, François – Sergeant, 103rd Line

Leslie, Charles – Lieutenant, 29th Foot

Light, William – Lieutenant, 4th Dragoons

Lindau, Friedrich – Private, 2nd KGL Light Battalion

Lindenthal, Lewis – British Major General

Long, Robert B. – British Colonel

Loureiro, José Jorge – Staff Officer, General Campbell's Portuguese Brigade

Loy, Casimiro – Cavalry Brigadier, Spanish 4th Army Expeditionary Corps

Lumley, William – British Major General

Lützow, Leo – Lieutenant, Legion Extrangera

Madden, Charles – Lieutenant, 4th Dragoons

Maransin, Jean-Pierre – Division General, Vth Corps

Miranda, José – Colonel commanding of Spanish Artillery

Moore, Matthew – Lieutenant, 39th Foot

Morrison, John – Assistant Surgeon, 3rd Foot

Morrow, Alexander – Lieutenant, 39th Foot

Nooth, Mervin – Major, 7th Fusiliers

Peacocke, Thomas – Captain, 23rd Portuguese Line

Penne-Villemur, Louis, Count of – Spanish Cavalry General

Pernet, Jean-Étienne – Captain, Vth Corps Artillery

Perrin de Solliers, ? – 2nd Lieutenant, 21st Light

Philipps, Grismond – Lieutenant, 23rd Fusiliers

Roverea, Alexander de – Captain, ADC to General Cole

Saunderson, Hardress W.R. – Captain, 39th Foot

Schepeler, Andreas Daniel Berthold von – Staff Officer for General Zayas

Sherer, Moyle – Lieutenant, 34th Foot

Smith, Harry – Lieutenant, 95th Rifles

Somerset, Edward – Lieutenant Colonel, 4th Dragoons

Somerset, Fitzroy – Military Secretary to the Duke of Wellington

Soult, Jean de Dieu – Marshal and Duke of Dalmatia, Commanding General, Army of the South

St George, Stepney – Lieutenant, 66th Foot

Stanhope, James – Lieutenant and Captain, 1st Foot Guards

Stephens, William – Captain, 3rd Foot

Stewart, Charles – Adjutant General

Stewart, William – British Major General

Unger, William – Second Lieutenant, KGL Artillery

Vivien, Jean-Stanislas – Captain, 55th Line

Wachholtz, Friedrich Ludwig von – Captain, Rifle Company, Brunswick Oels

Whinyates, Frederick C. – Second Captain, Royal Horse Artillery

Wilson, James – Captain, 1st Battalion, 48th Foot

Wojciechowski, Kajetan – 2nd Lieutenant, 1st Lancer Regiment of the Vistula Legion

Wood, William – Lieutenant, 2nd Battalion, 48th Foot

Zayas, Jose de – Mariscal de Campo, Spanish 4th Army Expeditionary Corps

# BIBLIOGRAPHY

A Die Hard, 'Letter from "A Die Hard"', *United Service Journal* (1829), Part 2, pp. 106–107

Aineville, Charles Marie-Blanche d'& Espérandieu, Antoine d', *'Autour de Deux Portraits de Famille: Le Général Baron Joseph Pépin'*, *Revue de l'Institut Napoléon*, No. 142 (1984), pp. 57–66

Aitchison, John, *An Ensign in the Peninsular War* (London, 1981)

Alten, Charles von, 'Narrative of General Count Alten, October 1833', H.N. Estrangeiros Caixa 205, Maço 166 (2), Portuguese Arquivo Nacional da Torre de Tombo, Lisbon, Portugal

An Old Soldier, 'Albuera', *United Service Journal* (1840), Part 3, pp. 107–108

_____, 'Battle of Albuera', *United Service Journal* (1835), Part 3, pp. 535–6

_____, *Army Officers Awards, Napoleonic Period* (London, 1853, reprint London, 1969)

_____, 'Bataille d'Albuera', File C8 72, Service Historique de l'Armée de Terre, Chateau de Vincennes, Paris, France

_____, 'The Battle of Albuhera', *Regimental Journal of the Worcestershire & Sherwood Foresters Regiment*, (April, 1931), pp. 7–18

_____, 'Biographical Sketch of G.J. Guthrie, Esq, FRS', *The Lancet* (1850), pp.726–36

_____ (Private, 3rd Foot), 'Extract from a letter from a private of the 3rd Regiment of Foot, or Buffs, who was taken prisoner and effected his escape from the enemy', *The Soldier's Companion; or, Martial Recorder, Consisting of Biography, Anecdotes, Poetry, and Miscellaneous Information Peculiarly Interesting to Those Connected with the Military Profession*, (London, 1824)

_____, 'Extract from a Letter dated Lisbon, 24 May 1811', *The Times*, 6 June 1811, p. 3, col. a

_____, *Further Strictures on Those Parts of Col. Napier's History of the Peninsular War Which Relate to the Military Opinions and Conduct of General Lord Viscount Beresford*, (London, 1832, reprint Sunderland, 1995)

_____ (Officer, 1/48th Foot), 'Letter from an Officer, 19 May 1811', *Evening Star*, 5 June 1811, p. 3, col. d.

_____, 'Life of Sir William Myers', *The Royal Military Chronicle*, (October 1811), pp. 469–74

_____, *Strictures on Certain Passages of Lieut.-Col. Napier's History of the Peninsular War Which Relate to the Military Opinions and Conduct of General Lord Viscount Beresford*, (London, 1831, reprint Sunderland, 1995)

_____, 'The 29th at Albuhera', *Regimental Journal of the Worcestershire & Sherwood Foresters Regiment*, (April, 1931), pp. 19–25

Arnold, James, 'A Reappraisal of Column versus Line in the Peninsular War', *Journal of Military History*, Vol. 68, No. 2 (2004), p. 547

Atkinson, C.T., 'The Composition and Organisation of the British Forces in the Peninsula, 1808–1814', *English Historical Review*, Vol. 17, No. 65 (1902), pp. 110–33

_____,'A Swiss Officer in Wellington's Army', *Journal of the Society for Army Historical Research*, Vol. 35 (1957), pp. 71–8

_____, *The Dorsetshire Regiment – Vol. 1, the 39th Foot*, (Oxford, 1947)

Ayres de Magalhães Sepúlveda, Christiovam, *Historia Organica et Politico do Exercito Portuguez*, Vol. 11 (12 vols., Coimbra 1902–17) [Volume 11 (Coimbra 1916) deals with Albuera]

Bakewell, Robert (17th Portuguese Regiment), Transcript of Bakewell Diaries (3 vols.), NAM Manuscript No. 7509–75, National Army Museum, London

Barrès, Jean-Baptiste (Bernard Miall, tr.), *Memoirs of a Napoleonic Officer* (London, 1925)

Barrett, C.R.B., *History of the XIII Hussars* (2 vols., London, 1911)

Bayley, Charles (Lt., 31st Foot), Letter to Miss Sally Smith, 'Camp near Albuera, 18 May 1811, 10 O'Clock Morning', Private Collection

Beamish, N.L., *History of the King's German Legion* (2 vols., London, reprint 1993)

Beauvais de Préau, G.T. (ed.), *Victoires, Conquêtes, Désastres, Revers et Guerres Civiles des Français de 1792 á 1815* (27 vols., Paris 1817–21) [Volume 20 (1820) deals with Albuera]

Belmas, J., *Journaux des Sièges Faits ou Soutenus par les Français dans la Péninsule, de 1807 à 1814* (5 vols., Paris 1836–7)

Benavides Moro, Nicolas & Yaque Laurel, José A., *El Capitán General Don Joaquín Blake Y Joyes, regente del Reino, Fundador del Cuerpo de Estado Mayor* (nl [Madrid] nd [1960])

Bennett, Thomas (Sergeant, 13th Light Dragoons), 'Memoirs of a Saddler Sergeant', in Fortescue, *Following the Drum*, pp. 81–103

Beresford, William C., Letter to Sir Charles Stewart, 25 May 1811, Letters of Lord Londonderry, Durham Records Office, D/LO/C –18/63I, Durham, England

_____, *A Second Letter to Charles Edward Long, Esq*, (London, 1843)

_____, *Letter to Charles Edward Long, Esq., on the Extracts Recently Published from the Manuscript Journal and Private Correspondence of the Late Lieutenant General R.B. Long*, (London, 1833)

_____, *Refutation of Colonel Napier's Justification of his Third Volume* (London, 1834)

_____, Official Report to Wellington, 18 May 1811, *London Gazette Extraordinary*, 4 June 1811 [This report is reproduced in many other sources including *The Times*, 4 June 1811, p. 2, and *Dispatches*, Vol. 7, pp. 588–93]

Blanco, Letter to the Editor, 15 November 1834, *United Service Journal* (1834, Part 3), p. 546

Boutflower, C., *The Journal of an Army Surgeon during the Peninsular War* (nl nd [1912])

Bouvier, J.-B., *Historique de 96e Régiment (ex 21e Léger)*, (Lyon, 1892)

Brasier de Thiry, ?, *Historique du 103e Régiment d'Infanterie* (Mamers, 1886)

Bremond d'Ars, Théophile, *Historique du 21e Régiment de Chasseurs à Cheval 1792–1814* (Paris, 1903)

Bridgman, George, *Letters from Portugal, Spain, Sicily and Malta in 1812, 1813 and 1814* (London, 1875)

Brooke, William (Major, 2/48th Foot), 'A Prisoner of Albuera' in Oman, *Studies in the Napoleonic Wars*

Burriel, Antonio (Chief of Staff, 4th Army), *Batalla de la Albuhera* (Cadiz, 1811)

Butler, Lewis, *Annals of the King's Royal Rifle Corps* (6 vols., London, 1913)

Caddell, Charles, *Narrative of the Campaigns of the 28th Regiment* (London, 1835)

Calvo Perez, Juan Luis, *El Regimiento de Infanteria de Linea de Castropol* (Madrid, 1996)

Cambon, Jean Pierre, *Jean-Pierre Maransin, General de Division [et] Baron d'Empire, 1770–1828* (Tarbes, France, 1991)

Carpue, Joseph C., *An Account of Two Successful Operations for Restoring a Lost Nose From the Integuments of the Forehead* (London, 1816, reprint Birmingham, Alabama 1981)

Chaby, Claudio de, *Excerptos Historicos e Collecçâo de Documentos Relativos a Guerra Denominada da Peninsula – Parte Terceira: Guerra da Peninsular* (Lisbon, 1863)

Challis, Lionel S., 'British Officers Serving in the Portuguese Army, 1809–1814', *Journal of the Society for Army Historical Research*, Vol. 27 (1949), pp. 50–60

Champion, B.W., 'James T. Morisset of the 48th Regiment', *Royal Australian Historical Society Journal and Proceedings*, Vol. XX, Pt. IV (1934), pp. 209–26

Ciefuego Linares, Julio, *La Albuera 16-V-1811* (Merida, Spain, 1996)

Close, Edward Charles (Lt., 2/48th Foot), *Diary of E.C. Close* (London nd)

Cobbold, Richard, *Mary Anne Wellington, the Soldier's Daughter, Wife and Widow* (3 vols., London, 1846)

Colborne, John (Lt. Col., 66th Foot), Letter to Rev. Duke Yonge, 18 May 1811 in Smith, *Life of Lord Seaton*, pp. 160–1

Cole, G. Lowry, *The Correspondence of Colonel Wade, Colonel Napier, Major General Sir H. Hardinge and General the Hon. Sir Lowry G. Cole, Relating to the Battle of Albuera* (London, 1841)

_____, (Maude Cole & Stephen Gwynn, eds.), *Memoirs of Sir Lowry Cole* (London, 1934)

Cole, John William, *Memoirs of British Generals Distinguished During the Peninsular War* (2 vols., London, 1856)

Combermere, Viscountess Mary & Knollys, W., *Memoirs and Correspondence of Field-Marshal Viscount Combermere* (2 vols., London,1866)

Conrady, G. von, *Leben und Wirken des . . . Carl von Grolman* (3 vols., Berlin, 1894–6)

Cooper, John Spencer (Sergeant, 7th Foot [Fusiliers]), *Rough Notes of Seven Campaigns* (London, 1869)

Crompton, George (Lt., 66th Foot), Letter to Mother, 18 May 1811, *Journal of the Society for Army Historical Research*, Vol. I (1921–2), p. 130

Daniell, D. Scott, *4th Hussars 1685–1958* (London, 1959)

Dessirier, ? (ed.), *Historique de 34ᵉ Régiment d'Infanterie* (Mont-de-Maisan, France, 1894)

D'Héralde, Jean Baptiste (Surgeon, 88th Line), *Mémoires d'un Chirurgien de la Grande Armée*, (Paris, 2002)

Dickens, Lt. S. (Lt., 34th Foot), Letter to Unidentified Correspondent, 24 May 1811, *Report on the Manuscripts of the Late Reginald Rawdon Hastings, Esq., of the Manor House, Ashby de la Zouch* (Vol. 3, London, 1934), pp. 289–93

Dobbin, Robert Brown (Lt, 66th Foot), Letter to Unidentified Correspondent, 23 May 1811, Regimental Archives of The Duke of Edinburgh's Royal Regiment, (Salisbury)

Drummond, Duncan (Sergeant, 66th Foot), Documents Concerning Duncan Drummond, NAM Manuscript 2003-12-9:47 (National Army Museum, London)

Du Casse, Robert, *Le Volontaire de 1793; Général du Premier Empire – Jean-Baptiste Girard* (Paris, nd [1880])

D'Urban, Benjamin (Portuguese Quartermaster General), Memorandum for Colonel Colborne, 29 April 1811, Private Collection

_____, Letter to H. Taylor, 29 August 1811, Private Collection, (previously on loan as NAM Manuscript 7805-46-143, National Army Museum, London)

_____, *The Peninsular Journal of Major General Sir Benjamin D'Urban, 1808–1817* (London, 1930)

_____, *Report of the Operations in the Alemtejo and Spanish Estremadura, During the Campaign of 1811* (London, 1817, reprint 1832)

Dutton, Corporal (3rd Foot), 'Extract of a letter from Corporal Dutton [nd]', *Historical Manuscripts Commission Report on the Manuscripts of Reginald Rawdon Hastings* (London, 1934)

Dutton, Geoffrey, *Founder of a City – The Life of Colonel William Light* (Adelaide, 1984)

E.M., 'Albuera, etc.', *United Service Journal* (1835, Pt. 2), p. 536

Eeckhoudt, Guy Van, *Les Chevau-Legers Belges du duc d'Arenberg* (Paris, 2002)

Ellis, J.D., 'Drummers for the Devil? The Black Soldiers of the 29th (Worcestershire) Regiment of Foot, 1759–1843', *Journal of the Society for Army Historical Research*, Vol. 80, No. 323 (Autumn 2002), pp. 186–201

Emerson, J., 'Recollections of the Late War in Spain and Portugal', in Maxwell, *Peninsular Sketches*, Vol. 2, pp. 205–42

Esdaile, Charles J., *The Peninsular War* (London, 2003)

_____, *The Spanish Army in the Peninsular War* (Manchester, 1988)

Espinchal, Hippolyte d', *Souvenirs Militaires, 1792–1814* (2 vols., Paris, 1901)

Everard, H., *History of Thos. Farrington's Regiment Subsequently Designated the 29th (Worcestershire) Foot 1694 to 1891* (Worcester, 1891)

Fletcher, Ian, *Bloody Albuera: The 1811 Campaign in the Peninsula* (Ramsbury, 2000)

_____, *Galloping at Everything – The British Cavalry in the Peninsular War and at Waterloo 1808–1815* (Staplehurst, 1999)

Fortescue, John W., *A History of the British Army* (20 vols., London, 1899–1930) [Volume 8 (text) and Volume 8 (maps) (1917) deal with Albuera]

_____, *Following the Drum* (London, 1931)

Fraser, Edward, *The Soldiers Whom Wellington Led – Deeds of Daring, Chivalry and Renown* (London, 1913)

Fryer, Mary B., *'Our Young Soldier': Lt Francis Simcoe, 6 June 1791 – 6 April 1812* (Toronto, 1996)

Fyans, Foster, *Memoirs Recorded at Geelong, Victoria, Australia by Captain Foster Fyans (1790–1870)* (Geelong, 1986)

Gazan, Honoré-Théodore-Maxime, Letter to Berthier, 19 May 1811, AF IV 1630, Plaq 1(111) (Archives Nationales, Paris)

Gell, Thomas (Captain, 29th Foot), Letter to Father [Philip Gell], 17 May 1811, Papers of the Gell Family of Hopton, Ms. D3287/28/20/1 (Derbyshire Record Office, England)

Gil, Ferreira, *A Infantaria Portuguese na Guerra da Peninsula – Segunda Parte* (Lisbon, 1913)

Gil, J., '*O Centenario d'Albuera*', *Revista Militar* (1911), pp. 210–22

Girard, Jean Baptiste (French General), 'Excerpts from Report to Marshal Soult, 16 May 1811' in Sainsbury, *The Napoleon Museum*, p. 481

Glover, Michael, 'The Royal Welch Fusiliers at Albuera', *Journal of the Society for Army Historical Research*, Vol. LXVI, No. 267 (Autumn 1988), pp. 146–54

Gómez de Arteche y Moro, José, *Guerra de la Independencia – Historia Militar de España de 1808 á 1814* (14 vols., Madrid, 1868–1903) [Volume 10 deals with Albuera]

Gómez Ruiz, Manuel, *El Ejército de los Borbones Pt. V – Reinado de Fernando VII*, Vol. 1, (Madrid, 1999)

Gordon, Arthur (Capt., 3rd Foot), 'Extract of a Letter from a Captain of the Buffs, who was wounded in the action at Albuera, to His Brother Officer in England, 20 May 1811', *The Star*, 8 June 1811, p. 4, col. l.

Gotteri, Nicole, *Le Maréchal Soult* (Paris, 2000)

_____, (Jaques-Olivier Bourdon, ed.), 'L'Entourage Militaire du Maréchal Soult', *Armée, Guerre et Societé à l'Époque Napoléonienne*, Paris, 2004

Gougeat, Louis-Antoine (Private, 20th Dragoon), '*Mémoires d'un Cavalier d'Ordonnance de 20e Dragons (1804–1814)*', *Carnet de la Sabretache*, Vol. 9 (1902), pp. 331–44 and 400–22

Graves, Donald E., *Fix Bayonets! A Royal Welch Fusilier at War, 1796–1815* (Toronto, 2006)

Griffon de Pleineville, Natalie, 'Fighting for Napoleon: General Gazan de la Peyriere', *History Today* (1 April 2003)

Groves, J. Percy, *The 66th Berkshire Regiment* (London, 1887)

Gurney, Russell, *History of the Northamptonshire Regiment 1742–1934* (Aldershot, 1935)

Guthrie, George J., *Commentaries on the Surgery of War in Portugal, Spain, France, and the Netherlands, From the Battle of Rolica, in 1808, to that of Waterloo, in 1815* (London, 1853)

_____, *On Gunshot Wounds of the Extremities* (London, 1815)

Hall, C.D. (ed.), 'Albuera and Vittoria: Letters From Lt. Col. J. Hill', *Journal of the Society for Army Historical Research*, Vol. LXVI, No. 268 (Winter 1988), pp. 193–8

Hall, John A., *The Biographical Dictionary of British Officers Killed and Wounded, 1808–1814* (London, 1998)

Hall, Samuel C., *Retrospect of a Long Life* (New York, 1883)

Halliday, Andrew, *Observations on the Present State of the Portuguese Army* (London, 1811)

Hardinge, Charles, Viscount, *Rulers of India – Viscount Hardinge* (Oxford, 1891)

Harris, R.G., 'Two Military Miniatures', *Journal of the Society for Army Historical Research*, Vol. LXIII, No. 254 (Summer 1985), pp. 99–103

Harrison, John (Lt., 23 Foot (Fusiliers)), Letter to Father, Lisbon, 22 June 1811 (Royal Welch Fusiliers Archives, Caernarfon Castle, Gwynedd)

_____, Letter to Mother, Elvas, 18 May 1811, *ibid.*; reproduced in Glover, 'Royal Welch Fusiliers', pp. 146–7

_____, Letter to Mother, Elvas, 24 May 1811, *ibid.*, reproduced in Glover, 'Royal Welch Fusiliers', pp. 149–54

Hartmann, Julius von, 'Beitrage zur Geschichte des Krieges auf der Pyrenaischen Halbinsel in den Jahren 1809 bis 1813', *Hannoversches Militairisches Journal,*Vol. 2 (1831), pp. 91–126

_____, *Der Königlich Hannoversche General Sir Julius von Hartmann – Eine Lebenskizze*, (Hannover, 1858)

Hayman, Peter, *Soult – Napoleon's Maligned Marshal* (London, 1990)

Haythornthwaite, Philip, *Die Hard! Dramatic Actions from the Napoleonic Wars* (London, 1996)

_____, 'Henry Hardinge', *Military Illustrated*, No. 25 (June 1990), pp. 49–50

Hill, John (Capt., 23 Foot (Fusiliers)), Letter to Mother, 18 May 1811 (Royal Welch Fusiliers Archives, Caernarfon Castle, Gwynedd), reproduced in Hall, 'Albuera and Vittoria', p. 193

_____, Letter to Mother, 22 May 1811, *ibid.*; reproduced in Hall, 'Albuera and Vittoria', pp. 194–5

Hobhouse, Benjamin (Ensign, 57th Foot), Letter to 'My Dear Father', 17 May 1811, *The Times*, 25 February 1915, p. 9, col. b

Holme, Norman & Kirby, E.L., *Medal Rolls: 23rd Foot – Royal Welch Fusiliers, Napoleonic Period*, (London, 1978)

Hope, John M. (Major, ADC to General Graham), Letter to General Sir John Hope, 29 May 1811, Hopetoun Papers Vol. 177, pp. 55–62 (Scottish Record Office, Edinburgh)

Hugo, Abel, *France Militaire: Histoire Militaire des Armées Françaises de Terre et de Mer de 1792 à 1837* (4 vols., Paris, 1838)

Inglis, Lady, Manuscript History of the Services of Major General William Inglis, compiled by Lady Inglis 1828 (?), Archive Item MAM Ms. No. 6504-52/33 (National Army Museum, London)

Inglis, William, Letter to the Editor, *United Service Journal*, (1832) Part 2, pp. 241–2

J.L., 'Captain Gibbons of His Majesty's Thirty-Fourth Foot', *The Royal Military Chronicle* (April 1812), pp. 431–2

Jackson, Lady (ed.), *The Bath Archives – A Further Selection From the Diaries and Letters of Sir George Jackson, K.C.H., From 1809 to 1816*, (2 vols., London, 1873)

Jones, John T., *Journals of Sieges Carried on by the Army under the Duke of Wellington in Spain, During the Years 1811 to 1814* (3 vols., London, 1846)

Jones, Rice, *An Engineer Officer Under Wellington in the Peninsula* (reprint (British Engineer Officer) London, 1986)

Juretschke, Hans, 'El Coronel von Schepeler – Caracter Y Valor Informativo de su Obra Historiografica Sobre el Reinado de Fernando VII', *Revista de Estudios Politicos*, No. 126 (1962), pp. 229–49

Kirkor, Stanislaw, *Legia Nadwislanska 1808–1814* (London, 1981)

Knight, C.R.B., *Historical Records of the Buffs East Kent Regiment (3rd Foot) 1704–1914, Part 1 – 1704–1814* (London, 1953)

Kujawski, Marian, *Z Bojow Polskich w Wojnach Napoleonskich: Maida-Somosierra-Fuengirola-Albuera* (nl [London] 1967)

Lamare, Jean-Baptiste (French Engineer Officer), *Relation des Sièges et Défenses d'Olivença, de Badajoz et de Campo-Mayor en 1811 et 1812* (Paris, 1837)

Lamathiere, Theophile, *Pantheon de la Légion d'Honneur* (17 vols., 1875–1911)

Lapène, Édouard (Artillery Officer, Vth Corps), *Conquête de l'Andalousie – Campagne de 1810 et 1811 dans le Midi de l'Espagne* (Paris, 1823)

Latour-Maubourg, Count V. de, Report to Marshal Soult, Usagre, 27 May 1811, Add. Ms. 37425, ff. 65-69 (British Library, London)

Lavaux, François (Alfred Darmon, ed.), *Mémoires de François Lavaux, Sergent au 103e de Ligne (1793–1814)* (Paris nd)

Lemaitre, L., *Historique du 4e Régiment de Dragons (1672–1894)* (Paris, 1894)

Leslie, Charles (Lt., 29th Foot), *Military Journal of Colonel Leslie, K.H., of Balquhain* (Aberdeen, 1887)

Leslie, J.H., 'Medals Which Were Awarded to Officers of the Royal Regiment of Artillery . . .', *Journal of the Royal Artillery*, Vol. LI, No. 6, pp. 403–409

L'Estrange, George B., *Recollections* (London, nd [1874])

Lievyns, A., *Fastes de la Légion d'Honneur – Biographie de tous les Décorés accompagnée de l'Histoire législative et réglementaire de l'Ordre* (5 vols., Paris, 1842–7)

Lillie, John Scott (Lt., Lusitantian Legion), Letter to the Editor, *The Times*, 26 September 1856, p. 8, col. a

Lindau, Freidrich (Private, 1st KGL Light Battalion), *Erinnerungen Eines Soldaten aus den Feldzügen der Königlich Deutschen Legion* (Hameln, 1846)

Lloyd, E.M., 'The Battle of Albuera', *Journal of the Royal United Service Institution*, Vol. 39, No. 21 (Sept. 1895), 903–11 plus map

Londonderry, Charles William Vane, Marquess of, *Narrative of the Peninsular War from 1808 to 1813* (2 vols., London, 1829)

Long, Charles Edward, *A Reply to the Misrepresentations and Aspersions on the Military Reputation of the Late Lieutenant General R.B. Long Contained in a Work Entitled 'Further Strictures . . .' Accompanied by Extracts From the Manuscript Journal and Private Correspondence of that Officer, and Corroborated by the Further Testimony of Living Witnesses* (London, 1832)

_____, *The Albuera Medal* (London, nd [1838])

_____, *Letter to General Viscount Beresford, GCB in Reply to his Lordship's Letter to the Author Relative to the Conduct of the Late Lieutenant General R.B. Long in the Campaign of 1811* (London, 1833)

_____, *Reply to Lord Beresford's Second Letter to the Author Relative to the Campaign of 1811 and the Conduct of the Late Lieutenant General Long, then Commanding the Allied Cavalry* (London, 1835)

Long, Robert Ballard, Letter to C.B. Long, 30 May 1811, printed in C.E. Long, *A Reply to . . . a Work Entitled 'Further Strictures . . .'* (London, 1832)

_____, Letter to Le Marchant, 5 June 1811, Le Marchant Papers, Packet 13a, Item 8, p. 4 (Royal Military Academy, Sandhurst)

Loureiro, José Jorge, Letter, 20 May 1811, *Revista Militar*, Vol. 55 (1903), pp. 364–6

Luz Soriano, Simão José da, *Historia da Guerra . . . em Portugal . . . desde 1777 até 1834 – Guerra de Peninsula*, Vol. 3 (1809–11) (Lisbon, 1874)

MacDonnell, Donald (Lt. Col., 11 Portuguese regiment), Letter to his Cousin [Archibald MacDonald], 23 May 1811 (Royal Welch Fusilier Archives, Caernarfon Castle, Gwynedd)

Madden, Charles Dudley (Lt. 4th Dragoons), 'The Diary of Charles Dudley Madden, Lieutenant 4th Dragoons, Peninsular War 1809–1811', *Royal United Services Institution Journal*, Vol. 58 (1914), pp. 334–49 and 501–26

Madden, George (Portuguese General), 'Narrative of the Operations of the 5th, or Spanish Estremaduran Army', *Royal Military Calendar* (5 vols., London, 1820), Vol. 4, pp. 66–93

_____, Letter to D'Urban, 18 May 1811 (Portuguese Arquivo Nacional da Torre do Tombo, Lisbon)

Malaguti, Captain, *Historique du 87e Regiment d'Infanterie de Ligne (ex-12e Léger) 1690–1892* (Paris, 1892)

Marmont, Marshal, *Mémoires du Maréchal Marmont, Duc de Raguse, de 1792 à 1814* (9 vols., Paris, 1857)

Martin, E., *Le 55e Régiment d'Infanterie* (Avignon, 1888)

Martinien, A., *Tableaux par Corps et par Batailles des Officiers Tués et Blessés Pendant les Guerres de l'Empire (1805–1815)* (Paris, 1899, reprint nl nd [1980?])

_____, *Tableaux par Corps et par Batailles des Officiers Tués et Blessés Pendant les Guerres de l'Empire (1805–1815) (Partie Supplementaire)* (Paris, 1909, reprint San Diego, 2000)

Matthews, Elizabeth, Letter to Marquis of Londonderry, 14 September 1828, in Appendix of Correspondence in Londonderry, *Narrative*, Vol. 2, pp. 317–19

Mayne, Richard, *A Narrative of the Campaigns of the Loyal Lusitanian Legion* (London, 1812, reprint Cambridge, 1986)

McGuffie, T.H. (ed.), *Peninsular Cavalry General 1811–1813: The Correspondence of Lieutenant-General Robert Ballard Long* (London, 1951)

Menuau, Maurice L., *Historique du 14e Régiment de Dragons* (Paris, 1887)

Message, Colin, 'Dying Hard – Military General Service Medals for the Battle of Albuera', *Medal News* (April 2000), pp. 26–7

Morillon, M., 'L'Artillerie de Montagne Sous le Premier Empire', *Soldats Napoléoniens*, No. 9 (March 2006), pp. 27–36

Muir, Rory, *Tactics and the Experience of Battle in the Age of Napoleon* (New Haven, 1998)

Mullen, A.L.T., *The Military General Service Roll 1793–1814* (London, 1990)

[Murray, George] (Wellington's Quartermaster General), Manuscript Account of the Battle of Albuera, Papers of Alexander Gordon, Ref. GD 364, Item 1216, Hope-Lufness Papers (Scottish Record Office, Edinburgh)

_____, Letter to Alexander Gordon, 22 May 1811, Item 1217, *ibid.*

Murray, John (Surgeon, 66th Foot), Letter to his Father, Lisbon, 29 June 1811, Ms. RAMC 830 (Wellcome Library, London)

Myers, Sir William (Colonel, 23rd Foot (Fusiliers)), 'Life of Sir William Myers', *The Royal Military Chronicle* (October 1811), pp. 469–74

Nadaillac, Colonel de, 'Lettres et Notes du Sigismond de Pouget, Marquis de Nadaillac (1787–1837)', *Carnet de la Sabretache*, Vol. 19 (1911), p. 473

Nafziger, George F., *The Armies of Spain and Portugal 1808–1814* (nl. [privately printed], 1992)

Napier, William F.P., *A Letter to General Lord Viscount Beresford Being an Answer to his Lordship's Assumed Refutation of Colonel Napier's Justification of his Third Volume* (London, 1834)

_____, *Colonel Napier's Justification of his Third Volume; Forming a Sequel to his Reply to Various Opponent, and Containing Some New and Curious Facts Relative to the Battle of Albuera* (London, 1833)

_____, *History of the War in the Peninsula and in the South of France from the Year 1807 to the Year 1814* (6 vols., London, 1828–40); Vol. 3 deals with Albuera

Napoléon I, *The Confidential Correspondence of Napoléon Bonaparte with his Brother Joseph* (2 vols., New York, 1856)

_____, *Correspondance de Napoléon Ier (Publiée par l'ordre de l'Empereur Napoléon III)* (32 vols., Paris, 1858–69)

Nettleship, Andrew, *That Astonishing Infantry – A History of the 7th Foot (Royal Fusiliers) in the Peninsular War 1809–1814*, (Chippenham, 1989)

Nunes, J. Lucio, *As Brigadas da Cavalaria Portuguesa Na Guerra Peninsular* (Lisbon, 1954)

Oatts, Lewis Balfour, *I Serve: A Regimental History of the 3rd Carabiniers (Prince of Wales's Dragoon Guards)* (Chester, 1966)

Oman, Sir Charles W., *A History of the Peninsular War* (7 vols., Oxford, 1902–30); Volume 4 (1911) deals with Albuera

_____, 'Albuera (A Lecture Delivered at the Royal Artillery Institution, Thursday, 7th January, 1909)', *The Journal of the Royal Artillery*, Vol. XXXVI (1909–10), pp. 49–69

_____, 'Albuera Once More', *The Army Quarterly*, July 1932, pp. 337–42

_____, *Studies in the Napoleonic Wars* (London,1929)

Painvin, Achille Paul Arsène, *Historique de 51e Régiment d'Infanterie* (Paris, 1891)

Palmerston, Lord, *Return of the Names of the Officers in the Army, Who receive Pensions for the Loss of Limbs, or for Wounds* (London, 1818)

Peacocke, Thomas (Capt., 23rd Portuguese Infantry), *Memoirs of Major General Thomas Peacocke* (Tours, 1855) [Microfilm copy at National Army Museum, London]

Pearse, Hugh W., *History of the 31st Foot, Huntingdonshire Regt., and 70th Foot, Surrey Regt., Subsequently the 1st and 2nd Battalions of the East Surrey Regiment* (2 vols., London, 1916)

Pearson, Andrew, *The Soldier Who Walked Away – Autobiography of Andrew Pearson, a Peninsular War Veteran* (London, 1987)

Pépin de Bonnerive, ?, 'Un Soldat de l'Empire: Le Général Pépin (1765–1811)', *Carnet de la Sabretache* (1932), pp. 62–91, 189–217, 274–89 and 354–77

Pernet, Captain Étienne (Capt., 5th Horse Artillery), 'Journal' in Remy & Rey, *Général Bourgeat.*

Perrin-Solliers, ? (Sous-Lt., 21st Light), [Review of *Examen Raisonné* by Okouneff] *Le Spectateur Militaire*, No. 13 (1832), pp. 353–78

Petiet, Auguste (ADC to Soult) (N. Gotteri, ed.), *Souvenirs Historiques, Militaires et Particuliers 1784–1815* (Paris, 1996)

Philipps, Grismond (Lt., 23rd Foot), 'Letters Home', *The Waterloo Journal*, Vol. 20, No. 2 (August 1999), pp. 20–6

Priego Lopez, Juan, *Guerra de la Independencia, 1808–1814 – Volumen 6, La Campaña de 1811 (Primer Periodo)* (Madrid, 1992)

Prieto Llovera, Patricio, *El Grande de España Capitan General Castanos, Primer Duque de Bailen Y Primer Marques de Portugalete (1758–1852)* (Madrid, 1958)

Rey, Jules & Remy, Emile, *Le Général Baron Bourgeat 1760–1827 d'après sa Correspondance et des Documents Inédits* (Grenoble, 1898)

Robinson, Thomas Gerald, *Los Sitios de Badajoz Y La Batalla de la Albuera* (Badajoz nd)

Roverea, Ferdinand de, *Mémoires de F. De Roverea* (3 vols., Paris, 1848)

Sainsbury, John, *The Napoleon Museum* (London, 1845)

Saint-Chamans, Alfred A.R. (ADC to Soult), *Mémoires du Général Comte de Saint-Chamans, Ancien Aide de Camp du Maréchal Soult 1802–1832* (Paris, 1896)

Schepeler, Berthold von (Spanish Staff Officer), *Histoire de la Révolution d'Espagne et de Portugal* (5 vols., Liège, 1831)

Scovell, George, Diary Vol. 2 (1810–1811), Public Records Office WO 37/7(a), Kew

Severn, John Kenneth, *A Wellesley Affair – Richard Marquess Wellesley and the Conduct of Anglo-Spanish Diplomacy, 1809–1812* (Tallahassee, FL, 1981)

Sherer, Joseph Moyle (Lt., 34th Foot), 'Kit Wallace – A Recollection', *The Museum of Foreign Literature, Science and Art* (January 1829), pp. 7–9

_____, *Recollections of the Peninsula* (London, 1824; reprint 1996)

Smith, G.C. Moore, *The Life of John Colborne, Field Marshal Lord Seaton* (London, 1903)

Smith, Harry, *The Autobiography of Lieutenant General Sir Harry Smith* (2 vols., London, 1902)

Smythies, R.H. Raymond, *Historical Records of the 40th (2nd Somersetshire) Regiment* (Devonport, 1894)

Société d'Hommes de Lettres et de Militaires, *Les Fastes de la Gloire ou les Braves Recommandés à la Postérité* (5 vols., Paris, 1817–22)

Somerset, Fitzroy, Letter to Duke of Beaufort [his brother], 23 May 1811, Manuscript Fm M 4/1/6(13) (Badminton Archives, England)

Soriano, S.J.L. da, *Historia da Guerra Civil e do Estabelecimento do Governo Parlemnetar em Portugal* (15 vols., Lisbon, 1866–92)

Soult, Jean de Dieu, Letter to Berthier, 4 June 1811, excerpted in Sainsbury, *The Napoleon Museum*, p. 483

_____, (Louis & Antoinette de Saint-Pierre, eds.), *Mémoires du Maréchal Soult – Espagne et Portugal* (Paris, 1955)

_____, 'Rapport de S. Exc. Le maréchal duc de Dalmatie à S.A.S. le prince de Neufchâtel, major général', 21 May 1811, *Le Moniteur Universel*, [Paris] 13 June 1811; this report is reproduced in a number of other different sources including *Supplementary Despatches*, Vol. 13, pp. 651–3. An English translation appears in *The Times*, 21 June 1811, p. 3, col. d.

_____, Unpublished Report to 'Prince de Wagram', 18 May 1811, File C8* 147*, pp. 196–203 (Service Historique de l'Armée de Terre, Château de Vincennes, Paris)

Spain, Escuela Superior del Ejercito, 'La Batalla de Albuera – Un Ejemplo de Coordinacion Hispano-Portuguesa (16 de Mayo de 1811)', Conferencia

Pronunciada en el Instituto de Altos Estudios Militares (Portugal) (Lisbon, 1983)

Spain, Seccion de Historia Militar, *Estados de la Organizacion Y Fuerza, de los Ejercitos Espanoles Beligerantes en la Peninsula, Durante la Guerra de España Contra Bonaparte* (Barcelona, 1822)

Stampa Piñeiro, Leopold, 'La Batalla de Albuera, 16 de Mayo de 1811', *Dragona*, Vol. 3, No. 6 (March 1995), pp. 45–9

Stanhope, Philip Henry, Earl, *Notes of Conversations with the Duke of Wellington, 1831–1851* (London, 1938)

Stewart, General Sir Charles (Wellington's Adjutant General), Letter to Unidentified Colonel, 22 May 1811, Letters of Lord Londonderry (Durham Records Office D/LO/C –18/62, Durham)

_____, Letter to Lord Londonderry, 30 May 1811, *ibid.*, D/LO/C –18/63

Stewart, Sir William, *Cumloden Papers* (Edinburgh, 1871)

Thompson, Mark S., *The Fatal Hill: The Allied Campaign under Beresford in Southern Spain in 1811* (Chapelgarth, 2002)

Thoumas, Charles Antoine, *Les Grands Cavaliers du Premier Empire: Notices Biographiques* (3 vols., Paris, 1890–1909)

Titeux, Eugene, 'Le Général Dulong de Rosnay', *Carnet de la Sabretache* (1901), pp. 3–15.

Tomkinson, William, *The Diary of a Cavalry Officer in the Peninsular War and Waterloo Campaign 1809–1815* (London, 1895)

Toreno, José M.Q. de L.R. de S. Count of, *Histoire de Soulèvement, de la Guerre et de la Révolution d'Espagne* (4 vols., Paris, 1836); Volume 4 deals with Albuera

Unger, William (Lt., KGL Artillery), 'Description to the Plan of the Battle of Albuera . . . 24 May 1811', *Journal of the Royal Artillery*, Vol. XIII (1885), pp. 126–7

Vere, Charles Broke (Assistant Quartermaster General), *Marches, Movements, and Operations of the 4th Division of the Allied Army, in Spain and Portugal in the Years 1810, 1811 & 1812* (Ipswich, 1841)

Vichness, Samuel E., 'Marshal of Portugal: The Military Career of William Carr Beresford, 1785–1814', (Ph.D. dissertation, Florida State University, 1976)

Vigo-Roussillon, François, *Grenadier de l'Empire* (Paris, 1981)

Vigors, Desmond D., *The Hanoverian Guelphic Medal of 1815 – A Record of Hanoverian Bravery During the Napoleonic Wars* (privately printed, 1981)

W.T., 'Battle of Albuera', *United Service Journal* (1836, Pt. 3), pp. 401–402

Ward, S.G.P., 'The Portuguese Infantry Brigades, 1809–1814', *Journal of the Society for Army Historical Research*, Vol. LIII, No. 214 (Summer 1975), pp. 103–12

_____, 'The Quartermaster General's Department in the Peninsula, 1809–1814', *Journal of the Society for Army Historical Research*, Vol. XXIII (1945), pp. 133–54

Warre, H.J., *Historical Records of the Fifty-Seventh, or, West Middlesex Regiment of Foot* (London, 1878)

Warre, William (Staff Officer, Portuguese Army), *Letters from the Peninsula* (London, 1909)

Welford, Richard, *Men of Mark 'Twixt Tyne and Tweed* (1895)

Wellesley-Pole, William, Letter to Wellington, 16 June 1811, Wellington – Ms. Letter No. 114, Raglan Papers (Gwent County Record Office, Cwmbran)

Wellington, Duke of (J. Gurwood ed.), *The Dispatches of Field Marshal The Duke of Wellington During His Various Campaigns in India, Denmark, Portugal, Spain, The Low Countries and France* (13 vols., London, 1838)

_____, *General Orders for Spain and Portugal* (6 vols., London, 1809–14)

_____, *Supplementary Despatches, Correspondence, and Memoranda of Field Marshal Arthur Duke of Wellington K.G.* (15 vols., London, 1858–72)

Whinyates, Edward C. (Lt., Royal Horse Artillery), Letter to His Sisters, 30 May 1811, in F. Whinyates, *Whinyates Family Records*, Vol. 2, pp. 233–4

_____, Letter to His Uncle, 20 and 22 May 1811, *ibid.*, pp. 230–3

Whinyates, Frederick T. (Comp.), *Whinyates Family Records*, (3 vols., Cheltenham, 1894)

Wilson, Sir James (Major, 1st/48th Foot), Manuscript Journal of Sir James Wilson 1810–1812 (The Newberry Library, Chicago)

Wojciechowski, Kajetan (Lt., Vistula Legion Lancers), *Pamietniki Moje W Hiszpanii* (Warsaw, 1978)

Woods, William (Lt., 2/48th Foot) (Timothy Cooke, ed.), 'A Second Prisoner of Albuera: A Letter from Lt. William Woods of the 48th Foot 29 May 1811', *The Waterloo Journal*, Vol. 26, No. 3 (Winter 2004), pp. 3–10

Woolgar, C.M., 'Writing the Dispatch: Wellington and Official Communication', *Welllington Studies II* (Southampton, 1999), pp. 1–25

Woollwright, H.H., 'Albuera, 16th May 1811', *United Service Magazine*, Vol. 82 (June 1911), pp. 306–18

_____, *History of the Fifty-Seventh (West Middlesex) Regiment of Foot 1755–1881* (London, 1893)

# INDEX